# The Modern State

## Theories and Ideologies

Erika Cudworth
Tim Hall and
John McGovern

EDINBURGH UNIVERSITY PRESS

© Erika Cudworth, Tim Hall and John McGovern, 2007

Edinburgh University Press Ltd
22 George Square, Edinburgh

Typeset in 11/12.5 Sabon
by Servis Filmsetting Ltd, Manchester, and
printed and bound in Great Britain by
Antony Rowe Ltd, Chippenham, Wilts

A CIP record for this book is available from the British Library

ISBN 978 0 7486 2175 0 (hardback)
ISBN 978 0 7486 2176 7 (paperback)

The right of Erika Cudworth, Tim Hall and John McGovern to
be identified as authors of this work has been asserted in
accordance with the Copyright, Designs and Patents Act 1988.

# Contents

| | |
|---|---|
| Acknowledgements | vi |
| Introduction | 1 |
|     More than an abstraction? The idea of the modern state | 2 |
|     Aims and approach: ideologies, theories and politics | 5 |
|     The structure of the book | 9 |
|     The chapters | 10 |
| 1  The Emergence of the Modern State | 20 |
|     Two concepts of sovereignty | 20 |
|     The modern state as a law-state | 24 |
|     Warfare and the making of the modern state | 26 |
|     The modern state and representation | 28 |
|     The modern state and democracy | 29 |
|     The growth of state power: the end of the law-state? | 33 |
| 2  Liberalism: the Pluralist State | 37 |
|     Context | 41 |
|     Definition | 44 |
|     Theorists | 50 |
|     Practical politics | 57 |

# Contents

| | | |
|---|---|---|
| 3 | The State and the Power Elite | 63 |
| | Context | 64 |
| | Definition | 70 |
| | Theorists | 75 |
| | Practical politics | 82 |
| 4 | Marxism: the State as a Real Illusion | 91 |
| | Context | 92 |
| | Definition | 95 |
| | Theorists | 99 |
| | Practical politics | 108 |
| 5 | The Social Democratic State | 113 |
| | Context | 115 |
| | Definition | 119 |
| | Theorists | 121 |
| | Practical politics | 130 |
| 6 | Anarchism: the Politics of Anti-Statism | 137 |
| | Context | 139 |
| | Definition | 142 |
| | Theorists | 143 |
| | Practical politics | 150 |
| 7 | Fascism: Overcoming the Modern State | 159 |
| | Context | 160 |
| | Definition | 163 |
| | Theorists | 167 |
| | Practical politics | 179 |
| 8 | Conservatism: Authority in the Modern State | 188 |
| | Context | 188 |
| | Definition | 190 |
| | Theorists | 194 |
| | Practical politics | 202 |
| 9 | Feminisms: the Gendering of the State | 214 |
| | Context | 215 |
| | Definition | 220 |
| | Theorists | 222 |
| | Practical politics | 229 |

# Contents

| 10 | The 'New' Right: the Minimal State | 240 |
|---|---|---|
|  | Context | 242 |
|  | Definition | 246 |
|  | Theorists | 248 |
|  | Practical politics | 255 |
| 11 | Fundamentalism: the Godly State | 265 |
|  | Context | 265 |
|  | Definition | 270 |
|  | Theorists | 272 |
|  | Practical politics | 277 |
| 12 | Futures: Theorising the State in a 'Global Age' | 289 |
|  | Context | 291 |
|  | Definition | 293 |
|  | Theories | 295 |
|  | Practical politics | 303 |
|  | The nation-state in the twenty-first century | 308 |
| Index |  | 315 |

# Acknowledgements

This book has emerged out of our collective experience of teaching undergraduates in politics at the University of East London. Some of those students read and commented on drafts for some of the chapters in this volume, and we would very much like to thank Melanie Farrell, Christine Hennessey, Pete Robinson, Daniel Washington and Ben Whitham for their time and their feedback. They now know that lecturers are less capable than students of sticking to deadlines. Erika would like to thank Steve Hobden for his comments on her chapters and his correction of her bad grammar. We would also like to thank Nicola Ramsey of Edinburgh University Press for initially commissioning the book, and James Dale, for his patience with our missed deadlines and his advice and help along the way.

# Introduction

*Erika Cudworth and John McGovern*

The 'state' has been seen as the key formation of modern politics (Tivey 1984: i) and often as indispensable to the maintenance of complex societies. However, within political writing and analysis it is difficult to find a consensus about the state. Theorists from different perspectives fail to agree on most of the important questions we might ask – what is the state? what does it do? how is it organised? who runs it? One of the aims of this book is to reflect the wide diversity of understandings about the modern state with reference to such questions, and to enable readers to compare and contrast the substance and quality of those answers.

In the last two decades, Western political theory has increasingly come to question any certainties there might have been surrounding the concept of the state. In the burgeoning literature on 'globalisation' the view most commonly expressed is that we are witnessing some kind of transformation of the state, and, concomitantly, a dissipated influence and role for nation states in a context of increasingly close and complex interrelations between polities and economies. Some Western states have also witnessed practical political attempts to restrain or reverse the tide of public expenditure and decrease the scale of state activity. Much political analysis and commentary has applauded or decried such attempts. Yet for all the apparent debate and concern, the state remains similar in size and perhaps more invasive in reach, than ever before (Gamble and Wright 2004: 1–6; Hay and Lister 2006: 2). Despite the enthusiastic obituaries produced by neo-liberalism and some of the latter's more pessimistic critics, the 'inexorable demise of the state' is mythic, and there is considerable evidence to suggest its continued health and vitality (Hay 2004: 38–9). This is not to suggest that the state has remained a static set of institutions and relationships. Rather, how one understands shifts in the state usually depends on a particular understanding of the state itself, and this in turn is dependent on specific theories of the character of political power.

## More than an abstraction? The idea of the modern state

Each chapter in this book contains a consideration of the ways in which different theories and ideologies understand the state. Even within different theoretical positions, there is not always consensus on how the state might be defined. This arises largely from the problematic nature of the concept of 'statehood'. As Patrick Dunleavy and Brendan O'Leary note, the state is a conceptual abstraction (1987: 1) and, as such, means different things to different theorists. This said, they consider, quite helpfully, that there are two distinct forms of definition. First, the state can be defined by its organisation. Here, it is seen as an interrelated set of governing institutions. While governance (some form and process of social regulation) is an intrinsic quality of the human condition, however, the state in this conception is seen as a specific kind of government associated with European modernity. Alternatively, the state can be defined functionally either as a set of institutions which pursue certain objectives, or as a set of institutions whose actions have particular consequences, such as the maintenance of social order. In this broad definition, any institution and social process which can be seen to have purposes and effects which overlap with those of the state can be seen as part of the state such as, for example, educational and religious institutions or the 'family' (Dunleavy and O'Leary 1987: 2–4). Certain theories and ideologies of the state emphasise one or other of these types of definitions more strongly. We will see, for example, that institutional definitions feature strongly in elite theory, while functionalist definitions can be found in some pluralism and feminism and in various kinds of Marxist and social democratic accounts.

Dunleavy and O'Leary (1987: 11) further suggest that 'there is no very tight fit between philosophy, methodology and substantive theories of the state', yet we cannot consider any theory of the state outside its broader philosophical, ideological, historical and material context. The values of any 'school' of state theory are key to situating its analysis – so for Marxism, for example, an analysis of capitalism is central to understanding the state as constitutive of class interests and as actant in the interests of the long-term health of capitalism as a social and economic system. Key questions we might ask of the state are answered, at least in part, by the ideological stance of the theorist. Can the state be value free or is it, as Marxists, feminists and some elite theorists suggest, inevitably partisan, reflecting power relations in wider society? What interests, if any, does it pursue – its 'own', or those of an elite group or class, gender or region? Alternatively, as some liberal pluralists have suggested, is the state a neutral regulator, arbitrating in disputes over resources between various social pressures? Should and could the state re-shape whole societies along religious or nationalist lines? Is the state, as most theorists concur, an inescapable feature of our modern condition or would we be better off if there were less of it, or even without it, as 'New' Right and anarchist writers presume?

This said, there is something more to conceptualising the state than the notion that one's definition depends entirely on one's ideology. There are various common elements to the notion of the state and these are elaborated in Chapter 1, which looks at the emergence of the modern state as an historical form in western Europe. For Quentin Skinner (1989), the development of the state is associated with Renaissance republicanism – the concept of a self-governing republic that would be an autonomous political authority, deriving its authority from the people over which it governed. The modern state is distinct from civil society. Skinner (1989: 90) argues that the development of 'absolutist' states in Europe signalled the formation of the state as a distinctive, autonomous set of institutions of governance that is independent from the people or subjects of its power, those who undertake the duties of state office and powerful interests and organisations in civil society such as the church.

The definition that has best stood the tests of fashion and time is that of Max Weber (1978) who has an organisational or institutional definition of the state as a 'compulsory political organization with continuous operations' that 'successfully upholds the claim to the monopoly of the legitimate use of physical force' in securing the enforcement of its decisions. The state for Weber is, first, a separate and recognisable set of institutions with dedicated personnel that is autonomous from the interests of various social groups. Secondly it has a monopoly over legitimate rule-making and enforcement (backed by a monopoly of the means of physical violence) within a bounded territory. In this definition, the state is seen as a supreme power, a sovereign body within such a territory. Important for Weber was the notion that the state is autonomous from the personnel who occupy bureaucratic, political and other positions within its institutions.

This definition has been particularly influential in shaping the understandings of the state produced by elite theorists (among whose ranks Weber might be counted), neo-pluralists and some neo-Marxists. It has made its presence felt in other perspectives such as conservatism and social democracy. It has also been critically interrogated. Some feminists, for example, consider this ideal type has little purchase on the ontology of statehood in which states are not the only legitimate sources of violence. There are Marxists, fundamentalists, some pluralists and various different theorists of 'globalisation' who reject the notion of the state as autonomous and sovereign, and many theorists have theories of the state as a set of institutions thoroughly compromised by their social and historical locations. Furthermore, there are those who endorse the notion of the state as a fiction, with the view that it is an illusion – a result of a range of mystifying and disciplinary strategies of 'governance' (Rose 1999).

It is fashionable to critique the ideal types put forward by classical political sociologists such as Weber. Many such critics, it seems, do not appreciate the notion of ideal types, which may fit more or less well with different forms of material objects in different places and at different historical junctures. While the state is, indeed, a theoretical abstraction, and a highly contested and 'messy' conception (Mann 1988: 4), it also has material objects of reference. Both historically and theoretically, it has been associated with the development of certain kinds of political and social institutions. The state does have, however compromised, an 'autonomy' of bothorganisation and function with respect to coercive power (Poggi 1990: 21). It is a specialised apparatus of governance, albeit that the specific form of that apparatus differs in its scope, size and level of operational complexity. Notwithstanding the growth of regional and global political formations and the contested process of nation-building and maintenance, states also remain fundamentally

# Introduction

affected by ideas of nationalism, and are sets of social and political institutions within bounded territories.

## Aims and approach: ideologies, theories and politics

How we understand politics and the distribution of political power in states and societies often has direct bearing on our views about politics, and, in particular, the distribution of political power within and across states and societies. In presenting a range of possible understandings and considering their manifestations in *realpolitik*, this book aims to engage the reader in appraising their own views on such matters. A premise for this book is that political theory has a direct bearing on the politics of everyday life, and can help the understanding of current political transitions and institutional formations and practices. Each chapter illustrates how state theory has been deployed in recent historical contexts and shaped policy initiatives. In so doing, this book uses a range of pertinent examples to illustrate the embedding of competing theories of how states can, do and should operate in the complexity of our political world.

Our aim is to give a comprehensive account of theories of the modern state. In our view it is too often assumed that such an account is the same as describing varieties of democratic theory. This seems to us to be a flawed approach for two reasons. First, the implicit assumption – that any satisfactory theory of the modern state must be democratic – simply prejudges the question. Secondly, such an approach does not, in fact, do justice to democratic theory itself, since it does not allow for the contrasts that reveal its truly distinctive features. In short, we believe that it is vital to recognise that there exist theories of the state which lie outside the democratic tradition, that some are pointedly anti-democratic and that it is not at all clear that the actual behaviour of even 'democratic' states is comprehensively accounted for in terms of democratic thought. The term 'modern' as it appears in the title of this book is interestingly ambiguous between a merely chronological sense ('recent' or 'contemporaneous') and a normative one. There are theories of the state that are 'modern' in the first of theses senses but not the latter. In this book we shall be considering state theory that, though recent or contemporary, is premised on a rejection of the 'modern' secular state. Thus, our account includes a range of non-democratic theories of the state, namely, elitism, fascism and fundamentalism, as well as those theories critical of liberal democracy, namely, anarchism, Marxism and (sometimes) feminism. The political 'mainstream' is accounted for by the presence of chapters on liberalism, social democracy, conservatism and the 'New' Right. We have not included a chapter on green political thought because the green movement has not so far produced a coherent theory of the state beyond municipal democracy and green anarchism, despite some moves in this direction (Barry and Eckersley 2005). Chapter 6 on anarchism, however, will include the work of the social ecologist Murray Bookchin.

Generally, our approach is 'scientific' in the modest sense that it is our intention to present, as clearly and impartially as possible, a range of different ways of thinking about the state. But it does not follow from the fact that an impartial account of the varieties of state theory is possible that state theory itself can be 'scientific' in another, stronger sense, according to which a 'scientific' theory of the state is one that is supposed to be 'objective', neutral between different political positions and, therefore, itself a-political. We are sceptical of this 'objectivist' view of state theory advanced by some political scientists and political sociologists. In our view, any supposedly 'scientific' state theory turns out to be motivated by a vision of what the state ought to be, in other words, by *political* principles. For instance, we examine pluralism and neo-pluralism as versions of liberalism.

The overall point of view taken of politics in this book is a practical one. A separate section of each chapter shows how different theories of the state have affected the framing and implementation of policies or the history of political parties and movements. Just as importantly, the practical point of view is also implicit in the view taken of political theory as such. This is the reason why the book does not cover many approaches (such as functionalism, structuralism, institutional analysis or rational-choice theory) that are claimed to produce supposedly value-free accounts using methods allegedly analogous to those employed in the natural sciences. It could not seriously be claimed of most of the political theories examined in this book that they are scientific. All of them, some more directly than others, prescribe how politics ought to be practised. They deal in dogma not in fact. If they appeal to facts, they do so selectively. Always, more implicitly in some cases than others, they subordinate apparently objective analyses to an over-riding concern to promote certain values. In other words, they are all 'practical theories' aiming to incite or justify political action and not to give a neutral analysis or an objective explanation of it.

But why look at political theory in this way? One reason is that the claim that political theory can be a value-free science is highly questionable. A test case is provided by two of the theories covered in this book, Marxism and elite theory. These two have claimed to be scientific. They arrive at quite incompatible conclusions. Marx claimed that scientific knowledge of the laws of history reveals that the coming of a truly egalitarian society is a matter of historical necessity. Elite theorists predicted that a minority would dominate the majority in even a socialist society because genuine political science reveals the inevitability of elite rule. It is obvious that two incommensurable theories each claiming to deliver scientific truth cannot both do so. Moreover, each theory unmasked the scientific pretensions of the other. Marxists have had little difficulty in showing that the conclusions of elite theory reflect the values and interests of its 'bourgeois' adherents. The prediction made by the early elite theorists proved to be true in all socialist parties, movements and wherever socialists took control of the state. If these allegedly scientific theories are not scientific at all, what reason is there to believe that more recent attempts to construct a value-free science of politics have succeeded? Marxists, feminists, 'post-structuralists' and conservative thinkers continue to demonstrate that the scientific aspirations of contemporary political science serve to conceal 'capitalist', 'patriarchal', 'ethnocentric' or 'liberal' values and interests.

It would seem, then, that any political theory is practical in the sense that, rather than describing how politics are, it prescribes how they should be. There will be as many such prescriptions as there are sets of socially prevalent values and interests in a given society, though some will tend to predominate. Because a way of thinking about politics is prescriptive it does not follow that the term 'theory' cannot be used to refer to it. If a body of political thought contains more or less definite and distinctive principles that are sufficiently rational and cohere with one another in a more or less consistent way, there is no compelling reason not to call it a 'theory'. In that sense, all of the ways of thinking about the modern state examined in this book might be regarded as 'theories'. Evidently, however, some of the ways of thinking about the state examined in this book appear to be less rational and coherent than others. Fascism, for instance, is often said to be too incoherent to rank as anything like a political theory. The popular understanding of fundamentalism is that it is irrational. One of the purposes of this book is to show that ways of thinking about politics that do not sit comfortably with the principles of liberal democracy should not be dismissed as irrational on that account alone. Other political visions, as well as being repudiated by critics on the grounds that they are unscientific, rule themselves out as theories. For different reasons, both conservatives and anarchists have been suspicious of the very idea of scientific political theory as oppressively systematic. Should the same term, 'theory', be used to refer to Max Weber's writings as well as the sermonising of Jerry Falwell? Is conservatism a 'theory' in the way that pluralism is? Are fascism or social democracy 'theories' at all?

The sub-title of the book mentions 'theories *and ideologies*'. The term 'ideology' can be understood in two quite different ways. It can be taken to refer to an unscientific way of thinking about politics that lacks truth because it is unscientific. On the other hand, 'political ideologies' can be understood to refer to different, more or less rational sets of political ideas that serve principally not to explain but to guide political action. This second sense is the one contained in the sub-title, the intention of which is to emphasise further the practical nature of political thought. That is to say, each of the ways of thinking about the state considered in this book is viewed as a theory and an ideology; a theory in so far as it discloses, according to its own distinctive assumptions, an intelligible vision of politics, and an ideology because the purpose of that vision is political action. Our intention is not to oppose but to connect theory with ideology. Although some of the chapters deal with ideas that seem more reflections of rather than reflections on political action, more 'ideology' than 'theory', while other chapters describe well-elaborated traditions of thought for which the term 'theory' seems perfectly appropriate, this is a matter of emphasis and style rather than a categorical difference.

All the chapters look at ways of thinking about the modern state that seek to understand it in order to act upon it, whether that is to conserve, abolish, reform, destroy or transcend it. In other words, all of the theories are ideologies as well. This is what accounts for their power. And it is their power that makes them worth studying. No one would make a revolution for the sake of functionalism. There is no mass movement marching under the banner of 'rational-choice'. Wars are not declared to defend a 'state-centred analysis' from a 'society-centred' one. Acts of terror are not committed in the name of discourse analysis. Nor is it clear that political science really affects policy-making unless it also happens to reflect the agonising practical imperatives operating on policy-makers. In that case it might provide a language that politicians and bureaucrats use to pass off as if they are objective decisions that were taken on wholly practical grounds.

## The structure of the book

Apart from the opening and closing chapters, which consider the historical emergence of the modern state and its possible futures, each chapter contains four parts. Each chapter begins with a 'context', an historical account of the theory in question. This is not be so much a 'history of ideas' as a matter of locating the theory in its proper historical context and showing how and why it has developed. Our intention is to draw out the self-interpretation of the theory, demonstrating how it emerged, when and where it did, and to consider how the state is conceptualised as a result.

This is followed by a section in which the ways in which the theory has been defined are discussed. The theories that we consider are rarely susceptible to simple definition. A number of different leading interpretations have been given. In this section we discuss why definition may be difficult and present to the reader different interpretations. However, in each case there are certain core beliefs or common themes. In this way we hope to help the reader to overcome a frequently encountered problem. Students are often puzzled when they read a definition in one text, which is at odds with or is not expressed in language commensurate with what they read in another. Our method of presenting a range of interpretations within a common framework, so allowing comparison and contrast, should help undergraduate readers particularly. We also consider how definitions of the 'state' are never politically neutral, but are shaped by values and beliefs and are inherently ideological. Each theory then, has a specific way of understanding what sort of entity the state 'is'.

An introduction to the work of some key 'theorists' (some contemporary) is then given in the third part of each chapter. The thinkers selected are each representative of different versions of the theory or, in some cases, they are chosen to illustrate the international character of the tradition in question. Thus, the theorists whom we consider subscribe to the tradition that they have developed. We have chosen them because they give powerful 'insider's' accounts of the theory. They are also selected because their views have contemporary relevance. By giving an account of a number of different thinkers the reader will gain some insight into the breadth and diversity of the traditions.

The final sections show how the theory can be seen in 'practical politics', in concrete political circumstances. It is our belief that state theory must illuminate practical politics. Where we can provide case studies showing the practical application of a theory or how a theory has informed political practice we do so. Our discussions of practical implications refer back to the previous sections, showing how theory relates (or does not relate, or relates in unsuspected or contradictory ways) to practice.

Throughout each chapter, the readers will find themselves referred to other chapters in the book, as often the criticism of one theory has been crucial to the development of another. In other words, we view criticism as a 'value-laden' affair, with the political point of view of the critic determining the view they take of the object that they criticise. In this way the book gives the reader the opportunity to view a particular theory in a wider context and to compare and contrast one tradition with another.

## The chapters

The modern state is a distinctive form of political society in that it is an impersonal, autonomous and differentiated structure of coercive power in which authority is centralised and exercised over a well-defined territory. Where, when and how did such a state emerge? This is the subject of Chapter 1. The appearance of territorial states which provided for the administration of law in western Europe during the twelfth century is linked to the development of the concept of sovereignty. Especially during the Italian Renaissance, the rise of cities and market economies was reflected in the emergence of the notion of popular sovereignty. In contrast, the ascendancy of early modern nation states gave rise to doctrines of state sovereignty in which the state, for the first time, was understood to be an impersonal structure of distinctively political authority autonomous in respect both of rulers and the people. The role of warfare in the development of the state is examined, with absolutist

# Introduction

and constitutional states seen as arising in response to different military and fiscal imperatives.

A description of the part played by representative assemblies in the evolution of the modern state leads to a consideration of the relationship between the modern state and democracy. The modern state has been related to democracy in two separate ways. Liberal democratic states emerged from within a constitutionalist tradition that, while not rejecting the doctrine of popular sovereignty, subordinated the will of the people to the rule of law. The 'total' democracy that emerged with the French Revolution identifies the two. This chapter closes with a brief consideration of the growth of state power after the early nineteenth century and the transition from the limited law-state of early modern Europe to the late modern state that intervenes in such spheres of life as education and health, the 'welfare state'. The progressive extension and intensification of state power from the early nineteenth century, the disciplining and homogenising of populations within territorial boundaries, should be viewed in relation both to the emergent system of nation states and to the demands laid upon the state as the regulator of newly industrialised societies from the 1830s. This highly activist state has departed from the limited style of politics associated with the law state as that developed between the sixteenth and the nineteenth centuries. It is this state that is the subject of the theories and ideologies discussed in the chapters which follow.

Chapters 2, 3 and 4 cover what is sometimes referred to as the mainstream of modern state theory: (liberal) pluralism, elite theory and Marxism. State theory has perhaps always been a more broadly-based affair, and other models differ in important ways from the traditional triumvirate. The social democratic model of the state is elaborated in Chapter 5, and later in Chapter 10, we find the criticisms and alternatives put forward by the 'New' Right. There are chapters on material rarely included in other collections, such as fascism and fundamentalism. In these cases, it may be the political undesirability of the ideas expressed that lead to their marginalisation, but these are ideas about what states should be and how they operate that have had significant practical impact, be it historical or contemporary. Other perspectives included are less well known, such as anarchism. It is sometimes contended that political perspectives such as conservatism and feminism, along with anarchism, do not have a 'theory если the state' as such, but 'simply' some understandings of political processes, or of political power.

## The Modern State

Chapter 2 focuses on post-war developments in liberal pluralist thought. Taking as its central theme the 'neutrality' of the liberal democratic state, it considers three different conceptions of the pluralist state: the political process model developed by the Yale school in which the state is neutral in respect of the pressures brought to bear on it; the neutrality of the liberal equalitarian state in respect of its indifference to different conceptions of the 'good life'; and the multicultural state that is neutral with regard to ethnocultural justice between ethnocultural groups within the state. In considering these different conceptions of liberal pluralism we move between different methodologies – the empirical democratic theory of the Yale school, on the one hand, and the normative political theory of liberal political philosophy, on the other. We also distinguish between different kinds of pluralism: the 'political pluralism' of the Yale school and the 'value pluralism' of the liberal equalitarian and multiculturalist schools. The state is, therefore, plural in respect of the multiple decision-making arenas that constitute it (political pluralism) and in regard to multiple forms of life that it makes possible (value pluralism). The key theorists whose works are reviewed include Robert Dahl and Charles Lindblom from the Yale school, John Rawls and Will Kymlicka. The inclusion of Rawls represents a departure from standard practice in surveys of contemporary state theory but we felt his influence in shaping the way the pluralism of the liberal polity has been thought, could not be ignored. Charles Lindblom's influential account of incrementalist policy process is reviewed in the practical politics section.

Elite theory represents a decisive break with the understandings of liberal pluralism in that it assumes that whatever the form of polity and organisation of governmental institutions, the state is inevitably run by an elite. Popular sovereignty is mythic and 'democracy' is a sham as all systems of government are 'actually' oligarchic. Chapter 3 begins with a brief history of the concept of an 'elite'. It examines the contribution of the 'classical' elite theorists, and of Max Weber and Joseph Schumpeter, whose conceptions of democratic elitism inform more contemporary approaches. The second section considers how elite theory might be distinguished and considers the ways in which elite theorists define the state. Thirdly, the work of a number of more contemporary theorists is considered: C. Wright Mills, *The Power Elite* is a seminal work here, and had a significant impact on future studies. It informs the work on the American political system conducted by William Domhoff and the

# Introduction

analysis of Britain undertaken by John Scott. The practical political footprint of elite theory is more difficult to assess, for no government, party or state claims to 'be' elitist. The final section will consider elite understandings of the nature of politics in three different historic forms of state: British liberal democracy; state socialism in eastern Europe; and military government in Brazil.

The Marxist tradition remains a rich resource for theorising the modern state, notwithstanding the demise of Marxism as a practical political ideology. Chapter 4 begins by reviewing classical accounts of the state found in the work of Marx and Engels. Particular attention is given to Marx's first attempt to theorise the state in the 1844 Manuscripts, as an alienation of civil society that is often overlooked by Marxist theorists of the state. The central argument of the chapter is that this early conception represents the basis for thinking together the instrumentalist and arbiter/structuralist model of the state often attributed to him (Hay 2006: 67). That is to say, on the basis of the social ontology sketched out in the 1844 Manuscripts and developed by subsequent Marxists – most notably Georg Lukács – there is a way of thinking about how the state is both real and ideological. On the basis of this idea – the state as a 'real illusion' – the writings of the contemporary Marxist theories of the state are surveyed (Miliband, Poulantzas, Jessop). Key debates between these theorists – such as the agency/structure debate – are reviewed from the perspective of the unifying idea of the early conception.

Social democratic approaches to the state are reviewed in Chapter 5. While there is some overlap between social democratic approaches to the state and the liberal pluralist and Marxists approaches considered in Chapters 2 and 4, respectively, it is their consistently interventionist and consensual character that, we think, warrants separate consideration. The chapter focuses on the central problems confronting social democratic theories of the state today including how the state 'intervenes' in pursuit of social democratic aims when its capacity to do so is ever more circumscribed by increasing economic interdependence between nation-states; how the 'retreat of the state' is managed; and how social consensus is to be arrived at in increasingly minoritarian political cultures. The review of contemporary theorists will focus on the different arguments for the renewal of social democracy by Fritz Scharpf, Claus Offe, Anthony Giddens and Paul Hirst. Scharpf's arguments for a renewal of social democracy through multi-levelled governance in Europe will be reviewed in the practical politics section.

Unrivalled and uncompromising anti-statism has been anarchism's defining feature, and is the subject-matter of Chapter 6. All anarchists understand the state as institutionalised repression. The chapter considers the emergence of anarchist state theory and takes account of differences between Western and non-Western themes and concerns. Theories include Peter Kropotkin's anarcho-communist analysis of the state as semi-autonomous of class and his contribution to the theories of spontaneous order. Drawing on Kropotkin, Murray Bookchin has presented the state as a hybridisation of social and political institutions that reproduce a range of relationships of domination, while Alan Carter's understanding of the autonomous state is a clear exposition of the anarchist view that the state has interests of its own. In contrast to these conceptions is the 'anarcho-capitalism' of Murray Rothbard, which suggests that the functions of the state can and should be superseded by the market. A number of different cases illustrate the practical politics of anarchist state theory. The ideas of Rothbard on privatisation of security, judicial and penal services have influenced new right thinkers and governments. Anarchist analyses of the latent authoritarianism of the state and notions of self-governance are endemic in the case of the Gandhian Sarvodaya movement in India, and latterly, anarchism has made its presence felt in movements opposing 'globalisation'.

The subject of Chapter 7, fascism, is too often not so much understood as condemned. An obstacle which presents itself in the definition of fascism is the widespread progressivist assumption that fascist politics represent an aberration. This assumption leads to diagnosis rather than analysis. In Chapter 7, fascism is seen, not as a regressive movement foreign to the normal politics of modern states, but as a product of political modernity, in particular of the populist stream of modern political thought. In so far as it represents an extreme version of elements within political modernity, understanding fascism must involve a reconsideration of the tradition within Western political thought stemming from Rousseau. The history of fascism is be traced back to various irrationalist tendencies which emerged in the modern period as well as setting fascist movements within the political, economic and social contexts from which they emerged during the inter-war period.

In its approach to the state fascism shows a marked ambivalence, at once anarchist and statist. This ambivalence will be shown to derive from its complete rejection of the modern state as an autonomous structure of authority in the name of a radical interpretation of the doctrine of popular sovereignty. The two theorists considered each repudiated the modern state. For Georges Sorel it represented the political expression of decadent liberal civilisation. In Sorel we find a candid apology for the virtues of violence and the necessity of political myth. Giovanni Gentile developed a disquietingly plausible vision of the 'total' state in which the individual is utterly subordinated to a type of democracy. That vision, a political religion, has attracted few adherents in post-war Europe, as the final section of the chapter argues, but continues to animate tendencies in post-Communist states, the identity politics of militant ethnic minorities and, above all, Islamism, one of the subjects of Chapter 11.

Chapter 8 looks at conservatism and the state. The traditional conservatism of the nineteenth century declined after 1918 to be replaced, on the one hand, by new forms of conservatism (the authoritarian right, 'radical' or 'revolutionary' conservatism and, most recently, neo-conservatism), while, on the other hand, a conservative tendency became an element among others within the political life of the representative democracies. Although the definition of conservatism as an ideology is notoriously difficult, the forms considered in this chapter are related to a number of themes – the vital importance of tradition, the vision of society as an organism, belief in the radical imperfection of human nature and, above all, the authority of the state.

Three thinkers illustrate the variety and development of conservative doctrine. An examination of Michael Oakeshott's scepticism, Carl Schmitt's statism and Leo Strauss' anti-relativism will show that conservatism is characterised by a tension between a communitarian impulse and a *laissez-faire* or libertarian tendency. This tension is the main theme of the discussion of the examples of practical politics that follow. Post-war European conservatism seems to have disavowed entirely its nineteenth-century inheritance except in so far as it remains committed to an anti-universalist vision of the state as the structure of authority required for the protection of concrete civil societies. By European standards American neo-conservatism is not conservative at all. Nevertheless, in the uniquely American context, it has sought aggressively to defend a certain principle of authority.

Chapter 9 begins by contextualising feminist state theory in terms of the exclusion of women as citizens in Western states in the nineteenth and early twentieth centuries. This was a regional phenomenon – in many non-Western states feminism and nationalism were closely entwined and the post-colonial state was gender inclusive. Feminism has been a challenge to mainstream state theory; particularly pluralism, and different varieties of feminism and feminist definitions of the state will be outlined. Theories include Catherine Mackinnon's 'classic' model of the state as an agent of patriarchal interests, and Carole Pateman's understanding of the liberal state as gender dichotomous. Sylvia Walby sees the state as an arena of competing interests and demands, however, and Iris Marion Young advocates a 'radical pluralism'. The model of the patriarchal state will be considered in relation to the 'Islamic state' in Iran after 1979, but even here, there are glimpses of 'state feminism'. Surprisingly, some theorists who have deployed the patriarchal model of the state have dallied with state feminism, the controversial 'anti-pornography' ordinances in parts of the USA being cases in point. The impact of feminism on the British New Labour Administrations since 1997 will be evaluated, with the question of quotas for parliamentary candidates, and domestic violence policy taken as illustrative examples.

Chapter 10 focuses on the New Right, and begins by discussing its emergence as a critique of the politics of social democracy in Western states in the 1960s and 1970s, and its links to developments in both conservative and liberal thinking. The New Right defines the state distinctively and unconventionally, usually as an agency delimited by the supply and demand of the political marketplace. Alternatively, it is seen as a series of institutions in a limited 'public sphere'. Theorists illustrate different strands and themes. James Buchanan and Gordon Tullock have used public or rational choice theory to understand voting and pressure group activity, party politics and the behaviours of politicians in liberal democratic states. William Niskanen considers that the role of the bureaucracy in particular leads to 'over supply'. The well-known New Right solution of the 'minimal state' is elaborated with reference to the work of Robert Nozick, and Fredrick von Hayek provides the critique of social democracy. Since the 1980s, New Right ideas have borne directly on practical politics and policy making, particularly in the US and Britain. The thesis of bureaucratic oversupply influenced attempts to slim down bureaucratic machines. The idea that pressure groups 'distort' democracy can be seen in British trades union policy from 1980–92, and changes in the

## Introduction

provision of social goods reflect the influence of the market. It is suggested that New Right thinking has had a sustained influence on the political landscape in countries such as Britain and the USA, and has impacted on international organisations.

Fundamentalist movements have emerged throughout the world during the twentieth century in opposition to what is perceived as coercive secularism. Chapter 11 contests the commonly held belief that fundamentalism represents little more than a reactionary tendency. It will be argued instead that fundamentalism is an essentially modern political phenomenon. Fundamentalism is to be distinguished from other modern ideologies in so far as it must be defined in the context of traditional religious belief, even if it invariably involves doctrinal innovation. It is characterised above all by the impulse to restore purity to a faith that, translated into political terms, leads to the desire to recreate purity in the state.

The theorists considered in this chapter represent the global nature of fundamentalism. Jerry Falwell and Tim LaHaye are prominent thinkers within the Christian Right in the USA. Sayyid Qutb's political theology of *jihad* continues to influence violent Islamist movements today. Practical implications of fundamentalism are discussed in two contexts related to the discussion of fundamentalist thought. The influence exercised currently over the American Republican Party by fundamentalist opposition to feminism and secular humanism, concerns for 'Christian values' and belief in apocalyptic prophecy in relation to US foreign policy will be examined. This chapter will also consider the Iranian Revolution of 1979 and the struggle to create a pure Islamic state. In each case the main theme is the essentially contradictory nature of fundamentalist political religion. Critics see fundamentalism, like fascism, as a regression to barbarism. This chapter considers fundamentalism to be not so much anti-modern as post-modern. Whereas its critics assume the superiority of a more or less secular way of life, fundamentalists are motivated by a feeling which others also experience, that secular modernity is spiritually empty and that it must be transcended by re-enchanting the world. In pursuing this vision as a matter of religious duty, the political expression of Islamic fundamentalism known as 'Islamism' resembles European fascism.

The final chapter considers the future of the nation-state in the twenty-first century with an examination of the impact of 'globalisation' and the ways in which theories of globalisation have differently conceptualised the future of the state. It unpacks the concept of globalisation, considers different definitions in relation to various perspectives in the globalisation debate and assesses the extent to which these perspectives are ideological. The possible futures for the nation-state are elaborated in relation to debates on territorialisation, trade flows and the sovereignty of decision making. Key theorists are drawn from different positions in the globalisation debate. Neo-liberal Kenechi Ohmae argues that the state has no future in what is increasingly a 'borderless world', whereas liberals like Ronald Robertson are encouraged by cultural effects of globalism as a mechanism of restraining 'national' and parochial interests. Marxists like Alex Callinicos see 'globalism' as a new form of imperialism. Sceptics like Paul Hirst argue that a 'global system' is not a new or recent development, whereas David Held considers that the state is undergoing a process of radical institutional transformation in a changed global context. Practical politics includes the global nature of certain aspects of policy making, the development of global 'supra-state' institutions and some social movement activity. The chapter, and the book, will conclude by evaluating what different theories of the state have to say about the health of the nation-state in the twenty-first century.

## Bibliography

Barry, J. and Eckersley, R. (eds) (2005), *The Global Ecological Crisis and the Nation-State* (Cambridge MA: MIT Press).

Dunleavy, P. and O'Leary, B. (1987), *Theories of the State: the Politics of Liberal Democracy* (Basingstoke: Macmillan).

Gamble, A. and Wright, T. (2004), 'Introduction' in A. Gamble and T. Wright (eds), *Restating the State* (Oxford: Blackwell).

Hay, C. (2004), 'Re-stating politics, re-politicising the state: neo-liberalism, economic imperatives and the rise of the competition state, in A. Gamble and T. Wright (eds), *Restating the State* (Oxford: Blackwell).

Hay, C. and Lister, M. (2006), 'Introduction: theories of the state', in C. Hay, M. Lister and D. Marsh (eds), *The State: Theories and Issues* (Basingstoke: Palgrave).

Mann, M. (1988), *States, War and Capitalism: Studies in Political Sociology* (Oxford: Blackwell).

Mann, M. (1993), *The Sources of Social Power, Vol. 2* (Cambridge: Cambridge University Press).

Poggi, G. (1990), *The State: Its Nature, Developments and Prospects* (Cambridge: Polity).

Rose, N. (1999), *The Powers of Freedom* (Cambridge: Cambridge University Press).

Skinner, Q. (1989), 'The state', in T. Ball et al. (eds), *Political Innovation and Conceptual Change* (Cambridge: Cambridge University Press).

Tivey, L. (ed.) (1984), *The Nation State: the Formation of Modern Politics* (Oxford: Martin Robertson).

Weber, M. (1978), *Economy and Society: an Outline of Interpretive Sociology* (Berkeley CA: University of California Press).

Weiss, L. (1998), *The Myth of the Powerless State: Governing the Economy in a Global Era* (Cambridge: Polity).

CHAPTER ONE

# The Emergence of the Modern State

John McGovern

Largely because of the influence of a tradition instituted by nineteenth-century sociologists, it is almost always assumed that the term 'society' refers unequivocally to a universal condition of human existence (Mann 1986a: 135). At the same time, there is also implicit in the normal use of the term the assumption that 'societies' are, or should, possess legal and administrative unity within well-defined borders. In fact, only *modern* societies may be characterised as politically unified territorial entities. Far from being the inevitable consequence of universally present principles of human association, that condition came about historically 'as a result of distinctive forms of social integration associated with the nation-state' (Giddens 1985: 2). When we speak of a modern society, then, more often than not we would do better to talk about a *state* as defined by Max Weber: 'a human community that (successfully) claims the *monopoly of legitimate use of physical force* within a given territory' (Weber 1970: 78, original emphasis). How, where and when did this territorially sovereign state emerge?

## Two concepts of sovereignty

There is a broad consensus among contemporary historians and sociologists that early modern Europe was unique in combining sovereign territorial power with the market economy (Anderson

1974; Downing 1992; Hall 1986; Mann 1986a; Tilly 1992). Observing that political unification remains to this day an aspiration rather than a reality in the Middle East, with political power still the possession of 'ruling castes', Nazih Ayubi has attributed this to the fact that 'the Arab state is not a natural growth of its own socio-economic history or its own cultural and intellectual tradition' (Ayabi 2006: 1–3). The modern state was a western European invention (Navari 1981: 31–2). Territorial states began to emerge by the mid-twelfth century with theorists developing the concept of sovereignty during the same period (Canning 1991: 349, 363). The notion of sovereignty, that is, the claim that there should be a single source of political authority within a given territory gradually emerged in western Europe alongside the basic elements of what was to become the modern state, namely, 'permanent institutions for financial and judicial business' (Strayer 1970: 9, 35). Between the ninth and eleventh centuries the activity of ruling had been carried out through a network of personal feudal relations between lords and vassals. Power tended to be held by local notables, members of a warrior caste who competed for entitlements to tax and exercise legal jurisdiction over dependent populations. Throughout continental Europe there existed small autonomous centres of power, differing in the ways in which they governed subjects and often warring with one another for the privilege, with little political unification over large areas. As power shifted downwards, away from territorial rulers, 'feudal anarchy' was the result. However, by the thirteenth century a system of rule that prefigured the modern state, the *Ständestaat* or 'polity of the Estates', had appeared. Parliaments, assemblies and diets emerged throughout Europe, bodies whose purpose was to represent the interests of the 'Estates' – cities, clergy and nobility – before territorial rulers (Myers 1975).

The *Ständestaat* involved 'power dualism' in that the ruler and the Estates appeared as two separate power centres. Through mutual agreement the two constituted the realm or kingdom, the Estates co-operating with rulers in those aspects of government that affected the realm as a whole. Although powerful rulers may have wished it otherwise, representative institutions were, as Charles Tilly has put it, 'the price and outcome of bargaining with different members of the subject population for the wherewithal of state activity, especially the means of war' (Tilly 1994: 24). Rulers were able to build territorially-based states only on condition that they co-operated with the Estates: 'the European state evolved slowly and doggedly in the midst of a pre-existing civil society' (Hall 1994: 21). Within this dualistic power structure, however, the notion of territorial sovereignty was present. Although the Estates were self-standing associates in the business of rule, the king, prince or duke came to be seen as the occupant of a non-feudal public office, the source of an authority superior to any other temporal power within the realm (Poggi 1978: 36–59). Crucial to this development was the rise of towns (Tilly 1994: 8–10). Both as centres of production and commerce and, increasingly, as politically autonomous forces, late medieval towns undermined the feudal system of rule in so far as the urban economy, with its more developed division of labour and large-scale commercial activities, required the creation of new non-feudal legal forms.

The growth of towns was a particularly notable feature of late medieval northern and central Italy, the population of which doubled between the tenth and fourteenth centuries with the emergence of densely settled urban centres accounting for almost all of the rise in population. In these Italian cities a commercial revolution occurred as the volume of overland trade increased greatly and long-distance seaborne trade in luxury items stimulated the evolution of banking and credit arrangements (Waley 1988: 4–5). Supplementing commercial power with the use of advanced military techniques, the Italian cities were able to maintain a remarkable degree of political independence until the beginning of the sixteenth century when they were subordinated to France, Germany and Spain. Generally, throughout late medieval western Europe cities enjoyed relative autonomy embedded within wider frameworks of rule. The tendency was for towns to act in concert in order to influence already existing territorial rulers, with their interests better served the more extensive and stable the territorial jurisdiction in which they operated (Poggi 1978: 42). Where territorial rulers could safeguard trade and enforce contracts towns allied with them against local feudal powers. Cities demanded the right of self-government, but only in so far as that was required to safeguard their productive and commercial enterprises. Unlike feudal lords for whom ruling was a vocation to which they would subordinate even their economic interests, townsmen were able to submit to the leadership of rulers providing that they were sufficiently powerful to protect, but not so powerful as to inhibit, the acquisitive and productive pursuits that constituted urban life (Tilly 1994: 11).

However, in their internal administration, guild organisations, commercial enterprises and banking arrangements, late medieval European cities also developed highly participatory forms of corporate representation and non-feudal 'rational' institutions characterised by the distinction between an office and the office-holder. This concrete historical experience lay behind a notable feature of late medieval Italian political literature that was to be especially important for the development of the concept of the state. As Quentin Skinner has shown, this was the way in which it elaborated a usage of the term *stato* that distinguished between a current regime and the institutions of government that exist independently of any particular ruler. The concrete context for the emergence of such an understanding of government lay in the contradiction between feudal patrimonial rule and the political requirements of the urban market economy. Instead of the state being thought of as the private possession of a ruler, the civic humanists, expressing the experience of the Italian city-states, spoke of 'the state' as an independent structure of laws and institutions which rulers are trusted to administer on behalf of the community. It is within this republican tradition that 'we first encounter the familiar understanding of the state as a monopolist of legitimate force' (Skinner 1989: 107).

The civic humanist understanding of sovereignty was not, however, the only one to emerge in early modern Europe. Originating in thirteenth-century Italy as a means of defending the autonomy of city-states, the republican tradition ascribed sovereignty to the community as a whole. By the fifteenth century the notion that the state is a distinct form of public authority which, rather than enjoying personal ascendancy over government, rulers have a duty to maintain had become a commonplace in the political thought of the Italian Renaissance. Like Marxists and other later advocates of direct democracy, republican theorists, ultimately identifying the state with 'the people', understood sovereignty as *popular* sovereignty (Skinner 1989: 112–13). That is to say, within the republican tradition the state was viewed as autonomous in relation to office-holders but not in respect of the people. In contrast, reflecting the rise of nation-states ruled by powerful monarchs in France, England and Spain, sixteenth- and seventeenth-century thinkers such as Bodin, Hobbes, Grotius and Suarez developed the concept of the state as a single and supreme sovereign authority distinct equally from those who rule and those who are ruled (Skinner 1989: 119–20). This ascription of sovereignty to the state was a response to the dangerous use to which radical interpretations of popular sovereignty had been put in the religious wars of sixteenth-century France and the seventeenth-century English Revolution. As a result of this 'earliest major counter-revolutionary movement within European history', *state sovereignty* supplanted the earlier notion of popular sovereignty (Skinner 1989: 121–2). As Skinner has shown, the modern idea of the state derives from the writings of the early modern theorists of state sovereignty. In the political thought of Hobbes especially, for the first time we find the notion that political allegiance is owed neither to a ruler nor to the community but to the state itself as an entirely impersonal legal structure (Skinner 1989: 123–6).

## The modern state as a law-state

As John Hall has argued, the economic development of late medieval cities was supported by a certain type of emerging state in which 'a limit to arbitrariness' was combined with 'ever increasing infrastructural power'. The Church also played a decisive role in the emergence of such a polity. Throughout Christendom there existed a common culture, which was 'necessary for the European market to emerge in the first place' (Hall 1994: 21, 23). Moreover, by refusing to sacralise politics, as well as through its own engagements in power politics, the Church undermined empire and stimulated the development of separate autonomous territorial states. A consequence of the Investiture Conflict of the eleventh century was the secularisation of government, with the temporal political sphere separated from the administrative structure of the Church. While this weakened the Empire, the secular power of territorial rulers reigning over kingdoms and principalities emerged strengthened from the struggle with the Gregorian reformers. Since the Church conceded that it was the responsibility of such rulers to dispense justice in their various realms, this led to the early development of those codes of law and judicial institutions that were to provide a necessary basis for state-building. In contrast to Islam, Christianity accorded legitimacy to secular power as such and, although it would be anachronistic to see the Investiture Conflict as a struggle between 'church' and 'state', the distinction between a temporal authority valid within its own limits and the spiritual realm of the Church 'profoundly influenced the development of Western constitutionalism' (Tierney 1964: 2). From the beginning 'their only excuse for existence' was that European states should administer justice: 'the ruler was bound morally (and often politically) by the law' (Strayer 1970: 23).

Late medieval states exhibited neither the scale of administration nor the concentration of power in a central authority that were to become progressively characteristic of modern states. They included empires and city-states that did not control well-defined, continuous territories. There was no separation of 'church' and 'state' as ecclesiastical and political powers overlapped when they were not unified (Tilly 1975: 26–7). Nevertheless, the ideal of the state as a 'law-state' permitted temporal rulers to win the allegiance of urban populations whose economic interests conflicted with the essentially arbitrary, personal exercise of feudal power. With increasing control over the administration of justice came 'infrastructural' state power, that is, the capacity of states as autonomous centres of power to penetrate and shape their societies (Mann 1986a). From the beginning of the thirteenth century fees levied by monarchs on legal transactions undertaken within their territorial jurisdictions boosted the revenues of the states over which they presided. Rulers also recognised that the administration of justice was a way of asserting their authority and acted to increase the number of cases that came before their courts (Strayer 1970: 29–33). In this they set a precedent that was to prove fruitful for the 'territorially continuous, centralized, differentiated, coercion-monopolizing state' that emerged throughout western Europe in the early sixteenth century (Tilly 1994: 5). When such states provided legal and other infrastructural services rather than exercising despotic control, paradoxically 'restraint on government in the end generated a larger sum of power' (Hall 1994: 21). Rulers promoted economic growth by creating internal single markets. With the exception of France until after 1789, rulers removed internal tariffs as an incentive to trade from which, in turn, they derived revenues in the form of customs and excise duties. By the seventeenth century even if departments of government were rudimentary, western European states possessed competent bureaucracies through which rulers were able to dispense justice, tax populations and provide welfare. Although far from democratic, early modern states were representative in that the consent of the socially significant sections of the population was required for the successful prosecution of national policy. They were not despotic states but 'law-states' which depended upon impersonally administered justice both to secure the loyalty of subjects and for the revenues that provided their material support.

## Warfare and the making of the modern state

They were also states that routinely made or threatened war with foreign enemies. It is widely accepted that the modern territorial state supplanted other rival forms of political organisation in early modern Europe – empires, city-states and feudal powers – in virtue of their superior military capacity. This was both a consequence of and a means of legitimating the fiscal powers these states employed to derive revenues from urban market economies and the coercive authority they were able to exercise over the peasantry (Tilly 1992). The future development of successful early modern states, their capacity to survive and flourish within a competitive system of states, was determined by military prowess (Mann 1986b). The historian Otto Hintze has been particularly influential in drawing attention to warfare as a cause of early modern state-building. Following Weber, Hintze rejected the Marxist emphasis on class conflict as 'one-sided' and proposed instead that the internal structure of political societies has been shaped more decisively by the external pressure brought about by conflict between them (Hintze 1975: 178–215). He used this militarist theory to account for the difference between what are generally recognised as the two main types of government that emerged in the early modern period, absolutism and constitutionalism. Where nations experienced military pressure from the land forces of contiguous enemies, they developed absolutist government and bureaucratic administration. Thus, continental rulers, faced with the territorial threat of land warfare, responded by subverting representative assemblies, undermining local self-government and creating professional bureaucracies and standing armies. The older power dualism of the *Ständestaat* was eroded in favour of effectively imperial rule exercised uniformly across territories using a bureaucratic apparatus dependent upon the ruler alone. In contrast, Hintze argued, as an insular power, England was able to maintain power dualism in the form of parliamentary government under a constitutional monarch and non-bureaucratic locally based administration.

## The Emergence of the Modern State

More recent accounts of the formation of the modern state draw heavily upon Hintze's militarist theory but supplement it with an emphasis upon the revenue-raising capacities of states as a further factor responsible for political and administrative differences between them. Charles Tilly has argued that variations in the formation of modern states are to be explained not solely with reference to the type of armed forces they mobilised and the amount of warfare required to resist hostile competitors. He suggests that differences in the way in which the resources required to sustain military power were extracted must also be taken into account. Where economies were commercialised, Tilly argues, a relatively large resource base could be drawn upon by a small and non-bureaucratised fiscal apparatus. This was the case, he claims, in eighteenth-century England. In contrast, taxes on land were both more expensive and more difficult to collect, so that continental powers dependent upon agricultural economies, such as Brandenburg-Prussia, were compelled to create bureaucratic administrations controlled by absolutist rulers (Tilly 1985: see also Downing 1992 and Mann 1986b).

However, the 'fiscal-military' model seems to be deficient in three main respects. As Thomas Ertman has observed, there were early modern states whose development did not take the form predicted by the model. Constitutional states emerged in Hungary and Poland. Yet during the relevant period both were threatened from the land, the Hungarians by the Turks and the Poles by Sweden and Russia, and neither had access to substantial commercial revenues. On the other hand, absolutist Spain and Portugal easily extracted massive resources from their American and Asian colonies (Ertman 1997). Nor is the assumption made by Tilly and others that it was more difficult to raise land taxes from rural populations a safe one. In fact, in late eighteenth-century Britain the collection of commercial revenues required a far larger and more bureaucratised staff than did the administration of land taxes in Frederick the Great's Prussia (Brewer 1989). Perhaps the most serious objection, however, is that in accounting for variations in the internal structure of states by reference to external geo-political pressure, the militarist theory tends to underestimate the contribution of different national political traditions. This is surprising since Hintze himself stressed the significance of differences in the nature of medieval representative assemblies for the future development of modern states.

## The modern state and representation

There were, Hintze argued, two basic types of medieval parliament. In England, Poland, Hungary and Scandinavia there had been 'two-chamber' systems of representation in which the higher nobility and clergy sat in one house with representatives from the counties and towns meeting in the other. In contrast, 'tricurial' parliaments existed throughout Germany and Latin Europe. According to this system assemblies were divided into at least three chambers in each of which sat representatives of only one status group, normally the nobility, the clergy and the burghers. Hintze claimed that the structure of systems of representation was a causal factor responsible for variations in state formation, with territorially-based parliaments of the bicameral type more resistant to the imposition of bureaucratic absolutism than tricurial assemblies composed of distinct and exclusive status groups. This was because with the latter each status group would be motivated to promote its own distinctive prerogatives and disinclined to co-operate with representatives of the other 'Estates'. Such an assembly would not act univocally to represent the nation as a whole. In bicameral territorially-based parliaments, on the other hand, members of different status groups were present in both chambers and members of the upper house were often bound to representatives in the lower house by ties of kinship, patronage or co-residence. Moreover, the representatives present in two-chamber assemblies were almost always also responsible for local government. As well as inclining them to view national parliaments as a means by which local interests could be protected, their association with localities made available to bicameral assemblies political, financial and military resources that could be drawn upon to defeat the ambitions of rulers. Such was the case with the English and Scottish parliamentary rebellions against the Stuarts, the Hungarian revolts against the Habsburgs and the struggles between the Polish nobility and monarchy (Ertman 1997: 20–2).

Although lack of military power eventually led to a loss of independence in constitutional Hungary and the destruction of the Polish state, the absolutist attempt to govern continental European states as if they were empires failed. The eighteenth-century British constitutional state was more powerful than absolutist France which suffered repeated military defeat at the hands of Britain (Hall 1994: 25). The eighteenth-century French state was already collapsing by virtue of internal contradictions before the Revolution finished it off. Like other absolutist regimes in Latin Europe, France was a patrimonial state characterised by proprietary office-holding, heritability of office and tax farming. It has been estimated that in late seventeenth-century Languedoc more than a third of tax revenues raised remained in the pockets of local notables. Despite taxing the population more heavily than anywhere except Prussia, where particularly brutal methods were employed to raise the revenues necessary to keep a huge army of 30,000 in the field, the French state was forced to resort to borrowing, largely from the venal notables who took tax money as a reward of office. By 1714 government debt in France was so high that repayments consumed almost all state revenue. Not only did the absolutist state slide towards bankruptcy because of venal administration, it made itself hated among the population because its taxation system was highly inequitable with the peasantry taxed heaviest and the upper classes lightest (van Creveld 1999). Nevertheless, it would be mistaken to regard the absolutist state as merely 'regressive'. The truth of Tocqueville's thesis that, by centralising administration and emasculating the provincial nobility, absolutism levelled French society and thus prepared the way for the modern revolutionary state must also be acknowledged (Tocqueville 1966). Moreover, it was in the period from the mid-seventeenth to the late eighteenth century that many of the most characteristic institutions of the modern state were created under absolutism – large bureaucracies, armed forces, police and prisons.

## The modern state and democracy

The relationship between the modern state and democracy is much more fraught than the routine use of the phrase 'democratic state' suggests. Apologising for royal absolutism in seventeenth-century France, Bossuet insisted that unless coercive power is monopolised by the state, and the authority of the state vested in the monarch, 'all is confusion and the state returns to anarchy' (Sommerville 1994: 350). Although Hobbes' absolutist theory of the state did not involve attributing to kings a divine right to rule, it too was designed to prevent the return to anarchy which Hobbes called 'the state of nature'. Similarly, Max Weber declared that the abolition of the state would signal the emergence of 'anarchy' (Weber 1970: 78).

However, it is not clear what difference there might be between the 'anarchy' which theorists of the sovereign state have always feared and democracy based on a radical interpretation of the doctrine of popular sovereignty. Hobbes wrote that his purpose in publishing a translation of Thucydides was to show to Englishmen the folly of democratic government (Peters 1956: 20). As we shall see in Chapter 3, Weber's theory of democracy was elitist. What Hobbes, Weber and many others have believed is that, if democracy means rule by the people, it is indistinguishable from anarchy and certainly incompatible with the modern state.

The historian Karl Dietrich Bracher has pointed out that until 1945 within the German political tradition it was traditional to regard the concepts of the state and of democracy as incommensurable (Bracher 1974: 3–29). Even for German liberals freedom was understood as an adjunct of necessary constraints imposed by a powerful and autonomous law-state rather than as the freedom of the individual from the state underwritten by belief in inalienable human rights. For Bracher the Hobbesian notion of the state as a non-political entity standing above all sections of society was an ideological illusion by means of which authoritarian conservative elites resisted democratic demands for social and political change. This conservative ideology, he argued, prepared the ground for the rise of National Socialism. At the same time, Bracher recognised that 'naturally democracy today cannot be direct self-government of the people by the people' and that 'a state there must be, since democracy can only function through a capable government and administration' (Bracher 1974: 27). It should also be noticed that a late modern democratic society requires the state not only to provide administration. As Bracher himself emphasised, it is principally through *law* that guarantees individual freedoms and political pluralism that a society becomes and remains democratic. It is clear that the sort of democracy that Bracher favours, like other critics of the modern state, is *liberal* democracy. What such critics tend to overlook is the fact that liberal democracy and popular sovereignty are not at all the same thing. As Samuel Finer has observed, the principle of popular sovereignty does not strictly imply any particular type of political regime and may accommodate autocracy, oligarchy and even, as the case of Germany in 1933 shows, totalitarianism just as much as liberal democracy providing 'only that the office-bearers are able to convince the public that they have received office by public mandate – whatever that is (and however contrived)' (Finer 1999: 1476).

Depending upon how it has been interpreted, the doctrine of popular sovereignty had given rise to two very different but equally modern types of polity. One, the modern form of republicanism or constitutionalism associated with the American Revolution, has succeeded in becoming identified with 'democracy'. The other, appearing first in Revolutionary and Napoleonic France, has come to be seen as the antithesis of 'true' democracy. In fact, both were expressions of the doctrine of popular sovereignty but neither were democratic in the full sense, which prescribes government not only of the people but *by* the people. The fundamental aim of the American Revolution was 'to provide legal guarantees for civil rights, most of which had long been recognized and exercised in Britain'. The goal was the 'rule of law' and not democracy which remained, as Finer put it, 'still a dirty word . . . understood to mean direct democracy where every citizen was consulted and the government was the simple servant of the resultant will' (Finer 1999: 1476). The system that provided for a 'government of laws' was what James Madison called 'a scheme of representation' through which not the people but elected politicians would govern (Madison et al. 1987: 126–8). The fact that modern states which imitate Anglo-American constitutionalism call themselves 'democratic' is testimony to just how successfully that tradition has redefined democracy.

The term has now come to connote features distinctive of that tradition, namely, government by elected representatives, the separation of executive, legislative and judicial powers, and legally protected civil rights. None of them are essentially democratic. If civil rights, especially the rights of minorities, are safeguarded it is the liberal constitutional state and not democracy which achieves this. Democratic polities tend towards the 'tyranny of the majority', as Tocqueville famously remarked. Nor is the principle of 'checks and balances' a democratic one. If, as the concept of genuine direct democracy implies, there exists a single sovereign popular will it should be transferred without impediment into political decision-making. The purpose of the separation of powers is precisely to frustrate the operation of undivided sovereign power. Because it was the sovereignty of ambitious rulers that eighteenth-century constitutionalists sought to restrain we should not overlook the fact that for exactly the same reason, to preserve liberty, a sovereign popular will would also require restraint. And, despite the fact that the practice of elections is now spontaneously regarded as a *sine qua non* of the democratic state, as the Greeks knew election is a method of allocating offices not to the common people but to members of an elite (Manin 1997: 8–41).

In describing modern states which emulate the Anglo-American republican model as 'democracies' we recognise in them a political system characterised by a limited style of government implying a sharp distinction between the public sphere and the private, a distinction which the democrats of ancient Athens would have found unintelligible or repulsive. Within the public sphere of so-called 'democracies' power is delegated to politicians and, increasingly, bureaucrats who are entitled to act on behalf of the people to the extent that their actions may be demonstrated to promote the public interest. The purpose of law in such a system is not to stipulate substantive goods to which citizens are bound but to bind office holders to act for the common good rather than for personal ends or to secure sectional interests, with constitutional and administrative law conceived of essentially as being composed of generally acknowledged procedural rules designed to ensure governmental impartiality and impersonal administration. In so far as a private sphere of 'civil society' exists in which individuals are subject to no political interference other than that supposed to serve the public interest, we call such systems 'democratic'. They are polities in which 'negative liberty' is enjoyed as a consequence of the legal protections and other infrastructural helps afforded by a certain type of state that derives legitimacy from its practice of self-restraint.

The dogma of popular sovereignty may also license a very different form of government. If instead of dividing and limiting sovereignty it is believed that the will of the people must be one and indivisible, as Article 25 of the French Constitution of 1793 prescribed, then legality is identified with the popular will. In the writings of Rousseau and the Abbé Sieyès we find the principles put into effect by the Jacobins and, later, Bolsheviks and Fascists. The popular or 'national will', Sieyès insisted, was 'always legal' because 'it is the law itself'. Not bound by law, 'it is the origin of all legality' (Sieyès 2003: 136–7). It is a more logically consistent understanding of the doctrine of popular sovereignty. As Finer has remarked, however, on this account of democracy 'any individual, however rough and ready, could be elected to power through a popular vote or plebiscite, or alternatively might seize power violently and have this confirmed by a popular vote' (Finer 1999: 1477). Such a popular government would then, following the logic of popular sovereignty, concentrate all legislative, executive and judicial powers in its hands alone and abridge or abolish civil rights whenever, as they must, they offered impediments to the expression of the general will.

Despite the warning contained in Jacob Talmon's phrase 'totalitarian democracy' (Talmon 1970), if we now spontaneously think of totalitarianism as the antithesis of democracy this cannot be because, from 1789 onwards, totalitarian regimes, dictatorships, one-party states and Third World 'people's democracies' have not been 'democratic' in the sense of claiming that power was conferred upon them by 'the people' in whose 'real' interests they act. On the contrary, such regimes have been at least as 'popular' in that sense as representative governments. The reason why we reserve the name 'democracy' for constitutional governments is because they are the inheritors or imitators of a certain type of state, a state that is not intrinsically democratic in that it operates by inhibiting rather than releasing the will of the people. It does so in the name of 'good government' where that is understood as the provision of responsible administration under the rule of law. Rather than law being identified with the general will, whenever popular sentiment collides with law the latter takes priority in what we have come to call, somewhat obscurely, 'democratic states'. What distinguishes the modern state from other types of polity is the fact that it is a structure identical neither with the rulers nor the ruled but, including both, claims legal authority over both (van Creveld 1999).

## The growth of state power: the end of the law-state?

After 1789 not only was the *ancien régime* finished, throughout Europe absolutist monarchy retreated before the apparently irresistible advance of what was called 'Progress'. With the rise of industrialisation and liberalism during the nineteenth century, monarchy itself entered a phase of terminal decline. It was not, however, always succeeded by the constitutional state. As Martin van Creveld has written, nineteenth-century nationalism transformed states 'from instruments for imposing law and order into secular gods' (van Creveld 1999: viii). In the name of the sacred nation every nineteenth- and twentieth-century European state moved to discipline its ordinary citizens in unprecedented ways by policing, imprisoning, educating and subjecting them to its welfare services. With central banks financing government debt, the tax burden rising massively and a larger proportion of citizens coming into contact with the state for the first time through the tax system, the state increased its power over civil society enormously. To the extent that they subjugated their citizens, even ostensibly constitutional states ceased to act as 'law-states'.

Whereas the early modern state was an instrument for dispensing justice, the late modern state has sought to promote 'the national interest'. This is an enterprise quite different from the early modern state's enforcement of generally acknowledged rules that had been directed towards protecting an independently existing civil society. The promotion of 'the national interest' involved the reconfiguration of civil society in order to render it more productive and, during the first half of the twentieth century, belligerent, as states declared total war on one another or, rather, visited war upon other populations and their own. The contemporary state has acquired unprecedented power over the lives of citizens. Its activities reach down into every sphere of existence. As members of families, consumers, pupils, beneficiaries of welfare, employers or employees none of us evade the powers of the state to tax, legislate, regulate, enforce and re-distribute resources. The state makes and unmakes identities whether national, communal, professional, sexual or religious. As we shall see in subsequent chapters, while the New Right hopes to curb its power, social democrats to reform it, anarchists to abolish it and fundamentalists make it holy, 'the state penetrates everyday life more than did any historical state' (Mann 1988: 7).

## Bibliography

Anderson, P. (1974), *Lineages of the Absolutist State* (London: Verso).
Ayabi, N. (2006), *Over-Stating the Arab State: Politics and Society in the Middle East* (London: I. B. Tauris).
Bracher, K. D. (1974), *The German Dilemma*, trans. R. Barry (London: Weidenfeld and Nicolson).
Brewer, J. (1989), *The Sinews of Power* (London: Unwin Hyman).
Canning, J. (1991), 'Introduction: politics, institutions and ideas', in J. H. Burns (ed.) (1991), *The Cambridge History of Medieval Political Thought c.350–c.1450* (Cambridge: Cambridge University Press).
Downing, B. (1992), *The Military Revolution and Political Change: Origins of Democracy and Autocracy in Early Modern Europe* (Princeton NJ: Princeton University Press).

Ertman, T. (1997), *Birth of Leviathan: Building States and Regimes in Medieval and Early Modern Europe* (Cambridge: Cambridge University Press).
Finer, S. (1999), *The History of Government Volume Three: Empires, Monarchies and Modern States* (Oxford: Oxford University Press).
Giddens, A. (1985), *The Nation State and Violence*, (Cambridge: Polity).
Hall, J. A. (1986), *Powers and Liberties* (Harmondsworth: Penguin).
Hall, J. A. (1994), *Coercion and Consent: Studies on the Modern State* (Cambridge: Polity).
Hintze, O. (1975), *The Historical Essays of Otto Hintze*, F. Gilbert (ed.) (New York: Oxford University Press).
Madison, J., Hamilton, A. and Jay, J. (1987), *The Federalist Papers*, I. Kramnick (ed.) (Harmondsworth: Penguin).
Manin, B. (1997), *The Principles of Representative Government* (Cambridge: Cambridge University Press).
Mann, M. (1986a), 'The autonomous power of the state', in J. A. Hall (ed.) (1986), *States in History* (Oxford: Blackwell).
Mann, M. (1986b), *The Sources of Social Power Vol. 1* (Cambridge: Cambridge University Press).
Mann, M. (1988), *States, War and Capitalism* (Oxford: Blackwell).
Myers, A. R. (1975), *Parliaments and Estates in Europe to 1789* (London: Thames and Hudson).
Navari, C. (1981), 'The origins of the nation-state', in L. Tivey (ed.) (1981), *The Nation State* (London: Martin Robertson).
Peters, R. S. (1956), *Hobbes* (Harmondsworth: Penguin).
Poggi, G. (1978), *The Development of the Modern State* (London: Hutchinson).
Sieyès, E. J. (2003), *Political Writings*, trans. M. Sonenscher (Indianapolis and Cambridge: Hackett).
Skinner, Q. (1989), 'The state', in T. Ball, J. Farr and R. Hanson (eds) (1989), *Political Innovation and Conceptual Change* (Cambridge: Cambridge University Press).
Sommerville, J. P. (1994), 'Absolutism and royalism', in J. H. Burns (ed.) (1994), *The Cambridge History of Political Thought 1450–1700* (Cambridge: Cambridge University Press).
Strayer, J. (1970), *The Medieval Origins of the Modern State* (Princeton NJ: Princeton University Press).
Talmon, J. (1970), *The Origins of Totalitarian Democracy* (London: Sphere Books).
Tierney, B. (1964), *The Crisis of Church and State 1050–1300* (Englewood Cliffs NJ: Prentice Hall).
Tilly, C. (1975), 'Reflections on the history of European state-making', in C. Tilly (ed.) (1975), *The Formation of National States in Europe* (Princeton NJ: Princeton University Press).

Tilly, C. (1985), 'War-making and state-making as organized crime', in P. Evans, D. Rueschemeyer and T. Skocpol (eds) (1985), *Bringing the State Back In* (Cambridge: Cambridge University Press).

Tilly, C. (1992), *Coercion, Capital and European States 950–1992* (Oxford: Blackwell).

Tilly, C. (1994), 'Entanglements of European cities and states', in C. Tilly and W. P. Blockmans (eds) (1994), *Cities and the Rise of States in Europe A.D. 1000–1800* (Boulder CO: Westview Press).

Tocqueville, A. (1966), *The Ancien Regime and the French Revolution*, trans. S. Gilbert (London and Glasgow: Collins/Fontana).

van Creveld, M. (1999), *The Rise and Decline of the State* (Cambridge: Cambridge University Press).

Waley, D. (1988), *The Italian City-Republics* (3rd edn) (London: Longman).

Weber, M. (1970), *From Max Weber*, H. H. Gerth and C. Wright Mills (eds) (London: Routledge and Kegan Paul).

CHAPTER TWO

# Liberalism: the Pluralist State

*Tim Hall*

It is fitting to begin a survey of approaches to the modern state with a discussion of the liberal pluralist state. The reasons for this are clear. 'Liberal democracies' make up the majority of states in the West, that is, the United Kingdom and western Europe, the United States and Canada, Australia and New Zealand. As a model of limited and accountable government liberal democracy also represents an aspirational model for emergent democracies in eastern Europe, South America and Africa. In this respect, the Westminster model and the United States federalist model, often regarded as the first historical examples of liberal democracy, have exercised a profound influence. As a theory of the state, liberalism has close affinities with the social democratic and New Right models (see Chapters 5 and 10, respectively), each of which could, with justice, be called variations on the liberal democratic state. A further reason for considering the liberal democratic model first in a book of this nature is that liberalism represents the critical target of so many of the alternative approaches. More often than not it is the liberal pluralist state that is the principal target of criticism from Marxist, feminist and elite-theoretical approaches on the one hand, to the anti-modernist perspectives of conservatism and fundamentalism on the other. A clear understanding of the sources and development of modern liberalism is therefore essential for an understanding of other approaches considered in this book. As we shall see, a number of different approaches to the state have been termed liberal pluralist and the sources of the approach are voluminous, often appearing equivalent to the history of modern political thought itself. Despite this it remains necessary to attempt to bring precision to the concept even if simply for the sake of avoiding the creation of a 'straw man'.

Given the predominance and the exemplarity of the liberal pluralist state today, it is hard to imagine how liberalism – and by extension the liberal state – were considered outmoded and surpassed not very long ago. Writing in the early 1960s, the American sociologist C. Wright Mills described liberalism as an ideology as all but defunct:

> As an articulation of ideals, liberalism remains compelling, but on each of the other aspects of political philosophy – as ideology, as designation of historical agencies, and as a set of theories about man, society, and history – its relevance is now largely historical only. (Mills 1963: 29)

For Mills liberal conceptions of liberty and polity had simply been swept aside by the emergence of complex society and mass politics with its characteristic large-scale organisations. By this he meant that not just the characteristic institutions of the nineteenth-century liberal polity – the 'night watchman' state, the 'Burkean' conception of the political party – were unfit for purpose, but that the very basis for the liberal way of life had been eroded. Complex modern societies were no longer composed of autonomous individuals but of 'masses' to be 'gripped by ideologies' (communism, nationalism) and mobilised for a variety of purposes, most importantly, electoral majority, revolution and war (Lukács 1971: 2). Political parties had been transformed from the loose associations of individuals bound by common principles as Burke had described them into 'machines' capable of mobilising the population in the pursuit of election victory. The state had grown from a minimal institution, primarily concerned with homeland security and protection against foreign invasion, to a vast monolith that administered over more and more areas of life including welfare, public health and education. Such developments appeared to put permanently out of play the nineteenth-century liberal ideal of limited government – versions of which were espoused by de Tocqueville and J. S. Mill – in which individual liberty was safeguarded and fostered by the plethora of intermediary institutions that comprised nineteenth-century civil society. Given the dominance of liberal pluralism today we might justifiably ask, what changed?

Clearly this question cannot be discussed in any detail here, but one possible answer is the reaffirmation of liberal values that occurred after the Second World War and the onset of the Cold War. The reaffirmation of liberal values took the form of the Universal Declaration of Human Rights (1948) and the setting up of the United Nations. These, however, very quickly became embroiled in the Cold War that brought a particular urgency to the task of distinguishing liberal democratic states from dictatorships.

Given this context it is perhaps little wonder that the liberal pluralist state in its modern form – that is to say, complex societies with large-scale political organisations – was first theorised by a group of political scientists working at Yale, who included David Truman, Robert Dahl and Charles Lindblom. Their work was principally concerned to show how democratic governments such as those found in the United States and the United Kingdom are held to account through the competitive party system and interest group activity. Ultimately they sought to show how such societies, marked by political competition, were the best guarantee of individual liberty and, as such, could be contrasted with dictatorial states. Their work very quickly became canonical for political science and no survey of liberal pluralist approaches to the state in modern times can afford to ignore it.

If the pluralist model of the state developed by the Yale school has been canonical for political science, then a similar claim could be made for John Rawls's account of liberal justice in respect of contemporary political philosophy. Similar to Yale pluralism, while few subscribe to Rawls's account of justice, it has set the terms of the debate on liberal equality since its first formulation in *A Theory of Justice* (1971). While the inclusion of Rawls in the roll-call of pluralist state theorists is a departure from standard practice, there are good reasons for his inclusion: first, due to the proximity – often under-acknowledged – of the pluralist model of the state developed by Dahl and others to central currents in the liberal tradition. As will be seen, one of the central concerns of Dahl and others, writing at the height of the Cold War, was a clear distinction between democracy and tyranny or dictatorship. For Dahl and others this involves showing how, as a matter of fact, governments and officeholders are constrained in their actions by the competitive party system and the activities of interest groups. It is, therefore, first and foremost an account of limited government and deserves to be considered alongside other accounts of the liberal state.

Second, the philosophical turn of liberal theory at the hands of Rawls could be read as a response to the evident breakdown in the notion of consensus to which the work of the Yale pluralists frequently appeals. It is widely acknowledged now – not least by themselves – that Dahl and others assumed a far greater degree of consensus in liberal democracies than was warranted and, as Husserl has noted, a characteristic response of a science in crisis is to rethink its fundamental concepts (Husserl 1970: 5–7). For this reason empirical democratic theory and normative political philosophy should not be seen as alternative and mutually exclusive projects in the liberal tradition but as related projects that can reciprocally illuminate one another.

Thirdly, Rawls's conception of liberal equality is the point of reference for contemporary debates in liberal theory about citizenship, multiculturalism and diversity. Any survey of contemporary liberal pluralist approaches to the state that wants to include a discussion of multiculturalism, therefore, inevitably runs up against what is problematic in conceptions of liberal equality. Inevitably this consideration of liberal equality and diversity will mean a shift in focus from models of the state. This does not mean, however, that the conception of liberal equality developed by Rawls (1971 [1972]) and Dworkin (1977), or the conception of ethnocultural justice developed by Kymlicka does not have a bearing on how the liberal state is theorised or how its pluralism is conceived.

The approach favoured here is to distinguish between two types of pluralism – and two ways in which the post-war liberal democratic state might be thought of as pluralist: first, 'political pluralism' which refers to the polyarchical character of liberal democratic societies; and second, 'moral' or 'value pluralism' referring to the capacity of the state to enable and make possible different ways of life with different conceptions of the good (Galston 2002: 38). An example of the first type can be found in the conception of the state developed by the Yale school. Different versions of the second type can be found in Rawls's account of the liberal state and Kymlicka's account of the multicultural state. This is not to suggest that political and moral pluralism are mutually exclusive. As we shall see in respect of the conception of the state developed by the Yale school, it is possible for the state to be polyarchical and yet relatively 'majoritarian' and this notwithstanding Dahl's own characterisation of polyarchical states as a government of minorities (Dahl 1956: 132). It is also possible that a state could be autocratic and yet relatively tolerant of different ways of life – Tito's Yugoslavia being a case in point. More often than not political and moral pluralism are complementary with ethnic minorities adapting quickly to group politics, although it should not be forgotten that value pluralism implies different and incommensurable conceptions of the good which set it beyond the brokering process of interest group politics.

In line with this distinction we shall consider, in the 'definitions' section of this chapter, three different versions of the liberal pluralist state, with three different conceptions of state neutrality: the polyarchical state which is neutral in respect of the interests to which it responds; the 'Rawlsian' liberal state which is neutral in respect of different conceptions of the good; and the multicultural state which is neutral in respect of ethnocultural bias. The 'theorists' section will consider the respective schools: Yale pluralism; liberal equality; and multiculturalism. The 'practical politics' section will consider the impact of pluralist ideas on policy-making and the conclusion will consider contemporary debates on the primacy of diversity or individual autonomy. The chapter begins, however, with a brief review of the sources of modern pluralist thought.

## Context

The sources of liberal pluralist thought are, unsurprisingly, multiple and diverse (Dunleavy and O'Leary 1987: 15). The origins of liberalism go back to John Locke and the notion of limited government. Locke, the theorist of constitutional monarchy, was the first in the modern period to develop the idea of government that held power in trust. A government that abused its trust by violating the natural rights of individuals, recognised in civil society, could be legitimately overthrown. This doctrine was taken up, albeit in different ways, by the American Declaration of Independence in 1776 and the French Declaration of the Rights of Man in 1789.

Particularly influential for the Yale pluralists was the doctrine of the separation of powers first developed by Montesquieu in *The Spirit of the Laws* (1748) and then taken up and developed by the drafters of the American Constitution. Montesquieu was responding to the development of executive power in the first half of the eighteenth century. James Madison in *The Federalist Papers* (1788) sought to guard against the possibility of a tyranny through a 'vertical' and 'horizontal' separation of powers. In this way individual liberty was safeguarded through a constitutional settlement that encouraged the proliferation of factions. Madison's account of federalism would be the starting point for Robert Dahl's discussion of polyarchies in *A Preface to Democratic Theory* (1956).

A telling characteristic of Yale pluralism is its tendency to remain equivocal as to whether it is closer to a 'protective' or a 'developmental' model of democracy. Where a protective model implies an institutional arrangement primarily aimed at safeguarding the liberty of the individual, the developmental model is concerned with securing opportunities for citizens to participate in politics (Held 2006: 56–95). While developmental models require individual liberty they also value participation for its own sake. If Montesquieu and Madison are the central sources of the protective aspects of Yale pluralism, de Tocqueville and J. S. Mill are undoubtedly the sources of its developmental aspects. Both de Tocqueville and Mill emphasised the value of intermediary institutions between individual and society for negative and positive reasons: for negative reasons insofar as a vibrant civil society created a buffer zone between state and individual, further protecting the liberty of the individual in addition to the separation of powers; for positive reasons insofar as the private sphere was the sphere of social self-expression – the domain in which human beings were to achieve fulfilment through a full immersion in social life (Freeden 1999: 154). The protective and developmental elements in Yale pluralism which ultimately refer back to contrasting notions of liberty in Madison and de Tocqueville – Hobbesian in the former and republican in the latter – go largely unexplored in Yale pluralism due to its positivist methodology. The important point, however, is that traces of both concepts of democracy and liberty can be found in the writings of the Yale school.

If Madison and de Tocqueville represent the key sources for Yale pluralism, the contract tradition – especially Rousseau and Kant – is the central point of reference for liberal theorists of equality. Both Rawls and Dworkin explicitly draw on these thinkers in their respective attempts to outline a political morality (Dworkin 1977; Rawls 1971 [1972]: 11). In particular, Kant's account of moral duty based on the concept of autonomy has been influential (Rawls 1971 [1972]: 251–7). Departing from both egoism and eudaemonic ethics, Kant argued that a concept of moral obligation could be successfully accounted for only if it was thought of as 'free', self-determining action. Without the concept of freedom or autonomy only a contingent basis could be attributed to moral duty. To this day the concept of autonomy represents the fundamental battle line in liberal political thought and beyond. Where protective and developmental models of democracy tend to depend on Hobbesian and Humean accounts of human nature and freedom, respectively, deliberative models attempt to base political obligation on reason rather than human nature. For the latter the public use of reason becomes central to the political decision-making process.

A further influence on the Yale school in particular was classical utilitarianism. The brokering of interests carried out by the pluralist state requires that different interests are commensurable. If different interests are not commensurable – as value pluralists maintain – then they cannot be brokered. For this reason the model of political competition advocated by the Yale pluralists presupposes a consensus or broad agreement on political values. For them political competition, like a game, has rules which must be scrupulously adhered to by the competitors. If not the political process quickly descends into anarchy.

More recent sources are the English pluralists and the American pragmatists (Smith 2006: 22). Writing in the early twentieth century and responding to the alarming growth of the state that followed the extension of the franchise, G. D. H. Cole, J. N. Figgis and H. J. Laski developed critiques of the centralised state with its monistic conception of sovereignty. Each adduced the case for a decentralised model of democracy in which voluntary associations would become self-governing and the state would be restricted to a co-ordinating role. While the work of the English pluralists has particular relevance to British political experience with its more centralised political institutions and greater propensity for elective dictatorship, their work has come to take on an increased significance in recent times, particularly in the work of Paul Hirst (see Chapter 5). For Hirst, associative models of democracy provide a basis for addressing the detrimental effects on democracy of social inequality – a problem that becomes increasingly central to the Yale pluralists, most notably, Lindblom's *Politics and Markets* (1977) and Dahl's *A Preface to Economic Democracy* (1985). Hirst saw in stakeholder capitalism and the democratisation of corporate governance the potential for redressing the claim of the democratic polity against the market (Hirst 1994).

Finally, the influence of the American pragmatists – in particular William James and John Dewey – should not be forgotten (Smith 2006: 23–4). Pragmatism was essentially a philosophical school engaging with scientific and idealist conceptions of truth. At the risk of gross oversimplification, the pragmatists were concerned to show how truth claims in science and philosophy could be 'cashed out' in terms of their practical significance. A theory was true or not depending on whether it worked. The eminently practical bent of Yale pluralism derives in part from pragmatism but also from others sources such as Adam Smith as will be seen from Lindblom's incrementalist approach to the policy process.

## Definition

The following accounts of the liberal pluralist state are drawn from three phases of post-war liberal thought: the empirical democratic theory of the Yale school; liberal theorists of equality and social justice; and multiculturalism. Each school of pluralist thought can be viewed as responding to specific concerns: the Yale school to distinguishing between liberal democratic and dictatorial government in the context of the Cold War; the theorists of liberal equality to the social cleavages that problematised consensus in liberal democracies; and multiculturalism to ethnocultural relations between ethnic minorities in the state. As none of these schools saw themselves as explicitly theorising the state each approach outlined is an extrapolation. This is especially true of the equalitarian and multicultural states where the principal focus in each case is a liberal concept of justice. In no sense are these three approaches to be conceived as definitive nor do they, of course, preclude the possibility of interpreting the shifts in liberal pluralist thought in the post-war period in other ways. Despite their differences, these three conceptions have one thing in common – each involves a conception of state neutrality: the first in respect of the interests it is responsive to; the second in terms of the multiple conceptions of the good it makes possible; and the third in terms of the reduction or elimination of ethnocultural bias. The aspiration towards state neutrality, albeit in the different senses mentioned, has, therefore, as good a claim as any to being an essential characteristic of the liberal pluralist state.

In the writings of the Yale pluralists at least two different conceptions of the pluralist state are discernible: the first is the responsive state that conducts policy in accordance with the outcome of competing interests in society. In this conception the state is viewed as impartial and without interests of its own. It functions to mediate group interests and adjudicate between demands emanating from civil society. The second is the broker state, with distinct interests of its own, that functions by forging alliances with key interests in society – above all capitalist interests – and governing in their favour (Held 2006: 173). The first is the classical model of the pluralist state developed in the early writings of the Yale pluralists; the second, often referred to as the neo-pluralist state (Held 2006: 173) or neo-corporatist state (McLelland 1995: 38), is to be found in the later writings. In many respects the neo-pluralist model of the state emerged from criticism from a variety of sources to which the first conception was subjected.

In the first conception, pressure is brought to bear on decision-makers from a variety of sources: through parliament or the representative assembly; through political parties; and through interest groups. In contrast to competitive elite theories that viewed the competition between political parties for office as essentially the competition between two elites, Dahl and others saw the competitive party system as the principal way in which political leaders were held to account by a variety of interest groups. This was because the electoral mandates that they secured were based on 'platforms' or manifestos that reached out to a wide variety of interests in society. Political parties for Dahl and others served to aggregate the different interests in society (Schwarzmantel 1994: 57). In addition to the electoral process, decision-makers were subject to pressure from organised interest groups that sought to influence government policy. If one takes into account the separation of powers, both 'vertical' and 'horizontal', the picture emerges of a complex political reality in which political leaders are constrained in multiple ways (Dahl 1956: 3). The state – or more correctly the sum total of government offices with decision-making powers – is heavily circumscribed in how it can act as a result of the institutional constraints that it acts under. These constraints derive from political competition manifested through the competitive party system and the direct activities of organised pressure groups. According to this account of the political process, the state was a fundamentally reactive institution that responded to different pressures exerted on it. It acted like a 'weather-vane' turning in whatever direction the outcome of political competition sent it (Dunleavy and O'Leary 1987: 27).

Political leaders were assumed to be moderate coalition builders without agendas of their own and the political process was seen as one of gradual reform not gridlock or radical change (Merelman 2003: 18).

Among the early writings of the Yale pluralists there was some ambiguity as to whether the state was restricted to a purely passive role or whether it actively intervened to ensure a fair contest between interest groups. Dahl and others tended to emphasise the parity in resources between different interest groups, with different kinds of resource (time, energy, money) cancelling each other out. At other times they acknowledged the inequality of resources between groups that prejudiced the outcome of some pressure group contests in advance (Held 2006: 160). This gave rise to the question as to what the responsive neutrality of the pluralist state consisted of. Did it consist simply in ensuring that the rules of the game were abided by? Or did it mean intervening to ensure that political competition between interest groups was fair? If the latter the state, at a minimum, would actively seek out the views of less well resourced interest groups to ensure full group representation in the policy process.

In contrast to this conception, the neo-pluralist state is viewed as fundamentally interested. It acts as a broker between different interests but like a broker has interests of its own. According to this position, not only are some interests more powerful than others but also some are necessary to the very survival of the government itself. The fact, for instance, that no government could be indifferent to the performance of the economy (that is, to inflation rates, unemployment levels, etc.) meant that it was necessarily partial to these interests and invariably favoured them in its policies (Dahl 1985: 54–5; Lindblom 1977: 122–3). The cost of not doing so was almost certainly defeat at the next election. While favouring business interests might be justified in terms of outputs, without question it led to a 'democratic deficit' through the under-representation of interests, as both Lindblom and Dahl came to realise.

In addition to recognising the dependence of the state on capitalist accumulation the neo-pluralist conception was forged through criticism from a variety of sources. Multiple elite theorists, such as Theodore Lowi, highlighted the ways in which policy areas came under the control of particularist coalitions or sub-governments (McFarland, 2004: 9). New Right theorists analysed the ways in which government departments developed their own interests such as maximising budgets and safeguarding jobs. The former indicated that the state was altogether less responsive than the early writings of the Yale school had suggested it to be; the latter proved the state to be one interest (or multiple interests) among others and certainly not the neutral arbiter it was initially taken to be (see Chapter 10). While the existence of counterbalancing interests – the tendency for two or more interest groups to emerge either side of an issue – gave back to the neo-pluralist state some capacity for independent action, the conception of the state that emerged was altogether more worldly and restricted by vested interests than the original pluralist conception that it replaced.

A very different conception of the pluralist state can be found in the writings of Rawls and other writers on liberal equality. Whereas for Dahl and others the liberal democratic state was plural in a political sense, that is, in respect of the institutional fragmentation of power and the process by which decisions were taken – for Rawls the state was plural in a moral sense, that is, in respect of diverse ways of life or conceptions of good that it makes possible. The pluralist state theorised by Rawls, therefore, stands in the tradition of tolerance and religious freedom that was integral to the emergence of the state in the early modern period. Rawls's specific conception of the state, however, has more in common with the way the pluralist state was subsequently developed by political philosophers of the Enlightenment. Since reason could not provide an answer to the age-old question of what the good life consisted of, the state was obliged to remain agnostic on this question and restrict itself to providing the political and moral 'infrastructure' for the pursuit of happiness in the private realm.

The relegation of the question of the good life to the private sphere had different implications for the development of the state in the United States and Europe. For the former, with its reference to God-given rights in the Declaration of Independence (1776), it meant the restriction of religion to the private sphere and the development of a public morality – Lockean in provenance – based on tolerance and respect for religious freedoms. For Europe, on the other hand, with its more secular orientation, it led to the development of public morality that increasingly displaced religious ethics. For Rousseau, Kant and Hegel individual rights were not God-given but social in origin and explainable rationally. Rawls's work belongs to this latter tradition and his attempt to derive principles of justice that would be binding on all members of the polity represents a major current in post-war liberal thought.

Our concern here is not with Rawls's general theory of justice, but in the manner in which it is derived and in the related claim that the state should be neutral in respect of different individual preferences when it comes to implementing principles of justice. For Rawls the state is the central mechanism by which all social primary goods – such as liberty and opportunity, income and wealth – are allocated in society. Liberal democratic states are ones that do this in accordance with principles of justice agreed – in principle at least – by all. The manner in which Rawls attempts to demonstrate this need not occupy us here. The key point is that the state is the primary 'allocator' of values in society and it carries out this function in accordance with principles of justice that are sharable, in principle, by all (Rawls 1971 [1972]: 11).

In determining who gets what, when and how, the liberal democratic state is characterised by its neutrality in respect of individual preferences. This is to say, whatever the preferences of individuals in society – whatever their respective notions of the good turn out to be – is a matter of complete indifference to the state in its role as 'allocator' of primary social goods. This is not to say that the state gives equal weight to all preferences but rather that these preferences are a matter of indifference to it (Kymlicka 2002: 220). As noted earlier individual preferences as different conceptions of the good are incommensurable and, therefore, not amenable to the interest brokering process advocated by the Yale pluralists.

This approach leads Rawls to follow in the footsteps of Rousseau, Kant and others in outlining a political morality. He does this by asking what principles of justice individuals would choose if they knew nothing of their social circumstance, individual talents or their particular notions of the good and only a rational self-interest were assumed (Rawls 1971 [1972]: 60). By inference, only if the values underpinning the state's allocation of primary social goods *were publicly shareable* could this lead to outcomes that were acceptable to all regardless of their particular conception of the good (Rawls 1982: 183).

In contrast to the broker model favoured by the Yale school, liberal equality theorists like Rawls view the state as implementing impartially the principles of justice that are shareable by all irrespective of their particular circumstance, talents or conception of the good. It is a normative conception of the state, which is to say, an account of what a democratic liberal polity should be rather than a description of the political process as it is found. The final conception of the pluralist state to be considered here – the multicultural state – developed by Will Kymlicka and others is akin to the Rawlsian approach. For Kymlicka, the most pressing problems facing the liberal state today relate to the status of ethnic minorities within the state. Part of his work has been concerned to adduce principles of ethnocultural justice that can orientate state policies in respect of ethnocultural minorities.

The accommodation of multiculturalism in a liberal framework is a relatively recent development. This is because questions of group rights and group representation were considered to be irreconcilable with liberal principles, particularly the notion of individual autonomy. If an ethnocultural group were claiming a right as a group to exemption from civil and political rights in order to maintain a traditional way of life, this was unassimilable to a liberal position that, of necessity, favoured the right of the individual over the community. The assumption here, however, was that ethnocultural groups sought group rights to preserve traditional (i.e., illiberal) ways of life. This ignored scenarios in which the group claiming the right did so in order to reverse the domination of an ethnocultural majority. The claim, for example, for greater Black and Asian representation in politics was not a claim to preserve a traditional way of life but rather to redress the domination of one group over another. This distinction formed the basis of what is referred to as the 'liberal culturalist' position. According to this position it was not legitimate to restrict basic liberties for the sake of preserving traditional cultures but it was legitimate to accord groups various rights against society as a whole, 'in order to reduce the group's vulnerability to the economic and political power of the majority' (Kymlicka 2002: 342).

What this implied for the state was that it recognise that individual autonomy and access to one's own culture were interrelated and that, consequently it should endeavour to redress the balance between ethnocultural groups within the state (Smith 2006: 36). A truly pluralist state could not remain aloof to ethnocultural diversity: it had to actively intervene to redress relations of domination between ethnocultural groups and ensure the capacity for autonomy of citizens was not impeded by lack of access to their culture.

## Theorists

There are, therefore, a number of different senses to the term liberal pluralism and it is important to distinguish between them: there is the pluralism of the political process analysed by the Yale school; the pluralism of the state in respect of different conceptions of the good analysed by liberal equality thinkers; and there is the pluralism of the multicultural state as theorised by liberal culturalists. In the following we consider the links between these different senses of the liberal pluralist polity with reference to the theorists for each and consider also some of the problems with each approach.

Despite important contributions from a number of political scientists, Yale school pluralism has come to be most closely identified with the work of Robert A. Dahl and Charles E. Lindblom. A constant theme in their work – which spans five decades – is the nature of democracy and its possible extent in modern societies. At the risk of over-generalisation, their early work tended to be optimistic about the possibilities for democracy in modern societies, while their later work tended to be more pessimistic in outlook. We focus, here, on the shift in Dahl's thought on democracy – specifically the criticisms to which it has been subjected and the revisions it has undergone and consider in the following section Lindblom's influential analysis of the policy process in democratic societies.

Dahl's early work on democratic theory exhibits considerable optimism about the extent of democracy in modern societies. In contrast to competitive elite theories that represented the electoral process in modern democracies as a competition between party elites, Dahl argued that 'citizens exert a relatively high degree of control over leaders . . .' (Dahl 1956: 3). This was a claim borne out, he maintained, by careful observation of the political process, most famously in his classic study, *Who Governs? Democracy and Power in an American City* (1961). In this study he argued that power was not concentrated in elites or classes as stratification theorists maintained but dispersed throughout the democratic polity. Moreover, this was not due primarily to checks and balances in the political system but to the nature of the political process itself. The fundamental characteristic of liberal democracies was political competition between interest groups. It was to such cross-cutting and overlapping interests that political parties appealed in their pursuit of office and for this reason they were heavily restricted in the policies that they could carry out. The ubiquity of interest group representation and the existence of distinct policy arenas led Dahl to liken democratic government to a rule of minorities (Dahl 1956: 132). Underpinning the rule of minorities in the democratic state, however, was consensus: consensus about the procedures of the democratic process and the policy options that were available (Held 2006: 164). For this reason the competition between interest groups was fundamentally different in character to the struggle for power between classes in stratification theories of power (for example, Marxist analysis of class conflict), for it was based on a broad social consensus.

The character and extent of this consensus, however, has been a constant point of debate amongst pluralist and non-pluralist commentators alike, and Dahl's own characterisation of it is suggestive. Consensus is determined, he maintains, by the politically active members of society and in this sense the majority could be said to rule. He continues as follows:

> Lest anyone conclude that these basic agreements are trivial: a century ago in the US it was a subject of political debate whether the enslavement of human beings was or was not desirable. Today this question is not subject to political debate. (Dahl 1956: 132–3)

The emergence of the Civil Rights movement during this period, however, indicated the contrary. Retrospectively, it appears that Dahl and others consistently overestimated the extent of the consensus in American society and underestimated the effect of social cleavages (race, class and gender) on political representation. The fact that black Americans during this period were campaigning for basic civil rights in the face of 'Jim Crow' laws in the South makes it difficult to understand how Dahl could have confidently asserted that 'political conflicts are no longer about the boundaries of the system but rather the distribution of resources within the system' (Dahl 1961: 329–40). The importance of agenda-setting in politics, and the limitations of Dahl's analysis of power, were also highlighted in Bachrach and Baratz's study, 'The Two Faces of Power' (1962). The problem with pluralist analyses of power relations, according to this study, was that they were restricted to decision-making processes. This left the kind of power exercised by the majority in setting the political agenda and establishing the range of policy alternatives unaccounted for in pluralist theory.

The tendency to affirm the status quo also extended to the methodology of Dahl's empirical democratic theory, as Gregor McLennan has pointed out:

> Put simply behaviourist and empiricist cannons of investigation are incapable of detecting or theorising the 'structural' constraints which frame any particular balance of power. Under the banner of scientific rectitude, the dominant paradigm, it was argued, effectively implied a conservative value-stance. Focussing on *overt* behaviour and ostensible political claims and confessions, the *underlying* social realities were being ignored. (McLennan 1995: 37, original emphasis)

David Held makes an analogous point when he links the empirical method to the failure of Dahl and others to justify their conception of democracy in the face of rival conceptions:

> their 'realism' entailed conceiving of democracy in terms of the actual features of Western polities. In thinking of democracy in this way, they recast its meaning and, in so doing, surrendered the rich history of the idea of democracy to the existent. (Held 2006: 166)

Later writings of both Dahl and Lindblom, most notably Lindblom's *Politics and Markets* (1977) and Dahl's *A Preface to Economic Democracy* (1985), engaged with these and other criticisms. One of the problems of the first pluralist model was that it assumed a greater capacity to influence decision-makers and generally hold governments to account than in fact was warranted. This ignored political inequalities deriving from racial, class or gender exclusion. It tended to emphasis the parity between interest groups rather than the disparity in resources. It further tended to view non-participation in politics as a sign of a settled political culture rather than alienation from the political mainstream. The assumptions are increasingly questioned in Dahl and Lindblom's later writings.

In *A Preface to Economic Democracy*, Dahl sets out an argument for addressing political inequalities deriving from the ownership and control of capital. These inequalities are twofold: the first relates to differences in 'wealth, income, status, information, control over information and propaganda, access to leaders', etc. which lead to inequalities in the 'capacities and opportunities' for political

## Liberalism: the Pluralist State

participation; the second relates to corporate governance and the lack of opportunities for citizens to participate in corporate decision-making despite the fact that they are affected by the outcome of these decisions (Dahl 1985: 54–5). In response Dahl advocates a 'stakeholder' model of capitalism (Dahl 1985: 109) and the democratisation of corporate governance along with the complete arsenal of social democratic regulative and redistributive instruments. These are presented as an antidote to neo-corporatist tendencies evidenced in liberal democratic states (Dahl 1985: 109–10).

Dahl's *A Preface to Economic Democracy* is the juncture at which his liberal pluralism becomes all but indistinguishable from social democratic approaches to the state and it is little wonder that it should have proved influential in this quarter. In particular, Paul Hirst's theory of associative democracy – considered in Chapter 5 – takes as its point of departure Dahl's later neo-pluralist thought and applies this in a British context (Hirst 1989: 3–4). Whereas for Dahl, however, pluralism remains at bottom a theory of political competition, Hirst – deriving inspiration from the English pluralists – seeks self-governing capacities for a wider range of associations in civil society (see Chapter 5).

The 'critical pluralism' of Dahl and Lindblom with its greater focus on political equality was in many respects anticipated by John Rawls and other liberal equality thinkers. It was precisely the 'boundaries of the system', however, that were at stake when Rawls and others enquired after the basis of consensus in modern society and turned to the contract tradition in liberal thought for assistance. For Rawls, Dworkin and others consensus was to be found in rational agreement about the basic values underpinning the principal social arrangements – most notably the state. In their view this required a conception of social justice that would strike the right balance between liberty – the first virtue of the liberal state – and equality. For Rawls, the liberal state was pluralist, not primarily because power was fragmented in it but because it made possible multiple forms of life with different conceptions of the good. The liberal state was pluralist because it was neutral in respect of the good.

Rawls's distinction between 'comprehensive' and 'political' liberalism was devised specifically for the problem of illiberal groups in liberal society (Rawls 1993). How might there be agreement between liberal and illiberal groups about the basic principles of justice underpinning the state? What consensus could exist between

53

liberal groups and illiberal groups that do not value the principle of individual autonomy? The problem with Rawls's original theory of justice was that it assumed liberal values among those agreeing to the two principles of justice. In other words it assumed rational self-interest and individual autonomy (the capacity to reflect on and revise our individual conception of the good), which are themselves values. This seemed to suggest that liberal principles of justice were only applicable to liberal peoples. Groups that did not value individual autonomy would not subscribe to these principles. This led to the question of whether the principle of autonomy could serve as a basis for government in a pluralist society (Kymlicka 2002: 232).

The concept of political liberalism dispenses with the principle of individual autonomy in an attempt to arrive at principles of liberal justice that are shareable by all (that is, by both liberal and illiberal groups). It does this through the notion of the overlapping consensus. While the two basic principles of justice remain the same for Rawls there is more than one way to establish them. He demonstrates the notion of the overlapping consensus with respect to the basic right to the liberty of conscience. While liberals would defend the principle on the ground that individuals should always remain free to revise their view of the good, illiberal groups would accept the principle on the ground that it protects freedom of worship. For Rawls it is the fact that we can arrive at an overlapping consensus on a range of basic liberties that provides the basis for consent in multicultural societies (Rawls 1982: 183).

The problem with the notion of the overlapping consensus is that it does not achieve what it sets out to. Illiberal groups may subscribe to the principle insofar as it grants a protective freedom of worship for the group but not insofar as it permits members of groups to question their beliefs and exit the group. At the time of writing, church groups are protesting against new legislation in the UK that prohibits discrimination in the provision of goods, facilities and services on the basis of sexual orientation. They are protesting against this on the grounds that it denies their right to deny services or equal representation to gay people in accordance with their beliefs (*The Guardian*, 10 January 2007). In protesting against the legislation, church groups appeal to the right to religious freedom while seeking to deny the right of their members to question their beliefs by restricting the teaching of life-style choice at schools. For reasons like this, Rawls supplements his concept of overlapping consensus with a distinction between public and private reason (Rawls 1985:

## Liberalism: the Pluralist State

241). The principle of individual autonomy is not dispensed with altogether. Rather it is limited to the public domain. In private citizens are free to hold what views they like. In this way individual members of illiberal communities have the legal right to question their views and exit the group even though it may be impossible for them to think of themselves as detached from their communities.

On the basis of this 'bicameral orientation of citizenship' the task of the liberal state is clear: in order to safeguard diversity it must ensure a vibrant public sphere and foster a sense of citizenship (Connolly 2005: 3).Without the latter and the day-to-day participation in the public life of the polity the overlapping consensus disintegrates. Additionally, the state must ensure that members of illiberal groups are aware of their rights and have the necessary basic education (that is, lifestyle choices in the school curriculum) to be able to exercise their autonomy. Unless the state carries this out through its educational policy the rights extending to illiberal group members will be in name only.

The central problem with this approach first pointed out by Marx in *On the Jewish Question* (1843) is that it sets up rival and ultimately irreconcilable commitments in citizens. Consensus in the multicultural state rests on a clear separation of private and public commitments even though this is seldom the case (McLellan 2000: 63). Moreover, in circumstances when these commitments come into conflict it is more likely that the private commitments will hold sway. An illiberal community that finds its practices questioned may experience this as an attack on its identity. Unless the state through its educational policy can foster attachment to citizenship it is unlikely that social plurality will be protected in this way.

In an attempt to advance beyond the 'liberal culturalist' paradigm in the recognition of cultural rights for ethnocultural groups, Kymlicka has focused on state activity to promote the integration of minorities (Kymlicka 2002: 339). For Kymlicka remedial action undertaken by the state to redress the relations of domination between ethnocultural groups did not suffice in itself to make the state multicultural. In addition, awareness was needed of how activities engaged in by the state actively disadvantaged ethnocultural minorities. Above all it was the activity of nation-building and the creation of what Kymlicka calls 'societal culture' that placed ethnocultural minorities at a relation of disadvantage to the majority culture. By 'societal culture' Kymlicka means: '[a] territorially concentrated culture, centred on a shared language which is used in a wide range of social institutions, in both public and private life (schools, media, law, economy, government etc.)' (Kymlicka 2002: 346).

This is to be distinguished from other forms of culture such as religious beliefs and personal lifestyles that do not involve a common language and shared institutions. Kymlicka claims that states routinely engage in such forms of nation-building in promoting an official language, establishing a core curriculum for education and creating citizenship tests for migrants (Kymlicka 2002: 347). The fact that states engage in such activities gives lie to the liberal state's claim to be 'blind' to ethnocultural diversity. While the liberal state might practise a 'benign neglect' towards religion it certainly does not do so, according to Kymlicka, when it comes to promoting integration through the creation of a societal culture. The truly multicultural state does not stop at remedial action to address the domination by the majority culture of ethnocultural minorities. It offers minority cultures fairer terms of integration and in some cases, where the minority constitutes a sub-state nation, the possibility of developing their own societal culture. In the first case, this may involve equal recognition for each ethnocultural group such as the marking of calendar days in shared institutions like universities and hospitals. The latter may involve the devolution of power and regional autonomy.

There are multiple forms of pluralism. If any trend is discernible, however, it is a gradual shift of focus from political pluralism to moral or value pluralism; from a concern with how in fact the political process is complex involving multiple centres of power to the role of the state in sustaining multicultural diversity. This is not to say that the states favoured by liberal theorists of equality and liberal multiculturalists are 'monolithic'. As Galston has noted there is a clear link between the political and moral pluralism:

> Moral pluralism lends support to the proposition that the state should not be regarded as all-powerful, while political pluralism helps define and defend the social space within which the heterogeneity of value can be translated into a rich variety of worthy human lives. (Galston 2002: 38)

The two kinds of pluralism could, therefore, be thought of as mutually reinforcing.

## Practical politics

Possibly one of the most enduring legacies of classical pluralist theory has been its influence on policy analysis. This should come as no surprise given its insistence on studying power relations in specific contexts and its generally pragmatic outlook. The early work of Charles Lindblom has been particularly influential in this regard. In a series of studies – most notably an article entitled 'The Science of Muddling Through' (1959) and the subsequent book-length study entitled *The Intelligence of Democracy* (1965) – Lindblom developed what has come to be referred to as the incrementalist model of policy analysis.

In contrast to rationalist models of policy analysis, incrementalist models are polycentred. Since, for pluralists, there are multiple centres of power in society, policy is not made and implemented by a single body but by a number of different bodies including different departments, different branches of government, supranational and sub-national government and interest groups (Lindblom 1965: 99). Housing policy in the UK, for example, will involve a number of different government departments including the Department of the Environment, the Treasury, Parliament, local government and other organisations such as housing associations, construction companies and campaign groups like Shelter. Whereas rationalistic policy analysis characterised the policy process as the rational pursuit, by a centralised body, of explicit objectives, Lindblom held that it was primarily means-orientated, often driven by political expedience, in which vaguely articulated objectives were pursued by multiple actors (Lindblom 1965: 97–8). Modern electorates are given – at the prompting of the media – to expressions of impatience at the vaguely worded manifesto commitments of political parties. From an incremental perspective, however, in which policy outcomes are the result of the activities of a range of organisations – and, therefore, always uncertain – it could not be otherwise. Only a highly centralised government, in which a single body oversees the making and implementation of policy, could give concrete commitments on policy objectives. In the real world, however, in which policy is conducted across different government departments, across different levels of government and subject to pressure from a range of different interest groups, these must necessarily remain nebulous.

Lindblom's central contribution to policy analysis is the theory of partisan mutual adjustment, which addresses the pivotal problem for policy implementation in the pluralist democratic polity: namely how policy is co-ordinated across a range of different organisations. Policy takes place, Lindblom maintains, in a crowded arena. Numerous groups try to influence policy undertaking partisan analysis. Policy emerges as a compromise – that is, as a result of the 'mutual adjustments' – between various interest groups.

The theory of partisan mutual adjustment presupposes a shared commitment on the part of all interested parties on reaching an agreement – an agreement, if you like, on the basic rules of the game. Since the implementation of policy is serial and fragmentary any loss suffered is temporary and there is always the possibility that 'losers' in the game of influencing policy could 'win' on a future occasion. What is noteworthy in the theory is the faith it places in the value of policy outcomes that result from the process of mutual adjustment, which far exceed what could be achieved by the most sophisticated of centralised co-ordinating bodies. Rather as the market delivers productive and distributive outcomes much more efficiently than is possible for any centralised planning agency, so the unanticipated outcomes of the process of mutual adjustment deliver policies that are both more efficient and, above all, more representative (Lindblom 1965: 229). Looked at from an incremental perspective, the end point of the policy process – to the extent that it could be said to have an end at all – is where the policy is accepted and agreeable to all interested parties, not when a specific objective, fixed by a centralised authority, is realised.

Critics have, however, pointed to very definite problems in the incrementalist account of the policy process. To begin with it appears essentially reactive and completely unable to deal with crises of a fundamental nature experienced by the state. The capacity for the government to anticipate problems before they have arisen is severely restricted in the incrementalist account. One only needs to think of recent crises in UK agriculture and fisheries such as bovine spongiform encephalopathy (BSE), or chronically depleted fishing stocks in the North Sea, to be reminded of this. Frequently, government responses to crisis problems such as these are 'too little too late'. Moreover, the reactive character of the policy process and the gradualist account of political change that it implies appear to wed the incrementalist model to the maintenance of the status quo. This, as we have seen, is a recurrent problem with all pluralist theory that understands itself in purely descriptive terms. By describing the policy process as it is one inadvertently precludes the possibility that it could be otherwise.

Lindblom's response to this – a response that is characteristic of pluralist approaches in general – was to seek to supplement the descriptive theory of incrementalism with a prescriptive theory (Lindblom 1965: 161–2). Complex problem-solving requires not a departure from incrementalism but a more skilful and deft practising of it. 'Disjointed incrementalism', as he refers to it, may involve the reduction of policy alternatives to tried and trusted policies; the piloting and subsequent rolling out of policy initiatives. In response to the criticism that incrementalism invariably comes down on the side of the status quo, he insists that fundamental change is often the consequence of a gradualist process (Lindblom 1965: 184).

Despite these innovations to the theory critics have pointed to a number of continuing problems with it. Incrementalism remains reactive and short-termist and often fails to address the underlying issue. The increasing use of 'policy tsars' with special executive powers over a specific area of policy is testament to this. An example of this was the appointment of Keith Hellawell as 'drugs tsar' by Tony Blair in 1997. This role involved co-ordinating policy across government departments including the Home Office and Education. The very creation of the role, however, signalled a failure of the incremental policy process to address the underlying issues of drug-related crime in the UK.

A critique of the incrementalist model was developed by Amitai Etzioni in an article entitled 'Mixed Scanning: A third approach to decision mixing'. Etzioni develops a twin critique of rationalist and incrementalist models. He argues that both rationalist and incrementalist approaches fail to distinguish between fundamental and non-fundamental problems (Etzioni 1967: 387). Fundamental problems set the context for society and imply a fundamental shift in the status quo; non-fundamental problems, on the other hand, are based on these decisions (1967: 387). An example of the former would be the consensus-creating policy of a government such as Roosevelt's New Deal or the neo-liberal reforms of the Thatcher governments. If the problem with rationalist policy analysis was that it ignored non-fundamental decisions, the problem for incrementalism was that it could not account for fundamental decisions. This meant that it was little use to governments seeking a radical change in direction of policy. It is difficult to imagine, for example, a radical shift in environmental policy in response to the crisis of global warning emerging from a series of incremental steps. In response Etzioni developed a third perspective that he called – after a weather satellite system – mixed scanning (Etzioni 1967: 388–90). This approach combined detailed policy analysis with a general overview of the policy process. Etzioni's ideas have been influential in the development of policy co-ordinating units at the centre of pluralist government – in the UK in the expansion of the Prime Minister's office. This development indicates a loss of confidence, to some extent, in the incrementalist model and its capacity to deliver co-ordinated and representative policy.

\* \* \*

> [t]he Kantian and Millian conceptions of liberalism (which rest on autonomy and individuality as specifications of the good life) are not adequate solutions to the political problem of reasonable disagreement about the good life. They have themselves simply become another part of the problem . . . (Larmore, in Galston 2002: 23)

Larmore pinpoints here perhaps the most surprising development in liberal thought in the last twenty-five years. That is the idea that individual autonomy might not be the best principle to which to appeal in order to defend a plural society. The idea of liberalism without the principle of individual autonomy at its base would have seemed unconscionable to previous generations of liberal theorists. The decline in the strong sense of individual autonomy deriving from Kant and Mill has, however, reaffirmed the importance of the liberal state, as Galston has noted:

> State power can legitimately regulate the terms of the relationship among social agents, provided the public structure is as fair as possible to all and allows ample opportunities for expressive liberty. In this respect like others the state enjoys a certain priority: it is the key source of order in a system of ordered liberty. (Galston 2002: 38)

Whether liberalism can dispense with individual autonomy and still remain liberalism is an open question, however, and precisely where the balance is set between autonomy and diversity is a matter of fierce debate among liberals today.

## Bibliography

Addley, Easter, 'Religious rally opposes new gay rights', *The Guardian*, Wednesday, 10 January 2007.
Bachrach, P. and Baratz, M. S. (1962), 'The two faces of power', *American Political Science Review*, 56(4): 947–52.
Connolly, W. E. (2005), *Pluralism* (Durham NC: Duke University Press).
Dahl, R. A. (1956), *A Preface to Democratic Theory* (Chicago IL: Chicago University Press).
Dahl, R. A. (1961), *Who Governs? Democracy and Power in an American City* (New Haven CT: Yale University Press).
Dahl, R. A. (1985), *A Preface to Economic Democracy* (Cambridge: Polity).
Dunleavy, P. and O'Leary, B. (1987), *Theories of the State: The Politics of Liberal Democracy* (Basingstoke: Macmillan).
Dworkin, R. (1977), *Taking Rights Seriously* (London: Duckworth).
Etzioni, A. (1967), 'Mixed scanning: a third approach to decision making', *Public Administration Review*, 27: 5.
Freeden, M. (1999), 'True blood or false genealogy: New Labour and British social democratic thought', in Gamble, A. and Wright, T. (eds) (1999), *The New Social Democracy*, The Political Quarterly in Association with the Fabian Society (Oxford: Blackwell), pp. 151–65.
Galston, William A. (2002), *Liberal Pluralism* (Cambridge: Cambridge University Press).
Held, D. (2006), *Models of Democracy* (Cambridge: Polity).
Hirst, P. (1994), *Associative Democracy* (Cambridge: Polity).
Hirst, P. Q. (ed.) (1989), *The Pluralist Theory of the State: Selected Writings of G. D. H. Cole, J. N. Figgis, and H. J. Laski* (London: Routledge).
Husserl, E. (1970), *The Crisis of European Philosophy and Transcendental Philosophy* (Evanston IL: Northwestern University Press).
Kymlicka, W. (2002), *Contemporary Political Philosophy: An Introduction* (Oxford: Oxford University Press).
Lindblom, C. A. (1959), 'The science of muddling through', *Public Administration*, 19: 59–70.
Lindblom, C. A. (1965), *The Intelligence of Democracy* (New York: Free Press).
Lindblom, C. A. (1977), *Politics and Markets* (New York: Basic Books).
Lukács, G. (1971), *History and Class Consciousness* (London: Merlin).
McFarland, A. S. (2004), *Neopluralism: the Evolution of the Political Process Theory* (Lawrence KS: University Press of Kansas).

McLennan, D. (2000), *Karl Marx: Selected Writings* (Oxford: Oxford University Press).
McLennan, G. (1995), *Pluralism* (Buckingham: Open University Press).
Merelman, R. M. (2003), *Pluralism at Yale: the Culture of Political Science in America* (Wisconsin WI: University of Wisconsin Press).
Mills, C. U. (1963), *The Marxists* (London: Pelican Books).
Rawls, John (1971 [1972]), *A Theory of Justice* (Oxford: Oxford University Press).
Rawls, John (1982), 'Social unity and primary goods', in A. K. Sen and B. Williams (eds), *Utilitarianism and Beyond* (Cambridge: Cambridge University Press).
Rawls, John (1985), 'Justice as fairness: political not metaphysical', *Philosophy and Public Affairs*, 17/4: 223–51.
Rawls, John (1993), *Political Liberalism* (New York: Columbia University Press).
Schwarzmantel, J. (1994), *The State in Contemporary Society: an Introduction* (Hemel Hempstead: Harvester Wheatsheaf).
Smith, M. (2006), 'Pluralism', in C. Hay et al. (eds), *The State: Theories and Issues* (Basingstoke: Palgrave).

CHAPTER THREE

# The State and the Power Elite

*Erika Cudworth and John McGovern*

Elite theory represents a decisive break with the understandings of much liberal pluralism in that it takes as axiomatic the elite domination of the state. Whatever the form of polity and organisation of governmental institutions, the state is run by an elite. 'Classical' elitism, associated with the work of Robert Michels (1911 [1999]), Vilfredo Pareto (1935 [1976]) and Gaetano Mosca (1896 [1939]), considered that political power was always and irresistibly concentrated in the hands of a small ruling elite. Popular sovereignty is mythic, for all systems of governments are 'actually' oligarchic and any institutions or processes that claim to be 'democratic' are a 'sham' (Runciman 1963, cited Birch 1993: 169).

In order to substantiate this claim, Anthony Birch (1993: 170) considers that elite theorists need to provide evidence to support at least one of the following propositions. First, that access to political office is restricted to a small cohesive group with common interests that are not shared by the majority of citizens. Secondly, that office-holders are rarely responsive to the opinions and interests of the general public and are able to use coercion, persuasion or manipulation in order to induce public compliance. Finally, and associated with more contemporary left/Marxist elitist approaches, that office holders take decisions in line with the interests of a privileged group (such as a capitalist class). Elite theorists are both realists and empiricists, seeking to unmask the facade of liberal democratic practices or of political organisations and practices committed to socialism. However, the efficacy and substance of their empirical work varies in levels of systematisation and rigour. Certainly the classical elite theorists, despite an often passionate commitment to the 'scientific' study of society, produced work infused with ideology.

This chapter contextualises elite theory through a history of the concept of 'elite'. It examines the contribution of the 'classical' elite theorists, and of Max Weber and Joseph Schumpeter whose conceptions of democratic elitism inform more contemporary approaches. The second section considers how elite theory might be distinguished and considers the ways in which elite theorists define the state. Thirdly, the work of a number of more contemporary theorists is considered. The move from 'classical' to 'contemporary' elite theory involved a double shift. From its European origins as anti-Marxist theory, elite theory influenced a significant group of US scholars to produce a radical critique of liberal pluralism (Dunleavy and O'Leary 1987: 143–4). C. Wright Mills, *The Power Elite* is a seminal work here, which had a significant impact on future studies and enjoyed wide public popularity when it was first published (Crockett 1970: viii). Certainly it informs the work on the American political system conducted by G. William Domhoff, and the analysis of Britain undertaken by John Scott. The practical political footprint of elite theory is more difficult to assess, for no government, party or state claims to 'be' elitist. The final section will consider elite understandings of the nature of politics in three different historic forms of state: British liberal democracy; state socialism in Eastern Europe; and military government in Brazil.

## Context

Ever since the rise of civilisation nothing has been more common than 'the rule of the few'. In the ancient civilisations of China, India and the near East, classical Greece and Rome, medieval and early modern Europe, the belief prevailed that a minority was entitled to rule the majority as of right. Although Ancient Greece is now strongly associated with democracy, 'the rule of the many' was practised in Athens for only a century and three-quarters. Other ancient Greek societies were monarchies, aristocracies or tyrannies and throughout the Hellenic period most of the Greek world was subjected to the rule of powerful kings who were, like the rulers of ancient India or China, conceived of as representatives of transcendent order (Gardner 1974: xxi). The political theory of the greatest of all the classical philosophers identified the best type of state with the rule of an enlightened minority. As John Dunn has remarked, for Plato democracy was 'an all but demented solvent of value, decency and good judgement . . . the rule of the foolish, vicious, and always potentially brutal' (Dunn 2005: 45).

Nor was Athens a democracy in the modern sense. Of the total population during the fourth century only one-tenth were full citizens participating in the government of the *polis*: 'non-Athenian residents . . . inhuman objects of property (the many slaves) and the unreasoning second sex (women) were excluded without question or hesitation' (Fox 2006: 94). Moreover, among the adult males of Athenian descent who did enjoy full citizen status most did not participate actively in the business of rule, neither always attending the supreme governing body, the Assembly, nor, crucially, addressing it. Mogens Hansen has shown that Athenian democrats did not understand equality as it is conceived of in the celebrated sentence from the American Declaration of Independence which claims that 'all men are created equal'. Only a few of the minority of full citizens who actually attended a meeting of the Assembly would speak: 'in the Athenian democracy the indispensable political initiative was stimulated by ambition . . . and competition . . . neither of which is compatible with natural equality' (Hansen 1999: 83–4).

Within the various institutions of the Athenian democracy 'the best' tended to predominate. In the fourth century the Areopagus was a high court trying cases of homicide against Athenian citizens and treasonable offences, as well as supervising the administration of law in other courts and sometimes over-ruling the results of popular elections. Although, as Hansen has remarked, 'it was not a forum for a political elite' in that those appointed to it were not professional politicians, the Areopagus 'contained a disproportionate number of the well-to-do' (1999: 290). The magistrates who prepared business for the Assembly and implemented its decisions were also recruited from 'the best'. They were chosen by lot but only from among those who chose to put their names forward. An ordinary citizen might well have hesitated to do so since on leaving office and at any time during their tenure magistrates had to account for their actions and face punishment if they were judged to have acted badly or incompetently. The result was, as Bernard Manin has observed, 'self-selection from among potential magistrates' (Manin 1997: 12–13). The most important magistracies, those connected with the conduct of war and financial management, were elected and it was in them, rather than the offices filled by lot, 'that persons of eminence would be found'. Throughout the history of democratic Athens, as Manin has noted, the most influential politicians and military leaders were elected from the ranks of landed and, later, wealthy families such that 'there was a certain correlation between the exercise of public office and membership in political and social elites' (1997: 16). However, the institutions of ancient democracy were designed to rule out the possibility of power being held by a distinct political elite in the modern sense, that is to say, a class of professional politicians.

Drawing selectively upon ancient Greek and Roman sources, the civic humanists of Renaissance Florence and, later, the classical republicans of seventeenth-century England and eighteenth-century America attributed to 'the few' the role of guardians of the state. Significantly, however, according to this tradition the minority who should hold public office because they could be trusted to uphold the *res publica* were not the feudal nobility but wealthy town dwellers (Pocock 1975: 100–1). Within the classical republican tradition the new political aristocracy which governed was not entitled to do so on account of the fact that it was an hereditary elite but, rather, on 'rational' grounds which would be 'naturally recognizable by the Many' (1975: 515). The now virtually unquestioned notion that traditional landed aristocracy is the natural enemy of liberty is a consequence of the prevalence of a specific understanding of freedom first articulated by the Renaissance humanists, most notably Machiavelli for whom liberty signified freedom from political oppression (Skinner 1981: 52). That understanding reflected the style of life of ascendant commercially powerful elites whose economic and political interests were incompatible with the rule of feudal powers and the universal Church (see Chapter 1).

Machiavelli also redefined the concept of political 'virtue' in such a way as to reflect the outlook of statesmen, lawyers, administrators and diplomats, the 'natural aristocracy' that created the early modern state. Detaching it from the belief in transcendent moral order to which pre-modern rulers had been bound, *virtù* came to represent those character traits necessary to establish and maintain civic autonomy (Skinner 1981: 39, 53–4). *Virtù* was no longer the endowment of feudal warriors whom destiny had made lords but belonged to the 'rational' ruler who, through a calculation of advantage and by showing the determined self-assertion that brought good fortune, was able to resist fate. Machiavelli's utterly this-worldly understanding of what it is that entitles an elite to rule is the antithesis of the divinely sanctioned right to dominate claimed by pre-modern rulers. It is equally incompatible with classical philosophy's insistence that rulers must possess moral virtue. It is the first authentically modern understanding of what, symptomatically, we call 'the business of rule'.

Only fifty-five delegates, almost all 'gentlemen, "natural aristocrats", who took their political superiority for granted as an inevitable consequence of their social and economic position', attended the Philadelphia convention of 1787 that created the American constitution (Wood 2005: 147). The convention was, in Thomas Jefferson's words, 'a power superior to that of the ordinary legislature' since it aimed at creating law more fundamental than that already embodied in the states' written constitutions (2005: 138). Both the outcome of the convention, the new constitution and the means by which it was arrived at reflected the power of an elite. Those whose political vision prevailed, the federalists, created a new central government vested with wide-ranging fiscal powers and control over foreign policy, a national republic, which was to be imposed upon the states. At the head of the new system stood the presidential office in which monarch-like executive power over the armed forces, diplomatic relations and appointments to the judiciary was concentrated. Although finally dependent upon popular consent, the new constitution 'involved a serious diminution of popular participation' (Kramnick 1987: 41) in that a system of representation involving indirect election was devised which ensured that the Senate would be composed of what the leading federalist, James Madison, called a 'temperate and respectable body of citizens' responsible for protecting the common people from 'the tyranny of their own passions' (Madison et al. 1987: 371). To this natural aristocracy would fall the duty of upholding the rule of law without which the people would be 'stimulated by some irregular passion, or some illicit advantage, or misled by the artful misrepresentations of interested men' (Madison et al. 1987: 371).

Much might be made of the difference between conservatism and aristocratic republicanism like Madison's. It is true that Burke saw heredity both as a qualification for ruling and as a force for political stability. On the other hand, there may be little practical difference between the republican view that the reason why the political elite tends to be recruited from the 'better' families and the reason why it should govern are the same, namely, because its members are superior to the rest, and the conservative belief that it is because they are propertied that commercially-minded landed aristocracies should rule. Burke himself claimed that merit was an indispensable requirement for high office, observing ruefully that even low-born Irishmen maintained the political nation upon which great aristocrats depended and that what he called a 'true natural aristocracy' would include leading professionals and businessmen as well as the titled nobility (Morrow 1998: 159). This notion of a 'natural' elite was central to nineteenth-century liberalism. Tocqueville's warning of the danger of a 'tyranny of the majority' indicated to liberals, notably John Stuart Mill, that the masses required political and moral leadership. Influenced by Coleridge's notion of a 'clerisy', an independent cultural elite responsible for providing rulers with moral education (Coleridge 1972), Mill sought to extend the role of the enlightened few to civilising the masses. He also proposed an electoral system that, while permitting mass enfranchisement, would nevertheless ensure that a political elite remained in command of the administration of the state (Mill 1991). Like Tocqueville, however, Mill believed that the forces of democracy were irresistible. The rule of the few was to be a necessary but passing phase during which the masses, under the benign tutelage of a 'progressive' elite, would achieve the political maturity required for self-rule.

Not all nineteenth-century thinkers were so optimistic about the future of democracy. Some took the view that elite rule had not been outmoded by history but was a permanent feature of any political society and that modern politics required the commanding presence of a self-conscious and resolute minority of 'the best'. 'For institutions to exist there must exist the kind of will, instinct, imperative that is anti-liberal to the point of malice,' wrote Nietzsche. As for democracy, that, he declared, is 'the *decaying form* of the state' (original emphasis). Empire, not democracy, embodies the vital anti-liberal and anti-democratic will that creates political order. The Roman Empire had once gloriously represented this political will to power. In his own day, when 'the entire West has lost the instincts out of which institutions grow, out of which the future grows', Nietzsche looked to the East and saw in authoritarian Tsarist Russia 'the only power today which has durability in it, which can wait, which can still promise something' (Nietzsche 1968: 93–4).

Nietzsche's hatred of democracy was the political consequence of his view that 'life simply is will to power' so that ' "exploitation" does not belong to a corrupt or imperfect or primitive society; it belongs to the essence of what lives' (Nietzsche 1966: 203). It would follow, of course, that any attempt to eliminate exploitation in the name of democracy and equality is not simply misguided. It would involve a denial of 'life'. 'Life', for Nietzsche, meant a will to transform the world. The best state would be one founded on 'exploitation', that is to say, the process of self-overcoming by which men destroy what is 'alien' and 'weak' in themselves or in others and take responsibility for creating themselves. Democracy, because it represents 'the diminution of man, making him mediocre' and reducing him to the level of 'the herd', is incompatible with the goal of life, self-overcoming. Only 'aristocratic society', where there is 'the long ladder of an order of rank and differences in value between man and man' and 'slavery in some sense or other', permits the expression of what Nietzsche, like Machiavelli, believed to be the distinctively human value of freedom as self-assertion. Nietzsche's rulers were neither courtiers nor bourgeoisie but 'barbarians in every terrible sense of the word, men of prey who were still in possession of unbroken strength of will and lust for power' (1966: 201) The 'finest type' of such a ruler was Julius Caesar (Nietzsche 1968: 93). The future would belong to a new 'higher aristocracy' whom Nietzsche conceived of as simultaneously a racial, spiritual and political elite, a 'new caste'. Although it is all too easy to see why Nietzsche has so often been taken to be protofascist (Detwiler 1990: 113), it is equally clear that no value was more central to his thought than that of liberty.

The concept of a political elite took a crucial turn in the writings of Nietzsche in that he understood it in a new context, that of modern mass democracy. Political thinkers from Machiavelli to Madison never questioned the inevitability of elite rule. Their concern was to establish the authority of new 'natural' elites. Nineteenth-century industrialisation, nationalism and the growth of the administrative power of the state created an environment in which socialism emerged and with it the notion that there might be a 'democratic' society in which there is no political elite and 'the people' would somehow rule themselves. In the eighteenth century Burke had regarded that notion as amounting to a logical absurdity: 'The people are the natural control on authority,' he argued, 'but to exercise and to control together is contradictory and impossible'

(Burke 1960: 52). By the late nineteenth century, however, a revolutionary movement had appeared whose enthusiasts believed fervently that there was nothing either contradictory or impossible in the prospect of the people exercising political power. As Nietzsche saw, this socialist vision of 'democracy' descended from secularised Judaism and Christianity and not from ancient Athens. Fundamentally mythical, its adherents would not be defeated by merely rational objections such as Burke's. It was in response to this millennialist revolt against the inevitability of elite rule that the theory of modern elitism emerged.

## Definition

The mere recognition of the existence of political elites does not make a theory 'elitist'. It is difficult to see how any political theory could fail to acknowledge the fact that, historically, those who have ruled have composed a minority. Certainly socialists do not deny the existence of elites. Marx's vision of history is a vision of exploitation of majorities by minorities. What makes a theory elitist is its insistence that elites are inevitable. The political theory of elitism could not have arisen until the nineteenth century because it was only then that the historical conditions emerged that made possible a movement, socialism, predicated on the assumption that elite rule can and should be eliminated.

Another nineteenth-century development, the emergence of 'social science' or the notion that there could and should be an extension of the mode of inquiry characteristic of modern natural science to the study of human affairs also contributed towards the emergence of elitism. In the work of some of its most prominent exponents, notably Vilfredo Pareto, the thesis that elite rule is inevitable was supported by what was supposed to be 'logico-experimental' reasoning. As Raymond Aron showed, Pareto offered two definitions of the concept of an elite or, as he also termed it, 'aristocracy' (Aron 1970: 159–61). First, elites were those minorities most successful within any sphere of activity, whether it was business, art or prostitution. Pareto supposed that it was possible to specify with scientific precision membership of such elites. To refer to an elite in this sense was to make a wholly neutral value-free judgement. The second narrower definition referred to the smaller minority of individuals who participated in the business of rule, the political elite. For Pareto the character of any given society is given by its elites and especially its ruling elite.

Although Pareto's ruling elite resembles the Marxian notion of the 'capitalist class', Pareto distinguished his theory from historical materialism by means of two further claims. The first was that a ruling elite had not simply achieved economic dominance but also emerged as a result of superior military power and by having won possession of the state. That is, Pareto refused to view political power as merely an emanation of economic strength or the state as nothing more than an instrument deployed by the wealthy. The second was that a political elite is a permanent feature of any society. It followed that the victory of the proletariat anticipated by Marxists would not issue in government by the people but would represent victory for a socialist elite who claimed to act on behalf of the people.

Pareto's contention that the political distinction between rulers and ruled is both universal and the most significant of all social phenomena (Finer 1976: 14) is the defining characteristic of elite theory. Gaetano Mosca also proposed that what he called 'a ruling class' is 'among the constant facts and tendencies that are to be found in all political organisms, one so obvious that it is apparent to the most casual eye' (Mosca 1939: 50). Robert Michels called this 'constant fact' a law, the 'iron law of oligarchy'. On the basis of an empirical study of European socialist parties, especially the German SPD, he argued that they displayed a characteristic common to all large-scale organisations, namely, a pronounced tendency for power to concentrate in the hands of a small minority of leaders regardless of the cherished belief that the will of 'the people' was authentically present in socialist movements (Michels 1999).

If Michels argued that bureaucracy defeats democracy because it creates an elite that is not the servant of 'the people' but its master, Max Weber took the view that bureaucratic elites might be controlled by a political elite. For Weber, centralised administration was an indispensable functional requirement of the modern state because of the size, complexity and diversity of modern societies. However, a developed bureaucratic structure serves not merely 'administrative purposes' but also, Weber argued, engages 'of necessity' with 'the exercise of rule' (Weber 1978: Vol. II, 951–2). Weber believed that bureaucrats could not be relied upon to provide effective political leadership principally because they are trained to accept and not to exercise authority. No less significant was the fact that bureaucracy works best 'the more it is "dehumanized", the more completely it succeeds in eliminating from official business love, hatred, and all purely personal, irrational, and emotional elements which escape calculation' (1978: Vol. II, 975). The spirit of bureaucracy was incompatible with the patriotism required of national leadership while the 'rationalization' of both the political and the economic spheres threatened personal freedom (Beetham 1985: 119–20, 46–7). Nevertheless, it was clear to Weber that the government of a modern nation could not take the form of direct democracy precisely because a technically effective and professionalised administration has become 'completely indispensable' (Weber 1978: Vol. I, 223). Moreover, mandated representatives acting as agents of their constituents would not possess the freedom of discretion required to negotiate between conflicting interests or alter policy in the light of rapidly changing circumstances (Held 1996: 163).

Weber concluded that only an elected elite, working within an assembly modelled on the British parliamentary system, where leaders proved their worth in competitive debate and party struggle, could provide leadership strong enough to control the bureaucratic power of the modern state. Weber believed that the result of mass enfranchisement had been the rise of 'machine' party politics and the decline of parliaments as places where policy was decided on rational grounds. The extension of the franchise had not created the conditions for rule by the many. It had brought into being the rule of the professional politician. Career politicians, 'normally nothing better than well-disciplined "Yes" men', had to be controlled by charismatic leaders, Weber argued, since the real choice faced in modern politics is 'between leadership democracy with a "machine" and leaderless democracy, namely, the rule of professional politicians without a calling' (Weber 1970: 106, 113). If Weber preferred the former it was because the latter represented the penetration of the 'dehumanizing' bureaucratic spirit into the political sphere. Bureaucratic 'leaderless democracy' threatened not only national self-determination but also the freedom of the individual understood in customary liberal terms as 'the possession of an independent sphere of activity, guaranteed by private property, over which the individual is master' (Beetham 1985: 48).

Weber's endorsement of democracy was highly qualified. Not a good in itself, it was a means subservient to two ends. One was national greatness. Weber denounced the inconsistency of conservatives who sought to secure Germany's position as a great power while at the same time rejecting the necessary political consequence, the mobilisation of mass support by means of democracy (1985: 119). The other was the liberal goal of individual freedom. Here democracy was required to counter the threat to liberty posed by bureaucratisation. For Weber it was 'a piece of crude self-deception' to imagine that the freedom of the individual was anything other than the highest of values in a modern society (Weber 1994: 159).

Whereas Pareto viewed democracy as the opposite of elite rule because of his instrumental understanding of democracy Weber was able to see a way in which the two could be linked – 'democratic elitism'. Rule by charismatic leaders under conditions of party competition or, as he called it, 'plebiscitary leadership democracy' was, for Weber, 'the only feasible approximation to a genuine representative democracy' (Dunleavy and O'Leary 1987: 142). Democracy must be 'plebiscitary' because mass elections were no more than votes of confidence in governments. It must be 'leadership democracy' or, to use Weber's even more candid term, 'Caesarist', because what was at issue in elections was not policy. Weber saw no reason to believe that electorates understand policy. What was at stake was the popular appeal of political elites (Held 1996: 172). On Weber's view, what makes a modern state 'democratic' is that it possesses an electoral system by means of which a political elite acquires power. Democracy, under modern conditions, could have nothing to do with popular sovereignty in anything other than the mythical sense to which leaders appeal in order to secure popular support.

Joseph Schumpeter advanced a very similar 'democratic elitist' theory of the modern state. Modern democracy, he wrote, is 'the rule of the politician' (Schumpeter 1987: 285). The part played by the people is not to rule but 'to produce a government'. Neither equality for all nor participation in political power, democracy was defined by Schumpeter in strictly electoral terms as 'that institutional arrangement for arriving at political decisions in which individuals acquire the power to decide by means of a competitive struggle for the people's vote' (1987: 269). Like Weber, Schumpeter endorsed democratic elitism both because it accounted for the necessity of leadership and, equally, because he believed that only a political elite could defend individual freedoms from the increasingly bureaucratic modern state. If electors can change governments by choosing between political parties then they can hope to preserve their freedom from a state, which, in the absence of competing elites, would become an irresistible force reaching into and controlling every department of life. Although Schumpeter thought of 'the typical citizen' as 'infantile' in his appreciation of politics, he attributed enough understanding to voters to enable them to know which of at least two political parties were most likely to implement policies that would satisfactorily co-ordinate their diverse demands and interests (1987: 262).

Nevertheless, if elite theory delights in unmasking the democratic pretensions of liberalism, this signifies a commitment on the part of its adherents to the value of freedom that is the essence of liberalism itself. According to Isaiah Berlin's influential account, it was by denying the existence of a substantive 'common good' in favour of a plurality of incommensurable values that Machiavelli effectively invented the modern concept of liberty (Berlin 1979). In subscribing to the belief in the irreducible heterogeneity of values the elite theorists followed Machiavelli. Socialists typically argue that elite theorists, by endorsing a cynical view of parliamentary government and emphasising the importance of political leadership, actually justified the utter subjection of civil society to the state that was to become characteristic of fascism. However, as we shall see in Chapter 7, fascism was predicated on the notion of a 'general will' or 'common good'. Like Nietzsche, Pareto denied that anything real corresponded to this notion. Societies are always more or less heterogeneous and between the different interests motivating diverse groups no rational choice is possible: 'there is no criterion save sentiment for choosing one or the other' (Pareto 1976: 45). Whenever a choice between different interests is made and then designated 'the good of the community' it remains a subjective one. Of course, passing off their private judgement of what is good as if that also represents 'the common good' is exactly what non-liberal political elites are able to do. Pareto could not have emphasised more how it is not reason but the irrational features of human motivation that account for the business of rule. It is not reason but violence and fraud that permit rulers to stay in power.

Pareto's 'scientific' view 'denies the possibility of a rational choice between one political regime and another' (Aron 1970: 172). That is to say, the choice is *free*. Similarly, Max Weber's declaration that the choice between 'which of the warring gods we should serve' is a subjective one with no justification other than the individual's feeling of commitment (Weber 1970: 152–3) indicates Weber's adherence to the fundamental value of freedom. Schumpeter also claimed that 'there is . . . no such thing as a uniquely determined common good that all people could agree on or be made to agree on by the force of rational argument' (Schumpeter 1987: 251). Although there is no genuine common good, Schumpeter pointed out that, using the same techniques as are used in commercial advertising, professional politicians and ideologues can produce 'a manufactured will'. To the extent that this succeeds 'the will of the people is the product and not the motive power of the political process' (Schumpeter 1987: 263). A preoccupation with freedom lies behind this vision of 'the common good' as a fraudulent imposition. For this reason, as we shall see in the following section, it was possible for thinkers of the libertarian left to make use of elite theory in the twentieth century.

## Theorists

More contemporary approaches in elite theory are often associated with 'radical elitism', emerging in the United States after 1930. Despite the fact that classical elitism was intent on refuting Marx (Parry 1969: 27), the metamorphosis of elite analysis is not altogether startling if we consider the incipient liberalism within the elite theory tradition. For Dunleavy and O'Leary (1987: 143) the likely explanation for the precise location of radical elitism was the absence of a significant socialist force in the US, which left open a niche for a left-thinking anti-pluralism. Urban sociologists such as Floyd Hunter (1953) began to use elite concepts to critique pluralist notions of democratic city politics, and suggested that power was in the hands of business and social elites. Those such as C. Wright Mills attempted to integrate aspects of Marxism into a 'ruling elite' model of the national state. Mills was also influenced by Weberian notions of status, and acknowledges a debt to Thorstein Veblen's theory of the 'leisure class' in America, in this regard (Mills 1956: 58–9). Left critiques of class and power in the US were also influenced by a concern around the policing of status reflected in informed public opinion and journalistic accounts (Packard 1961).

Mills's study of *The Power Elite* (1956) proposed a model with a trinity of elite groups 'centred in the command posts of the major institutional hierarchies' political, economic and military (Mills 1956: 4), united by a common consciousness of their interests and institutional power (1956: 296). The political elite is composed of members of the executive branch of Federal government – the presidency and Whitehouse staff. The economic elite was centred on the corporate rich in the expanding large business corporations. The Pentagon establishment clustered around the Joint Chiefs of Staff constitutes the military elite.

Mills (1956: 167–9) argued that there was a single 'power elite' composed of overlapping and interlinking elite groups attached to various state functions. The organisation of these centres of power had become increasing linked through institutional intersections and the osmosis of personnel in 'overlapping crowds and intricately connected cliques' (1956: 11). The power elite has a common social basis in urban family clusters evidenced in the Social Registers kept for the major US cities. Its member's live exclusive lives 'set apart from the rest of the community' (1956: 57). They attend the same kind of schools and universities from which they gain privileged entrance and access to certain kinds of professions. This is utterly political, for it is Mills's contention that the power elite is drawn from a highly class-conscious and self-aware group which actively reproduces itself (1956: 283). The power elite directs public policy to suit the ends of its constitutive groups, which are intrinsically compatible due to the 'coincidence of interests' (1956: 292).

Mills allows that the pluralist picture of a politics of groups and competing interests might apply to some aspects of the US polity, such as the compromises secured in the legislative houses, but not to the powerhouse, the executive (1956: 255–9). However, he is scathing of the effectiveness of voting and participation in parties and pressure groups in terms of exercising any real control over the 'power elite'. Rather, Mills sees increasing centralisation in US politics wherein elected representatives decrease in significance and corporate interests are represented in the form of political advisers on the Whitehouse staff (1956: 235). There are also elements of similarity with Marxist approaches such as that of Ralph Miliband (1969, 1982; see Chapter 4), in that Mills identifies the ways in which economic and political elites are drawn together by a web of close relationships and overlapping interests. However, the Marxist belief that 'the political apparatus is merely an extension of the corporate world' (Mills 1956: 170) is for Mills, an economistic reductionism that underestimates the significance of the political.

## The State and the Power Elite

Certainly his point that 'the military capitalism of private corporations exists in a weakened and formal democratic system' (1956: 276) has been pursued by more contemporary theorists and has resonance with current debates on America's role as a 'world power'.

Unlike the classical elitists, Mills does not presume that societies are always and inevitably elitist. His argument is also one for a process of historical change – America has moved from a democratic society in the nineteenth century to an oligarchy by the 1950s. The causes of this change are the structural social developments and institutional weaknesses that facilitate the concentration of political power. First, American democracy, in terms of voting and pressure group activity, is weak, and the elected houses have limited and fragmented power (Mills 1956: 256). Secondly, expansion in international trade has increased the power of multinational corporations, who seek to influence the 'political directorate' in order to best secure markets and conditions. Thirdly, the expansion of the US role abroad has increased the political influence of the military elite, and the economy has become increasingly dependent on the defence industries. Finally, US popular culture is highly consumerist, and corporate advertising influences both individual political choices and collective political culture. Mills emphasises the abilities of the power elite to shape the conditions within which power can be exercised – to manipulate and indoctrinate or to condition power (1956: 305–17).

Mills has been particularly criticised for arguing that the power elite is a single political formation. Individual incumbents changing roles do not, in Tom Bottomore's view, substantiate the unity of the power elite (1973: 274). In addition, he (1993: 23–4) suggests that Mills cannot provide any more than a descriptive account of the solidarity of the power elite, because he will not accept the idea that the elite is a ruling class with particular systemic functions. For pluralist scholars such as Robert Dahl (1961, 1963), the 'elite' Mills specifies is more fragmented than unitary, and elements act in terms of issues pertinent to their specific memberships. Seen through the pluralist lens, the 'power elite' is a plethora of small elite groups advancing their interests. Mills argues that history is not the product of social forces but is made by individuals from certain backgrounds, in positions of power, making certain kinds of collective decisions. For Marxists however, the question of social origins is limited in value, as the state is functional for the perpetuation of the system of capitalism, and bias towards corporate interests is built in to the policy making process because of the structural constraints of the system (Miliband 1982: 31).

While Mills has a dualistic conception of the US polity, with the power elite sitting atop elements of a pluralist system (in state government and in Congress), G. William Domhoff suggests that national power elites are supported by and intrinsically linked to a vast support network of regional and local elites. Policy makers at these levels are highly important and both channel and shape diverse interests from more localised elites, integrating a mass of diverse elite interests (Domhoff 1967: 137).

For Domhoff, the state is run by a 'governing class' (1967: 3) which 'owns a disproportionate amount of a country's wealth, receives a disproportionate amount of a country's yearly income, and contributes a disproportionate number of its members to the controlling institutions and key decision-making groups in the country' (Domhoff 1967: 5). By allowing the elite to be a class, Domhoff can draw on the explanatory power of Marxism in suggesting that the liberal democratic state is functional for that particular group. However, Domhoff (1987: 190) stresses the distinctiveness of his 'class-and-institutions-theory' in which the institutions of the state have 'potential' autonomy from class. This distinction is overdrawn, for there are Marxists who allow for such potential autonomy of the political (Poulantzas 1978).

Similarly to Mills, Domhoff outlines an American upper class by drawing on Social Registers, histories of 'high-society', social clubs, preparatory schools and more in a mass of thick description. Domhoff links the upper class to control of the corporate economy through stock ownership and determination of general policy priorities (1967: 40–50), which he exemplifies with statistical data and cases of individual influence. Business dominates the process of the articulation of interest in the US political system and thereby controls the political agenda from which issue-based decisions are drawn and confirmed. A key mechanism by which this is achieved is the import of 'political outsiders' to the policy-making process, overwhelmingly, from the corporate executive and the military (1967: 104–5). Such processes construct a general consensus on political matters, facilitating a broad legitimacy for the specific decisions made by the governing elite. Electoral success depends on politicians being seen to deliver on economic performance and thereby the political elite is beholden to the demands of the capitalist class, in addition to the funding of political parties from corporate coffers (1967: 86–7). This can be seen in nominations for electoral candidates and in nominees for key offices in the main political parties and in the networks of affiliations between political parties (Domhoff 1972) and the upper echelons of the corporate community (Domhoff 1987: 195–9).

Domhoff's method also involves defining elite groups and examining their social origins and intersections, but his is a less polemical and more empirically detailed account than Mills's. Whether this makes it a better account is debateable. It certainly meets pluralist criticisms head on (Dahl 1970: 38–42). Domhoff is clear in defining the basis, scope and magnitude of the power of the governing elite, he accounts for differences and divisions within the elite and plurality of opinion within elite circles. His use of the concept of social class also allows him to counter the Marxist critique that raises the question of elite cohesion. Domhoff's governing class has a collective interest (1967: 147–2), but how this articulates itself explicitly within the political executive is not addressed. Domhoff avoids the question of decision making on grounds that it involves a focus on observable political behaviour, on key issues and on decisions made, which underestimates the mobilisation of bias and the articulation of interest in the political system (Bachrach and Baratz 1962; Lukes 1974). This question of substantiating interest is one that is perhaps better attended to by more strongly Marxist influenced elite approaches.

In the British polity, John Scott (1979) has demonstrated that there remains a great concentration of family wealth which has strong connections with the ownership and control of corporate property. The key corporate executives and property owners are intimately connected and form a single, cohesive social group, while the 'service class' of middle and lower levels of management, although organisationally significant, do not make crucial strategic decisions about the deployment of capital (Scott 1979: 175–6). This understanding of the British class structure underpins Scott's analysis of the state.

Scott's *Who Rules Britain?* intends to substantiate the view that the ruling elite is not a nominal category but a 'real and active social group' (1991: 2). He (1991: 4) considers that the term 'ruling class' usefully combines the economic concept of class with 'the political concept of rule'. Scott argues that there is a ruling class in Britain, and contends that as a result of an historical symbiosis, representatives of this class group act in concert to reproduce the conditions of their economic dominance (1991: 31).

Scott outlines the development of the British capitalist class in the twentieth century, arguing that we have seen the development of a unified capitalist business class with linked interests in land, commerce and industry (1991: 80–90). He compares corporate interests and personnel, arguing that groups of finance and executive capitalists have a 'direct supervisory position in the affairs of the system on which their privileges depend' (1991: 91). Their political recruitment depends both on their location within the capitalist economy and the possession of a particular kind of social background. Scott considers traditional social networks and prestige institutions including schools, universities and private clubs in accounting for the ways in which industrial capitalists in the nineteenth century came to accept the 'hegemony' of the values of the traditional propertied classes (1991: 128–9). The cohesiveness of that elite is maintained by strategies of closure (limiting the entry of outsiders, usually dependent on common social background) mediated by incorporation of wider social groups in order to reproduce the legitimacy of the elite (1991: 138). The ruling class sustains a policy consensus and hegemony of political culture more widely, particularly in relation to business practices, by guaranteeing the framework and substance of property, company and commercial law and pursuing policies conducive to private property and capital accumulation (1991: 23; Scott 1997: 2–10). However, the processes of incorporation results in shifts in policy consensus and some element of variety in the composition of the political elite, which Scott maps across the twentieth century (1991: 133–7) through which the capitalist class becomes organised around an 'inner circle' of finance capitalists.

More recently, Scott (1997) has sought to broaden the analyses of the power of finance capital and the power of multinational corporations in a comparative framework covering various countries and regions of the globe. Here, he attempts to demonstrate both the diversity of formations of corporate governance and the interlocking networks of financial flows, ownership patterns, class structures and policy regimes. Scott (1997: 262–73) argues that nation-states continue to be powerful in shaping the process of capital accumulation, both in striving to maintain the integrity of their national economies and enhancing the power of multinational corporations. This means that the interests of the capitalist ruling class operate on an internal and external level, collectively orchestrating a policy consensus, which realises their interests on a globalised scale (see also van der Pijl 1989: 254–61).

Scott's Marxism invites the standard pluralist attacks. The policy consensus he argues is constituted in line with dominant class interest could be a genuine consensus of opinion among parties, policy makers and the public. However, he provides a careful account of the various historical processes that draw elite groups together and result in a coalescing of interests. He considers how these map on to political agendas in a more convincing way than either Mills or Domhoff, who remain overly occupied with social background. The latter does not lend itself to an analysis which takes account of international context, whereas Scott's work fits with a genre of Marxist theorising of the state, class and corporate capital that has formed an important element of the globalisation literature (see Chapter 12; also Bottomore 1989). For Dunleavy and O'Leary, elite theorists do not test their suppositions sufficiently as their focus is on 'surrogates for power rather than the exercise of power itself' (1987: 150). This is evident in the preoccupation with analysing the social backgrounds of elite groups, and taking these as indicators for how they behave and what their interests are. As we have seen in Scott's work, not all elite theory is reliant on such inference. If the 'exercise of power itself' is taken to mean actual decision making, then pluralism is also open to the criticism of inference. In the classic study *Who Governs?* Robert Dahl states that even if a political decision appears not to reflect certain groups of social interests, those interests will have been attended to in the process of making the actual decisions (1961: 181–3). This process of attention is, however, beyond the scope of this work. Additionally, as Paul Bachrach and Morton Baratz argue, a focus on decision making 'takes no account of the fact that power may be, and often is, exercised by confining the scope of decision making to relatively "safe" issues' (1962: 948). Perhaps the most damaging critique of elite theory involves the assumption that political power is cumulative (Parry 1969: 136). However, in Domhoff and particularly Scott, political power is complex, multi-layered and crosscut with tensions. In these accounts power does not breed power in a simple way but may be contested and contravened, with the exercise of power by elite groups always being the result of a complicated process of political struggle through which interests are formed, refined and promoted.

## Practical politics

Elite theory has had a lasting academic impact in encouraging a refocusing of intellectual energy on the state. Marxist influenced theorists such as Theda Skocpol (1979) have argued for an approach that balances an analysis of the structural constraints of capital with the relative autonomy of state institutions, allowing for the possibility that the state may act against the interests of the economically dominant class. Here, the state is not a passive receptacle of social forces and pressure but can transform society on its own initiative, particularly in order to reproduce the conditions for its own legitimacy. Domhoff (1987: 160) sees such approaches as direct descendents of C. Wright Mills (see also Jessop 1990: 283). Other perspectives have also deployed elite theory, for example, feminist studies of women's representation and operation within US state government (Moore 1987) and large corporations (Ghiloni 1987). There has been continued interest in applying elite analyses to different kinds of policy making from community and urban studies, through central and local government studies to international relations (Evans 2006: 50–7). State communist regimes have also been analysed in terms of a relatively unified centralised elite that fuses political and administrative power and monopolises decision making. Authoritarian capitalist regimes, such as those in some developing countries, have been understood with plural elite models, often focusing on relations between military states and social and economic elites.

When Mills first published the *Power Elite*, his understandings of US politics were given a surprising endorsement. President Eisenhower's farewell address of 1957 warned of the influence of a 'military-industrial complex' that was to be found 'in every city, every State House, every office of the Federal Government' (quoted in Parry 1969: 64). It is notable that this was a public warning. A marked contrast between this and some other chapters is that we cannot use self-ascription as a device in selecting examples of elitism in practical politics. Elite theory seeks to unmask the facade of states, government and parties based on ideologies such as liberal pluralism, Marxism and social democracy, and posit a rule by elite. The remainder of this section will focus on analyses of different types of state in the twentieth century – British liberal democracy, state socialism in eastern Europe and the 'military republic' in

Brazil, considering the ways in which an understanding of elite theory may or may not give us a purchase on political 'realities'.

The journalist and writer Anthony Sampson has been producing his 'anatomies' of Britain since the early 1960s, and his writings about the mechanisms of political power in British society have been highly influential. Sampson examines a range of institutional power locations in Britain and argues that centres of both executive and financial power have become more centralised and concentrated, more integrated, and more divorced from the 'people' (Sampson 2004: xii).

For Sampson there is no one centre of power in Britain, but numerous hierarchical structures around which power coalesces. The House of Commons has become less powerful, certainly compared with the mid 1800s, but its members have become more professionalised and socially homogeneous forming a 'political class' of insular, full-time politicians, dependent on re-election (2004: 10). The British party system is in a condition of terminal decline, certainly in democratic terms of grassroots organisations attempting to represent their communities, and trades unions, vehicles of functional representation in the pluralist view, have negligible influence. The Prime Minister, and his or her staff, is increasingly powerful; a trajectory begun over forty years ago and promoted in particular by Margaret Thatcher and Tony Blair. The cabinet is divorced from both public and Parliament and bypassed by the Prime Minister. The bureaucracy remains an elite in terms of its social homogeneity, but is compromised by outside advisers, mainly from the business elite (2004: 125). Oxbridge and the British public schools are still found to be highly disproportionate in educating members of all elite groups (2004: 199). The secret services and military have become increasingly influential in defence decisions, gaining power as the politics of diplomacy declines (2004: 175). Significant changes involve the increasing influence of the news media (2004: 261) and private companies, particularly multinational corporations which are incredibly powerful yet lack any kind of accountability (2004: 295).

The most recent picture that Sampson paints is one of increasing openness of certain institutions and cosmopolitan diversity. Yet change is a shield for a creeping centralisation within central government. Earlier 'anatomies' of Britain (Sampson 1962, 1982) showed an establishment which ruled, but through a plural elite model in which the centres of power link and overlap to different degrees and with different sets of other elite groups without a clear focus or centre. What Sampson suggests he has been documenting across the decades is a marketisation of the British political system. In the new circles of power Sampson draws the circles are half as many, some are large in influence and others, more heavily drawn, have little accountability and much power. He argues that the British concept of pluralism is now outdated for the new British establishment is of one colour – the colour of money (2004: 360). In Britain then, we have the suggestion that an 'old' establishment has gradually been superseded by one more apparently open, but perhaps more pervasive, powerful and unaccountable.

What then of polities in which the old order has been swept away in its entirety, and the historic powers of aristocratic and capitalist classes are no more? Did the end of social inequality in state socialist eastern Europe mean the absence of a power elite? Milovan Djilas (1957) made explicit application of Weber's understanding of bureaucracy and its relation to political parties in arguing that a 'new class' emerged in the state socialist counties of eastern Europe in the post-war period, composed of the highest ranks of the state and party bureaucracy. Due to their administrative monopoly, members of this social elite were able to accrue privilege and even property in the Soviet system and to enjoy special relationships with and over other social groups (1957: 39–40). As such, the former Yugoslavia was characterised by rule by a bureaucratic class elite.

David Lane has spent much time considering social stratification in Russia during and after the communist period. With respect to the former, Lane (1971: 21) argues that the 'planned equalitarianism' of the Bolshevik revolution was compromised by the chaos of the revolutionary period and civil war. Later, Stalin's rapid industrialisation policy required technical expertise and skills, which resided in groups of 'bourgeois' extraction (Lane 1971: 25). Lane argues that that CPSU engineered elite groups from previously underprivileged backgrounds, through a rigorous programme of education and training in order to fulfil its economic, political and administrative staffing needs (1971: 25–34). Members of this elite were defined by their membership of the inner core of the CPSU or their positions in the state bureaucracy. They enjoyed a wage approximately nine times that of the average Russian worker (1971: 74) and other status benefits such as health care, cars, housing, holiday and shopping facilities. It is interesting, in the light of the rapidly changing landscape of eastern Europe and the

Russian Federation though the 1990s, to consider the ethnic homogeneity of the Soviet elite, with a preponderance of Slavic white groups and a long-term political marginalising of other ethnicities, such as Armenians, Kazakhs, Uzbekistanis and Chechens (1971: 91–9). Lane argues for a strong link between relatively privileged social and economic groups, ethnic stratification and the political and administrative elite in the Soviet system (1971: 121–8). This elite was manufactured and legitimated by a revolutionary regime committed to an ideology of equality. For Lane, the explanation for elitism within state socialism involves economic imperatives, technical necessity and political expediency. However, these imperatives resulted in a 'certain identity of interests' (1971: 136) among an identifiable privileged group.

Observers of Latin American politics have long used elites and masses as analytic tools, but from the 1980s, there was a tendency to suggest a plurality of elites in Latin American politics, focused around industrialists, politicians, the military and the Church (Conniff and McCann 1991: xi). For some, such elites were not seen as integrated and overlapping in the sense of Mills's power elite, whereas for others, there had been interlinking elite groups in Brazil from the fifteenth century and a concentration of elite power from the mid-twentieth century resembling Mills's model. It is likely that both models have purchase on differing political realities, with the mid-1980s seeing a transition from military government to democracy.

The officer corps of the Brazilian army has been key in the development of Brazilian politics, having a constitutional role in maintaining 'national well-being', a role that legitimated a coup and military government between 1964–85 (McCann 1991: 49). The officer corps, from whom the military government was drawn, was reminiscent of Pareto's 'lions' in considering themselves impartial, competent and not affiliated with any particular interest to justify military government in terms of a 'national interest' and public order agenda. Frank McCann argues that the Brazilian officer corps is a relatively small group characterised by close personal and often familial ties (1991: 51) in addition to an urban middle-class background. After the 1930 revolution the government was militarised, the army professionalised and the officer corps was reconstructed around a nationalist and modernising agenda. Army officers replaced civilians as government leaders, industrial managers and propagandists (Conniff 1991: 63). By 1945 there existed a 'civilian–military technocracy'. In the economic and political crisis of 1960's Brazil, the officer corps came to believe that they were the only institution willing and able to make the necessary changes to the economic and political structure in order to facilitate economic development and guarantee security (1991: 75). The military had intervened with such objectives in 1930, 1945, 1954 and 1955, but in 1964 they did not relinquish power to other civilian groups, but established a military republic which endured until 1985, by which time, Brazil had gone from being an arms importer, to being the fifth largest exporter in the global arms trade. From 1960–85, the military became the political elite, but sought alliances with other elites in order to defend specific common interests. Eli Diniz argues that industrial elites supported the military state in its promotion of capitalist development with strong government intervention and oligopoly in certain sectors, alongside censorship, curtailment of civil liberties and control of labour (Diniz 1991: 108–13). Thus, the military drew in other powerful groups, but was the institutional cement that effectively ruled for twenty-one years.

Out of fashion and favour for some time, elite theory has seen something of a renaissance as political scientists and political sociologists become more 'state-centred' in their theorising. For Bottomore (1993: 120–1) a revival of elite theory may well be prescient given recent developments. These include the increased influence of neo-liberal and New Right thinking in a range of national and supra-national political institutions. Currently, the strength of capitalism seems assured, there is cynicism and distrust towards political institutions even in the most liberal and democratic of liberal democracies and much of the world is characterised by impoverishment and conflict. In such conditions, the power of political elites to make decisions may be manifest.

Part of the classical triumvirate of state theory, we have seen that elite theory is engaged in dispute with both pluralism and Marxism. It rejects an understanding of political power as diffused among communities of interest, and also critiques conceptions of politics as (reducible to) class domination. This said, there are those who would dispute the distinctiveness of elite theory, as pluralism moves both left and right in various neo-pluralisms (Dunleavy and O'Leary 1987), and as the left-thinking intersections increase as Marxism becomes more pluralist (McLennan 1989). The latter, is something for consideration in the following chapter.

## Bibliography

Aron, R. (1970), *Main Currents in Sociological Thought 2: Pareto, Weber, Durkheim*, trans. R. Howard and H. Weaver (Harmondsworth: Penguin).
Bachrach, P. and Baratz, M. (1962), 'Two faces of power', *American Political Science Review*, 56: 947–52.
Beetham, D. (1985), *Max Weber and the Theory of Modern Politics* (Cambridge: Polity).
Berlin, I. (1979), 'The originality of Machiavelli', in I. Berlin (ed.), *Against the Current* (London: Hogarth).
Birch, A. H. (1993), *The Concepts and Theories of Modern Democracy* (London: Routledge).
Bottomore, T. (1973), 'Ruling elite or ruling class?' in J. Urry and J. Wakeford (eds), *Power in Britain* (London: Heinemann).
Bottomore, T. (1989), 'The capitalist class', in T. Bottomore and R. J. Brym (eds), *The Capitalist Class: an International Study* (Hemel Hempstead: Harvester Wheatsheaf).
Bottomore, T. (1993), *Elites and Society*, 2nd edn (London: Routledge).
Burke, E. (1960), *The Philosophy of Edmund Burke*, L. I. Bredvold and R. G. Ross (eds) (Ann Arbor MI: University of Michigan Press).
Coleridge, S. T. (1972), *On the Constitution of Church and State*, J. Barrell (ed.) (London: Dent).
Conniff, M. L. (1991), 'The national elite', in M. L. Conniff and F. D. McCann (eds), *Modern Brazil: Elites and Masses in Historical Perspective* (London: University of Nebraska Press).
Conniff, M. L. and McCann, F. D. (1991), *Modern Brazil: Elites and Masses in Historical Perspective* (London: University of Nebraska Press).
Crockett, N. L. (ed.) (1970), *The Power Elite in America* (Lexington MA: D. C. Heath and Co.).
Dahl, R. (1961), *Who Governs?* (New Haven CT: Yale University Press).
Dahl, R. (1963), *Pluralist Democracy in the United States: Conflict and Consent* (Chicago IL: Rand McNally).
Dahl, R. (1970 [1958]), 'A critique of the ruling elite model', in N. L. Crockett (ed.), *The Power Elite in America* (Lexington MA: D. C. Heath and Co.).
Detwiler, B. (1990), *Nietzsche and the Politics of Aristocratic Radicalism* (Chicago IL: University of Chicago Press).
Diniz, E. (1991), 'The post 1930 industrial elite', in M. L. Conniff and F. D. McCann (eds), *Modern Brazil: Elites and Masses in Historical Perspective* (London: University of Nebraska Press).
Djilas, M. (1957), *The New Class: an Analysis of the Communist System* (New York: Praeger).

Domhoff, G. W. (1967), *Who Rules America?* (Englewood Cliffs NJ: Prentice-Hall).
Domhoff, G. W. (1972), *Fat Cats and Democrats* (Englewood Cliffs NJ: Prentice-Hall).
Domhoff, G. W. (1979), *The Powers that Be: Processes of Ruling Class Domination* (New York: Vintage Books).
Domhoff, G. W. (1987), 'Where do government experts come from? The CEA and the policy planning network', in G. W. Domhoff and T. R. Dye (eds), *Power Elites and Organizations* (Newbury Park CA: Sage).
Dunleavy, P. and O'Leary, B. (1987), *Theories of the State: The Politics of Liberal Democracy*, (Basingstoke: Macmillan).
Dunn, J. (2005), *Setting the People Free: The Story of Democracy* (London: Atlantic Books).
Evans, M. (2006), 'Elitism', in C. Hay, M. Lister and D. Marsh (eds), *The State: Theories and Issues* (Basingstoke: Palgrave).
Finer, S. (1976), 'Introduction', in S. Finer (ed.), trans. D. Mirfin *Pareto: Sociological Writings* (Oxford: Blackwell).
Fox, R. L. (2006), *The Classical World: An Epic History of Greece and Rome* (Harmondsworth: Penguin).
Gardner, J. F. (1974), *Leadership and the Cult of Personality* (London: Dent).
Ghiloni, B. W. (1987), 'The velvet ghetto: women, power, and the corporation', in G. W. Domhoff and T. R. Dye (eds), *Power Elites and Organizations* (Newbury Park CA: Sage).
Hansen, M. H. (1999), *The Athenian Democracy in the Age of Demosthenes* (London: Bristol Classical/Duckworth).
Held, D. (1996), *Models of Democracy* (Cambridge: Polity).
Hunter, F. (1953), *Community Power Structure* (Chapel Hill NC: University of North Carolina Press).
Jessop, B. (1990), *State Theory: Putting Capitalist States in Their Place* (Cambridge: Polity).
Kramnick, I. (1987), 'Introduction' in Madison, Hamilton and Jay (1987), *The Federalist Papers* (Harmondsworth: Penguin).
Lane, D. (1971), *The End of Inequality? Stratification Under State Socialism* (Harmondsworth: Penguin).
Lukes, S. (1974), *Power: A Radical View* (London: Macmillan).
Madison, J., Hamilton, A. and Jay, J. (1987), *The Federalist Papers* (Harmondsworth: Penguin).
Manin, B. (1997), *The Principles & Representative Government* (Cambridge: Cambridge Cambridge University Press).
McCann, F. D. (1991), 'The military', in M. L. Conniff and F. D. McCann (eds), *Modern Brazil: Elites and Masses in Historical Perspective* (London: University of Nebraska Press).

McLennan, G. (1989), *Marxism, Pluralism and Beyond* (Cambridge: Polity).
Michels, R. (1911 [1999]), *Political Parties*, trans. E. and C. Paul (New Brunswick NJ and London: Transaction).
Miliband, R. (1969), *The State in Capitalist Society: An Analysis of the Western System of Power* (London: Weidenfeld and Nicholson).
Miliband, R. (1982), *Capitalist Democracy in Britain* (London: Oxford University Press).
Mill, J. S. (1991), 'Considerations on representative government', in J. Gray, (ed.) *On Liberty and Other Essays* (Oxford: Oxford University Press).
Mills, C. W. (1956), *The Power Elite* (New York: Oxford University Press).
Moore, G. (1987), 'Women in the old-boy network: the case of New York state government', in G. W. Domhoff and T. R. Dye (eds), *Power Elites and Organizations* (Newbury Park CA: Sage).
Morrow, J. (1998), *A History of Political Thought* (New York: New York University Press).
Mosca, G. (1939), *The Ruling Class*, trans. H. D. Kahn (New York: McGraw-Hill).
Nietzsche, F. (1966), *Beyond Good and Evil*, trans. W. Kaufmann (New York: Vintage Books).
Nietzsche, F. (1968), *Twilight of the Idols and The Anti-Christ*, trans. R. J. Hollingdale (Harmondsworth: Penguin).
Packard, V. (1961), *The Status Seekers: An Explanation of Class Behaviour in America* (Harmondsworth: Penguin).
Pareto, V. (1935 [1976]), *Pareto: Sociological Writings*, S. Finer and trans. D. Mirfin (eds) (Oxford: Blackwell).
Parry, G. (1969), *Political Elites* (London: George Allen and Unwin).
Pocock, J. G. A. (1975), *The Machiavellian Moment* (Princeton NJ: Princeton University Press).
Poulantzas, N. (1978), *State, Power, Socialism* (London: New Left Books).
Sampson, A. (1962), *The Anatomy of Britain* (London: Hodder and Stoughton).
Sampson, A. (1982), *The Changing Anatomy of Britain* (London: Hodder and Stoughton).
Sampson, A. (2004), *Who Runs this Place? The Anatomy of Britain in the 21st Century* (London: John Murray).
Schumpeter, J. (1987), *Capitalism, Socialism and Democracy* (London: Unwin Hyman).
Scott, J. (1979), *Corporations, Classes and Capitalism* (London: Hutchinson).
Scott, J. (1991), *Who Rules Britain?* (Cambridge: Polity).

Scott, J. (1997), *Corporate Business and Capitalist Classes* (Oxford: Oxford University Press).

Skinner, Q. (1981), *Machiavelli* (Oxford: Oxford University Press).

Skocpol, T. (1979), *States and Social Revolutions* (Cambridge: Cambridge University Press).

van der Pijl, K. (1989), 'The international level', in T. Bottomore and R. J. Brym (eds), *The Capitalist Class: an International Study* (Hemel Hempstead: Harvester Wheatsheaf).

Weber, M. (1970), *From Max Weber*, H. H. Girth and C. W. Mills (eds) (London: Routledge Kegan Paul).

Weber, M. (1978), *Economy and Society*, trans. and ed. G. Roth and C. Wittich (Berkeley: University of California Press).

Weber, M. (1994), *Political Writings*, P. Lassman and R. Spiers (eds) (Cambridge: Cambridge University Press).

Wood, G. S. (2005), *The American Reduction: A History* (London: Phoenix).

CHAPTER FOUR

## Marxism: the State as a Real Illusion
*Tim Hall*

'Marxism' takes its name from the German Jewish philosopher Karl Marx (1818–83) who, together with Friedrich Engels (1820–95), developed a critique of capitalist societies in the nineteenth century. Such societies were identifiable by the principled separation of the labourer from the means of production (in contrast to feudal serfs who owned the instruments of production), the existence of the notionally free wage-labourer (in contrast to the feudal bondsman whose labour was owned by the feudal lord) and the existence of private property laws (in contrast to the time before the various enclosure acts in which land was held in common). Above all they were characterised by the production of goods for exchange (rather than use) in a complex civil society itself characterised by increasing specialisation and division of labour. Marx's central claim was that such societies, while appearing free and uncoerced – that is, with individuals free to produce and consume what they like, entering into contracts as they see fit, etc. – were actually founded on the domination and exploitation of wage-labour by capital.

It is frequently stated that Marx did not develop a theory of the state (Wells 1981: vii; Wetherly 2005: 10), and the reasons adduced for this are various. Some trace these back to 'economistic' tendencies in Marx's later 'economic' thought and his tendency to view politics as the mere superstructural effect of antagonisms occurring in the economic base of societies. Others attribute this to the fact that his magnum opus – *Das Kapital* (1867) – was incomplete and that projected sections on class struggle and its relation to the state were never written (Marx 1990). Still others point to the apparently contradictory characterisations of the state throughout his writings – at some points a simple instrument of class rule, at others an autonomous institution acting as arbiter between classes – as evidence that he never properly developed a theory of the state (Wells 1981: vii). This has led some Marxist theorists of the state to view their own projects as completing or supplementing Marx's original theories (Miliband 1969; Poulantzas 1978a). Prior to a consideration of these, and by way of contextualisation, it would be helpful to survey Marx's own writings on the state.

## Context

Marx's concern with the state begins with his critique of the Hegelian conception of the state in *Critique of Hegel's 'Philosophy of Right'* (1843), *On the Jewish Question* (1843) and in *The Economic and Political Manuscripts* (1844). Hegel viewed the state as the realm of actualised freedom. In contrast to Kant and other idealist thinkers who elaborated an abstract conception of freedom in terms of the autonomous self-legislating moral subject, Hegel sought to develop a more concrete account of the subject by showing how it was supported (or mediated) by social institutions such as the family, civil society and the state. Marx drew deeply on this critique but, in the above-mentioned texts, challenged Hegel's claim that the state was the domain of actualised freedom and therefore universal. Instead, Marx views it as the alienation of civil society: 'It [the state] stands in the same opposition to civil society and overcomes it in the same manner as religion overcomes the limitations of the profane world . . .' (McLellan 2005: 53). By likening the Hegelian conception of the relationship between the state and civil society to the relationship between the heavenly and the profane world he means to criticise the claim that it represents the realm of actualised or achieved freedom. The state does overcome the particularity and egoism that characterised civil society but in a mystifying way: through the positing of the state and ourselves as citizens, as members of political communities, who somehow transcend the self-interest that characterises our actions as members of civil society. Marx points out the mutual dependence of the Hegelian conceptions of the state and civil society (the fact that the

## Marxism: the State as a Real Illusion

existence of civil society is the condition of the existence of the state even while the latter transforms and dominates the former) and draws out the latent antagonism between our egotistical and political selves. To transcend this alienated form of the state – the existence of the state as an abstraction – would mean, minimally, the resolution of this antagonism between our private and public selves; it would mean, as Marx puts it, 'taking the abstract citizen back into ourselves' (McLellan 2005: 64). If our freedom as citizens is constantly being undercut by our private interests then, for Marx, the universality that our participation in politics is supposed to embody is neither universal nor actual. Actualised freedom would involve the overcoming of the antagonism of our private and political selves through a human (rather than merely political) emancipation and the recovery of our 'species-being' – that is, our intrinsically social existence denied and suppressed in egoistic civil society. It would further imply the transcendence of the particularity and egoism characterising civil society in non-alienated form – that is, not in the form of the emergence of the modern state that embodies this in a mystifying way but in the emergence of a genuinely human society and authentic democracy.

Marx's early writings on the state are generally seen as formative only, principally because they contain no developed concept of capitalism or class conflict. For this reason they have come to exercise little influence over contemporary Marxist theories of the state. This neglect, however, is unjustified for, as David Wells has perceptively argued, the ambiguity at the heart of this early conception of the state – on the illusory or apparent independence of the state – is one that comes to characterise Marx's entire thinking on the state (Wells 1981: viii). Whether the state has only the semblance of independence and really is an instrument of class domination or has a genuine independence from society and, therefore, calls forth a more complex account of capitalist domination (one in which class domination is mediated by or filtered through the prism of relatively autonomous state power) is a question that Marx apparently never adequately resolved.

This ambiguity is evident in his central pronouncements on the state. In *The Communist Manifesto* (1848) Marx famously referred to the executive of the modern state as 'but a committee for managing the common affairs of the bourgeois' (McLellan 2005: 247). This implied that the state was little more than an instrument of class domination in which the capitalist relations of production were secured through the repressive activities of the state (police, military, law courts, etc.) and its universalistic ideology of popular sovereignty, the rule of law, separation of powers, etc. This conception of the state was repeated by Engels in *The Origin of the Family, Private Property and the State* (1884) where he refers to it as 'an instrument for the exploitation of wage-labour by capital' (Engels 1985: 141). The capitalist state gave the appearance of being independent from society and class interests but this independence was chimerical and served to conceal the naked class interests that it served. Thus, for this instrumentalist conception it was important that the state appeared to be independent even though, in reality, the interests of the state and the capitalist class were identical.

Marx appears to offer a different model of the state a couple of years after the publication of *The Communist Manifesto* (1848) in his analysis of the 1848 revolutions in France and the resulting regime of Louis Bonaparte. In *The Eighteenth Brumaire of Louis Bonaparte* (1851) he analyses the factors that made possible the seizure of power by Louis Bonaparte. The analysis is detailed and fine-grained in terms of the chronology of events and the politicians, parties and ideologies involved. What stands out, however, is the range of capitalist class interests or what Poulantzas calls 'fractions' of capital (Poulantzas 1978a). This complex account of the composition of capital and the range of interests it comprises is developed by Marx to explain the incapacity of the bourgeoisie to manage its own affairs. This failure opens the door to the Bonapartist regime. As Marx puts it, the bourgeoisie are driven to the position where they must give up political power: 'It declared unequivocally that it longed to get rid of its own political rule in order to get rid of the troubles and dangers of ruling' (McLellan 2005: 336).

The Bonapartist state then, far from representing the executive committee of the bourgeoisie, appears as a 'parasitic body' that forms on the surface of society with its criss-crossing class interests (McLellan 2005: 345). It consolidates and extends its power, not by representing bourgeois interests in general but by playing off one fraction of capital against another and one social class against another. This implies an autonomy and independence on the part of the state in respect of societies and social classes that appeared impossible on instrumentalist assumptions. Not only was the state capable of acting against the interests of the bourgeois but also it had to do so in order to secure the longer-term interests of the class.

## Marxism: the State as a Real Illusion

The Bonapartist state was not an aberration or a backslide into pre-capitalist political forms but a necessary consequence of the development of the capitalist economy based on the realisation – evidenced in the immediate aftermath of the 1848 revolutions – that the bourgeoisie were incapable of managing their own affairs.

Marx's analysis of the Bonapartist state has been profoundly influential both in the analysis of the relationship between capitalism and authoritarian forms of state and also – as we shall see with the work of Nicos Poulantzas – for the analysis of the state in general. It offers a model of the state that, while determined by the economy in myriad ways, is capable of arbitrating between different fractions of capital and, when necessary, between different social classes. For this reason the conception of the state developed here is sometimes referred to as the arbiter model and explicitly contrasted with the instrumentalist model (Dunleavy and O'Leary 1987: 202). Contemporary Marxists have generally developed one conception of the state at the expense of the other. Thus, the state is either the instrument of class domination and ideological (Miliband) or independent and objectively real (Althusser, Poulantzas). This rules out the possibility that the state could be both, that is, ideological and real; a product of class-related practices and an objective realm constraining and determining in its own right. Put differently, it may be possible to unite instrumentalist and structuralist approaches to the state in Marx if they are read through his account of the relation between appearance and reality – the ideological and the real – to which we will turn later.

## Definition

In state theory generally, a distinction is usually drawn between organisational and functional definitions of the state (Dunleavy and O'Leary 1987: 6; see Introduction). That is, between the state as a set of institutions consisting of definite power relations on the one hand and as a specific function or end that necessitates a certain institutional ensemble on the other hand (Hay et al. 2006: 10). Weber's definition of the state as a compulsory political organisation with a centralised administration that successfully upholds the claim to the monopoly of the legitimate use of physical force in a bounded territory is usually given as an example of the first type of definition. Talcott Parson's definition of the state as a collection of specialised agencies associated with the division of labour in advanced societies which functions to mediate and reduce tensions between sectors of societies is generally given as an example of the latter (Vincent 1987: 231). It is worth noting that both kinds of definition are prevalent in Marxist approaches to the state. For Miliband the state is ultimately an instrument of class domination and his analysis proceeds along Weberian lines as an analysis of state institutions and power relations. Similarly, Cornelius Castoriadis looks to reserve the term 'state' for a state apparatus with separate, hierarchically organised bureaucracies with distinct areas of competence (Castoriadis 1991: 157). Nicos Poulantzas, on the other hand, in *Political Power and Social Classes* (1978a: 273) defines the state in explicitly functionalist terms. The role of the state, he holds, is to take charge of the political interests of the bourgeoisie and realise the function of political hegemony – a task that the bourgeoisie is incapable of realising (Poulantzas 1978a: 273).

A significant factor in determining whether an organisational or functional approach to the state is adopted in a Marxist analysis is how one interprets Marx's philosophy of history. Paul Wetherly, basing his analysis on Gerry Cohen's analytic reconstruction of the Marxist philosophy of history, defines the state in functional terms: capital accumulation requires the fulfilment of certain political functions carried out by the state (Wetherly 2006). Cohen's reconstruction sets out to transform Marx's metaphysical speculations on the philosophy of history into a set of empirically testable and verifiable hypotheses. Thus, if the Marxist definition of the state could be placed in a comprehensive theory of social formation, then its precise function could be specified, including its degree of relative autonomy, and its interrelation with society in general. However, as a number of Marxists have pointed out there is something deeply paradoxical and self-defeating about the project of Marx's philosophy of history – at least if we understand this as the attempt to articulate the fundamental 'laws of motion' of history (Castoriadis 1991: 33–46; Lukács 1991 [1971]: 149–59). For the attempt to comprehend the eternal laws of history – even in the rigorous empirical form that Cohen's approach seeks to bring to this – would straight away indicate that history had come to an end. History 'comprehended' would lead to a predictive system equivalent to that provided by the natural sciences in respect of 'comprehended' nature. Arguably, however, it is the explicit recognition of the impossibility of such a predictive system in respect of history that is the central characteristic of a rigorous historical theory (Castoriadis 1991: 33–46). This is especially the case with political theory, which, if it were based on a predictive system, would effectively be denied any historical novelty on which to reflect and respond. Lenin famously (although by no means uniquely) defined 'the present' as the proper object of politics. Any theory that would convert this in advance into anything less than the singular and the novel – that is, into some permutation of immutable structures or the 'as yet to be comprehended' empirical realm – would be departing from this conception of politics and aligning itself with behaviourism or one of its transcendental equivalents. Similarly, any theorisation of the state that bases itself on a denial of history and the present would be equally problematic.

Marxist approaches to the state today are generally separated into three kinds: instrumentalist; structuralist approaches; and what is referred to as the strategic-relational approach. The former approach, as the name implies, tends to view the state as an instrument of class domination. The structuralist approach, on the other hand, attempts to dispense with the notion of a subject (that is, social classes) acting behind the state and seeking to direct it in accordance with its interests. Instead, they tend to see agency as distributed across or inscribed in state structures and state policy as the complex or structurally determined effects of this process. This further implies that for structuralist approaches, the state has a much greater autonomy and independence from society: instead of merely reflecting class domination existing in society the state constitutes a distinct apparatus capable of independent action. This greater independence enables it to arbitrate between class interests. As we have seen both instrumentalist and arbiter models of the state can be found in classical Marxian theory. We shall be looking at representatives of these 'schools' in the following section. In terms of defining the state, however, it is interesting to see the different perspectives this throws up on the kind of thing that the state is.

For instrumentalists the state is generally seen as a theoretical abstraction – albeit a necessary one. At bottom all the state is a system of interrelated institutions – the executive, parliament, the police and military, the judiciary, etc. and all these institutions are is a set of office holders and the power relations obtaining between them. Thus, the state system can be analysed down to its composite institutional parts and these in turn can be analysed down to the individuals (state managers and office holders) who operate them. At best the state is an analytical reference point for this set of formalised and non-formalised relations between individuals. Although such a reference point is useful and necessary for the purposes of theorisation the state has no corporate reality in itself and is nothing more than the complex sum of its parts. For structuralists, by contrast, it is an objective structure, whose system of relations has a unity and operation that cannot be understood in terms of its composite parts. Thus, while for instrumentalists it is an unavoidable abstraction which reduces to networks of interpersonal relationships, for structuralists it is a different type of 'object' altogether which requires a distinct type of cognitive enquiry – an approach that attends to how the object is constituted.

Between these approaches emerges the strategic-relational approach that aims to combine in a single complex model the view of the state as theoretical abstraction with that of objective structure (Jessop 1990). This appears first and foremost as an attempt to merge the twin poles of personal agency and structural effect. The state is a social relation or 'a condensation of the relationship of forces between classes' which expresses itself in the specific form that it takes (Poulantzas 1978b: 132). What this formula represents is an attempt to understand agency (differential force) as mediated by structure. Thus, while state managers are clearly restricted in their actions by structural factors their actions are not wholly reducible to systemic effects in the way in which structuralists claim. The strategic-relational approach, therefore, represents an attempt to reconcile the opposition between instrumental agent-centred approaches to the state, on the one hand, and structuralist approaches, on the other hand. It focuses on the 'dialectic' between agency and structure. Whether this succeeds in overcoming the opposition between structure and agency and advances Marxist theories of the state is a question that will be taken up later.

For instrumentalists then the state is nothing more than an 'analytic reference point' – a fiction albeit a necessary and useful one (Barrow 2002: 48). For structuralists it is an objective structure, while for strategic-relational approaches it is both and neither. Significantly, none of these approaches raise the question of the ontology of the state in the manner that Marx did in his critique of the Hegelian state. All remain at either the empirical or epistemological level with the strategic-relational approach adopting a dual standpoint. One of the problems for the strategic-relational

## Marxism: the State as a Real Illusion

approach and its claim to have arrived at a dialectical conception of the relationship between structure and agency will be that it has no account of the ontology of the state, that is, no account of how the state appears as distinct object – both from subjects (classes) that would influence it and from other realms of social activity or social objects – and must necessarily appear as such. In evaluating the strategic-functional approach the question will be raised as to whether a 'dialectic of agency and structure' is possible if not on an ontological basis (that is, the dialectic of appearance and reality). This is to say any account of the state that purports to overcome the dualism of agency and structure and the opposition between instrumental and structuralist approaches to which this gives rise, must account for why the state appears as it does and how our (class-related) social activity and our self-understanding as agents is implicated in this appearance.

### Theorists

Of these three distinct approaches to the Marxian state, the instrumentalist approach is generally identified with the work of Ralph Miliband, *The State in Capitalist Society* (1969), and the structuralist approach with Louis Althusser and Nicos Poulantzas, especially the latter's early work *Political Power and Social Classes* (1978a). The strategic relational approach is generally attributed to the later work of Poulantzas – in particular *State, Power, Socialism* (1978b) – and the work of Bob Jessop, *State Theory* (1990) and *The Future of the Capitalist State* (2002).

Ralph Miliband's background was in empirical sociology. His own work must be seen in the context of its engagement with and critique of pluralist models of the state – in particular Robert Dahl's. For pluralist's like Dahl the state was nothing more than a conduit for social forces (see Chapter 2). Contra Dahl and the pluralist conception, Miliband maintained that there was such a thing as the capitalist class; that underpinning the apparently variegated interests in civil society were real class divisions and exclusions based on ownership of the means of production; and that the relationship between the capitalist class and the state had to be empirically investigated. As noted above, the state consisted of nothing more than the institutions of which it comprised. For Miliband it comprised five elements: the government (executive and legislature); the administration; the police and military and the judiciary and sub-central government. The interaction of these elements constituted the state system (Barrow 2002: 48–50). Significantly for Miliband, the government was not identical to the state and had to be sharply distinguished. The fact that the government spoke in the name of state power did not mean that the government could be identified with state power (Miliband 1969: 49–50).

This immediately raises the question of who wields state power – if not the government, then who? Miliband's response was the capitalist class. By colonising the state apparatus – in particular the key administrative and regulatory posts – the capitalist class are able to control state power and exercise an effective veto over a range of state policies (Barrow 2002: 21). Central to this is control over the economy, for while Miliband acknowledges a range of intra-class interests, what unites the capitalist class is the unquestioned assumption that the capitalist relations of production provide the necessary context of state rule. The capitalist class is not homogeneous and their various interests are more complex than had often hitherto been acknowledged by the Marxist tradition. The various 'fractions' of capital are, however, capable of united co-ordinated action whenever the basic assumptions of capitalist accumulation are thrown into question. In order to demonstrate this thesis it is only necessary to look into the social origin, status and milieu of those holding the key executive and regulatory offices (Miliband 1983: 31). Simply stated, by analysing the composition of the judiciary, senior civil service, the military, heads of industry, etc. one could come to see how the capitalist classes hold onto state power regardless of which political party forms the government of the day. Indeed, the leadership of the main political parties reveals the same class biases.

There is much to be said for Miliband's approach. By analysing the control exercised over the state by the capitalist class he can account for the tenacious hold on power of capitalism. This was a question that exercised Marxists particularly at the time of the publication of *The State in Capitalist Society* immediately after the events of May 1968 in Paris. For Miliband it was not simply a matter of a political party gaining control over the state apparatus because state power is vested in a range of key offices. By strategic control over these offices the capitalist class is able to exercise control over society in general. Moreover, by distinguishing sharply between the government and the state Miliband is able to account

## Marxism: the State as a Real Illusion

for the de-radicalisation of parliamentary socialist parties when they enter government. He could also account for how it is that the state is able to act contrary to the interests of capital from time to time. The state in capitalist society is capable of this because the control that the capitalist class exercise over the state is not absolute. While it exercises effective power of veto over state policies that could undermine its capitalist basis, these policies are otherwise subject to the relative state of the class struggle. A balance of class forces in favour of the working classes can and does lead to reform in terms of labour and welfare rights, if not to the transformation of the fundamental relations of production and society generally. Indeed, this is how Miliband analysed the New Deal and the post-war entrenchment of the welfare state (Finegold and Skocpol 1995).

Poulantzas, also writing against the background of the failure of the left, student-led protests in the late 1960s, is also concerned to account for the persistence and tenacious character of capitalist social domination. His approach, however, diverges significantly from Miliband's. For Poulantzas it is not a question of accounting for the capture of state power by the capitalist class rather it is a question of showing how state power is intrinsically capitalist – without the appeal to extraneous class forces. In a critique of Miliband's *The State in Capitalist Society* published in the *New Left Review* in the same year, Poulantzas criticised the work for failing to comprehend the state and social classes as 'objective structures' and relying instead on historicist and 'finalist explanations' (Poulantzas 1972: 242). Following Althusser, Poulantzas asserted the priority of structures in Marxist social scientific explanation. Each mode of production is to be understood in terms of the functional interrelations between economic, legal-political and ideological levels. Each level is comprised of structures that serve to reproduce capitalist relations of production. Structures are composed of institutions but – unlike Miliband's conception of the state system – structures are not reducible to institutions. Social agents – agents of production – are to be understood as 'bearers' of 'ensembles of structures'. Rather than agents creating structures it is the other way around (Poulantzas 1978a: 62). Structural ensembles at the economic, political and ideological level function in a complex integrated manner to extend the capitalist relations of production but in doing so generate contradictory class practices. In this way 'class practices', of which social agents are the 'bearers', can be thought of as 'structural effects'. An example that

Poulantzas gives of this is the pursuit of higher profits by capital and higher wages by wage-labour at the economic level. These practices, rather than being the result of voluntarisitic collective activity, are the 'effects' of structural and systemic contradictions of which individual subjects are the 'bearers'. Class struggle at the economic level is not something that one 'opts for' or 'decides'. The whole language of choice is misplaced and ideologically charged here. The interrelated system itself generates contradictory class practices that individuals find themselves the bearers of. Class practices define who one is rather than pre-formed subjects deciding which practices they will undertake.

This contrasting account of agency gives rise to a different understanding of the state in capitalist society. The primary function of the state is to ensure the reproduction of the capitalist relations of production, but in order to be able to do this the state must have a relative autonomy from society and class forces. In *Political Power and Social Classes*, Poulantzas offers an extended reading of Marx's *Eighteenth Brumaire* to elaborate and support this thesis. Although he agrees with Marx's analysis of Bonpartism as a concrete historical phenomenon in which equilibrium of class forces gives rise to an authoritarian government, he goes one step further than Marx and calls this a 'constitutive theoretical characteristic of the very capitalistic type of state' (Poulantzas 1978a: 258). This is an important difference: what for Marx is an exceptional state resulting from a fateful balance of class forces, becomes for Poulantzas a constitutive feature of the capitalist type of state in general. It is not just in exceptional circumstances that the capitalist classes manifest an inability to rule, this is a general characteristic of the class that creates the need for a semi-autonomous state to secure what the class is incapable of securing for itself – the reproduction of capitalist relations of production.

It does this through a three-fold regulation of class practices through which three functions of the state – a general, an economic and a political function – are discernible. In its general maintenance function the state constitutes the factor of cohesion between the separate levels of social formation (that is, the socio-economic, the legal-political and the ideological). In its specifically economic function it is concerned with the labour process and the productivity of labour. Additionally it regulates the capitalist process of exchange through private property and contract law and organises labour through training and education. In its specifically political function it is also concerned with the maintenance of order, the punishment of disorder and the surveillance of subversive activity. In general terms it functions to organise the capitalist classes and disorganise the working classes. Its relative autonomy helps in this regard enabling it to broker deals between various fractions of capital (for example, manufacturing and finance capital) and intervene, for or against, the long-term interests of one fraction against another.

One of the problems with Poulantzas's analysis of the state in *Political Power and Social Classes* – and indeed structuralist analysis in general – is its seeming contentment to continuously analyse the synchronic systemic and structural relations, in all their combinatory forms, that obtained in the capitalist type of state without being able to account for how these structural ensembles emerged. This is a problem encountered by all typical analysis that purports to be doing anything more than providing ideal types for interpreting history. Miliband himself levelled this criticism at Poulantzas in his review of the English translation of *Political Power and Social Classes* in 1973 when he complained about the absence of any empirical analysis of contemporary capitalist states in the book (Barrow 2002: 28). While there are genuine methodological differences between Poulantzas and Miliband – the later empiricist and the former neo-transcendental – this criticism did touch on a problem with Poulantzas's approach that he was to take up and address in his later work. Like other structuralist thinkers, Poulantzas is good at accounting for how subjectivity/agency was inscribed in – or distributed across – pre-existing structural ensembles but not very good at explaining how one set of structural ensembles came to displace another. For this the 'time-slice' synchronic account of structural agency had to be supplemented with a concept of differential force in which structural relations were themselves seen as the outcome or product of forces.

In *State, Power, Socialism* (1978b) Poulantzas attempts to develop just such a conception. Here the state is defined not as an entity in its own right but as a 'material condensation of forces between classes and fractions of classes, such as this is expressed within the state in a necessarily specific form' (Poulantzas 1978b: 128–9, 132). Rather than classes and class fractions (or representatives of such classes) setting out to capture state offices with the aim of pursuing their own class interests as Miliband maintains, Poulantzas views class forces as 'objectively inscribed' in state institutions. In other words, the state as objective apparatus is the outcome of the balance of forces between dominant and dominated classes and between different fractions of the dominant class. Thus, while there may be antagonisms between the different fractions of the dominant class – between, say, large landowners, monopoly capital, industrial and financial capital – these each find expression within the state apparatus. Each branch of the state apparatus represents the power base of a certain fraction or conflictual alliance between fractions (Poulantzas 1978b: 133). The state, however, retains its relative autonomy from social classes and class interests because its very form or structure is the product of differential class forces. The state is, therefore, wrongly assumed to be a 'united mechanism, founded on a homogeneous and hierarchical distribution of the centres of power' (1978b: 133); rather it is an ensemble of structures 'shot through' with contradictions which 'traverse' the bureaucracy. Instead of confronting a state apparatus united around a univocal political will, one encounters a collection of fiefs, clans and factions – 'a multiplicity of diversified micro-politics' (1978b: 135).

Such a conception of the state runs the risk of not being able to account for the unity and coherence of state activity and policy. It cannot, for example, account for this by appeal to ideology and social milieu in the way that Miliband did. If the very state institutions and structures themselves are the product of conflictual class forces how are capitalist interest organised and what prevents the state apparatus from simply disintegrating? In addition to the strategic alliances between class fractions in the power bloc, Poulantzas also appeals to the 'apparatus-unity' exhibited by the state. The overall policy of the state is 'massively orientated in favour of monopoly capital' because the capitalist division of labour is reproduced with its hierarchic-bureaucratised framework. Poulantzas gives as an example the reproduction of the division of labour between manual and intellectual labour in the division between industrial and financial capital: the apparatus unity of the state reflects this hierarchy (Poulantzas 1978b: 136).

Poulantzas's conception of the state as a material condensation of a relationship of forces has been taken up and developed by Bob Jessop. In his *State Theory* (1990) he elaborates the strategic-relational approach to the state, as outlined by Poulantzas, as a distinct theory but presents it almost as a rapprochement of instrumentalist and structuralist theories. The critique of instrumentalism implicit in the approach does not deny that 'the state can be used to some effect', it's just that 'the form of the state gives it certain structural biases and it is important to examine how these affect its accessibility to, and the utility for, different social forces' (Jessop 1990: 150). The picture, therefore, emerges of a 'structural selectivity' performed by the state on class forces that endeavour to shape it. The state is not a subject in its own right and does not exercise power in the way that the structuralist contends:

> its powers are activated through the agency of definite political forces in specific conjunctures. It is not the state which acts: it is always specific sets of politicians and state officials located in specific parts of the state system. It is they that activate specific powers and state capacities inscribed in particular institutions and agencies. (Jessop 1990: 336–7)

Like Poulantzas in *State, Power, Socialism* he holds that state power is a 'form-determined condensation of the balance of forces' (Jessop 1990: 149). This is to say that class forces, localised in specific arenas, are mediated, in their attempt to influence state policy, by complex state structures. It is noticeable, however, that Jessop is altogether less reticent than Poulantzas in deploying agent-centred analysis of political structures. This is partly motivated by the desire – not uncharacteristic among British Marxists – to bring an analytical clarity to Marxist concepts. Whether talk of politicians and state officials 'activating specific powers' 'inscribed' in political institutions is one that Poulantzas would have accepted is a moot point. Admitting the concept of (differential) force into immobile structuralist forms is one thing and is a feature which the work of Poulantzas shares with other structuralist theorists of the time (for example, Foucault). Recanting the critique of humanist categories and 'finalist explanations' is, however, quite another. This is not to necessarily defend the anti-humanist approach adopted by Poulantzas but it is to acknowledge a certain truth moment in it. This it to say, what the structuralist and post-structuralist approaches to the state capture, albeit in a one-side way, is the imperviousness of the state in its objectivity to social control or at least its recalcitrance to any control – the fact that any attempt to subject the state to social control comes out in unanticipated ways. The problem with overcoming the dualism of structure and agency – a task that Colin Hay et al. (2006: 73–6) credits Jessop's work with accomplishing – is that it runs the risk of downplaying this recalcitrance to direction or control and with this, downplaying the extent to which the state is a reification of social activity.

The strategic-relational approach purports to overcome the dualism of structure and agency and with that, the related concepts of the state as instrument and ensemble of structures. Much would rest on what such an overcoming would putatively involve. At times the strategic-relational approach appears more like an attempt to externally combine an agent-centred and structuralist perspective rather than an attempt to forge a genuine dialectical approach. What is significant, however, is that proponents of the strategic-functional approach do not take up Marx's own attempt to mediate agency and structure or the way this was developed in the Marxian tradition. In his analysis of the commodity form in *Capital* he outlines a process in which a social relation between people – in this case private producers – comes to take on the form of an objective characteristic of a thing (its value-in-exchange or price). This leads to the situation in which individual producers are subject in their productive activities to 'objective laws' of supply and demand. It also implies, however, that private producers could relate to one another immediately and organise their productive activities collectively rather than mediately through the impersonal market. Here, in other words, Marx presents an account of how productive (social) activity appears as the objective characteristics or property of a thing and, by implication, an account of how this 'alienated subjectivity' could be recovered. By coming to see the movements of commodities on the market as represented in 'inexorable' laws of supply and demand as nothing other than our own uncomprehended social activity ('uncomprehended' because not interpreted in class terms), the economic sphere ceases to be an objective realm that externally constrains human activity.

This is the simplest and most abstract account of how the agency/structure opposition is overcome in Marx's thought. However, if one applies this to the complexly structured account of the reproduction of capital that one finds in *Capital* a more complex and complete picture emerges – a picture in which multiple constraints are imposed in economic agents. What one finds, therefore, is a more complex account of the dialectical mediation of agency and structure than that found in the strategic-relational approach – an account that allows for the possibility that state-mediated social relations could be transformed by 'releasing' sources of agency that are misrecognised as objective structure.

## Marxism: the State as a Real Illusion

It might be objected that Marx's analysis is restricted to the economic sphere and has no application to the political realm and the agency/structure oppositions that obtain there. This, however, would be to ignore how Marx's account of the dialectic of agency and structure in *Capital* was developed and generalised by other Marxists. Georg Lukács's theory of reification is one such account. Reification, like fetishism, describes the process in which a relation between people takes on the character of a thing, acquiring a phantom objectivity with 'an autonomy that seems so strictly rational and all-embracing as to conceal every trace of its fundamental nature: the relation between people' (Lukács 1991 [1971]: 83). For Lukács, however, this process is not restricted to the economic sphere. All social relations take on this thing-like character functioning in accordance with autonomous laws that conceal their social origin. Thus, the state and the institutions and procedures that comprise it take on an independent reality that conceals its social origin. The state and the institutions that comprise it 'peel off' from collective social activity and become an objective reality in their own right whose objective operation (organisational, functional) is to be captured by political science/theory.

Lukács restricted his analysis of the fetishisation of the political realm to an analysis of the abstraction involved in the centralised administrative process and did not develop a theory of the state. The only work in recent times that has set out to develop a Marxist theory of the state on the basis of the related concepts of fetishism and reification is David Wells's *Marxism and the Modern State* (1981). For Wells, as noted above, the ambiguity exhibited in Marx's work between the state as instrument of class domination (subjective) and the state as structural apparatus (objective) is ultimately the ambiguity of the necessary appearance form of the social world. The state appears autonomous – and must necessarily appear as such – in two senses; it must, first, appear autonomous from subjects (social classes) that seek to direct it in accordance with their own interests; and secondly, it must appear autonomous from other realms of social activity, in particular the economy. Belying this appearance of autonomy, however, is real interdependence; the state that appeared to be autonomous from subjects (classes) reveals itself to be dependent on (class-related) social activity and practices to reproduce it much as the autonomous and self-regulating activity of markets rely on 'unconscious' social activity; the state that appeared independent from other realms of social activity reveals itself to be dependent on these other realms for its own reproduction. (The economic conditions the political; the cultural conditions the economic, etc.) For Wells the biggest fallacy of the structuralist and strategic-relational approach is the supposition that the capitalist state can be understood in its specificity as structuralist and post-structuralist Marxists frequently claim (Poulantzas 1978a: 142): 'The state cannot be understood simply by analysing its specific form because the mystification of this form lies precisely in its specificity' (Wells 1981: 67). The idea that we could strip away the layers of determination to apprehend a pure state operation is a fallacy for Wells. The state is fetishised or, in terms of the early Marx, comprehended only it its alienated form as long as its dependence on the social activity that reproduces it remains unthought and its concrete interdependence with other spheres of social activity are left unexplored.

## Practical politics

Despite the collapse of the Soviet Union and the eastern bloc states – or even because of this – Marxism continues to exert considerable influence in radical politics. With the questioning of the 'productivist' bias, Marxism has taken its place with a range of critical discourses such as post-colonialism and feminism. While Marxists tended to view all forms of social domination – race, gender, sexuality – as ultimately class related there is greater acceptance among contemporary Marxists that the overcoming of social domination inherent in capitalist productive relations would not necessarily mean the overcoming of social domination *per se*. A good deal of contemporary neo-Marxist work is concerned with the interrelation between various forms of social domination and the mutually entailing critiques that these imply (Bulter 1999; Fraser 1997).

The questioning of the same 'productivist' paradigm has also led to fruitful engagement with environmental politics over critiques of waste in capitalist society and lost relations to nature in deep ecology theories. In the former approach the huge amount of waste generated by the market system and the economic problem of externalities is the central focus. Additionally Marx's early romantic theories and dialectic of nature drawn from his 1844 Manuscripts have been taken up by 'deep ecologists' in attempts to develop non-anthropocentric approaches to ethics (Benton 1996; Naess 1989).

## Marxism: the State as a Real Illusion

The internationalisation of Marxian class analysis in international political economy has also led to critical engagement with liberal theories of global social justice, which have influenced the anti-globalisation movement. While the line between Marxist approaches and contemporary left liberal political philosophy on global social justice are increasingly blurred, a substantial difference remains in the way it is seen as being realised (Kymlicka 2002: 190). A distinctive feature of liberal approaches to global economic inequality is its moral perspective. Invariably the onus is on wealthy Western states to initiate material transfers to poorer developing states (Beitz 1979), or to abide by a set of obligations that would constrain a range of international actors (O'Neill 1991). In this context Marxist approaches to global economic inequality with its greater attention to political conflicts arising from structural inequalities in the global economic system remain relevant. Whereas liberals see greater global social justice resulting from voluntary restraints taken on by a range of international actors, including states and multinational corporations, Marxists tend to be less optimistic and emphasise the ways in which justice is gained by social movements through struggle.

There is also growing interest in Marxist state power models, particularly Poulantzas, and Miliband, after twenty-five years of comparative neglect as non-statist approaches to power such as Foucault's, held sway (Aronowitz and Bratis: 2002). The process of the state's 'hollowing out' – upwards and downwards towards supra- and sub-national governance, respectively – has also been accompanied by greater centralisation and an increase in its powers of security and surveillance. Draconian legislation in the United States and the United Kingdom following the attack on the Twin Towers and the London bombings – the Patriot Act (2001) in America and the Anti-Terrorism, Crime and Security Act 2001 and subsequent Acts in 2005 and 2006 in Britain – gave sweeping new powers to the police that impact on fundamental liberties. Such developments make claims of the state's immanent demise appear summary. It is to the sophisticated models of state power, above all those developed by Poulantzas, that are increasingly being turned to (Aronowitz and Bratis: 2002).

\* \* \*

Generally, Marxists point up contradictions and emphasise their imperviousness to methodological dissolution. In a nutshell, Marx's riposte to Hegel was that contradictions were real and only resolvable through action and the actual transformation of the social world, not through thought, philosophy or methodology for that matter. While Marxist writers have long debated what such a conscious, transformative human activity would entail, it is clear that Marx intended neither the crude rejection of theorisation in favour of action nor (the other extreme) the theory-dominated methodological paradigm shift. One could even take the claim that 'the real' is antagonistic a step further, as some Marxist's have done, and maintain that theory itself is not free of the contradictions that it purports to apprehend in the social world.

If we now link this up with Marx's early critique of the Hegelian state and the ambiguity that seems to inhabit his later writings on the state, the point appears to be that we should not seek to reconcile these two approaches to the state by importing into Marxist theory a sociological method that purports to overcome the dichotomy between structure and agency. If Marxism teaches us anything it is that significant contradictions and ambiguities do not disappear with a shift of methodological standpoint alone. Rather we should look to understand the real source of the contradiction. The state appears autonomous and self-regulating – both from subjects (social classes) that would influence it and other spheres of social activity (the economic and the cultural sphere) that condition and are (in turn) conditioned by it – because it has to. Like the fetishised commodity relations that Marx analysed in *Capital* the state represents a real illusion. The state really is autonomous and self-regulating, serving to constrain and limit human action externally just as market laws constrain and limit economic agents. But just as the reified laws of the market-place can be mitigated by coming to see them as misrecognised forms of collective social activity so the fetishised forms of the state can be resolved back into the collective social activity of which it is made. The dualism of structure and agency and the forms of state to which this gives rise are overcome by taking the alienated form of the state 'back into ourselves'. But as Marx made clear this is not achieved by a shift in methodological standpoint or 'paradigm shift' but through 'conscious practical activity'.

To view the state as a reified (Lukács), as an alienation of civil society (early Marx), or as a fetishisation (Wells) is to see it as the product of class-related social practices even while it appears to be an objective structure. By reading Marx's theory of the state through his social ontology – articulated through his early concept of alienation;

the concept of fetishism developed in *Das Kapital* of Lukács' theory of reification – we can dispense with false oppositions foisted on it and arrive at a conception that is both distinctive and critical.

## Bibliography

Aronowitz, S. and Bratis, P. (eds) (2002), *Paradigm Lost: State Theory Reconsidered* (Minneapolis MN: Minnesota Press).
Barrow, C. W. (2002), 'The Miliband–Poulantzas debate', in S. Aronowitz and P. Bratis (eds), *Paradigm Lost: State Theory Reconsidered* (Minneapolis MN: Minnesota Press).
Beitz, C. (1979), *Political Theory and International Relations* (Princeton NJ: Princeton University Press).
Benton, T. (ed.) (1996), *The Greening of Marxism* (London: Guilford Press).
Butler, J. (1999), *Gender Trouble: Feminism and the Subversion of Identity* (London: Routledge).
Castoriadis, C. (1991), *Philosophy, Autonomy, Politics: Essays in Political Philosophy* (Oxford: Oxford University Press).
Dunleavy, P. and O'Leary, B. (1987), *Theories of the State: the Politics of Liberal Democracy* (Basingstoke: Macmillan).
Engels, F. (1985), *The Origin of the Family, Private Property and the State* (Harmondsworth: Penguin).
Finegold, K. and Skocpol, T. (1995), *State and Party in America's New Deal* (Wisconsin WI: University of Wisconsin Press).
Fraser, N. (1997), *Justice Interruptus: Critical Reflections on the Post-Socialist Condition* (London: Routledge).
Hay, C., Lister, M. and Marsh, D. (2006), *The State: Theories and Issues* (Basingstoke: Palgrave).
Jessop, B. (1990), *State Theory: Putting the Capitalist State in its Place* (Cambridge: Polity).
Jessop, B. (2002), *The Future of the Capitalist State* (Cambridge: Polity).
Kymlicka, W. (2002), *Contemporary Political Philosophy: An Introduction* (Oxford: Oxford University Press).
Lukács, G. (1991 [1971]), *History and Class Consciousness* (London: Merlin).
Marx, K. (1990 [1976]), *Capital: Volume One*, trans. B. Fowkes (Harmondsworth: Penguin).
McLellan, D. (2005), *Karl Marx: Selected Writings* (Oxford: Oxford University Press).
Miliband, R. (1969), *The State in Capitalist Society* (New York: Basic Books).
Miliband, R. (1983), *Class Power and State Power: Poetical Essays* (London: Verso).

Naess, A. (1989), *Ecology, Community, Lifestyle* (Cambridge: Cambridge University Press).
O'Neill, O. (1991), 'Transnational justice', in D. Held (ed.), *Political Theory Today* (Cambridge: Polity).
Poulantzas, N. (1972), 'The problem of the capitalist state', in R. M. Blackburn (ed.), *Ideology in Social Science: Readings in Critical Social Theory* (London: Fontana).
Poulantzas, N. (1978a), *Political Power and Social Classes* (London: Verso).
Poulantzas, N. (1978b), *State, Power, Socialism* (London: New Left Books).
Vincent, A. (1987), *Theories of the State* (Oxford: Blackwell).
Wells, D. (1981), *Marxism and the Modern State: An Analysis of Fetishism in Capitalist Society* (Sussex: Harvester Press).
Wetherly, P. (2006), *Marxism and the State: an analytic approach* (Basingstoke: Palgrave).

CHAPTER FIVE

# The Social Democratic State

Tim Hall

Few models of the state have been subject to the charge of obsolescence more frequently in recent times than the social democratic state. Where once the goals of social democratic government – full employment via a managed economy, greater equality in society through welfare provision and progressive taxation systems – represented the unquestioned credo of any post-war European government, they have, from the first period of their crisis in the late 1960s, come increasingly under fire. Thus, Ralf Dahrendorf, writing at the end of the 1970s after the Thatcher government came to power in the United Kingdom, described the social democratic model as 'exhausted' (Dahrendorf 1980: 2). For Dahrendorf the reasons for this were economic, political and cultural: economic because in an increasingly internationalised world, national governments had lost the power to manage the domestic economy; political because the sheer growth in the size of the state had reached the point where it began to restrict individual freedoms and, therefore, lack legitimacy; and cultural because the collectivist values underpinning it were more and more at odds with the increasingly individualist and 'opt-out' society that was beginning to emerge at this time (Dahrendorf 1980: 2).

John Gray in a pamphlet from 1996 repeats this charge, albeit for different reasons. Social democracy as a project, he argues, depended on the geo-strategic environment of the Cold War. This project, however, came to an abrupt end with the collapse of the

Soviet Union and the globalisation of capital. With a ready supply of skilled labourers from the former Soviet bloc countries, previously social democratic European states engage in a race to the bottom in which hard-fought-for labour and welfare rights are stripped away. 'In this changed historical circumstance,' he writes, 'the central economic programme of social democracy is unworkable and social democracy itself a bankrupt project' (Gray 1996: 12).

At the same time this verdict has been questioned by a number of theorists and social scientists in the field. Focusing on the different experience and response to crisis of western European states many have argued that the judgement that the social democratic model of the state is obsolete is summary. A seminal work in this respect is Fritz W. Scharpf's *Crisis and Choice in European Social Democracy*. Scharpf contends that the different experiences of western social democracies during this period – and their different capacities to cope – are due largely to the differences in the 'institutional repertoires' at the disposal of national governments. An example of this would be the existence of robust corporatist structures, in which labour and capital could meet in an *ad hoc* way to respond to crisis (Scharpf 1991). In a similar manner David Marquand in *The Unprincipled Society* (1988) argues that the demise of the social democratic or corporatist state in Britain was not an inevitable consequence of globalisation but the result of its own shortcomings. For Marquand it was the technocratic character of this state and its lack of consensus-generating institutions that made it moribund and opened the door to its dismantling at the hands of the New Right (see Chapter 10). The assumption of the inevitable and irreversible demise of the social democratic state has been further questioned by the emergence of supranational institutions of governance. While most social democratic theorists accept that domestic governments have lost the capacity to manage domestic economies in accordance with desired aims, the emergence of supranational institutions makes it possible to manage the economy at a global or regional level. For this reason social democratic theorists have championed projects of regional economic integration such as the European Union on the ground that they represent the opportunity of recovering regulatory instruments lost at the national level. For such theorists social democratic aims of managed growth and social fairness are redeemable in and through an account of multi-levelled governance. In this account the state

# The Social Democratic State

acts in concert with sub-national and supranational layers of governance.

This chapter considers this argument over the future of social democracy. It begins by tracing its historical emergence as a recognisable 'model' distinct from other forms of state (Marxist, socialist and liberal). It then looks at the central characteristics of the social democratic state before considering some of the key theoretical writings on it in recent times. The extent to which the loss of the state's capacity to manage capital at the national level is compensated at the supranational level will be explored in the section on debates around 'negative' and 'positive' integration in the European Union. The final section will focus on some ongoing problems in renewed conceptions of the social democratic state.

## Context

Social democracy has a variety of diverse sources from Marxism to non-conformist religion. In its northern European form (Germany, Austria and the Scandinavian countries) it is the product of the split between 'reformist' and 'revolutionary' wings of nineteenth-century European worker's movements. By contrast the development of social democracy in Britain was largely untouched by Marxism. To the extent that it had an ideology at all it was the product of the progressive liberalism of the Fabian Society and non-conformist religion (Freeden 1999).

The German Social Democratic Party (SPD) was formed in 1875 and was shaped by the history and fate of the Socialist Internationals. During the period of the Second International, Marxist and social democratic approaches represented left and right wings of the SPD. This was due to the dominance of evolutionary accounts of Marxism with their emphasis on innate maturation processes in society and their gradualist account of social change. The progressive and gradualist elements of Second International Marxism came increasingly under fire from more revolutionary currents of Marxism emerging in eastern Europe. The two wings of the party divided over their different responses to the First World War and the 1917 revolution, the latter culminating in the hard left turn of the international socialist movement and the ultra purism of the Third (communist) International. The split became irrevocable when some members on the right of the SPD colluded with the Nationalists in the suppression of the 1919 post-war uprisings in Germany.

The interwar years were a period of disorientation and ideological uncertainty for social democratic parties and the first social democratic governments produced little in the way of reform. Social democratic parties, attempting to steer a course between *laissez-faire* liberalism and communism, were arguably parties in search of a unifying ideology. This was provided by the unorthodox economics of John Maynard Keynes.

Keynes has claim to being the first theorist of the 'mixed economy' in which the state intervenes to correct imperfections arising from the free operation of markets. The key lesson that Keynes's political economy drew from the Great Depression was that governments could spend their way out of a recession. Through increased public spending, a government could stimulate demand in the economy generally and bring about an increase in production and employment. While it was not just social democratic governments that adopted Keynesian policies, the fact that first, they enabled democratic management of the economy; second, vindicated the ideals of justice by showing how growth itself was dependent on an ever broadening consumer base; and third, brought labour and capital together in pursuit of a high performing economy, made them particularly attractive to social democrats (Padgett and Patterson 1991: 22). More than anything else Keynesian economic policies have a claim to being the principal ideology of the post-war democratic state. They provided the theoretical framework for balancing the twin claims of individual liberty and social citizenship that came to characterise the social democratic approach in the post-war era.

In an unprecedented period of growth for the economies of western Europe in the immediate post-1945 era, social democracy entered its heyday. The combination of increasing affluence and the seeming capacity to manage the economy for social ends, led some social democrats to believe the problems of industrial society were largely solved (Padgett and Paterson 1991: 36). It was in this period of almost unlimited optimism that some of the classic programmatic statements of social democracy emerged. Anthony Crosland's *The Future of Socialism* argued for a rethinking of socialism in the light of post-war experience. The fiscal instruments provided by Keynesian economics now meant that governments could exert an unprecedented level of control over the economy, allowing them to pursue policies of full employment and social

## The Social Democratic State

equality (Crosland 1956). The very success with which post-war governments met in managing the economy rendered the oppositional politics of traditional socialist parties obsolete. Through the careful management of high performing economies standards of living of the working classes had been raised. This flatly contradicted the pessimistic prognoses of the Marxian left that predicted ever greater exploitation and 'immiseration'. Although inequalities in society remained – the inevitable consequence of wealth-creating free market institutions – traditional inequalities could gradually be eroded by the democratising effects of the educational system.

Crosland's work both articulated and influenced the optimistic mood among social democrats in Britain in the immediate post-war era. The equivalent to this in Europe was the SPD programme set out in the Bad Godesberg congress of 1959. At this and other conferences, the SPD re-defined itself as a broad-based 'people's party' with humanistic sources. Emphasis was placed on technology and progress and the capacity of human beings to control and direct their natural and social environments. The fiscal instruments now at the disposal of national governments were continuous with the increasing technical control exerted over the natural world.

No account of the history of social democracy would be complete without mention of Sweden. Sweden has a claim to being the first Keynesian social democracy – the first, that is, to use reflationary economic policies to pursue social democratic goals. However, it also assumed its distinctive shape in the post-war years. Distinctive features of the Swedish social democratic model include an emphasis on social partnership rather than public ownership and an importance given to individual fulfilment through education and culture. This implied a deep aversion to oppositional (that is, class) politics in all its forms and particularly close links between the state and the peak organisations of labour and capital. State intervention and direction such as the creation of public boards of administration to oversee the running of firms was favoured over outright public ownership. The long established and highly institutionalised form of social democracy makes it a paradigm case to this day.

Prior to the period of their crisis from the late 1960s onwards, social democratic governments had displayed marked elitist tendencies. The emphasis on technology and progress in the Bad Godesberg programme gave rise to the charge of 'technocracy' particularly from the Marxian left in West Germany. The new ideology of the social democratic parties with its emphasis on technical control of social economic life appeared to pave the way for the creation of a new stratum of social technocrats. The consequence of this was the undermining of its newly won democratic credentials. In Britain this took the form of the corporatist state in which the peak associations of labour and capital met behind closed doors to determine price increases and income levels. While different, the charge of technocracy and corporatism came down to the same thing – an increasingly unaccountable government.

These criticisms prefigured the slide into crisis that occurred towards the end of the 1960s. The first indication of the breakdown of attempts to manage the economy was the phenomenon of 'stagflation' – the concurrence of low growth, high unemployment and high inflation. This flew in the face of received Keynesian wisdom in which the management of the economy involved a 'trade-off' between full employment and low inflation. This crisis was then exacerbated by the international economic recession precipitated by the oil crisis of 1973–4. What was becoming steadily apparent during this period was the increasing economic interdependency of the world economy. This was rendering piecemeal all attempts by national governments to manage domestic economies. Domestic economies were increasingly exposed to outside shocks from which the state could provide little or no protection.

Social democratic parties in government adjusted to increasing economic interdependency by becoming governments of crisis management rather than demand management. This involved a shift of focus from the management of demand to the tight control of public expenditure to ensure that inflation remained at manageable levels. While no social democracy escaped austerity measures the experience of countries differed during this period. They faired more or less well depending on the extent to which their institutions were capable of generating consent to see through necessary reforms and spread the burden of any austerity measures. Thus in the 1980s, while Sweden responded to increased austerity with workers' share offers, the United Kingdom in successive Conservative governments experienced the dismantling of its corporatist structures.

Historians of social democracy tend to emphasise the singularity and uniqueness of the post-war period in which social democracy was in its ascendancy. Quite specific conditions – such as the return to protectionism after the Great Depression, the rebuilding programmes after the Second World War – made the pursuit of growth primarily through national economies possible. With the re-emergence of the

## The Social Democratic State

global economy in the 1960s, however, the Bretton Woods system came under increasing strain and the system that consolidated the period of protected national growth finally collapsed under the pressure of international currency speculation in 1971. With this the peculiar economic conditions that made the management of domestic economies possible came to an end (Scharpf 1991).

The emergence of supranational layers of governance, however, has led to a resurgence of social democratic thinking in more recent times. Simply stated the emergence of supranational institutions of governance opens up the possibility of the re-deployment of interventionist policies at the supranational level. The neo-liberal orthodoxies adopted by the International Monetary Fund and the World Bank after the breakdown of the Bretton Woods agreement have come increasingly under fire from neo-Keynesian economists particularly in the light of very public fiascos like the collapse of the Argentinean currency in 1997–9. In Europe, however, the development of the European Union from common market to economic union has given social democrats particular cause to hope. The extent to which this hope is justified will be explored below. In the proceeding section, however, attention turns to the central characteristics of the social democratic model of the state.

## Definition

'Strictly speaking there is no such thing as social democracy, if by that label is meant a singular fixed list of beliefs and practices' (Freeden 1999: 152). If, however, anything is to qualify as the credo for social democratic theorists it must be the belief that capitalism can and must be managed, in some sense, by the state. Capitalism must be managed because otherwise it produces, if not crisis as Marxists contend, then at least undesired social and political outcomes. It leads to great disparities in wealth and the consequent erosion of the social basis in which markets are embedded; to environmental disaster because unregulated markets create no incentives for meeting the cost of 'externalities' such as a clean and safe environment; above all it leads to a crisis of political legitimacy as political communities lack the power to govern themselves.

From its inception social democracy in contrast to Marxism has sought an accommodation with capitalism. While accepting that the market mechanism is the best and most efficient way of allocating resources, social democracy believes that the primary role of the state is to intervene and correct the economy when it delivers undesirable outcomes. This leads to a paradoxical conception of the social democratic state, as Claus Offe has argued (Offe 1984: 120). For insofar as it regulates and corrects the imperfections of the market, it is itself reliant on the (taxable) wealth generated by the free market economy. The state, therefore, has a vested interest in capital accumulation without which it is unable to exercise any power.

The consensus among social democratic theorists today, however, is that the state is much more heavily circumscribed in its capacity to intervene in the economy than it was. An interventionist government that pursues reflationary policies is immediately confronted with a 'capital flight' overseas resulting in a direct reduction of its power. Moreover, it also finds itself restricted in its capacity to regulate markets through legislation (for example, through the provision of employment rights) as states in a globalised economy vie with one another to attract overseas investment. This has led to pessimistic forecasts of a 'race to the bottom' in which labour rights fought for and won over the last hundred years are pared down to the minimum again. Most social democratic theorists tend, however, to reject this prognosis and point to emergent layers of supranational and sub-national governance as providing non-statist forms of intervention and regulation (Scharpf 1996). If the state is both unable and incompetent to intervene in a range of problems confronting it, then perhaps these problems could be solved through the sub-national governance exercised by voluntary organisations.

It is at this point that social democratic models of the state shade off into liberal pluralist conceptions and, indeed, in some conceptions, the social democratic state is all but indistinguishable from them (Giddens 1998). One of the ways, however, in which it continues to differ is in the importance that it gives to what Claus Offe has called 'institutional repertoires and practices' that provide alternative sources of 'problem-solving capacity' outside the formal channels of mass democracy and policy implementation (Offe 1984: 68). By this he means sources of political community and solidarity that would augment the state's problem-solving capacity. Social democratic models of the state would then differ from liberal pluralistic ones on account of their greater reluctance to accept the loss of the capacity for autonomy. To this end they tend to emphasise the sources of solidarity within political communities that augment the state's reduced capacity to act in an increasingly interdependent world.

If the desire to manage the capitalist economy for social democratic ends is one invariant characteristic of the social democratic approach, the other is the instinctive aversion to oppositional politics especially the class politics of the radical left. Whereas the Marxian left judged the state incapable of resolving the antagonisms/contradictions of modern (capitalist) society, social democrats saw in the interventionist state the capacity to resolve conflicts of interest arising at the social level. This debate about the nature of social transformation – whether interruptive and violent or gradualist and non-violent – can be traced back to Marx himself and debates around Second International Marxism. Generally though for social democrats the state is an essentially consensual institution in which divisions arising in civil society are potentially and actually reconciled. The sources for this are various, ranging from Hegel's conception of the state as universal to Durkheim's account of the emergence of a new moral order in response to the 'anomie' engendered by modernity and the division of labour. In post-war West Germany this consensual account of politics and the role of the state was given philosophical articulation by social democratic philosophers such as Karl Otto Apel and Jürgen Habermas. Habermas in particular developed a 'communicative theory of rationality' and a 'consensual theory of truth' that provided social democracy with a philosophical foundation (Habermas 1984). His distinction between 'system' and 'life-world' has been particularly influential for the state theory of Claus Offe and Fritz Scharpf, who have sought to account for how complex modern economies, understood in systemic terms, can be 'steered' in accordance with consensually derived 'norms'. However, if social democratic approaches to the state share beliefs in the 'manageability' of the economy and an aversion to conflictual politics, then there are significant differences as well. It is to such differences in some recent theorists that we now turn.

## Theorists

As stated there is general agreement among social democratic theorists that the state has lost a good deal of its power to pursue social democratic objectives such as full employment and social equality. There is disagreement, however, on the extent of this loss, with German political theorists like Offe and Scharpf arguing that it tends to be exaggerated in contrast to theorists like Giddens and Gray who tend to argue that it is not exaggerated enough. There is also disagreement about whether the waning of the power of the state is a cause for concern insofar as it represents the loss of the capacity for self-determination or a moment for cautious optimism in as much as it represents the opportunity to escape the ideologies of the state. Scharpf sees the loss of 'national problem-solving capacities' as potentially catastrophic leading to a loss of democratic legitimacy on a par with that suffered by some countries in the Great Depression (Dettke 1998: 31). Anthony Giddens, on the other hand, sees the advance beyond left and right entailed by globalisation as making possible the radical renewal of social democracy along cosmopolitan lines (Giddens 1998: 152). Such differences lead to profoundly different conceptions of the renewed social democratic project; the former a question of preserving institutional repertoires and traditions that run the risk of being liquidated in the face of globalising capital; and the second a question of capitalising on the possibility of a politics of the 'radical middle' presented by the demise of the state and the ideologies coterminus with it. The differing conceptions of social democratic renewal are themselves generated by profoundly different analyses of the problems confronting it.

For Scharpf (1996) the breakdown of the Bretton Woods system in 1971 and the oil crises that followed it in 1973–4 were clear indications of the increasing interdependence of the world economy signalling the end of the post-war period of nationally managed economic growth. Interventionist governments were confronted with the ineffectiveness of their fiscal instruments as reflationary policies led to 'capital flight' with investors looking for more secure and more lucrative investment opportunities at home and abroad. If governments could no longer regulate the level of demand in the domestic economy this meant they were increasingly powerless in the face of high unemployment.

It also meant a reduction in the capacity of governments to pursue redistributive policies through spending on welfare, health and education. Significantly, for Scharpf the performance of the domestic economies of western European states and their capacity to pursue welfarist policies differed markedly during this period. In

## The Social Democratic State

particular he points to the high level of taxation and welfare sustained in Scandinavian countries, most notably in Denmark (Scharpf 1996: 16). Also of particular importance for Scharpf is the existence of corporatist structures capable of generating a broad-based agreement across society for necessary economic reforms. This contrasts with the British experience under the Conservative government of Margaret Thatcher, in which what remained of the corporatist state was systematically dismantled in a return to oppositional politics.

In addition to greater economic interdependence there has also been a drift of power away from the state 'upwards' towards supranational institutions and 'downwards' towards emergent layers of sub-national governance. For Scharpf both the emergence of supranational governance and the process of decentralisation are inevitable consequences of greater internationalisation on the one hand and greater social complexity on the other hand. While Scharpf sees policy networks as a necessary aspect of modern government he stops short of advocating a functional model of democracy like Hirst or, to a lesser extent, Offe. Policy networks, he argues, are meant to precede or accompany decisions taken in national legislatures, not replace them (Scharpf 1999: 20). This is part of his broader argument that while the state has seen a reduction in its regulatory capacity it is far from powerless to intervene and shape domestic affairs. In this regard he points to competitive advantages secured through a more educated and skilled workforce, more co-operative industrial relations and the more effective use of advanced production techniques – all areas in which the state retains a predominant influence. The most distinctive feature of Scharpf's defence of the social democratic state is its avowed supranationalism, particularly in respect of the European Union, which we shall consider in the next section.

Claus Offe's work shares many characteristics with Scharpf's such as its emphasis on corporate structures and institutional repertoires particular to nation-states. He tends, however, to be less sanguine about the possibilities for pursuing social democratic aims at supranational level. In his early work he focused on the contradictory character of the modern welfare state. Drawing on the work of Marx and Karl Polanyi he argued that the imperfectly commodifiable character of labour – the fact that 'labour power' cannot be wholly separated from its owner – necessitated the creation of non-commodified support systems charged with the task of re-commodifying labour

(Offe 1984: 263). This leads to *ex ante* rather than *ex post* justifications of the welfare state. Precisely because there could not be a pure labour market, support systems (welfare, health, education) are an integral and necessary part of any market economy.

The contradictory character of the modern welfare state leads to contradictory and self-thwarting state policies, as the very attempt to re-commodify labour leads to the expansion of non-commodified support systems (Offe 1984: 127). To some extent Offe's analysis of the welfare state concurs with the overload theory of the New Right (see Chapter 10). Unlike the New Right, however, the appropriate response to the growth of the state is not the reduction of its size, the introduction of managerial forms drawn from the private sector and a heavy dose of traditional morality. This fundamentally misrecognises the necessity of non-commodified forms of production – like health and education – and the reliance of the market economy on these. Any government that pursues such policies would simply succeed in disembedding the economy with huge social costs.

Offe's approach to the modern state is neo-Marxian in many respects. What makes it distinctively social democratic is its adoption of the system/lifeworld distinction drawn from the work of Habermas. Contradictions in the welfare state are ultimately to be understood in structural and systemic terms (Offe 1984: 262). For example, the exercise of state power, considered as a functional system, reveals its dependence on capital accumulation (Offe 1984: 120). The state can manage and regulate the economy only if the latter generates wealth – an insight also arrived at by critical pluralists (see Chapter 2). Structural contradiction – the interdependence of functionally-orientated systems – while not ultimately resolvable (a thoroughgoing socialisation of production along Marxian lines) can be subjected to normative control and 'steered'. In this regard Offe attributes an important role to new social movements in bringing such contradictions to the attention of society to enable more effective and more consensual steering.

Offe's more recent work on the state focuses on the ways in which it retains its capacity to act in the face of its 'decomposition' and is notable for its unapologetic 'statism', albeit tempered by elements of associationalism. The decomposition of the state is due to the instruments at its disposal (fiscal instruments, positive law, force) which are simply unsuited to many problems that modern governments face; the sheer complexity of modern government and difficulty of co-ordinating policy across a range of actors; and the loss of sovereignty to the 'past' or to supranational organisations like the EU or NATO (Offe 1996: 64–5). Despite this Offe remains resolutely statist and points, like Scharpf, to 'repertoires of traditions, symbols, institutional patterns, and established routines that are characteristic for individual nations' (Offe 1996: 68). The existence of such traditions increase the problem-solving capacity of nation-states 'outside the formal channels of mass democracy and administrative policy implementation' (Offe 1996: 68). Unlike Scharpf he is more sceptical about the prospect of emergent supranational institutions of governance compensating for the lost regulatory powers of the state. Beyond a certain size, he argues, social systems undermine their capacity for autonomous democratic self-determination (Offe 1984: 273).

In contrast to both Scharpf and Offe, Anthony Giddens has presented the case for a more radical renewal of the social democratic state. For Giddens, rather than lament the loss of state powers, we ought to focus on the opportunities it presents for a post-ideological renewal of social democracy. Giddens sees four problems with the classical social democratic model: the first is increasing economic interdependence, or globalisation, that makes Keynesian fiscal instruments redundant; the second is an increasing individualism and the transition to a new politics that focuses on 'life choices' rather than 'life chances'; the third is the breakdown of the distinction between left and right; and the fourth new forms of political agency. The first requires little comment. The others require more comment as they are central to his conception of the renewal of the social democratic project.

For Giddens the most significant characteristic of modern societies is the extent to which all aspects of social life are subject to critique and open to individual choice. Whereas, for example, in traditional societies, marriage and having a family would have been largely assumed, today one is confronted with a plethora of life choices (for example, to remain single, to cohabit, to adopt rather than have children, not to have children at all, same-sex relations, etc.). In short, what in traditional societies represented a vast horizon of unquestioned assumptions becomes in modern society a matter of individual preference and choice. This has far-reaching implications for politics and the state. If one looks, for example, at systems of welfare or taxation it is easy to see the extent to which they have been tailored to traditional conceptions of the family.

At bottom the problem is the universalistic assumptions of traditional conceptions of the state. State policies have been based on functionalist analyses of society that enable a clear distinction to be drawn between 'normal' and 'deviant' social behaviour. Such distinctions have simply between swept away through processes of critique and modernity.

The problem with traditional ideologies of the state – ideologies like Marxism, liberalism, social democracy, etc. – is that they all appear tied to universalistic conceptions of the good life which seem to preclude life choices. To take the promethean pronouncements of Bad Godesberg, for example, in which political contestation is largely viewed as surmounted as a result of technological development and the success of modern governments in managing the economy: such a vision leaves little room for life choices and the inevitable contestation resulting from them. The emergence of the individual as the subject of life choices appears to call for a post-ideological politics in which governments at a minimum display less hubris.

This also demands recognition of new forms of political agency. Giddens refers here to Ulrich Beck's conception of the 'sub-political' and cites Greenpeace's campaign against Shell and its planned sinking of the Brent Sparr oil rig in 1995 as a case in point (Giddens 1998: 49–50). A concerted campaign via non-orthodox political channels led to a reversal of Shell's policy. For Giddens it is not that modern electorates are becoming less political. It is just that their political interests reflect emergent life choices such as the environment, human rights, animal rights, sexual identity, countryside, etc., and that such 'life politics' are pursued outside the traditional channels of party politics.

In response to this evident demise of the classical social democratic model Giddens calls for its renewal and two core ideas in this renewal are equality as inclusiveness and positive welfare. An inclusive society is a participatory society. Exclusion, for Giddens, is about 'mechanisms that detach groups from the social mainstream' (Giddens 1998: 104). This can take the form of the voluntary exclusion of the elites at the top or the (presumably) involuntary exclusion of the least advantaged at the bottom. From the point of view of realising the inclusive society, preventing the involuntary opt-out of the elites is at least as important as preventing the emergence of an underclass with little connection to the social mainstream (Giddens 1998: 104). The notion of the inclusive society which is pursued by renewed social democracy is to be contrasted with the egalitarianism of the old style social democracy.

Central to this notion of inclusiveness is the concept of positive welfare in which protections afforded by the state are met halfway with commitments by citizens to search for new employment and take risks. Aside from the provision of welfare protection (negative welfare) the state and voluntary associations in civil society must seek to foster a risk-taking culture (positive welfare) to enable individuals to help themselves out of welfare dependency and help civil society generally. On this basis, Giddens proceeds to define welfare as 'in essence' a psychic concept rather than an economic one and to propose counselling as an alternative or supplement to direct economic support (Giddens 1998: 117). Arguably this is where Giddens's project is at its weakest because it is difficult to see what is inclusive about a society that relies so centrally on the general diffusion of entrepreneurial spirit. Although Giddens maintains that welfare should have a redistributive function rather than act as a safety net, there is little to distinguish his own position from the 'soft' neo-liberal prescription of minimal state (counselling) and doses of self-help morality.

Moreover, Giddens's account of the inclusive society has little to say about underlying social inequalities. The general application of the concept of risk does not distinguish between the types of risk undergone or what individuals stand to lose beginning from unequal starting points. The new politics provides little basis for thinking social justice because the latter involves questions of political community and social solidarity. Giddens's focus on individuals and the life choices confronting them means that he has little to avail himself of in this regard except the 'thin' communitarian values in which rights come with corresponding responsibilities. Individuals may well fear the consequences of not helping themselves but it is difficult to understand why they would be positively obligated to society given radically unequal starting points. For, arguably, questions of social justice cannot ultimately be separated from notions of political community and social solidarity. How else could high tax burdens or comparable sacrifices be accounted for if not with reference to 'civic values' and an attachment to a distinctive but shared way of life? Giddens has little or nothing to say about sources of social solidarity and thus little or nothing to say about social justice.

An interesting alternative to the variants of social democracy proposed by Offe and Giddens is the associationalist model proposed and developed by the late Paul Hirst. 'Associationalism' is distinguished by the claim that individual liberty and human welfare are enhanced when 'as many affairs of society as possible are managed by voluntary and democratically self-governing associations' (Hirst 1994: 19). It derives from functionalist accounts of democracy originally outlined by Durkheim, Cole and Laski and proposes a radical decentring of power away from the state and towards the voluntary associations that comprise civil society. It views the state as an organ of social co-ordination rather than a medium for the registration of the wills of the majority. This sets it apart from liberal pluralist accounts of the state in which voluntary associations are viewed as secondary associations that ensure the democratic nature of the primary association (that is, the state). For associative democracy this relationship is 'turned on its head' and voluntary association becomes the primary means of democratic governance and organising social life (Hirst 1994: 26; see Chapter 2).

In contrast to Giddens, Hirst does take account of underlying social inequalities. Indeed, he views the attempt to reduce major unjustifiable social inequalities in power and wealth as one of the essential and enduring elements of the social democratic project (Hirst 1999: 87). While the question of private property no longer occupies the central position that it did in politics, the absence of social justice leads to the breakdown of society as a co-operative system (Hirst 1994: 10). For Hirst, however, problems of social justice are not necessarily solved by state intervention. Greater social equality, he argues, can best be achieved by the voluntary sector working in partnership with the poor and excluded (Hirst 1994: 10).

A key plank of the proposed renewal of social democracy along associationalist lines is the democratisation of corporate governance. Decentralisation in the form of substantive powers given to the governing bodies of schools and hospitals is all very well but unless the regulatory framework extends to companies the potential for participation will be minimal. Hirst proposes greater accountability to a range of stakeholders rather than simply being driven by shareholder profits. The democratisation of corporate governance, he argues, will not only increase the chances for participation but also increase the efficiency of the market economy. This is due to the essentially embedded character of the market, which enables it to be judged in terms of employment, investment and the composition of output. If it does not deliver acceptable levels of each 'social actors will intervene to correct it and provide the appropriate means of regulation and inputs to achieve the substantive outcome desired. The market system is thus a viable economic mechanism in the right kind of social context' (Hirst 1994: 65).

A favoured example of Hirst's is the regulation of rail networks by consumer groups, but while Hirst's model appears to work well for former public utilities it is less clear how it applies to multinational corporations where the stakeholders are dispersed across continents. It is unclear, for example, how corporations such as Starbucks are going to be held to account in this way. Admittedly Hirst's argument rests upon scepticism about the more breathless and exaggerated claims of globalisation. For a variety of reasons capital is less mobile than it is sometimes claimed to be. Nevertheless, there remains more than a trace of the altogether smaller-scale society in which the pluralist theory of democracy emerged. In order to exercise a regulative function the various interest groups must be able to associate. This implies that they are not presented with insuperable temporal and spatial barriers.

Associationalism represents an alternative to forms of 'left' social democratic thought that emphasise political community and/or social movements. Hirst rejects what he calls the 'new republicanism' that privileges the notion of a single self-governing political community. Such notions are anachronistic insofar as they conceive of the nation-state as an autonomous bounded community. Also they are at odds with a pluralistic society in which values and objectives increasingly diverge. What is needed, he argues, is a political community that enables citizens to be different rather than to 'exhort them to be the same' (Hirst 1994: 13–14). Similarly, he rejects an over-reliance on social movements on account of their oppositional character and inherent statism. Without a change in political institutions, he contends, and a state more accommodating to the creation of social communities, the impact of such movements will be limited and constrained (Hirst 1994: 14). His rejection of the old-style politics of opposition bears some comparison with Giddens. The question that this raises, however, is whether such institutional reform will suffice on its own to perform the regulative function, particularly the redistributive function formerly performed by the state, which Hirst (contra Giddens) recognises as necessary for a social democracy.

For Hirst associations are nothing more than groups that individuals voluntarily enter and leave (Hirst 1994: 52). If social groups are nothing more than the consolidation of the interests of their members then it is difficult to see what sources of social solidarity can be called upon to support redistributive policies. His rejection of such sources also leads him to make improbable claims for the inherently politicising function of associationalism. It is not clear, for example, how sitting on the board of governors of a tennis club is to provide 'a schooling in the arts of freedom and an enhancement in the political capacity of the individual' in the way that Hirst claims (Hirst 1994: 52).

## Practical politics

Scharpf, Offe and, to a lesser extent, Hirst on the one hand and Giddens on the other hand offer competing versions of the social democratic project. The former is the European social model and the latter the social market economy model. One place where these competing visions of the social democratic project have repeatedly collided in recent times is over the nature, institutions and policies of the European Union.

The European Union is often described as the most advanced experiment in regional integration in the world. While its origins in the post-war era were strategic (to prevent future conflict between European states), it has gradually come to take on the role of ensuring social and economic stability in Europe. As an economic and monetary union it seeks to eliminate frictions and disruptions resulting from divergent national interventions in the common market (Scharpf 1999: 47). Generally, social democrats of all stripes have welcomed the transition from common market to economic union on the grounds of the increased regulatory powers that it affords – powers generally agreed to have been lost at the national level. Neo-liberals, by contrast, have been more comfortable with the notion of a completed common market. For social democrats, much hangs on the character and extent of this integration. Does economic integration, for example, imply social rights or is it restricted to the economic narrowly defined (for example, monetary policy and competition law)? As suggested earlier, battle lines between neo-liberals and social democrats have been drawn around the distinction between negative and positive integration – roughly the distinction between 'market-creating' and 'market-correcting' regulation. Within different accounts of the social democratic project they tend to be divided over the character and extent of the embeddedness of the market system in society.

The problem for social democrats is that the EU has been altogether more successful at achieving negative integration than it has at achieving positive integration. This is due principally to the neo-liberal agenda driving processes like the 'constitutionalisation' of EU competition law and other 'market-making' processes. The EU also holds substantive powers in this regard such as Commission directives and the judgements of the European Court of Justice on a case-by-case basis that have overridden and 'struck down' national legislation. By contrast, 'market-correcting' measures such as social rights and environmental protection generally require intergovernmental agreement at the Council of Ministers. The problem is that consensus at these meetings is often very difficult to achieve with individual member states using the threat of veto to pursue narrowly defined national interests. This means that Europe is capable of positive action in these areas if and only if there is a possibility of common gains for all member states.

In addition there are, as Scharpf has noted, serious ideological, economic and institutional barriers to positive integration (Scharpf 1999: 79). On ideological grounds some states following neo-liberal agendas will be hostile to positive integration. The United Kingdom, for example, frequently cites the loss of competitive advantages *vis-à-vis* other member states as a reason for resisting EU legislation on employment rights. There are also seemingly insuperable economic barriers to positive integration on account of the different stages of development of the economies of member states. The consequence, for example, of fixing welfare payments at north European levels for countries like Portugal and Greece would be devastation for their economies. A final barrier to positive integration is the different institutional structures of European welfare states, which would make harmonisation very difficult, if not impossible. An example would be the employer-related insurance schemes in countries like Austria in contrast to the state provision of other countries. For each of these reasons then, in addition to the problems of securing a consensus at intergovernmental level, positive integration is difficult to achieve.

Euro-sceptics would point to the unrepresentative character of EU institutions as the principal reason why legislation on positive integration is difficult to achieve. Quite simply EU bodies lack a mandate for carrying out such policies. As Scharpf has persuasively argued, however, EU institutions represent the possibility of enhancing democratic accountability by restoring regulatory powers to elected bodies. In making this argument he draws on the distinction between 'input-orientated legitimacy' (government by the people) and 'output-orientated legitimacy' (government for the people) – roughly, the distinction between the legitimacy deriving from our capacity for self-government and that deriving from the increased problem-solving capacity of government. The representative character of political institutions would have a bearing on the first kind of legitimacy and the capacity to subject to control what previously eluded political control would have a bearing on the second type. Whereas the former requires a strong notion of collective identity if the will of the majority is to be accepted by the minority, the latter requires 'no more than the perception of a range of common interests that is sufficiently broad and stable to justify institutional arrangements for collective action' (Scharpf 1999: 11). For Scharpf, then, EU institutions meet the criteria of the latter 'output-orientated legitimacy' rather than the former. Democracy is enhanced by rendering decisions that were previously compelled by external necessity, or taken by an unaccountable authority, the object of collective choice (Scharpf 1999: 26–7). However imperfectly representative EU institutions are, the fact that they offer solutions to problems that require collective, co-ordinated action between states puts them in the credit rather than the debit column of the democratic deficit.

Scharpf's contention about the output-orientated legitimacy of EU institutions brings to the fore the importance for social democrats of recent attempts to replace the individual treaties that comprise the Union with a single constitution. The importance of the EU constitution lies in the fact that it seeks to simplify the process of European governance by consolidating the provisions of the preceding treaties in a single document. It seeks to render the activities of the European Council more transparent through subsidiarity, the creation of an EU president and through the extension of the powers of the European Parliament. It also aims at enhancing the effectiveness of the EU governance by extending qualified majority voting (QMV) in certain areas. In many respects the EU constitution represents little more than the 'tidying-up' exercise that realists and 'intergovernmentalists' claimed. In contrast to the provision under the existing treaties the actual extension of powers is quite minor. On the other hand, there is undoubtedly a grain of truth in the euro-sceptic fears of a creeping federalism. The ratification of the constitution would mean that the Union would for the first time have a distinct legal personality. Moreover, even though the extension of QMV is quite minor, particularly in its application to social rights, the constitution does indeed represent the legal framework for multi-level European governance. This is especially the case with the incorporation of the principle of subsidiarity into the constitution and the clarification of competencies and powers. While this falls a long way short of the restoration of problem-solving capacities at the supranational level that Scharpf and other social democrats envisaged, it certainly represents a step in that direction.

So much could have been reasonably concluded had the constitution been ratified. At present, however, we are still in the period of reflection following the 'No' vote of the French and the Dutch electorate – the former ironically on the grounds that the constitution was too neo-liberal. The sheer impracticality of the existing arrangements makes it likely that there will either be another attempt to ratify the treaty in the near future or that it will be implemented in its separate parts.

\* \* \*

In current social democratic thinking about the state there is a difference between the social market approach represented by Anthony Giddens and the European social model represented by such thinkers as Scharpf and Offe. While both approaches agree about the essentially embedded character of the market system and the need to manage the economy in order to arrive at socially desired goals they differ in their respective assessments of the extent of this embeddedness and the character of the management. Whereas Giddens and Hirst prefer self-regulation – the latter in particular emphasising the decentralising potential implicit in it – Scharpf and Offe argue for a more interventionist state. While they concede that this must occur in the context of the emergence of multi-level governance, the historical existence of a political community with its tradition and attachment to political institutions makes the state irreplaceable. It is fair to say that for both the disappearance of the state would be tantamount to the loss of political liberty itself: in other words, the ability of a political community to be self-determining. For each the existence of such a community along with its distinctive institutions and practices is the central bulwark against the 'race to the bottom' caused by regulation competition between states in the increasingly internationalised world.

Both Hirst and Giddens deny the existence of such communities. Each downplays the importance of 'existential communities' or 'communities of belonging' in modern politics. Both contrast the difference between old and new politics on the basis of the modern individual. While Hirst presses the case for the democratisation of corporate governance it is difficult to see how this will be effective in an international context unless it is supplemented by regulatory powers in supranational organisations like the EU. Giddens's position, on the other hand, particularly his conception of the inclusive society and the related concept of positive welfare, looks indistinguishable from neo-liberalism. At best the state co-ordinates the activities of voluntary organisations which in turn seek to activate the risk-taking capacities of individuals for the benefit of themselves and society.

On this account then the central difference between the social market approach and the European social model is the reliance of the latter on 'organismic' notions of community. The central question posed is whether it is possible for the state in a system of multilevel governance to pursue redistributive policies without an organismic notion of community. For Scharpf and Offe the answer is definitely not, even given the former's arguments about the output-orientated legitimacy of the recovery of problem-solving capacity at supranational level. Unless this is accompanied by the greater 'input-orientated legitimacy' of EU institutions themselves and unwillingness on the part of member states to accept the 'race to the bottom' driven by 'regulation competition', these powers will never be recovered. Offe argues along similar lines when he puts the case for an 'ordered retreat of the state' in which the state retains its centrality by initiating its own retreat rather than see its power gradually undermined. For Giddens an organismic or 'thick' notion of community is not necessary for an inclusive society which, in the transformed politics of the post-Cold War era, replaces the egalitarian society as the central goal of the social democratic state, but as we have seen with respect to the related concept of positive welfare, it is hard to see how this differs in essentials from neo-liberal conceptions.

Hirst does claim redistributive powers for the associative democracy but these are not powers that the hollowed-out state

## The Social Democratic State

retains. Much hangs on the thorny issue of the democratisation of corporate governance and the stakeholder conception of capitalism but it is difficult to see how this would work in an international context or which agency, other than the state, would have the legitimacy to initiate and carry through such far-reaching reform. Hirst sets great store by the spontaneous capacities of civil society but arguably without justification. Unless this account of the redistributive capacity of the associative democracy can be made good, his claims for a pluralist conception of freedom – the freedom to be different – will be idle. The question to which it would immediately give rise is how citizens in the associative democracy have access to the basic social goods to enable them to develop their differences?

The ideals of the social democratic state – the socially managed capitalist economy and an end to confrontational politics – continue to engage contemporary theorists of the state after the emergence of the global economy seemed to signal their demise. The sustained criticism of the performance of international organisations like the IMF following neo-liberal agendas – particularly in relation to the developing world – have led to a revival of Keynesian (non-orthodox) economics. The emergence of regional international organisations such as the European Union has also placed questions of positive integration between member states high on the agenda. Rethinking the role of the state in this context looks set to be an ongoing question in state theory.

## Bibliography

Crosland, C. A. R. (1956), *The Future of Socialism* (London: Jonathan Cape).

Dahrendorf, R. (1980), *After Social Democracy*, Unservile State Papers No. 25 (Dorset: The Blackmore Press).

Dettke, D. (ed.) (1998), *The Challenge of Globalization for Germany's Social Democracy* (New York: Berghahn).

Freeden, M. (1999), 'True blood or false genealogy: New Labour and British social democratic thought', in Gamble, A. and Wright, T. (eds) (1999), *The New Social Democracy*, The Political Quarterly in Association with the Fabian Society (Oxford: Blackwell), pp. 151–65.

Giddens, A. (1998), *The Third Way: The Renewal of Social Democracy* (Cambridge: Polity).

Gray, J. (1996), *After Social Democracy: Politics, Capitalism and the Common Life* (London: Demos).

Habermas, J. (1984), *The Theory of Communicative Action, Volume One: Reason and the Rationalisation of Society*, trans. Thomas McCarthy (Cambridge: Polity).

Hirst, P. (1994), *Associative Democracy* (Cambridge: Polity).

Hirst, P. (1999), 'Globalisation and social democracy', in Gamble, A. and Wright, T. (eds) (1999), *The New Social Democracy*, The Political Quarterly in Association with the Fabian Society (Oxford: Blackwell).

Marquand, D. (1988), *The Unprincipled Society: New Demands and Old Politics* (London: Cape).

Offe, C. (1984), *Contradictions of the Welfare State* (London: Hutchinson).

Offe, C. (1996), *Modernity and the State: East, West* (Cambridge: Polity).

Padgett, S. and Paterson, W. E. (1991), *A History of Social Democracy in Postwar Europe* (Harlow: Longman).

Scharpf, Fritz, W. (1991), *Crisis and Choice in European Social Democracy* (Ithaca: Cornell University Press).

Scharpf, Fritz, W. (1996), *A New Social Contract? Negative and Positive Integration in the Political Economy of European Welfare States*, European University Working Paper RSC No. 96/44 Badia Fiesolana: San Demenico (FI).

Scharpf, Fritz, W. (1999), *Governing Europe* (Oxford: Oxford University Press).

CHAPTER SIX

# Anarchism: the Politics of Anti-Statism

*Erika Cudworth*

Despite its uncompromising anti-statism, anarchism has been largely ignored in discussions on state theory, and sometimes seen as unilluminating or implausible (Dunleavy and Leary 1987: 10). Anarchist state theory is difficult to consider given the fact that anarchist writing on the state is focused on specific aspects of institutions (for example, education provision). In addition, anarchism has been accused of having a moral objection to the state but no theory of the operation of the state, for it is 'stronger on moral assertion than on analysis' (Heywood 2003: 190). Much anarchist writing has centred on encouraging our instincts of freedom and autonomy rather than analysing the state as an oppressive social formation, thus, anarchism has a smaller contribution to state theory than might be expected.

This is perhaps because anarchists reject a state-centric focus in their own theorising. While some (social democrats, fundamentalists, some liberal pluralists) see the state as a tool for positive social change others (some liberals, conservatives old and new) are more cautious, seeing the state as a 'necessary evil' fulfilling the imperative function of maintenance of law and order. Like instrumentalist Marxists and feminists, anarchists consider the state to be an instrument of social domination serving those with power and privilege but, in all its variants, anarchism is distinguished by its rejection of the state. For anarchist anthropologists like Harold Barclay (2003: 11) a problem for anarchism is that statism is a 'universal myth' of modernity, and bedrock of both theoretical and practical political understandings of the world.

This chapter considers the emergence of anarchism and the themes that have, historically, made anarchism distinct in its contribution to state theory. Despite radical differences between variants and exponents, defining the state has been relatively uncontroversial for anarchism. The state is defined not according to its organisation but with respect to its function, and this is seen as institutionalised repression. The compulsory and coercive powers of the state are not regarded as authoritative, and the processes of institutional democratic politics, such as the electoral process in liberal democracies and the role of parties and pressure groups, is seen as elitist and morally palpable. Key theories include Peter Kropotkin's anarcho-communist analysis of the state as semi-autonomous of class and his understanding of spontaneous order. Alan Carter's conception of the autonomous state further develops this notion and illustrates some of the synergies, as well as the differences, between anarchism and Marxism. In direct contrast, Murray Rothbard suggests an 'anarcho-capitalism'. The eclectic work of Murray Bookchin has presented the state as a hybridisation of social and political institutions that reproduce a range (gendered, natured, class based, (post-) colonial) of relationships of domination.

A number of different cases will be discussed in considering the practical political implications of anarchist state theory. The ideas of Rothbard on privatisation of security, judicial and penal services influenced New Right thinkers and governments in the 1980s. Anarchist analyses of the latent authoritarianism of the state and the development of ideas about self-governance are endemic to the Gandhian movement in India, particularly in the 1970s. A rather different historical example is the influence of anarcho-syndicalism in the powerful Confederación Nacional de Trabajo (CNT) union in Spain in the 1930s, which set up workers' collectives as an alternative form of political organisation. Anarchism has recently made its presence felt in movements opposing 'globalisation'. Anarchism can be evidenced in a variety of contemporary social practices, but it has had limited impact in practical political terms when we consider the organisation of contemporary states.

## Context

In the history of Western political thought, anarchism has often been equated with disorder, chaos and sporadic acts of violence. Its literal meaning, however, is an absence of authority, or, as Michael Bakunin put it, 'an absolute rejection of any principle of authority' (cited in Lehning 1973: 65). Consequently, anarchism might be defined as a conviction that the state is unnecessary (Woodcock 1986: 36–9) and a preference for a stateless social condition. Given the wide variety of forms which 'authority' assumes, it is unsurprising that anarchism has had an eclectic range of preoccupations – from the social system of capitalism, to a range of forms of social domination including those based on gender inequalities, sexual repression, racism, imperialism and warfare. Anarchists generally agree that forms of political authority restrict individual actions and beliefs and constitute a violation of their freedom (Goodwin 1982: 110–12). In light of this, they endorse egalitarianism, voluntary co-operation, self-management, individualism and decentralisation (Goodway 1989: 2). Like many feminists, anarchists tend to define politics very broadly and their analysis of political power is not restricted to the 'state' and 'government' (see Chapter 9). This said, an antipathy towards institutionalised authority has meant that historically a key feature of anarchism has been the contestation of authority exercised by the state. While anarchism emerged in eighteenth-century Europe in the context of political authoritarianism, it has remained staunchly critical of liberal intimations of 'democracy'. Liberal or 'bourgeois' democracy with the representative institutions of parliamentarianism is seen as inherently incapable of providing anything more than a justification for oligarchy.

There are a variety of different kinds of anarchist theorising and, almost inevitably, individual thinkers may slip across the lines drawn by a typology. All anarchists have provided some broader critique of social and economic structures and processes than simply a denunciation of the state. In the nineteenth century, most anarchists were also involved in workers' political organisations and most contemporary anarchists subscribe to some form of 'anarcho-communism' (Miller 1984) or more commonly, 'social anarchism', which is collectivist and in many ways, communitarian. In sharp contrast, 'anarcho-capitalism' (Miller 1984) or 'individualist anarchism', exemplified by the work of Murray Rothbard

(1978), is an extreme form of liberalism based on the absolute sovereignty of the individual (also Nozick 1974: Part 1). In the nineteenth century an important advocate of such individualism was Max Stirner (1845), whose suggestion that we are all (essentially) self-interested and self-seeking has been an element of conservative and liberal approaches (see Chapter 10).

What is often referred to as 'classical anarchism' however, was a left-orientated response to nineteenth-century developments, specifically the processes of industrialisation and new forms of labour relations, the increasing powers of the state and a concern with the escalation of the scale of warfare. Anarchism as an organised political force stemmed from the debates between followers of Marx and those of Bakunin in the First International. Both 'anarchists' and 'Marxists' agreed on the exploitative nature of capitalism, but differed on the nature of the state itself. Whereas the predominant view of Marx and Engels was a form of class instrumentalism, anarchists argued that the structure and actions of the state cannot be read off as either functional for the logic of the capitalist system, or as a direct instrument of class interests. This said, there are anarchists who have argued for the strong commonalities between Marxian and anarchist theory. Daniel Guérin (1989: 118) considers that there are grounds for fertile theoretical relations between anarcho-communism and 'authentic Marxism'. In my view, there are five elements which make anarchist state theorising distinctive: the conception of human nature; an understanding of social contract; a broad notion of social domination; the articulation of interest by the state; and the possibility of the state as an agent of political change.

For eighteenth-century anarchists such as William Godwin, humans are rational and can become perfect through self-education (Marshall 1989: 130). Godwin argues that the collective development of reason will obviate the need for the state. Most anarchists differ from Goodwin, however, on the notion of 'perfectibility' and consider that the structures and processes of governance bring out the worst in fallible creatures rather than having a crude assertion of 'natural goodness' (Crowder 1992: 344). For Peter Kropotkin, in the later nineteenth century, and for contemporary thinker Murray Bookchin, evidence from evolutionary biology, anthropology and ethology suggests that the human condition, like that of non-human animal species, is one of a struggle against adverse circumstances. Species with effective networks of mutual co-operation and aid are most likely to flourish and, in the absence of government, human communities will develop effective forms of social regulation and provision. Such theorising has been critiqued as naively positing a 'natural goodness' argument, yet this is an endemic problem for all political thought. Most political theory is based on some conception of 'human nature', and theories of the state are consistently imbued with such normative understandings (see, in particular, the chapters on liberalism (Chapter 2), Marxism (Chapter 4) and the New Right (Chapter 10)).

According to Robert Graham (1989: 150) the concept of contract has a significant purpose in anarchist theory. First, it is a means of ensuring economic justice through equivalent exchange of goods and services. For Pierre-Joseph Proudhon, the worker must be entitled to the full product of their labour and should be free to exchange what they have produced for goods/services of equivalent value with other free and equal producers (Proudhon 1970: 117–18). Secondly, it guaranteed individual liberty, for voluntary contracts would replace the economic coercion of the capital-labour relationship and the politico-legal coercion imposed on citizens by the state. Proudhon (1970: 113) considered that the compulsory nature of the state had defrauded the citizens of their liberty, and that alienation is endemic not just in the workplace but also in our relation with the state. Anarcho-communists argue that the market model endemic in Proudhon's notion of contract is problematic. Kropotkin advocates distribution of goods according to need rather than in a process of equivalent exchange. He also considered the difficulties in evaluating goods and services as 'equivalent' in the first place (Berkman 1977: 13). Despite these difficulties, Proudhon's notion of free exchange has been practically influential in some forms of radical politics, as we will see in the final section.

Similarly to Marxists and feminists, anarchists see a world shaped by social hierarchy and institutionalised oppression and domination. Most contemporary anarchists claim to be opposed to a range of social hierarchies that they see as interlinked and interdependent. Since the 1970s some Marxists and feminists have considered the multi-faceted interests articulated by the state, but nineteenth-century anarchists like Kropotkin also suggest that a range of social groups have been marginalised and disadvantaged by state actions. Thus, there are similarities between Marxist and feminist understandings of the state as an instrument of domination, but anarchism has been more historically eclectic in considering the range of interests articulated. In addition, anarchists argue that the state is not just a conduit for the interests of social hierarchies, but has interests of its own. One final distinction between Marxism and anarchism involves the possibility of utilising the state as an agent of political change. Marx and Engels considered that the state was a necessary tool for revolutionary change but would eventually 'wither away'. Bakunin, however, argued that such a statist revolution would result in the development of a repressive apparatus of a different kind (Harrison 1990).

## Definition

There are various ways in which anarchists have defined the state. For Errico Malatesta (1974) the state is the sum total of political, legislative, judicial, military and financial institutions through which the behaviour of the 'people' is controlled by manipulation and/or collective force. Kropotkin (1997: 10), however, wishes to distinguish between the notions of the state as a recent social formation based on a distinct territory, and that of government, which he suggests, is a practice of social regulation. Kropotkin is making the distinction here, between governance as a process of rule making and decision making, which all societies and organisations have in some form, and the institutional arrangements of the modern nation-state.

Proudhon saw the emergent nation-state with its increased abilities to monitor publics and extract goods and services, as an oppressive and destructive set of institutions, for:

> To be governed is to be watched over, inspected, spied upon, legislated, regimented, closed in, indoctrinated, preached at, controlled, assessed, evaluated, censored, commanded; all by creatures that have not the right, not the wisdom, nor the virtue . . . To be governed means that, at every move, operation, or transaction one is noted, registered, entered in a census, taxed, stamped, priced, assessed, patented, licensed, authorised, recommended, admonished, prevented, reformed, set right, corrected. Government means to be subject to tribute, trained, ransomed, exploited, monopolised, extorted, pressured, mystified, robbed; all in the name of public utility and the general good. (quoted in Marshall 1993: 245)

Here the state is seen as a coercive body that reduces people's freedom far beyond any point necessary to ensure social co-existence. It enacts restrictive laws and other measures which function in terms of its self-preservation and enhancement. For example, it interferes excessively with people's private lives by prescribing sexual conduct. It is also an exploitative body, which deploys its powers of taxation and economic regulation to transfer resources into the hands of a privileged elite. For others it is also a destructive agency in its preoccupation with international conflict and the enlistment of its subjects into the military (Goldman 1969: 59). In some ways, anarchists accept a Weberian definition of the state in which the state claims the monopoly of the legitimate use of violence within a given territory. It deploys that force to maintain both internal and external order – to ensure its territorial integrity and to defend itself against internal dissention. The authority of the state is also seen as compulsory, and there is no differentiation made between authoritarian forms of state and those that are conceived as liberal democratic in that 'its aim is the absolute subordination of the individual' (Goldman 1969: 56–7).

Perhaps the most influential contemporary anarchist thinker, Murray Bookchin, has taken anarchism beyond the denunciation of the state and capitalism. Bookchin is keen to use terminology that captures a range of hierarchies of social domination. Hierarchy is Bookchin's most important concept and the way in which he defines it is not only as a social condition but also as a state of mind. Thus, for Bookchin the state is not simply an interrelated set of bureaucratic and coercive institutions and practices but a psychological phenomenon, a way of thinking about the world and understanding social organisation (Bookchin 1991: 94–5). This notion that the state is both a set of institutions with particular functions and an internalised power relationship appears in most anarchist accounts, which as we see below, vary quite significantly.

## Theorists

In social anarchism or anarcho-communism, the human capacity for social solidarity is a foundation upon which state theory rests. This is most clearly and fully articulated by the geographer Peter Kropotkin in *Mutual Aid*, the purpose of which was to tackle the influence of social Darwinism in nineteenth-century

European politics. Thinkers such as T. H. Huxley and Herbert Spencer used a Darwinian notion of a process of evolutionary selection in biology to bolster a view of social selection in terms of bourgeois meritocracy. For Kropotkin, such theorisations had a flawed scientific foundation and were clearly political in their implicit support for competitive capitalism (Miller 1984: 72). *Mutual Aid* stressed the process of evolution as one where successful adaptation and exploitation of evolutionary niches is secured by species' propensity for mutual aid, co-operation and solidarity (van Duyn 1969: 21). This is a very similar notion to what contemporary microbiologist Lyn Margulis calls 'symbiogenesis' (Margulis and Sagan 1986: 119). Kropotkin's political argument was that the strong state and the capitalist market are not inevitable developments of our human condition, but dysfunctional social constructions based on inequities of power.

Kropotkin's political theory follows a historically evolutionary model in which societies move through stages, acquiring increased complexity and diversity (Miller 1984: 182). Kropotkin provides an historical account of the emergence of the modern state from the medieval period in Europe, wherein there is a coalescing of military elites with new forms of judicial authority and a breaking down of 'primitive village communities'. The modern state is a product of feudal class relations and is a class-based structure that is seized by the emerging bourgeoisie with the development of capitalism (Kropotkin 1997: 17–21). There is an important difference from Marxist instrumentalist accounts, however, for Kropotkin does not consider class to be the only factor in the establishment of social domination. Also important is the 'Triple Alliance' of the state with the institutions and practices of military power with judicial and (Christian) religious authority (1997: 33). The development of capitalism centralised and further enhanced the powers of state institutions.

Any reform in the direction of 'representative government' is seen as an entrenchment of the interests of the middle classes in Europe (Kropotkin 1997: 159). Yet Kropotkin does not see economically-derived class-based interests as the sole, or often even the dominant force in this development. The state is a self-serving bureaucracy and the process of legislative reform is a form of 'enchantment', which may convince the citizenry that change is happening, but has a mythic function in dispelling potential grievances and the articulation of protest (Kropotkin 1988: 32–42). Kropotkin is clear that

## Anarchism: the Politics of Anti-Statism

the state cannot be reformed, or be effectively used as a tool to ensure social justice. Rather, those parties and individuals who engage with the practicalities of liberal democratic politics become co-opted by the minutiae of legislative process and the normative liberal parameters of parliamentary debate. Here there are similarities with elite theory, that the tendency to oligarchy is systemically endemic in liberal democratic processes (for example, Nordlinger 1981). This is not to suggest, however, that all non-revolutionary efforts toward social change should be opposed so, for example, he was not hostile to co-operative socialism in Britain (Kropotkin 1988: 42–7). His view was that incremental changes were part of the evolutionary process and as inevitable as the punctuation of outbursts of revolutionary change.

Kropotkin's understanding of the state as semi-autonomous from both capitalism and the direct influence of capitalists has resonance with some neo-Marxist accounts of the politics of liberal democracy. There are elements of similarity in particular, with Nicos Poulantzas's notion of 'authoritarian statism' (Poulantzas 1978: 239). For Poulantzas, the institutional separation of the state from the capitalist class is substantial and important, and functions to make the 'democratic state' appear class neutral and open to the various interests of citizens. The difficulties of 'statism' meant that Kropotkin eschewed any form of 'proletarian state' as an agency of political change, and his exchanges with Lenin after his return from exile in 1917 reflect earlier exchanges between Marx and Bakunin.

Many of Kropotkin's ideas (in particular, from Kropotkin 1987) are elaborated in the work of the prolific contemporary anarchist theorist, Murray Bookchin, who has been instrumental in linking anarchism to green social and political thought in his advocacy of 'social ecology'. In *The Ecology of Freedom* (1991), Bookchin gives a complex account of how social hierarchies emerged with the oppression of women, proceeding to the exploitation and oppression of other groups of humans, socially stratified according to age, 'race', class and sexuality. Bookchin argues that these oppressions adopt different forms (social institutions and practices) and degrees of severity across different cultures and over time. Bookchin is keen to distinguish the specific characteristics of human sociality from those of 'natural' ecosystems (Bookchin 1995a), while elaborating the ways in which social hierarchies are embedded in environmental contexts (Bookchin 1971: 58–60, 1986: 26) with which we 'co-evolve' (Bookchin 1991: 21–5). Bookchin suggests that social hierarchy emerged in the early Neolithic period with the establishment of rudimentary government, but the modern nation-state is an historically recent form of domination that builds onto pre-existing social hierarchies, while also re-shaping and reproducing these relationships. Bookchin's understanding of the state is of a complex array of institutions some of which (such as education and welfare agencies) have social rather than clearly political functions. All state institutions undertake a range of functions – from the coercive and punitive to the distributive, welfarist and regulatory (1991: 123–8). What is particularly pernicious about the encroaching role and institutional presence of the state is that in modernity, functional expansion has been through 'social' rather than overtly 'political' institutions. The social functions of the state are perhaps the most highly political because their purpose is to make the state appear to disappear, embedding it firmly in the social fabric and making autonomous social provision seem outlandish or even impossible:

> The State's capacity to absorb social functions provides it not only with an ideological rationale for its existence: it physically and psychologically rearranges social life so that it seems indispensable as an *organizing principle* for human consociation. (Bookchin 1991: 127, original emphasis)

This 'hybridisation' of social functions with political institutions enables differing forms of state encroachment into ever more areas of contemporary social life, and here clear parallels can be drawn with the work of the post-structuralist thinker Michel Foucault (2000). Further, Bookchin suggests that the state reproduces the conditions of its own emergence and success – it restructures 'society around itself' to enable further colonisation of social life. The contemporary political 'problem' for anarchists is the embedding of modern states in the politics of our everyday existence. Thus, we are presently witnessing in powerful Western states increased bureaucratisation of large institutions such as schools, universities, local government service and business corporations (Bookchin 1991: 135–9).

Bookchin posits an 'ecotopia' of self-governing communes in federation (Bookchin 1989a: 159–207) and he has given extended reflection to questions of radical grassroots democracy. Although he has made strong criticism of what he calls 'lifestyle anarchism' (Bookchin 1995b), he does see 'lifestyle politics' as tapping into the more political stance of radical social movements across a range of social issues, from various kinds of environmental, animal welfare/'liberation', anti-corporate and feminist campaigns. For Bookchin, the cross-cutting links between various social movements involves an encouragingly anarchic politics which is, appropriately, deeply sceptical of both state action and mainstream politics, and mobilises masses of those who in various ways challenge forms of social domination and desire social transformation (Bookchin 1989b). Bookchin provides a complex analysis of social hierarchy and of the ways state institutions reproduce this, but in the incredibly diverse and ambitious scope of Bookchin's projects his theory of the state sometimes becomes rather lost in the mass of complex threads he wants to weave together.

A very clear anarchist position on the state is present in Alan Carter's (1989) reflections on anarchism, Marxism and theories of historical change. Carter argues that 'the fact' that the modern state tends to protect bourgeois interests does not adequately substantiate an instrumentalist theory of the state. As we saw in Chapter 5, the predominant explanation in Marx is of the state as a tool of the collective interests of the capitalist class, or relatedly, as an instrument which acts functionally to ensure the maintenance of the capitalist system over time by enabling profit accumulation. Carter argues that in order to preserve its territory, the state is compelled to maintain forces of coercion, the development and maintenance of which is financed via taxation. In addition, the state has an interest both in maintaining social order and in ensuring a healthy labour force, for which ends progressive taxation may be instituted (Carter 1989: 183–4). Neo-Marxists such as Poulantzas have considered this in terms of the relative autonomy of the capitalist state in perpetuating the long-term stability of capitalist society, yet Carter suggests they have mistaken 'a contingent correspondence between the state and bourgeois interests for an instrumental relationship' (1989: 184).

The modern state, in Carter's account, does not act as the instrument of the dominant class, but carries out its own interests which 'just happen' most often to correspond to the long- or short-term interests of the dominant class. Carter argues that whatever the structure of the state and whatever the political hue of its government, 'all the programmes chosen serve the state' (1989: 185) in addition to whatever other interests they may serve, and herein lies the basis for the state's autonomy from class, or gender or whatever. There is an overlap here with the view of elite theorists such as

C. Wright Mills (1956) who argued in the case of the United States political system that whoever runs the state has limited room for political manoeuvre in policy terms in liberal democratic governance (see Chapter 3). Carter goes further than this in suggesting that the state might even 'transform the mode of production', as was the case in the post-revolutionary Soviet Union or China, if it felt it was in its interests to so do (Carter 1989: 185). One of the features of the development of contemporary capitalism is the direction of surplus towards the 'development of forces of coercion' (1989: 186). For Carter, political executives select specific kinds and forms of relation of production in order to develop coercive capacity. The state acts in its own interests and harnesses the productive powers of capitalism towards expanding its functions – acquiring increasing roles and powers as it does so. Thus, the state is selectively appropriating the powers of capitalism to serve its own long-term interests in the maintenance of coercive forces to ensure social order and stability (1989: 189–90). In order to justify this practice, a range of state agencies encourage citizens to identify with a particular community usually through the ideology and practice of nationalism and the notion that the polity is in need of protection from external forces. In this model, the state is analytically central – it is not an instrument of the dominant economic class – a conduit of class power or a condensed or reified form of class struggle. Rather, the state is opportunist and acts to promote the type of productive forces and social relations that best serve its own short- and long-term interests.

Clearly, this is an inverse of a Marxist model where production relations and social class determine the state's composition and actions – 'superstructures' are selected according to their ability to stabilise relations of capitalism. Rather, for Carter, the state actively selects and shapes these relations in specific ways when it is in its interests to do so. This model allows for the autonomy of politics from economic relations and also for the changing composition and direction of the state that may impose different types of relations at different times. Thus, the state may act as neo-conservatives might wish, as an agent of a social democratic model of 'egalitarianism' or in a minimally (liberal) feminist way. This allows different kinds of politics to be articulated that may appear to serve the interests of different social groups that may have been historically marginalised. What Carter makes clear in all this is that the state serves its own interest in expanding its functions, scale and scope. It is these very

## Anarchism: the Politics of Anti-Statism

things to which anarchists object, but in the latter decades of the twentieth century it seemed to be the political right which appeared most successful in making the case for a reversal of this trend.

As we will see in Chapter 10, neo-conservative/neo-liberal/'New Right' arguments for a 'minimal state' (Nozick 1974) have been influential in the practical politics of liberal democracies, particularly since the early 1980s. Anarchist state theorists have strongly differentiated neo-conservative/liberal critiques of 'statism' from anarchism. Frank Harrison (1983), for example, argues that the apparently anti-state position of neo-conservatism in the United States is designed to produce a stronger state in respect to functions of coercion and a weaker state only in respect to a lack of market regulation and social provision. Some 'anarcho-capitalist' thinkers have taken such ideas further, however, in asserting that even a minimal state with a remit to protect the rights of the individual and retention of a monopoly on the use of coercive force is illegitimate and a hindrance to the proper operation of the free market.

For Murray Rothbard (1978), even a minimal state is a significant threat to liberty and is morally unacceptable due to a monopoly on legitimate violence. Neither the state or any private individual or group can threaten or use force against any person, nor can they threaten their property (Rothbard 1978: 46). Rather, individuals are able to regulate their own affairs by contracts that are binding, yet voluntarily entered into, and private arbitration firms could settle any disputes that might arise. The monies acquired by the state for the purpose of social provision, economic regulation and the maintenance of order amount to protection racketeering. The actions of states fetter the proper operation of the market mechanism, and the market more effectively and efficiently provides any service. Thus, for Rothbard, the courts and penal system, policing and the armed services should all be privatised. Government should be abolished and replaced by completely unregulated market competition. Sovereign individuals are property owners who many voluntarily enter into contracts with others to pursue mutual interests. Protection agencies, operating in the competitive market place would ensure 'consumers' seeking protection from one another would have a 'choice' and compel such agencies towards efficiency, 'value for money' and effectiveness. For example, private courts would need to develop a reputation for 'fairness' in the settling of disputes. Rothbard, like all other anarchists, bases much of his theorising on an understanding of what it is to be human. For Rothbard, libertarian capitalism reflects our 'human nature', and statism will collapse due to its contradictions in attempting to 'manage' a free market and free individuals. Unlike the state, Rothbard assumes the capitalist market has somehow emerged 'naturally' rather than being a social construct. Further, he seems to ignore any evidence of 'market inefficiency' when critiquing the insufficiencies of the state, and uncritically to assume the self-seeking and utility maximising 'nature' of individuals who have sufficient knowledge to make their utility maximising decisions. The notion that material conditions may severely impede our abilities to 'choose' in the market-place is entirely absent from his account.

Even right-thinking sympathisers have difficulties with Rothbard's anarcho-capitalism. Robert Nozick (1974: 16–17) suggests that the flaw in Rothbard's model is his inability to see that a dominant protective agency would emerge through free competition, and the en mass buying of 'justice' would in effect result in a minimalist state (for further discussion see Chapter 10). There is much, however, that draws Nozick and Rothbard together. Their critique of the state rests on an interpretation of liberty as the rights of private property, and their opposition to the state really amounts to little more than an uncompromising defence of the market. Most anarchist thinkers and activists are both egalitarian as well as libertarian, and Marshall (1993: 565) suggests Rothbard et al. are best seen as 'right-wing libertarians' rather than anarchists. There is certainly a limited view of 'freedom' expressed by Nozick and Rothbard, for the social consequences of capitalism are unrecognised or irrelevant – we are at liberty to be impoverished, ignorant and powerless. Sadly, it is such liberties that have made right-wing libertarianism attractive to parties of the right in liberal capitalist states. Perhaps unsurprisingly, the ideas of those who argue both against the state and for social justice, have found more resonance with social movements.

## Practical politics

It would certainly be an exaggeration to claim that anarchism has had a strong influence on the state in practical political terms, certainly from the mid-twentieth century onward. It has, however, had an impact on other kinds of state theory, and in particular, the work of people such as Rothbard in the United States have influenced New Right thinkers and politicians. In market-orientated forms of liberal democratic capitalism there has been increased use of the private sector in the ways anarcho-capitalists have suggested. In the United States, some states already make use of private courts, penal and arbitration services. There are private prisons and protection agencies in the United Kingdom and community-based schemes for the maintenance of public order such as 'Neighbourhood Watch'. Murray Rothbard (1977) has not only been a theoretical contributor to right-libertarianism, but helped to found the Libertarian Party in the United States. This campaigns for the abolition of the entire federal regulatory apparatus, the taxation system, social security, public education and welfare, and demands that the United States withdraw from the United Nations and drastically reduce the size of its military to constitute a defensive force with no foreign engagements. As suggested in the previous section, however, whether right libertarians can be seen as anarchists is moot. In this final section, I suggest that left libertarianism and anarcho-communism has had a sustained, albeit a very light, influence on the politics of the twentieth century. There are also those suggesting that its influence may be a little more pronounced in the twenty-first (Purkis and Bowen 1997; Roussopoulos 2002), but it is not my purpose to speculate here.

In the nineteenth century, anarchist revolutionaries sought to overthrow the state by spontaneous revolt of the masses, particularly in the form of peasant revolts as encouraged, for example, by Zapata in Mexico. In many cases, however, by the end of the century they had lost support and momentum to the better organised and tightly disciplined communist movements. The end of the nineteenth century was marked by incidents of anarchist violence and the deployment of terror by groups such as the 'Narodaya Volya' – 'People's Will' in Russia. A century later, in the 1970s, anarchist violence was deployed by groups such as the 'Baader-Meinhof Gang' in West Germany, the Red Brigades in Italy, the Red Army in Japan and the Angry Brigade in the United Kingdom. These activities encouraged the state to extend its repressive machinery and act quickly and harshly against such groups (as was their intent), yet oppressive measures often had the backing of 'public opinion'. For some anarchists political violence is a form of revolutionary justice; it arises from oppressive/repressive contexts and is directed against individuals, groups and institutions that are seen as culpable. However, various forms of direct action have involved use of the mass media to draw attention to anarchist issues and concerns, and have sometimes used comic drama to humiliate in the administration of 'revolutionary justice'. For example, in the early 1970s, the 'Zippies' in Miami, Florida, launched edible missiles at unsuspecting politicians, industrialists and media figures. Contemporary groups of 'flanarchists', such as the 'Biotic Baking Brigade' continue this tradition, focusing attention on those representative of transnational corporate power and politicians, academics and journalists who endorse neo-liberalism and anti-environmentalism.

Self-management in the workplace has been an important element of anarchist praxis. Anarchists were active in the Russian revolution and in its aftermath, large areas of the Ukraine were organised as systems of communes or 'work soviets', and were often also involved with the insurrectionary army of Nestor Makhno until its effective suppression in 1921 (Marshall 1993: 473–6). Anarcho-syndicalism became increasingly attractive to anarchists in the early decades of the twentieth century, eschewing representative politics and exerting direct pressure on employers through product boycotts, sabotage and strikes. The most significant anarchist political engagement of the twentieth century took place in Spain in the 1930s. The anarcho-syndicalist CNT claimed a membership of over one million at its peak, and after the outbreak of the Spanish Civil War in 1936 following a nationalist coup, anarchist and socialist workers and peasants began to seize land and collectivise it, along with factories and public utilities (Goodway 1989: 2). The defeat of the anarchists by Franco was mirrored by the repression of anarcho-syndicalism in Mussolini's Italy, and the elimination of anarchist organisations by national socialism in the 1930s. Syndicalism was a significant current in Britain until 1920, when the majority of trades unions became persuaded that 'managerialism' represented a more politically 'astute' path for the betterment of industrial workers than workers control, and the British Labour Party became a key institution in the deliverance of such an objective (Ostergaard 1997).

There are some commentators who 'write-off' the impact of anarchism after the Second World War as an active and significant political force (Joll 1979: ix; Woodcock 1986: 7–8). This ignores the sustained influence of anarchism in countries such as India. Mohandas Gandhi referred to his anarchism as 'of a different kind' in its emphasis on 'non-violent resistance' (Sharp 1979) or 'satyagraha' in political transformation (Bondurant 1959). He suggested that the post-colonial nation-state was largely unnecessary. His 'constructive programme' of radical reform suggested the establishment of village-based decision-making (Bandyopadhyaya 1969) and a federal system similar to that of Kropotkin. He suggested the gradual diminution of the Indian state as even its minimally coercive functions were unnecessary – prisons would become education centres and law courts would be replaced by local arbitration (Gandhi 1954: 70–1). After Gandhi's assassination in 1948, a range of different kinds of 'Gandhian' associations came together to form the Sarvodaya movement. Sarvodaya intended a revolution in the ownership and management of land – a communal village system with common ownership, local self-sufficiency, and an ethos in which all work was equally shared (see Ostergaard and Currell 1971; Ostergaard 1985). Sarvodaya became confrontational in the mid-1970s, particularly in response to Indira Gandhi's authoritarianism, but fell apart after a disastrous experiment with Indian parliamentary politics. Geoffrey Ostergaard (1989: 210–11) explains this by noting the gradualism of Indian anarchism and its faith in radical reformism, which enabled such an experiment. He also notes that Indian anarchism extends the 'community' beyond the human to animals and the planet and there is a strong link here to ecologism. In contemporary India, many of the protests of movements for environmental justice are a continuing reflection of Gandhian ideas in the twenty-first century.

In the West, anarchism had some influence in radical social movement politics in the 1960s. Its presence can be seen in some of the ideological shifts of the New Left from the 1950s through the 1970s, which stressed decentralisation, workers' control, direct action and critiques of consumerism and cultures of work and in some cases, ecologism (for example, Gorz 1982, 1985). The counter-cultural movement, particularly among American students in the 1960s and 1970s mined the seam of anarchist ideas and critiques (Marshall 1993: 543–7), as can be seen in the student uprising in France in the spring of 1968. Situationism was clearly influential here, drawing analogies between the economic vulnerability and poverty of both students and workers and seeing them both as victims of the 'spectacle' of consumer society. Guy Debord's (1967) *Society of the Spectacle* and Raoul Vaneigem's (1983) *The*

*Revolution in Everyday Life* had widespread influence. Both these works argued that capitalism had reduced contemporary life to a 'spectacle' in which we (the workers) are alienated from the 'real' world and ourselves, and seek and find satisfaction in consumption by internalising the 'spectacle' (see in particular Debord 1988). In their critique of state communism and liberal capitalism, Debord and Vaneigem echo anarchist concepts and sympathies, and they argue that the bureaucratic mechanisms of the state are in and of themselves structures for the oppression of the mass of the population.

In place of the 'society of the spectacle' the Situationists argued for a society without a money economy, commodity production, wage labour and the state (Gray 1998). The state would be replaced by workers and community councils based in workplaces and neighbourhoods (Vaneigem 1983: 211). Although the life of the 'Situationist International' was brief, the notion of 'revolution in everyday life' has inspired other similar movements such as the 'Provos' and 'Kabouters' in Holland (Marshall 1993: 555). These groups, influenced by the anarchist thinker and activist Roel van Duyn (1969), emphasised sabotage and direct action and their combination of left-libertarianism with environmental concern makes them forerunners of the Green 'party-movement' in Europe in the 1980s and 1990s. The influence of anarchist ideas can be seen snaking through social movements of the late twentieth century such as ecologism, feminism, and those opposing militarism, homophobia and globalisation, alongside decentralising and 'localising' political projects. The 'alternative' or 'counter-culture' social living experiments of the 1970s in particular suggest ways in which political contestation is embedded in everyday life (Rigby 1986).

Colin Ward (1982) has emphasised that anarchism is a profoundly practical politics. Human society is full of spontaneous organisation – informal, transient, voluntary, self-organisation in networks of human relations. Ward has written about a diverse range of social practices as exhibiting such a form of organisation in the areas of education, housing, town planning, welfare provision and 'work'. He has been keen to show that the self-provisioning and organisational abilities of communities question the need for compulsory provision and state dependency. Tom Cahill (1989) traces the history of the co-operative movement in Britain, arguing that co-operativism has had 'a distinct anarchist flavour' (Cahill 1989: 236) in its grassroots, spontaneous, anti-hierarchical and profoundly democratic organisation and practice. These networks of self-managed groups are opposed to statism, albeit quite subtly, in their attempt to provide a replacement for elements of the capitalist system of production and exchange. These kinds of practices continue to be seen in mutual credit associations, work and time banks, local exchange and trading (LETS) networks – all examples of non-statist mutualism involving free agreement and voluntary exchange.

In the twenty-first century, the influence of anarchist ideas and practices in social movements pertains and can be seen in environmental justice campaigns, wilderness protection, anti-militarism and contestation of a variety of forms of 'globalisation'. However, because of the eclecticism and ambiguity of anarchist thought, and the tangential nature of some anarchist state theory, the anarchist contribution to understanding the autonomy of state power is sometimes overlooked. Some of the most famous anarchist theorists were writing in the context of European autocracy, but the questions they raised about the legitimacy of state authority and the increasing scope of state power remain pertinent. Despite the globalisation of some aspects of policy making, nation-states retain incredible power, and that power is increasingly exercised in the regulation of social life – from prescribing appropriate parenting, legitimating partnerships to instructing us in the demonstration of certain kinds of 'citizenship'.

## Bibliography

Bandyopadhyaya, J. (1969), *Social and Political Thought of Gandhi* (Calcutta: Allied Publishers).
Barclay, H. (1991 [1982]), *People without Government: an Anthropology of Anarchy* (London: Kahn and Averill).
Barclay, H. (2003), *The State* (London: Freedom Press).
Berkman, A. (1977), *ABC of Anarchism* (London: Freedom Press).
Bondurant, J. V. (1959), *Conquest of Violence: the Gandhian Philosophy of Conflict* (Oxford: Oxford University Press).
Bookchin, M. (1971), *Post-Scarcity Anarchism* (Berkeley CA: Ramparts Press).
Bookchin, M. (1986), *The Modern Crisis* (Philadelphia PA: New Society).
Bookchin, M. (1989a), *Remaking Society* (Montreal: Black Rose Books).
Bookchin, M. (1989b), 'New social movements: the anarchist dimension', in D. Goodway (ed.), *For Anarchism* (London: Routledge).

Bookchin, M. (1991), *The Ecology of Freedom* (Montreal: Black Rose Books).
Bookchin, M. (1995a), *Re-Enchanting Humanity* (London: Cassell).
Bookchin, M. (1995b), *Social Anarchism or Lifestyle Anarchism?* (Oakland CA: AK Press).
Cahill, T. (1989), 'Co-operatives and anarchism: a contemporary perspective', in D. Goodway (ed.), *For Anarchism* (London: Routledge).
Carter, A. (1989), 'Outline of an anarchist theory of history', in D. Goodway (ed.), *For Anarchism* (London: Routledge).
Crowder, G. (1992), 'Freedom and order in nineteenth century anarchism', *The Raven – Anarchist Quarterly* 20, 5, 4: 342–58.
Debord, G. (n.d. [1967]), *Society of the Spectacle*, trans. K. Nabb (London: Rebel Press).
Debord, G. (1988), *Commentaries on the Society of the Spectacle* (Paris: Gerard Lebovici).
Dunleavy, P. and O'Leary, B. (1987), *Theories of the State: the Politics of Liberal Democracy* (Basingstoke: Macmillan).
Foucault, M. (2000), 'Governmentality', in J. Faubion (ed.), trans. R. Hurley, *Power: Essential Works of Michel Foucault 1954–84*, Vol. 3 (Harmondsworth: Penguin).
Gandhi, M. K. (1951), *Satyagraha* (Ahmedabad: Navajivan).
Gandhi, M. K. (1954), *Sarvodaya* (Ahmedabad: Navajivan).
Gandhi, M. K. (1982 [1927]), *My Experiments with the Truth* (Harmondsworth: Penguin).
Geoghegan, V. (1987), *Utopianism and Marxism* (London: Methuen).
Goldman, E. (1969), *Anarchism and other essays* (New York: Dover).
Goodway, D. (1989), 'Introduction', in D. Goodway (ed.), *For Anarchism: History, Theory, Practice* (London: Routledge).
Goodwin. B. (1982), *Using Political Ideas* (Chichester: John Wiley).
Gorz, A. (1982), *Farewell to the Working Class: an Essay on Post-Industrial Socialism* (London: Pluto).
Gorz, A. (1985), *Paths to Paradise: on the Liberation from Work* (London: Pluto).
Graham, R. (1989), 'The role of contract in anarchist ideology', in D. Goodway (ed.), *For Anarchism* (London: Routledge).
Gray, C. (1998 [1974]), *Leaving the 20th Century: the Incomplete Work of the Situationist International* (London: Rebel Press).
Guérin, D. (1989), 'Marxism and anarchism', in D. Goodway (ed.), *For Anarchism* (London: Routledge).
Harrison, F. (1983), *The Modern State: an Anarchist Analysis* (Montreal: Black Rose Books).
Harrison, F. (1990), 'The crisis of Soviet statism', in D. Roussopoulos (ed.), *The Anarchist Papers 3* (Montreal: Black Rose Books).

Heywood, A. (2003), *Political Ideologies* (3rd edn) (Basingstoke: Palgrave).
Iyer, R. N. (1973), *The Moral and Political Thought of Mahatma Gandhi* (Oxford: Oxford University Press).
Joll, J. (1979), *The Anarchists* (2nd edn) (London: Methuen).
Kropotkin, P. (1927), *Revolutionary Pamphlets* (Vanguard Press).
Kropotkin, P. (1987 [1902]), *Mutual Aid* (London: Freedom Press).
Kropotkin, P. (1988), *Act for Yourselves: Articles from Freedom 1886–1907*, N. Walter and H. Becker (eds) (London: Freedom Press).
Kropotkin, P. (1997 [1897]), *The State: Its Historic Role* (London: Freedom Press).
Lehning, A. (1973), 'Intoduction', *Michael Bakunin: Selected Writings* (New York: Grove Press).
Malatesta, E. (1974 [1891]), *Anarchy* (London: Freedom Press).
Margulis, L. and Sagan, D. (1986), *Microcosmos* (New York: Sumit).
Marshall, P. (1989), 'Human nature and anarchism', in D. Goodway (ed.), *For Anarchism* (London: Routledge).
Marshall, P. (1993), *Demanding the Impossible: A History of Anarchism* (London: Fontana).
Miller, D. (1984), *Anarchism* (London: Dent).
Mills, C. W. (1956), *The Power Elite* (New York: Oxford University Press).
Nordlinger, E. (1981), *The Autonomy of the Democratic State* (Cambridge MA: Harvard University Press).
Nozick, R. (1974), *Anarchy, State and Utopia* (Oxford: Basil Blackwell).
Ostergaard, G. (1985), *Non violent Revolution in India* (Delhi: Gandhi Peace Foundation).
Ostergaard, G. (1989), 'Indian anarchism: the curious case of Vinoba Bhave, anarchist "Saint of the Government"', in D. Goodway, *For Anarchism* (London: Routledge).
Ostergaard, G. (1997), *The Tradition of Workers Control* (London: Freedom Press).
Ostergaard, G. and Currell, M. (1971), *The Gentle Anarchists* (Oxford: Clarendon Press).
Poulantzas, N. (1978), *State, Power, Socialism* (London: New Left Books).
Proudhon, J. P. (1970 [1840]), *What is Property? An Enquiry into the Principle of Right and Government* (New York: Dover).
Purkis, J. and Bowen, J. (1997), *Twenty-First Century Anarchism: Unorthodox Ideas for a New Millennium* (London: Cassell).
Rigby, A. (1986), 'Be practical, do the impossible: The politics of everyday life', in G. Chester and A. Rigby (eds), *Articles of Peace* (Bridport: Prism Press).
Rothbard, M. (1977), *Power and Market* (Kansas City KA: Sheed Andrews and McMeel).
Rothbard, M. (1978), *For a New Liberty: a Libertarian Manifesto* (New York: Macmillan).

Roussopoulos, D. (2002), 'Introduction', *The Anarchist Papers 5* (Montreal: Black Rose Books).
Sharp, G. (1979), *Gandhi as a Political Strategist* (Boston MA: Porter Sargent).
van Duyn, R. (1969), *Message of a Wise Kabouter* (London: Duckworth).
Vaneigem, R. (1983 [1967]), *The Revolution of Everyday Life*, trans. D. Nicholson-Smith (London: Rebel Press).
Ward, C. (1982 [1973]), *Anarchy in Action* (London: Freedom Press).
Woodcock, G. (1986), *Anarchism: a History of Libertarian Ideas and Movements* (2nd edn) (Harmondsworth: Penguin).
Wrabley, R. (1990), 'Neo-conservatism and social ecology 1960–1980', in D. Roussopoulos (ed.), *The Anarchist Papers* 3 (Montreal: Black Rose Books).

CHAPTER SEVEN

# Fascism: Overcoming the Modern State

*John McGovern*

Within what is called 'fascism' there seem to be two very different visions of the state. 'Down with the state in all its forms!', declaimed Benito Mussolini in 1920, addressing his fellow *fascisti* in the most explicitly anarchist terms: 'To us, who are the dying symbols of individualism, there remains, during the present gloom and the dark tomorrow, only the religion, at present absurd, but always consoling, of Anarchy!' (cited in O'Sullivan 1983: 158–9). Before 1932 there had been no official statement of Fascist political ideology but in that year there appeared under Mussolini's name a text, *The Doctrine of Fascism*, co-authored by the philosopher Giovanni Gentile. In this document it is said that 'for the Fascist, everything is in the State, and nothing human or spiritual exists, much less has value, outside the State', and that 'in this sense Fascism is totalitarian' (Oakeshott 1939: 166). Renzo de Felice has emphasised the division within Italian Fascism between those for whom authentic Fascism was a movement, not a party bureaucracy, and those who saw in Fascism the opportunity to create a mass political party of national unity which would, in turn, provide the underpinning for the establishment of a new Italian state (de Felice 1976: 44–5). What united these two apparently very different views, however, was a common antipathy towards the ideal of the autonomous law-state.

## Context

Noel O'Sullivan has argued persuasively that fascism has been demonised because of the virtually all pervasive influence of progressivist political beliefs. Because socialists and liberals share the belief that human beings possess a common humanity which is or should be developing towards an ever more rational and peaceful historical destination, when the fascist movements of the inter-war period irrupted this was viewed as a 'regressive' event which should not have happened. The notion that fascism represented a perversion of the 'true' course of European history, so that it was not a 'genuine political ideology', is a commonplace. In fact, central features of fascist ideology show an essential continuity with elements of modern European political thought which are not ordinarily considered to be mythical or irrational (O'Sullivan 1983).

Though very often it is to conservatives such as Joseph de Maistre that liberal intellectuals like to trace the origins of fascist ideology (Berlin 1990), Rousseau's political thought prefigures those themes which were to become distinctive of fascism. By identifying the state and society, Rousseau instigated a way of thinking about politics hostile towards the concept of the state described in Chapter 1 of this book. When, especially in the aftermath of the First World War, individual states experienced severe crisis and the European state system seemed to have collapsed, historical conditions were present in which Rousseau's thought could find real application in two forms: communism and fascism. If fascism appears contradictory, both worshiping the state and denouncing it, this is because the concept of the state that fascism idolised was not the one it condemned, namely, the concept of an autonomous state which formed European politics from the Renaissance until the twentieth century. The first exponent of its different vision of the state was Rousseau, who imagined a state with vastly greater power but without the properly political power to remain independent of both the regime and 'the people'. While it is difficult to avoid referring particularly to Italian Fascism as 'statist', it must be recognised that Fascist ideology imagined a radically different type of state.

The affinities between Rousseau's political theory and fascism derive from the claim made in *The Social Contact* that the principal condition for the emergence of the good state is 'the total alienation of each associate, together with all his rights, to the whole

## Fascism: Overcoming the Modern State

community' (Rousseau 1973: 174). Since the individual is a part of the state, 'each man, in giving himself to all, gives himself to nobody' (1973: 174). Here Rousseau introduces the notion of 'the general will'. The state is conceived of as a moral and collective body, a 'public person' complete with 'its unity, its common identity, its life and its will' (1973: 175). When placed under political obligation, the citizen does not bend to an alien power but finds himself in accordance with his own 'true' will. Rousseau's state is supported by, indeed it *is*, the voluntary activity of the citizens who compose it. The sovereign, that is, the state as an active power, because it is composed of the citizen body, 'neither has nor can have any interest contrary to theirs' and, so, 'merely by virtue of what it is, is always what it should be' (1973: 177). Because it represents the 'higher self', the most noble and rational aspirations of each and every citizen, the state cannot dominate or oppress them. It should also be noted that a nationalist element appears in Rousseau's concept. The general will is the moral force latent in a particular society or nation. There are as many general wills as there are genuinely distinct political societies. This nationalism is evident in some of Rousseau's minor writings, such as *The Government of Poland*, where he also recommends public spectacles as a means of political indoctrination (Rousseau 1985: 4).

Naturally, there is no place for what Rousseau calls a 'particular will', the will of the individual who wishes to enjoy the rights of the citizen without fulfilling the corresponding duties. Hence, anyone who disobeys the state 'will be forced to be free' (Rousseau 1973: 177). The individual is so thoroughly identified with the state that 'his life is no longer a mere bounty of nature, but a gift made conditionally by the State' (1973: 189). Whereas individual wills can and must be impeded, the general will must not be bound because it always promotes the interests of 'the people'. 'Partial associations' intermediate between the individual and the state should be eliminated since their very existence provides an obstacle to the formation of the general will (1973: 185). Because he distinguishes it from the mere aggregate of 'the will of all', the general will as representative of the highest aspirations of the people may be expressed by one person, 'universal silence' may be taken for consent and the state 'need give no guarantee to its subjects' (1973: 176, 183). Rousseau describes the state as if it were a church. In this his writings anticipated the modern political religions, fascism and communism. The legislator, a 'father of the nation' like Moses or

Muhammed, 'feels himself . . . capable of changing human nature, of transforming each individual . . . into a part of a greater whole . . . altering man's constitution for the purpose of strengthening it' (1973: 194). A charismatic leader whose authority depends upon popular consent only because he is the creator of the general will of his people, the legislator is self-authorising. The 'great soul of the legislator,' Rousseau says, is 'the only miracle that can prove his mission' (1973: 197).

Before it was to emerge in the guise of fascism, the 'activist style of politics' articulated by Rousseau (O'Sullivan 1983: 62–3, 94–8) took socialist forms, including revolutionary syndicalism. Also known as 'anarcho-syndicalism' because of its roots in the nineteenth-century anarchism of Proudhon and Blanqui, this was a movement that became prominent in France before the outbreak of the First World War. Proudhon was highly influential among French fascists whose thought, in turn, was crucial for the formation of Italian Fascism (Sternhell 1986, 1994). Proudhon expressed the syndicalist view of the state when he announced 'that the revolutionary formula cannot be *Direct Legislation*, nor *Direct Government*, nor *Simplified Government*, that it is NO GOVERNMENT' (Proudhon 1989: 126). The state was not needed for the minimal administration required in a truly free society in which workers would associate on an entirely voluntary and contractual basis. Although limited administrative functions would survive the revolution, political power, that is, the state, was to be dissolved in an economy organised by means of direct democracy. The state was to be submerged in society, as Rousseau had recommended. Although Proudhon loved to profess his loathing for Rousseau, this was because he took the author of the *Discourse on the Origin of Inequality* to be an anarchist of the wrong sort, the inventor of the radically asocial 'noble savage' whose essentially bourgeois ideas had fuelled the French Revolution. Nevertheless, Proudhon's vision of a self-organising direct democracy from which the state has been eliminated is not at all inconsistent with the collectivist Rousseau of *The Social Contract*. For Proudhon and his syndicalist followers, there was no real difference between authority and liberty, the state and the individual, because, as for the religious believer, 'to be is within the group' (Sternhell 1994: 104).

Animated by a hatred of the existing capitalist state, Proudhon's anarchism was equally motivated by a desire to restore a social order which he believed had been supplanted by the rise to power of the bourgeois class. This commitment to social order eventually led him to argue in favour of a federal state, the principal purpose of which was to prevent the emergence of economically dominant groups within society (Proudhon 1979). However, Proudhon failed to acknowledge that, if the state is reduced to no more than a set of delegates representing various economically-based interest groups, with no power to act autonomously of those groups, it will be powerless in practice to achieve the urgent end to which Proudhon appointed it, to rescue 'the people' from the domination of elites. Fascists recognised this. One of Proudhon's French followers, the syndicalist leader turned fascist, Edouard Berth, had already seen in 1908 that, because 'the people feels and sense itself to be a collective social being', a transfer of legal authority from the existing state to the syndicate was required. This entailed that the syndicate would take the place of the state, exercising a 'constraint' that is 'salutary, beneficial and creative' (Sternhell 1994: 104). The French syndicalists were not opposed to the state 'in any form'. Like the Italian Fascists, who often began as anarcho-syndicalists, they stood against a certain type of state, the existing liberal state, and for another, different type of state.

## Definition

Various attempts have been made by political theorists and sociologists to define 'generic' fascism, that is, those features common to any fascist movement or regime, which may also be attributed to parties not described by their adherents as 'fascist', whether during the period of 'historical fascism' or after 1945, either within or outside Europe. Ernst Nolte gave the first important non-Marxist definition of 'the fascist minimum' in the post-war period. Stanley Payne's influential description of 'generic fascism' amplifies it (Payne 1980). Nolte posited three 'fascist negations': anti-Marxism; anti-liberalism; and anti-conservatism. It is not, however, obvious that these negations are either genuinely or distinctively fascist. Clearly fascists were violent enemies of communism and liberal democracy but conservatives also oppose socialism and, to varying degrees, political liberalism. It should also be noted that Italian Fascism and French *faiscisant* movements originated among socialists, while what is referred to as 'fascism' in Germany was known to its adherents as 'National *Socialism*'. Marxists have always disputed the claim that fascism was anti-liberal (Kitchen 1976). Its political purpose, in the Marxist view, was to combat revolutionary socialism in conditions of crisis and, therefore, to maintain in existence the capitalist economy which normally finds political expression in liberalism. Even if the Marxist account of the relationship between fascism and liberalism is highly contentious, none the less, it demonstrates that the belief that parliamentary government was out-dated, if not utterly corrupt, has been no less characteristic of the extreme left than of fascists and the authoritarian right. Finally, it has been claimed, again by leftists, that anti-conservatism is not a characteristic of fascism at all on the grounds that fascists invariably allied themselves with conservative elites. As we shall see, it does not follow from this that fascism did not remain essentially anti-conservative. It might seem, then, that there is nothing especially 'fascist' about any of the 'fascist negations'.

Nolte also stipulated three positive elements: the leadership principle; a party army; and totalitarianism as definitive of fascism (Payne 1980: 5). Again, however, there are grounds for claiming that these are not generic because they are particularly characteristic of German National Socialism. While the importance of the *Führerprinzip* for the Nazis is indisputable, there was no exact equivalent to the 'leadership principle' within Italian Fascism or, arguably, in any of the other inter-war movements labelled 'fascist' (1980: 55). As for party militias, the *Sturmabteilung* (SA) and the *Schutzstaffel* (SS), were an especially prominent feature of National Socialism, which, as a movement, was more militarised than any other. It must also be noted that paramilitary politics has never been uniquely fascist. The usefulness of the notion of totalitarianism has been questioned for two different reasons. One is that it is debatable whether either of the two regimes which are called 'fascist' with most confidence, Mussolini's Italy and Hitler's Germany, were genuinely totalitarian states. The other, of course, is that if fascism was totalitarian, so was its avowed enemy, communism.

If the principal difficulty with older definitions of generic fascism is that they over-generalise, more recent definitions tend to be excessively abstract. For instance, Roger Griffin has proposed that 'fascism is a political ideology whose mythic core in its various permutations is a palingenetic form of populist ultra-nationalism' (Griffin 1993: 26). This stresses the fundamentally non-rational character of fascism and, in particular, specifies the presence of some or other version of a myth of rebirth ('palingenesis'), whether it is the nation, race or a type of civilisation that is to be reborn. However, it is not clear that this is a definition of a political ideology at all. Griffin seems to have confused two quite different things. It does not follow from the evident fact that many fascist ideologues celebrated the non-rational aspects of human existence that fascism itself, whether as an ideology or a movement, was inherently non-rational. As Zeev Sternhell has said, although many find it very difficult to accept, as a matter of fact fascism possessed 'a body of doctrine no less solid or logically defensible than that of any other political movement' (Sternhell 1986: ix). Similarly, Michael Mann has argued that viewing fascist ideology as essentially mythical is difficult to square with the fact that fascists themselves tended to be 'rather hard-headed', advancing economic policies and devising political strategies that were not obviously less coherent than those of their opponents. For Mann, Griffin's definition 'is lacking in any sense of *power* . . . even a sense of practicality' (Mann 2004: 12).

It should be noted that Griffin's catalogue of contemporary 'fascisms', including skinheads, numerically insignificant and ephemeral paramilitary organisations, nationalist political parties and a handful of little-known writers, is only possible given the very abstract definition which he has elected to employ (Griffin 1995). There is a risk of conceptual inflation in using 'fascism' generically. A. J. Gregor has shown how the generic approach was first taken during the Second World War, when Italian Fascism, German National Socialism, Spanish Falangism, Portuguese National Syndicalism, the Hungarian Arrow Cross and the Romanian Legion of the Archangel Michael were all dubbed 'fascist' for purposes of propaganda (Gregor 2004: 4). Since 1945, there has been a widespread tendency to label states, parties, organisations and individuals considered by some liberals and socialists to be anti-democratic, excessively nationalistic or racist as 'fascist', 'neo-fascist', 'para-fascist', 'quasi-fascist' or 'crypto-fascist'. Phrases in common contemporary usage, such as 'far right', 'radical right' and 'extreme right' turn out to be synonyms for 'fascist' (Gregor 2004: 3; see Eatwell and Mudde 2004). In general, 'fascism' has become 'a meaningless term of abuse' (Gregor 2004: 2). Ever since 1945, 'anything deplored by prevailing "political correctness"' may enter a list of 'fascisms' as long as it is absurd, including football hooligans, graveyard vandals, anti-feminists, homophobes, tax protestors, libertarians, sexists, anti-environmentalists and people who see no good reason for believing that animals have 'rights'

(Gregor 2001: xii; see Gregor 2004: ch. 1). The IRA, the RUC, Robert Mugabe, Margaret Thatcher, Slobodan Milošević, Bill Clinton, the *Daily Telegraph*, Winston Churchill, General de Gaulle, the Tate Modern, Opus Dei, New Labour, Old Labour, some university vice-chancellors, publicans and the Pope have all been called 'fascists' (Griffiths 2000: 1).

Roger Eatwell defines fascism as 'an ideology that strives to forge social rebirth based on a holistic-national Third Way . . . and to engage in Manichean demonization of its enemies' (Eatwell 2001: 33). Acknowledging that fascism did possess 'a genuine ideology', Eatwell has criticised those, like Griffin, who take insufficient account of the fact that, historically, fascism was seen as providing a coherent 'corporatist' economic programme designed to steer a 'third way' between capital and labour, right and left (Eatwell 1996). Michael Mann similarly claims that 'fascism is the pursuit of a transcendent and cleansing nation-statism through paramilitarism' (Mann 2004: 13). Fascists aimed at 'transcendence' in that they sought to overcome socio-economic and political divisions in a distinctive way, not by class struggle or conservative nationalism but through revolutionary mass politics which were 'neither right nor left'. However, Mann's assertion that 'fascists worshiped state power' (Mann 2004: 14) should be qualified. In fact, some were essentially anarchists for whom it was through the movement, not the state, that 'transcendence' was possible, while fascists who saw the state as 'transcendent' certainly did not worship the state as it had been customarily understood. The 'transcendent' state was a 'total', not an autonomous, one.

While Gilbert Allerdyce's claim that there is no such thing as generic 'fascism' at all may be exaggerated (Kallis 2003: 49–56), it must be recognised that the definition of fascism has involved stipulating general or abstract features the selection of which has been politicised. For this reason, as one historian has put it, 'no definition of "fascism" can ever be universally accepted or objectively "correct" ' (Blinkhorn 1990: 2). While all central, southern and eastern European regimes veered towards the authoritarian right during the inter-war period, with many expressing admiration for some of the achievements of Italian Fascism, few actually described themselves as 'fascist'. Nevertheless, Italian Fascism, German National Socialism, the Austrian *Heimwehr* and other new movements of the 1920s were significantly different from the broad current of the authoritarian right, more virulently nationalist and populist, explicitly opposed to traditional conservative elites and influenced by leftist revolutionary thought while, simultaneously, more violent in their opposition to the left. Historians tend to divide right-wing politics in the inter-war period between movements and regimes. Some movements may safely be called 'fascist' because they referred to themselves in that way. Others were movements of the authoritarian right. Most regimes were conservative and authoritarian. In two cases, Italy and Germany, the labels 'Fascist' or 'National Socialist' were adopted in self-description (Blinkhorn 1990: 3). In this chapter, 'fascism' is identified with historical fascism, that is, Italian Fascism together with the French anarcho-syndicalist and national socialist currents that influenced it. After Mussolini's successful seizure of power, Italian Fascism was emulated elsewhere during the inter-war period. Because of its racialism, the inclusion of German National Socialism under the description 'fascism' is contentious.

## Theorists

### Sorel: myth and violence

According to Georges Valois, the leader of the French *Faisceau*, Sorel was 'the intellectual father of fascism' (Winock 1998: 180). Mussolini's life-long admiration for Sorel is well-documented. 'I owe most to Georges Sorel', he once said. Sorel repaid the compliment (Talmon 1991: 451). At the time of writing his most important text, *Reflections on Violence*, Sorel was a revolutionary socialist. It has been plausibly argued that fascism should be seen as a nationalist form of socialism (Sternhell 1986) or a 'deviant' type of Marxism (Gregor 1979a, b). This is evident in the writings of Sorel who, it has been said, 'is the point where left and right meet' (McClelland 1970: 117). Sorel's contribution to fascism derived from two themes in his writings, the celebration of political violence and the necessity of political myth. Both sprang from his preoccupation with civilisational decline. Late nineteenth-century France seemed to him to have become a society in which vigorous, militant life had given way to decadence and despair. By 'civilisation' Sorel understood not a peaceful, prosperous and materially advanced society but an order which gave meaning to human life, one in which men could enjoy ecstatic experiences of passionate commitment. Seeking a society that was peaceful so that they could be guaranteed an uninterrupted experience of merely material enjoyments, the bourgeoisie had created a liberal state in which the heroic, martial virtues, the spirit of self-sacrifice and devotion to a cause had no place. A life without struggle was, for Sorel, one without meaning, because it was only through pain and sacrifice that human beings discovered their true worth and dignity. It is not too much to say that, for Sorel, strife was a means to a form of secular salvation. It was the means by which 'we . . . create within us a new man' (Sternhell 1994: 61). As we shall see in Chapter 11, religious fundamentalists share this vision of modernity as a scene of decadence and radical Islamists, such as Sayyid Qutb, have interpreted *jihad* as political struggle in a way which closely resembles Sorel's doctrine of revolution.

Even during his Marxist phase, Sorel had been remarkably disinterested in the bread and butter politics of working-class poverty. Socialist revolution could be justified only on ethical grounds. Sorel saw the proletariat 'not as paupers fighting for a larger share of the cake but as a force predestined by history to enthrone a new civilization and a heroic morality on the ruins of the decaying bourgeois world' (Talmon 1991: 458). He arrived at a highly distilled version of Marxism in which all that remained was the conviction that apocalyptic class conflict, understood in a voluntarist manner, was the motive force in history (Sternhell 1994: 50–1). If orthodox Marxism was rejected on the ground that the proletariat should be moved by ethics, not economics, for the same reason there could be no compromise with democratic socialism. 'Progressive' politicians who claimed to represent the interests of the proletariat professed socialism only in order to secure 'the object of their cupidity', state power (Talmon 1991: 459). The purpose of the revolution, for Sorel, was to abolish the state, together with the decadent society that it served, and to replace it with an utterly new moral order. Representative democracy, as it had developed since the eighteenth century, was inherently corrupt. Sorel condemned the fundamental principles of eighteenth-century rationalism as monstrous falsehoods. The intransigent realities of human existence were glibly ignored by the optimistic *philosophes* and their positivist followers in the nineteenth century, the intellectuals whom Sorel never ceased to denounce, as they dreamed of a world from which both conflict and, therefore, nobility had been banished by the power of reason.

One idea above all, the idea of progress, was a particular source of corruption. For Sorel, what is taken for democracy in modern societies, whether liberal or parliamentary socialist, is really the expression of the decadent illusion of progress. From this idea sprang the notion of the general will, 'the unitary dogma that democracy constantly opposes to the class struggle' (Sorel 1972: xliii). 'Anti-patriotism', he wrote, just before the beginning of the First World War, 'becomes an essential element in the syndicalist programme' (Talmon 1991: 467). The unity of the nation is an illusion, for Sorel, but democratic politicians, thanks to 'cunning language, smooth sophistry, and a great array of scientific declamations', succeed in working a kind of magic upon the population (Sorel 1972: xlv). Trumpeting the slogan of 'progress', party politicians lead the proletariat to believe that the sum of collective happiness is ever increasing. The truth is that representative democracy is a corrupt game played by professional politicians in which they offer false promises and the satisfaction of base desires in return for power. The non-confrontational politics of welfare represented by social democracy is the contemporary expression of the type of politics against which Sorel inveighed. His boundless contempt for democracy was an inspiration for later fascist ideologues. In place of democratic politics, Sorel advocated class warfare. In early Christianity, later when the monastic orders arose to purify the Church, and again at the Reformation with the emergence of extreme Protestant sects, Sorel perceived the appearance of movements which had given men unshakeable confidence and a determination to engage in unequal struggle with far more powerful enemies. Sorel believed that it was the presence of myth within such movements that was responsible for their irrepressible vitality. Only belief in a myth would sustain workers in the arduous task of creating an utterly new, morally rejuvenated, vital social order. Sorel's intention in *Reflections on Violence* was to supply just such a political myth.

The general strike was to be the content of the myth. Aiming at nothing less than the violent overthrow of the state by means of strikes, shut-downs and factory occupations, the proletariat was to disengage completely from democratic politics. There was to be no compromise with employers. The more self-reliant the workers became, the more intensely militant their self-consciousness as a revolutionary force would grow. Within the revolutionary syndicates new and more profound values would emerge: heroism; devotion; solidarity; and honour. A new system of justice, in which wrong-doing was conceived of in strictly ethical terms, would replace the sham that was bourgeois legalism. Similarly, the relationship between leaders and followers would be based, not on money, status or cunning, but on morality, with leaders showing a greater capacity for self-sacrifice and a genuine will to serve the interests of those whom they lead. Sorel read Rousseau in the some highly selective way as Proudhon. Instead of the abstract general will which Sorel considered Rousseau to have proposed, and which he saw as representing the bourgeois illusion of national unity, there would be a concrete general will, with workers submitting themselves to a cause because it was truly theirs. The society to come would be a 'total' community. It would be brought into existence by acts of political violence. Physical combat with police and strike-breakers would make the class enemy visible, revealing the capitalist ruling class for what it truly was, a bellicose antagonist prepared to intimidate, wound and kill in order to preserve its power (Sorel 1961). Sorel's vision is genuinely Manichean. He interpreted revolutionary socialism as a political religion.

Whereas Proudhon, while celebrating the heroism of pre-capitalist society, had repudiated violent revolution as a means of overcoming capitalism, Sorel celebrated it. He distinguished between 'force', the hidden coercion which maintains the unjust liberal state in existence, and 'violence', an open and ethically warranted reaction to bourgeois hegemony. In his view the liberal state was not so much 'the executive committee of the bourgeoisie', as it had been for Engels, as the creature of politicians and intellectuals whom Sorel, like all fascists, despised. In an 'electoral democracy', he wrote, 'it is necessary to work upon the simplicity of the masses, to buy the co-operation of the most important newspapers, and to assist chance by endless trickery'. The elected representative 'promises endless reforms to the citizens which he does not know how to bring about, and which resolve themselves simply into an accumulation of parliamentary papers' (Talmon 1991: 465). The deception practised on the people by politicians was a type of 'force' that did not declare itself openly, an unrecognised form of coercion which succeeded precisely because it went unnoticed. 'The middle class have used force since the beginning of modern times,' he insisted, 'while the proletariat now reacts against the middle class and against the state with violence' (1991: 465). In contrast to the disguised force used by the political classes, working-class violence was an expression of authenticity and nobility. As Jacob Talmon has observed, this characterisation of the liberal state as resting on 'force' has become 'a commonplace among ideologists of violence of all kinds' (1991: 464).

Sorel's insight, that human beings are not in essence rational, but creatures who require a mythical vision in order to realise their creative, truly human powers, was to be reasserted by Mussolini in an often quoted speech given in 1922. 'We have created our myth,' Mussolini declaimed, 'The myth is a faith, a passion. It is not necessary for it to be a reality. It is a reality in the sense that it is stimulus, is hope, is faith, is courage' (Griffin 1995: 44). Recognition of the political power of myth is a central feature of fascism. 'Progressives' tend to underestimate the mythical aspect of politics because of their commitment to 'reason', even though belief in progress is itself a myth, as Sorel never ceased to insist. Significantly, in the same speech, Mussolini went on to insist that 'Our myth is the Nation' (Griffin 1995: 44). Later, when he had been in power for a decade, he proclaimed that the fascist myth was also a myth of the state. In *The Doctrine of Fascism*, co-authored with Giovanni Gentile in 1932, he declared the state to be 'an absolute before which individuals and groups are relative' (Lyttelton 1973: 53). Sorel, of course, was opposed to nationalism and, far from providing a theory of the state, anticipated its abolition. It should be noted, however, that it was not because nationalist sentiment is 'irrational' that Sorel condemned it but, rather, because 'national unity' was a slogan used by the bourgeoisie to trick the working class. This left open the possibility of a revolutionary form of nationalism which truly served the interests of the people. Might just such a nationalism provide an even more compelling political myth than Sorel's vision of the general strike? Might there be a *national* socialism?

Already, even before the surge of working-class nationalism occasioned by the outbreak of war, it was clear to Sorel's disciples Georges Valois and Edouard Berth that the myth of the nation alone possessed the potency required to galvanise the French people to overthrow the decadent liberal order. By 1910 syndicalists such as Valois and Berth had allied themselves with extreme French nationalists whose contempt for liberal democracy equalled their own. This alliance was motivated by the belief that the general strike, even if successful in destroying the power of industrial capital, would fail to transform French society (Talmon 1991: 474). The route from anarcho-syndicalism to fascism is less indirect than might be supposed. Sternhell has shown how Sorel's French followers turned towards fascism partly because, though they remained true to Sorel's opposition to the liberal state, they developed another, rival conception of the state, at once nationalist and authoritarian (Sternhell 1994: 127–9). Sorel's socialism was never motivated by what he would have regarded as a merely materialist, envy-ridden preoccupation with wages, conditions of work and living standards. It was always the expression of an heroic ethic. If revolutionary syndicalism turned to nationalism, as the last years of his life showed, this was by no means incompatible with Sorel's vision. Nor was the statism which began to characterise Italian Fascism once Mussolini had seized power wholly at odds with Sorel's revolutionary doctrine. Certainly the state could not be liberal. If, however, the state was seen as 'not reactionary, but revolutionary' (Lyttelton 1973: 54–5), a 'corporatist' state, demanding the submission of the individual to a glorious cause, and giving an ethical justification for that self-sacrifice by requiring it of all social classes equally, then it was possible for fascists to view it as the object of the martial virtues which Sorel insisted must supplant the rationalism and hedonism characteristic of bourgeois decadence. Giovanni Gentile set out to give the theory of just such a state.

## Gentile and the total state

Until his assassination at the hands of communist partisans in 1944, for more than twenty years 'Gentile served Fascism as one of its principal intellectual spokesmen' (Gregor 2001: 3). As early as 1897, in his *A Critique of Historical Materialism*, the professor of philosophy offered a criticism of 'vulgar Marxism' which was remarkably similar to Sorel's interpretation (2001: 10). The same emphasis on volition is apparent in both. If the distinction between thought and action is an error produced by the fatally mistaken philosophy of materialism and, instead, thought is 'pure act', as Gentile argued, then a general conclusion to be drawn about politics is clear. The mistake involved in divorcing thought from action, as Hegel had taught, lies in a failure to recognise that, so distinguished, thought and action become one-sided abstractions. From the point of view adumbrated by Idealist philosophy, in reality, thought and action compose one indivisible whole or 'totality'. Politics should not be considered apart from other spheres of human existence such as education, religion and family life. A certain 'totalitarianism' is already evident in the Idealist philosophy, 'actualism', which was Gentile's starting point. This philosophy led him to reject 'bourgeois individualism' as vehemently as any Marxist. He rejected its founding assumption, namely, that the individual exists in a state of pure freedom prior to its entry into society. For Gentile, the individual in this sense was a fiction. Were human beings absolutely free in relation to society, they would not have liberty but its opposite. Real freedom, he argued, is possible only for the individual who is wholly enmeshed within a collective. It has been plausibly argued that 'this view of man as an integral part of an organic whole is the basis of fascism's political philosophy' (Sternhell 1979: 345).

However, among fascists there are two different views of the nature of the collective. Sorel, as we have seen, looked to the emergence of a militant, quasi-religious movement as the type of collective to which the individual should abandon himself. For anarchist fascists, only a fluid movement, unencumbered by a fixed ideology and requiring no political aim other than self-expression, could provide the collective experience in which true freedom is possible. There were those for whom fascism represented the 'religion of Anarchy' celebrated by Mussolini in 1920. The state in any form, with its legal and administrative structures, represents an obstacle to the anarchist fascist who desires a collective life because it promises a more vital type of experience and not on account of the stability it might provide. Gentile, in contrast, identified the collective with the state. For him, liberalism proposed an aggregate of atomised individuals for whom the security required to make genuine freedom possible would be absent, since that security is provided by society, especially by its laws and political constitution. In fact, Gentile argued, the concept of society coincides with the concept of the individual (Oakeshott 1939: 166). For the fictitious 'negative freedom' attributed to the individual by liberals, Gentile substituted what he regarded as authentic freedom, Rousseau's 'positive freedom' which is enjoyed by the member of a society who thoroughly identifies with its collective will, especially its legal and political forms, that is, with the state. Gentile's was a thoroughly statist interpretation of Fascism elaborated after the Mussolini regime was established (Lyttelton 1973: 14; Sternhell 1979: 344–5).

In referring to fascism as 'religious' or 'spiritualized', Gentile's intention was not to claim that it was a 'religion' (Gentile 1928; Lyttelton 1973: 302) but to contrast it with 'the flabby materialistic positivism' of 'doctrines . . . that put the centre of life outside man, who with his free will can and must create his own world'. According to the 'spiritualized conception', the individual is viewed as the embodiment of 'an objective Will' which 'raises him to conscious membership of a spiritual society' (Oakeshott 1939: 164–5). Like Sorel, Gentile viewed human beings, not as material creatures determined by blind forces, but as persons endowed with 'spirit', that is, creative will. The capacity to 'create his own world', however, cannot be exercised by the bare individual. Only the person who consciously and voluntarily, that is, in Gentile's sense, spiritually identifies himself with a collective, itself a 'higher personality' (Oakeshott 1939: 167), may perform the act of self-creation which is distinctively human. Gentile chose to call this view of man 'religious' because, historically, religion has offered the most familiar example of one aspect of the 'spiritual' type of experience which, he argued, would be more perfectly represented by fascism. In religion, the self discovers a collective identity transcending mere individuality, 'an objective Will'. In fact, religion, at least the Catholicism which must inevitably have come to mind for a man like Gentile, describes 'objective Will' in such a way as to *limit* man's capacity to 'create his own world'. Nevertheless, despite his emphatic denials that fascism was a religion, Gentile did construe fascism as a political religion in which ethics were confused with politics and the feeling of participation proper to religious experience was transferred to the relationship between the individual and the state.

Gentile's 'objective Will' was rigorously this-worldly. He identified the 'spiritual society' with which the individual must fuse his will as, progressively, 'the family or social group', 'the nation' and, finally, 'the State' (Oakeshott 1939: 165–6). The state was 'spiritual society' in the fullest sense for Gentile. Nationalists, he argued, typically conceive of the nation, not as something which men create through 'spiritual activity', but as 'a datum of nature' (Gentile 2002: 26). The nation in that sense is not a spiritual society but a merely territorial or ethnic and, therefore, material entity. 'Nationalism . . . bases the State on the concept of the nation', Gentile observed, but, while it is true that the nation 'transcends the will and the personality of the individual', this is because 'it is conceived of as objectively preexistent, independent of the consciousness of individuals' (2002: 25–6). For Gentile, therefore, the nation conceived of in this inert way, 'inflexible, illiberal, retrograde, and crudely conservative' (2002: 26), could not be the genuine embodiment of an 'objective Will'. Nationalist sentiment was neither sufficiently conscious nor volitional for it to be 'spiritual' in the sense required, Gentile insisted, for it to disclose the type of collective with which the individual could be thoroughly identified.

This is not to say that, though opposed to conservative nationalism, Gentile failed to recognise the value of the nation. The nation could be the embodiment of an authentically 'objective Will' if it was understood in a different, revolutionary way, not as 'a race' or 'a geographically determined region', but 'as a community historically perpetuating itself, a multitude unified by a single idea, which is the will to existence and to power' (Oakeshott 1939: 167; see Gentile 2002: 47–8). Only a collective which was itself 'spiritual', that is, a 'higher personality' brought into and maintained in existence by conscious, voluntary action, in accordance with 'a single idea', would be capable of commanding the full allegiance of the people because it would actively substitute for their separate, individual wills a truly 'objective Will'. This collective was the state. 'It is not the nation that generates the State,' he insisted, 'rather the nation is created by the State, which gives to the people, conscious of its own moral unity, a will and therefore an effective existence' (Oakeshott 1939: 167). A nation, its traditions, memories, language and customs, could become 'this higher personality' only 'in so far as it is the State' (Oakeshott 1939: 167). The religious origins of this notion of a 'higher personality' are obvious. Other fascist ideologues would candidly describe the fascist state as a 'church state' (Griffin 1995: 32).

Gentile, Mussolini and other Fascists, including the syndicalist Panunzio, used the term *totalitarianismo* in an ethically positive sense. The individual, family, all social groups and even the nation itself were to be subordinated to the state because only such a 'total state' would be able to make concrete the highest ethical aspirations of the people. For Gentile, fascism represented a noble form of life, 'serious, austere, religious'. Dedicated to struggle and sacrifice in a quest for the authentically human goal of collective self-creation, 'supported by the moral and responsible forces of the spirit', the Fascist, he pronounced, 'disdains the "comfortable" life' (Oakeshott 1939: 165). The 'defining trait of Fascism' was, Gentile wrote, 'to take life seriously', avoiding the pursuit of mere pleasure in favour of 'labour, effort, sacrifice and hard work' (Gentile 2002: 57). It is the same ethical impulse, scornful of base self-interest, calling men to a collective Nietzschean self-overcoming, that motivated Sorel. Gentile's theory of the 'ethical state', 'a tutorial state with greater authority than the old liberal regime to develop the resources of the entire people and realize the higher ("ethical") aspirations of the nation', as Stanley Payne has noted, was 'a Rousseau-derived ambition that has become increasingly common in the twentieth century' (Payne 1980: 74). As we shall see in Chapter 11, the twentieth-century welfare state has been criticised by conservatives and Christian fundamentalists for its attempt to play a tutelary role similar in some respects to the one Gentile recommended.

The good citizen of the fascist state would not distinguish between loyalty to family and allegiance to the state that Gentile described as 'the form, the inner standard and the discipline of the whole person' which 'saturates the will as well as the intelligence' (Oakeshott 1939: 168). As for 'civil society', Gentile's ethical state was 'the purest example of a totalitarian ideology' (Sternhell 1979: 356). 'Outside the State,' he urged, 'there can be neither individuals nor groups (political parties, associations, syndicates, classes)' (Oakeshott 1939: 166). It was to be a 'corporatist' state from which, as Rousseau had urged, 'partial societies', whether independent trade unions, political parties or churches were to be eliminated. It has been said that 'the denial of diversity is the central characteristic of Gentile's political thought' (Lyttelton 1973: 34). Certainly, he repudiated the value of a certain type of diversity for reasons which might seem less repugnant than the totalitarian conclusions he drew from them. As he observed, those who accuse fascism of eliminating 'diversity' subscribe to the liberal ideal of 'a free independent personality' for which the state is 'nothing other than the external limit' (Gentile 2002: 54). If the liberal state's elevation of 'tolerance' as an ideal means that, in practice, it serves merely to manage conflict between individuals who consider it their indefeasible 'natural right' to pursue self-interest without regard for society at large, not only fascists have found the value of such 'diversity' questionable. It is not clear that the liberty of the individual in this sense amounts to anything more than economic freedom or that 'diverse' is not simply another word for 'divided'. Gentile's 'denial of diversity' was a response to what he saw as liberalism's 'denial of every moral reality' (2002: 54).

The stumbling block for any non-liberal politics in modern societies is that it is difficult to see how increasing the power of the state over the individual or, what is the same thing, over the market economy may be justified. Gentile's genuinely radical solution to the problem involved moving beyond the terms in which it is presented by liberals. It was not simply the notion that the limits to individual freedom are 'external' but the fact that they are, therefore, imposed by the liberal state which had to be challenged. It is mistaken, he argued, to believe that 'Fascism presumes to impose the State upon the individual'. On the contrary, 'the State is the very personality of the individual'. Only when 'the individual feels the general interest as his own, and wills therefore as might the general will' can a society compose a truly moral order (Gentile 2002: 55). Like Rousseau's, Gentile's political thought essentially derives from his acknowledgement of a particular sentiment the intrinsically satisfying quality of which cannot be denied, the feeling of religious participation. It was this that led him to claim that 'immanent in the concept of an individual is the concept of society . . . Man is, in an absolute sense, a political animal' (Sternhell 1979: 344–5).

If he rejected 'diversity', Gentile did not deny democracy. However, the type of democracy which he advocated in a remarkable passage in *The Origins and Doctrine of Fascism* was consistent both with his denial of liberal diversity and his opposition to conservative nationalism. The state must not be 'imposed from on high', as the 'Nationalist State' dominated by traditional conservative elites was, Gentile urged. This 'aristocratic state' was such that 'the people depended on the State', its authority nothing more than 'force'. The fascist state, in contrast, depended on the people. A truly 'popular state' because it represents the people as a totality, in that laudable sense it is 'totalitarian' (Gentile 2002: 28). Thus, Gentile subscribed to the doctrine of popular sovereignty but not to its liberal interpretation. For him, representative democracy had for its counterpart 'a deferential society, where achievement and wealth had replaced distinction of birth, but where the concept of distinction as such survived and the elector, who respected his representative, trusted him to serve his interests' (Sternhell 1979: 348). In place of liberal democracy, Gentile argued that the people as a whole, the masses, could be truly represented only by a leader, 'so that the thought and will of the solitary person, the Duce, becomes the thought and will of the masses' (Gentile 2002: 28–9). Having substituted the nation for the individual and the state for the nation, he proposed that the state and the leader were one. True democracy required dictatorship.

Italian Fascists of the inter-war period generally insisted that parliamentary representatives served sectional interests, when they were not motivated by personal profit, and were incapable of acting on behalf of the people as a whole. Only a leader could recognise and, more importantly, implement the true needs of the people. For such a leader to be 'representative' it was enough that he should act. If the masses failed to appreciate his leadership, 'that explains the necessity of the Fascist Party and of all the institutions of propaganda and education that foster the political and moral ideals of Fascism' (Gentile 2002: 28). It was not necessary that he should occasionally receive a majority of votes at elections, depend upon the support of a class of professional politicians or constantly seek to satisfy that 'public opinion' which is created by journalists and other *leterati* to serve powerful sectional interests. Acceptance of his leadership, whether active or passive, signified consent on the part of the people. As Gregor has noted, for Gentile, 'a politically gifted individual would be able to sense the mood of the times and the sentiments of the people – and marshal a nation to the fulfillment of aspirations long held' (Gregor 2001: 57). In and through the leader, individual and nation, nation and state, thought and action would coincide in 'pure act'.

Gentile referred to the fascist state as 'an autonomous state'. By 'autonomous', however, he meant 'a creation . . . that is revealed and works in its own consciousness' (Gentile 2002: 47). The fascist state, the theory of which Gentile elaborated, was certainly not 'autonomous' in the sense described in Chapter 1. For the rule of law as the bond of society, Gentile substituted participation in a common purpose. Against the separation of state from society, he insisted upon their unity in one 'total' community. Constitutional protections against the abuse of power were deemed not only unnecessary but unwanted obstacles in the path of a leadership, which was deemed incapable of misusing the absolute monopoly it should, ideally, command. The fascist state was not defined in territorial but 'spiritual' terms. Territorial conquest was always, therefore, warranted in principle. 'The State is always *in fieri*', Gentile wrote, always, that is to say, a movement (2002: 28). As Noël O'Sullivan has said, fascism 'deliberately and explicitly set out to destroy the state concept upon which the western style of limited politics had been based for five centuries and to replace it with something very different, *viz.* a "movement"' (O'Sullivan 1983: 39). Nevertheless, Gentile's fascist state was also populist–nationalist, an 'ethical' state deriving legitimacy from its capacity to realise the higher national aspirations of the Italian people. Gentile associated 'force' with the old conservative-nationalist state and, while he condoned its use against enemies of state, the fascist state was not to use coercion as a routine political instrument in its relations with 'the people' (Gentile 2002: 49–51). In place of force, a political education in fascist ideology, propagated through the PNF, was to bind the individual to the state, just as a religion binds together individuals through ritual and doctrine without using force. In this way, because it represented a politicised version of Christianity, *totalitarianismo* was moderated.

## Practical politics

*Fascism 1918–1945*

Only in Italy, after Mussolini formed his first government in 1922, and in Germany after 1933, could it be said that there were Fascist regimes. Even that is debatable. Historians have questioned the extent to which Mussolini's internally divided regime was genuinely Fascist. Payne has noted that ex-Marxists and syndicalists militated for a revolutionary national socialism, revisionists saw fascism as providing a new elite to command the existing political system, paramilitary groups used terror to establish a dictatorship, and nationalists worked for an authoritarian state under the monarchy. De Felice's distinction between fascism 'as movement' and 'as regime' draws to our attention the disparity between the clerical, corporatist, capitalist and conservative Mussolini state and the revolutionary, anti-bourgeois and national-socialist Fascist movement (de Felice 1976). To fascist revolutionaries the Mussolini regime represented an imperfect embodiment of the fascist ideals which inspired the movement because of its alliances with the monarchy and the Church and its accomodation of capitalism. Contemporary historians tend to agree that, even at the height of his power, Mussolini was unable to institute a fully fascist regime. As early as 1927, the PNF was widely perceived by revolutionary Fascists as having become conservative (Payne 1980: 68–9).

The Italian state before the Fascist seizure of power had been weak, divided and, especially in the aftermath of the First World War, barely capable of governing. When Mussolini spoke of *totalitarianismo* his intention was to claim for the Fascist state genuine sovereign power, the capacity to make and to enforce decisions wherever there was conflict within Italian society. This presupposes that society exists independently of the state, even if such a society would not be one in which liberals would feel comfortable. Despite the hyperbolic language that he could not resist, Mussolini neither glorified nor presided over the type of state described by theorists of totalitarianism (Kershaw 2000: 21). It is true that he established a one-party state, ruled by decree, centralised political power in Rome and placed trades unions under state control. However, throughout the years of Fascist rule, Victor Immanuel III remained head of state and, under the provisions of the Lateran Treaty of 1929, the special position of the Catholic Church in Italy was protected. The PNF was subordinated to the state and controlled neither the judiciary nor the police, both of which remained organs of the state, as did the regular army. Although trades unions were regulated, business, industry and finance were autonomous. There was no Ministry of Propaganda until 1936, when the German model was imitated with far less enthusiasm or efficiency than would have been required to create a department exercising control over all aspects of culture such as Goebbels's *Propagandaministerium*. Throughout the sixteen years of its existence, the court instituted to try political crimes, the Special Tribunal for the Defence of the State, sentenced forty-two men to death of whom thirty-one were executed (Farrell 2004: 181). Compared with Nazi Germany, Stalin's Soviet Union and Mao Tse-Tung's Communist China, Fascist Italy was not 'totalitarian' as that term is now most often understood (Payne 1980: 75). To the extent that it was 'totalitarian' at all, it was in Gentile's 'ethical' or 'spiritual' sense. However, even Gentile's vision of a tutelary state was beyond the reach of the Fascists. As Hannah Arendt recognised, despite the rhetoric of *totalitarianismo*, Italian Fascism, in practice, remained essentially nationalist and statist in conventional terms. Once the Mussolini regime was established, 'their movement had come to an end with the seizure of power' (Arendt 1973: 257).

Nor was the Third Reich unambiguously 'fascist'. German National Socialism was dedicated to the creation of a racial state (Burleigh and Wipperman 1991). Biological racism played little or no part in Italian Fascist ideology (Sternhell 1994). Gentile remained true to Italian culture when he defined the nation in 'spiritual', not racial or ethnic, terms. Whereas traditional anti-semitism received political expression in many other nations, in Germany it took a pseudo-scientific, lethal form. Motivated above all by racialism, the terrible fate to which they delivered the German nation itself showed that the Nazis were not nationalists in either the conservative or even the populist sense adhered to by Italian Fascists. Hitler's vision was one in which the fundamental realities were forces, understood in strictly racial terms, pitted against one another in a struggle for survival. It was a more terrible political religion than Gentile's. Moreover, it might be argued that the Third Reich was as imperfectly national socialist as Mussolini's Italy fell short of the Fascist ideal. Hitler purged the Nazi movement of its more socialist, revolutionary elements in 1934, within a year of seizing power, as much in order to conciliate conservative political, industrial and military elites as to establish personal dominance within the NSDAP. The 'neo-paganism' of less politically astute Nazi ideologues such as Alfred Rosenberg was sidelined because Hitler, rightly, recognised that a precipitate assault on Christianity would be imprudent and that Catholic Germany especially would have to be appeased in the short term (Conway 1968). Post-war historians such as Martin Broszat and Hans Mommsen have shown how the Third Reich was riven by conflicts between different institutions and individuals within a complex structure composed of various, often competing, power blocs (Broszat 1981; Mommsen 1979). If anything blocked its totalitarian ambitions, it was the essentially lawless, anarchist nature of German National Socialism itself. This was already evident to wartime emigres such as Ernst Fraenkel and Franz Neuman for whom the Third Reich was a chaotic 'polycratic' state approaching the condition of statelessness (Gregor 2000: 146–52). The state mattered to the Nazis only in so far as mobilising the German people for racial war required considerable bureaucratic organisation. Not an autonomous state, neither was the Third Reich the 'ethical state' imagined by Italian Fascists. Racialism was substituted for nationalism and, whereas in Italy the PNF became an instrument of the state, the German state was subordinated to the profoundly anarchic NSDAP and its religion of race.

While Mussolini always found his scope for action restricted by compromises he had been compelled to make in order to seize power, Hitler, especially after 1936 when he was able to dispense with the formal alliance with the authoritarian right which had brought him to power, enjoyed far greater freedom to pursue National Socialist policies. Between 1918 and 1933, the Weimar state had been characterised by political violence, inflation, unemployment and instability, with seventeen governments formed in less than fifteen years, as the Republic struggled with non-democratic extremes on both the left and the right. It was in this context of insupportable political crisis that conservatives entered into an alliance with the Nazis in 1933, fatally mistaken in their belief that control of the German state would remain in their hands. Economic and, after 1939, military imperatives meant that the Third Reich continued to accommodate conservative elements for reasons of expedience. Marxists claim that the fact that fascists were less hostile towards conservatives than they were towards liberals or socialists shows that fascism was not genuinely anti-conservative. In this respect, however, Nolte was right. Identifying conservatism as the ideology of a fraction of the ruling class, and fascism as a reactionary attempt to save capitalism, Marxists have mistaken the tactical compromise with conservatism that fascists made for a genuine affinity. What Marxists ignore is the fact that the aims and ideology of fascism remained fundamentally incompatible with conservatism. Fascists set out to transcend even the most authoritarian forms of conservatism. In Germany they succeeded.

## Fascism after 1945

Historians who rightly stress the historically specific political and cultural factors responsible for the rise of fascism are not inclined to predict its return (Payne 1980: 206–7). It is true that there are today in western Europe and North America proscribed or 'underground' organisations for whom the term 'neo-fascist' is not inappropriate, such as the American National Alliance, the Italian Armed Revolutionary Nuclei (NAR), and Combat 18 in Britain. Membership of such organisations is numerically tiny, they are regarded as pariahs by the populations among whom they live and are subject to incessant state surveillance and infiltration. Their political significance is nugatory.

There are also political parties that are alleged to be 'neo-fascist'. There are two types of such parties, one of which is more safely described thus than the other. The Italian *Movemento Sociale Fiamma Tricolore* (MS-FT), the German *Nationaldemokratische Partei Deutschlands* (NPD) and the British National Party (BNP) are political parties widely regarded as neo-fascist. Because they stand at elections, such parties must take care not to use overtly fascist language or symbols in public if they wish to avoid prosecution. State authorities barely tolerate their existence. During 2003 the German federal government attempted to ban the NPD on the grounds that its existence violated the terms of the German Constitution. The trial failed because it was discovered that so many senior members of the party were undercover agents working for the German secret services that it was impossible to determine whether allegedly illegal activities had been undertaken on behalf of the state in order to secure a ban on the party or whether such activities had been performed by genuine neo-fascists. Public opinion, which states do so much to manufacture, ensures that parties of the 'far right' are generally regarded as unwholesome extremists, with the result that the electoral support for such parties is marginal. The NPD collected 1.6 per cent of the votes cast in the 2005 German national election and 0.7 per cent of voters chose a BNP candidate at the 2005 British general election. The price paid by a party espousing disguised but, none the less, recognisably fascist politics in a contemporary liberal democracy is impending criminalisation and electoral impotence.

The other type of party to which especially leftists freely apply the label 'fascist' are more accurately described as 'populist-nationalist', the French *Front National* (FN), the Austrian *Freiheitliche Partei Össterreichs* (Freedom Party), the Belgian *Vlaams Blok* or 'Flemish Block' (re-titled *Vlaams Belang* in 2004) and the Italian *Alleanza Nazionale* (AN). This second type of 'extreme right' party tends to enjoy significantly higher levels of electoral support than the first. At the 2001 Italian elections the 'National Alliance' won ninety-six seats of 630 in the Chamber of Deputies and forty-six of 324 in the Senate. At the time of writing, its leader, Gianfranco Fini, is Italian Foreign Minister. *Vlaams Blok* received 24.1 per cent of the vote at the Belgian regional elections of 2004. The Freedom Party took 10 per cent of the vote at the 2002 Austrian Parliamentary election. In the first round of the 2002 French Presidential election the leader of the FN, Jean-Marie Le Pen, came second, with 16.9 per cent of votes cast, only 3 per cent less than the eventual winner, Jacques Chirac. Certainly successful in electoral terms, it is not clear that such parties are fascist. They are called 'fascist' by their political opponents. The FN are particularly disposed to taking legal action when the party is smeared, as they see it, with this accusation.

Their enemies take the view that when men like Fini, Le Pen and Jörge Haider claim that they are not fascists, this is opportunism designed to permit them to engage in democratic politics, as if subscribing to the legal norms required of any constitutional political party and offering electorates programmes which differ markedly from historical fascism but resemble those of legitimate right-wing parties were mere ploys. If, as their opponents believe, such parties are composed of fascists attempting to fool the public, then they have fooled themselves. In renouncing an authentic fascist lineage, in the case of the AN or Freedom Party, or repudiating one which has been attributed to them, as the FN does, these parties have not merely distanced themselves verbally from fascism. The Freedom Party rejects extra-parliamentary tactics and appeals to working-class voters on the basis of an Austrian nationalist programme which is both monarchist, pro-clerical and, in some respects, neo-liberal in economic policy. Two-thirds of AN supporters are in favour of neo-liberal policies such as the privatisation of state enterprises. The FN is a populist conservative party which receives support to the extent that it expresses nationalist fear over the consequences of globalisation for the French economy and society. Such parties represent attitudes towards economic policy, law and order, immigration and defence similar to those found among sections of the British Conservative Party and American Republican Party (Mudde 2000). These are evidently not parties like Hitler's NSDAP or Mussolini's PNF which mobilised paramilitary violence behind electoral campaigns mounted with the intention of destroying parliamentary politics. Contemporary parties of the 'far right' such as these accept pluralist democratic politics. This has been the condition for their electoral success, just as the perception that parties like the NPD and the BNP are not genuinely pluralist has been the reason for their lack of it. Contempt for liberal democracy is an article of faith, which no authentic fascist will renounce.

In Italy, France and Germany, fascism is dead. It never lived in Britain or, traditionally, in the Anglophone world. Nevertheless, understanding fascism remains important. The modern 'activist style of politics' (O'Sullivan 1983) was present before historical fascism and it has survived its comprehensive defeat, though not in central or western Europe. Elements of the 'fascist style of politics', such as the leader-principle, ultra-nationalism, national socialism, ethnocentrism, racism and the cult of violence, are discernible in many different contexts. It has reappeared in communist and post-communist regimes in Asia, including China, Cambodia, North Vietnam and North Korea where there exist ethnocentric or racist, nationalist, authoritarian regimes given to militarism and the cult of the leader. Ultra-nationalist, racist movements have emerged in eastern Europe since 1989, most notably in Russia and the Ukraine. Ethnically based 'identity politics' among Black Americans is often motivated by the same impulses as was Italian Fascism (Garvey 1926) and the politics of Jewish fundamentalism depends upon notions of racial purity similar to those adhered to by the Nazis (Kahane 1987). Where the modern autonomous state never took root, or where the attempt to build it has failed, ethnic or religious nationalism can produce politics comparable to those of historical fascism which, in both Italy and Germany, was itself a consequence of state failure. Most significantly of all, as will be argued in Chapter 11, radical Islamism shows remarkable affinities with historical fascism.

*Note:* It is customary to use a capital to distinguish the Italian Fascist movement from generic fascism.

## Bibliography

Arendt, H. (1973), *The Origins of Totalitarianism* (New York: Harcourt Brace Jovanovich).
Berlin, I. (1990), 'Joseph de Maistre and the origins of Fascism', in H. Hardy (ed.), *The Crooked Timber of Humanity* (London: John Murray), pp. 91–174.
Blinkhorn, M. (ed.) (1990), *Fascists and Conservatives* (London: Unwin Hyman).
Broszat, M. (1981), *The Hitler State*, trans. J. W. Hiden (London: Longman).
Burleigh, M. and Wippermann, W. (1991), *The Racial State: Germany 1933–45* (Cambridge: Cambridge University Press).
Conway, J. (1968), *The Nazi Persecution of the Churches* (London: Weidenfeld and Nicolson).
de Felice, R. (1976), *Fascism: An Informal Introduction to its Theory and Practice* (New Brunswick NJ: Transaction).
Eatwell, R. (1996), 'On defining the fascist minimum: the centrality of ideology', *Journal of Political Ideologies*, 1, 3: 303–19.
Eatwell, R. (2001), 'Universal fascism: approaches and definitions', in S. Larsen (ed.), *Fascism Outside Europe* (New York: Columbia University Press), pp. 15–45.
Eatwell, R. and Mudde, C. (eds) (2004), *Western Democracies and the New Extreme Right* (London: Routledge).

Farrell, N. (2004), *Mussolini: A New Life* (London: Weidenfeld and Nicolson).
Garvey, M. (1926), *Philosophy and Opinions of Marcus Garvey: Volume Two* (New York: Universal Publishing House).
Gentile, G. (1928), 'The philosophic basis of fascism', *Foreign Affairs*, 6 (2): 290–304.
Gentile, G. (2002), *The Origins and Doctrine of Fascism*, ed. and trans. A. J. Gregor (New Brunswick NJ: Transaction).
Gregor, A. J. (1979a), *Italian Fascism and Developmental Dictatorship* (Princeton NJ: Princeton University Press).
Gregor, A. J. (1979b), *Young Mussolini and the Intellectual Origins of Fascism* (Berkeley CA: University of California Press).
Gregor, A. J. (2001), *Giovanni Gentile: Philosopher of Fascism* (New Brunswick NJ: Transaction).
Gregor, A. J. (2004), *Mussolini's Intellectuals: Fascist Social and Political Thought* (Princeton NJ: Princeton University Press).
Gregor, N. (ed.) (2000), *Nazism* (Oxford: Oxford University Press).
Griffin, R. (1993), *The Nature of Fascism* (London: Routledge).
Griffin, R. (ed.) (1995), *Fascism* (Oxford: Oxford University Press).
Griffiths, R. (2000), *An Intelligent Person's Guide to Fascism* (London: Duckworth).
Kahane, M. (1987), *Uncomfortable Questions for Comfortable Jews* (Secaucus NJ: Lyle Stuart Inc).
Kallis, A. (ed.) (2003), *The Fascism Reader* (London: Routledge).
Kershaw, I. (2000), *The Nazi Dictatorship: Problems and Perspectives of Interpretation* (4th edn) (London: Arnold).
Kitchen, M. (1976), *Fascism* (London: Macmillan).
Lyttelton, A. (ed.) (1973), *Italian Fascisms: From Pareto to Gentile* (London: Cape).
Mann, M. (2004), *Fascists* (Cambridge: Cambridge University Press).
McClelland, J. S. (ed.) (1970), *The French Right From de Maistre to Maurras* (London: Cape).
Mommsen, H. (1979), 'National socialism: continuity and change', in W. Laquer (ed.), *Fascism: A Reader's Guide* (Harmondsworth: Penguin), pp. 151–92.
Mudde, C. (2000), *The Ideology of the Extreme Right* (Manchester: Manchester University Press).
O'Sullivan, N. (1983), *Fascism* (London: Dent).
Oakeshott, M. (ed.) (1939), *The Social and Political Doctrines of Contemporary Europe* (Cambridge: Cambridge University Press).
Payne, S. (1980), *Fascism: Comparison and Definition* (Madison WI: University of Wisconsin Press).
Proudhon, P.-J. (1979), *The Principle of Federation* (Toronto: Toronto University Press).

Proudhon, P.-J. (1989), *General Idea of the Revolution in the Nineteenth Century* (London: Pluto).
Rousseau, J.-J. (1973), *The Social Contract and Discourses*, trans. G. D. H. Cole (London: Dent).
Rousseau, J.-J. (1985), *The Government of Poland* (Indianapolis IN: Hackett).
Sorel, G. (1961), *Reflections on Violence*, trans. T. E. Hulme (London: Collier).
Sorel, G. (1972), *The Illusions of Progress*, trans. J. and C. Stanley (Berkeley CA: University of California Press).
Sternhell, Z. (1979), 'Fascist ideology', in W. Laquer (ed.), *Fascism: A Reader's Guide* (Harmondsworth: Penguin), pp. 315–71.
Sternhell, Z. (1986), *Neither Right Nor Left: Fascist Ideology in France*, trans. D. Maisel (Princeton NJ: Princeton University Press).
Sternhell, Z. (with M. Sznajder and M. Asheri) (1994), *The Birth of Fascist Ideology*, trans. D. Maisel (Princeton NJ: Princeton University Press).
Talmon, J. (1991), *Myth of the Nation and Vision of Revolution* (New Brunswick NJ: Transaction).
Winock, M. (1998), *Nationalism, Anti-Semitism and Fascism in France*, trans. J.-M. Todd (Stanford CA: Stanford University Press).

CHAPTER EIGHT

# Conservatism: Authority in the Modern State

John McGovern

Its more thoughtful adherents have always recognised and, indeed, lauded the ideological paucity of conservatism. For Roger Scruton, 'conservatism is a stance that may be defined without identifying it with the policies of any party'. Rather than aiming to remake political arrangements in the light of fixed principles, he has insisted, 'the conservative attitude seeks above all for government'. In characterising conservatism in this way, Scruton's implicit claim is that neither socialists nor *a fortiori* liberals seek to govern in the sense of ruling. Despite the indisputable fact that, historically, conservative political practice and liberal ideals have converged, Scruton considers liberalism 'the principal enemy of conservatism'. The reason he gives for this is that 'for the conservative, the value of individual liberty is not absolute, but stands subject to another and higher value, the authority of established government'. Regarding 'no citizen as possessed of a natural right that transcends his obligation to be ruled', the essential feature of conservative politics, on Scruton's account, is 'an ideal of authority' (Scruton 1980: 15–16, 19).

## Context

Although there were more European monarchies in 1914 than a century earlier, during the nineteenth century their supremacy was steadily undermined by the forces of liberalism, nationalism and socialism. In the words of Norman Davies, they survived only 'by profoundly modifying the nature of the bond between rulers and ruled' (Davies 1997: 802). Political liberalism, with its urgent emphasis upon government by consent, the rule of law, constitutional procedure, religious toleration, universal human rights and individual liberty opposed hereditary prerogative in Church and State. Economic liberalism, free trade and *laissez faire* tended to increase the social power of the new middle classes *vis-à-vis* their traditional masters even if it was also welcomed by some established elites, most notably the Whig aristocracy in Britain, while early nineteenth-century Germany demonstrated the fact that political liberalism is by no means a necessary consequence of its economic counterpart as free trade was successfully introduced within the German confederation under the authoritarian rule of Frederick-William III. Davies makes the often ignored but vital point that conservatism 'began to crystallize as a coherent ideology in conjunction with liberal trends' (1997: 812). Political theorists, including some conservative thinkers, tend to regard conservatism and liberalism in the abstract as very different and, indeed, antithetical ideologies. At the level of doctrine, of course, an 'ideal type' of conservatism can be constructed which represents the ideological reverse of liberalism. Nevertheless, historically, the relationship between conservatism and liberalism has always been rather closer (Greenleaf 1983: 193, 265).

Conservatism should not be regarded merely as the reactionary antagonist of liberalism because it has never stood against either democracy as such or resisted change *tout court*: 'what it did was to insist that all change should be channelled and managed in such a way that the organic growth of established institutions of state and society ... should not be threatened' (Davies 1997: 812). Indeed, not only have conservatives embraced the distinctively liberal principle of 'negative liberty' and, therefore, the need to limit the action of the state in the name of individual freedom, conservatives such as Peel and Disraeli 'often turned out to be the most effective of would-be reformers'. In real political terms, the difference between conservatives and liberals is 'a fine one', Davies points out, with 'the large area of agreement between them' defining 'the middle ground' of politics in stable democracies ever since the nineteenth century (1997: 812).

## Definition

While left-wing intellectuals prefer to believe, with John Stuart Mill, that the Conservatives are 'the stupid party', the absence of conservative ideology a sure sign of the ignorance of those who, representing the status quo, have no interest in thinking 'critically' about it, thoughtful conservatives draw the conclusion that conservatism is non-ideological as a matter of principle. Scruton's remark that conservatism is a stance not to be identified with the ideology of any particular party echoes the judgement of the most important English-speaking conservative thinker of the twentieth century, Michael Oakeshott, who defined conservatism in pointedly non-ideological terms as a very common and highly general 'disposition', an inclination 'to prefer the familiar to the unknown' (Oakeshott 1991: 408). It is only too obvious, as has often been pointed out, that, on this account, there is nothing to distinguish conservatism from any other political ideology (McClelland 1996: 783).

The American intellectual Samuel Huntington spoke for a certain type of conservatism when he claimed that conservatives are inclined to preserve not any institutions in particular but, recognising the value of institutions as such, existing ones (Huntington 1957). The underlying principle of such conservatism has been called 'historical utilitarianism', that is, the notion that the value of a political institution is to be measured by its usefulness and that, in turn, utility is demonstrated by historical longevity (Muller 1997: 6–7). However, as even sympathetic commentators such as Gertrude Himmelfarb have pointed out, simply because a tradition exists it does not follow that it should exist, let alone that it should be conserved (Himmelfarb 1986: 210–28). Hostile critics like Ted Honderich object that conservatism in this sense is no more than self-serving rhetoric the evident purpose of which is to protect the power of those who happen to enjoy it (Honderich 1991). Because conservatives are rather more discriminating than Huntington suggests, valuing some institutions more than others, and some not at all, irrespective of how well established they happen to be, were there not some principle by means of which they choose from among 'existing institutions' those which should be conserved on rationally defensible grounds it is difficult to see how Honderich's objection could be answered.

Anthony Quinton has argued that such a principle is found in 'belief in the imperfection of human nature' (Quinton 1978: 13). Sometimes this belief takes a religious form but, as Quinton has shown, it may also be expressed in secular terms. For conservatives, human imperfection is both moral and intellectual but, according to Quinton, 'of the two imperfections it is the intellectual one that is specifically emphasized by conservatives' (1978: 13). The value of tradition, then, may be seen as rationally justified in terms of a more fundamental principle. The rational person will recognise that human reason is radically imperfect and, resisting the temptation to 'conduct their political affairs under the impulsion of large, abstract principles of change arrived at by individual thinkers working in isolation from the practical realities of political life', reasonable men and women 'should be guided rather by the accumulated political wisdom of the community' (1978: 13). In addition to a rationally justified traditionalism in this sense, Quinton has derived two further distinctively conservative political principles from the central belief in human imperfection. There is organicism 'which takes a society to be a unitary, natural growth, an organized, living whole, not a mechanical aggregate'. In stressing that real men and women are not 'bare abstract individuals' but 'social beings' conservatism stands opposed to liberalism. Traditional institutions, for conservatives, are not 'external, disposable devices of interest to men only by reason of the individual purposes they serve; they are, rather, constitutive of the social identity of men' (1978: 16). The other principle is political scepticism. Because of their conviction that human reason is an irremediably flawed instrument, conservatives mistrust theoretical speculation in politics and prefer, instead, to place their faith in 'the deposit of traditional customs and institutions that have survived and become established and also those people who, in one way or another, have acquired extensive practical experience of politics' (1978: 17).

It seems to me, however, that Quinton's justification of conservative traditionalism depends upon an ideal of authority that he failed to clarify. His account implies that the political value of tradition lies in the type of authority that belongs to it, its capacity to enjoin political obligation without recourse to either force or consent. It is difficult to see why the citizen should recognise in traditional institutions 'the accumulated wisdom of the community', rather than merely conventional devices or relics, unless they solicit a particular type of response from her, such that the rules of which they are composed are given assent, neither through compulsion nor on account of their content, but because of the source from which they issue. Nor is it clear that the disposals of those who 'in one way or another' have acquired political power should be accepted just because they happen to have grown used to exercising it. Tradition must appear 'right', 'fitting' or even 'natural', the rules which it prescribes accepted on trust, rather than subject to some rational assessment, because of the source from which they derive. Thus, political value should be ascribed to traditions, not because they happen to be established, but because they support a peculiarly binding type of authority that it is distinctive of conservatives to regard as politically indispensable. For conservatives, there can be no genuinely political society in the absence of authority. If collective decisions are to be made, those who make them should be authorised to do so. Political order, at once an effect of and a necessary condition for successful decision making, must be maintained and the best means of its maintenance is authority. Institutions persist and acquire traditional status only because they possess such authority in the first place. While it is true that historical longevity consolidates authority, it can not create it. It is, however, true that tradition can supply something politically invaluable to authority: to the extent that authority is shrouded in tradition, its rulings perceived as part of an immemorial order, political obligation is experienced as unforced and without need of justification.

Conservatives ascribe political value to authority and, hence, to tradition because they subscribe to the idea normally associated with liberalism that freedom should be understood as negative liberty. As an illustration of conservative adherence to liberal doctrine, consider the principles listed in one recent exposition of doctrinaire conservatism where, as well as human imperfection, organicism, gradualism, constitutionalism and nationalism, the authors mention 'the limited state' and the preservation of 'private life', 'the prosperous economy' attributed to *laissez-faire* economic doctrine and 'respect for property' as 'an extension of personality' (Seldon and Snowdon 2001: 19–24). Such liberal principles derive from the notion of negative liberty. From that notion follows a vision of 'civil society' which conservatives uphold no less than liberals. It is a vision of society as an autonomous sphere, composed of non-coercive relations embedded within institutions the rules of which are endorsed voluntarily. According to this vision, no force, whether political or religious, may legitimately interfere with the self-ordering of the social sphere.

An idea of the state follows accordingly, one which prescribes that its principal function is to protect civil society from whoever or whatever would threaten the autonomy of the social sphere. Clearly, this implies that the state must act so as to remove obstacles to the exercise of freedom and, given that what the acceptable exercise of such liberty consists in is always contentious, it follows that the state must decide upon what counts as an impediment and enforce its decision. It must, therefore, intervene. However, state intervention is legitimate, on this account, to the extent that it does not suppress the exercise of individual freedom or overrule the activity of social institutions when no impediment is offered to the autonomy of the social sphere as a whole. However, this characterisation of the state raises a question. What is the source of its legitimacy? Within the tradition of modern liberalism the action of the state is said to be legitimated by reference to the consent of 'the people'. That is, society is the source of the state's legitimacy.

In sharp contrast, it is axiomatic for genuine conservatives that the source of the power to take decisions for society as a whole cannot be located within society. A power distinct, even if not really separate, from society is required. That power, the state, cannot be understood in the liberal terms of consent or contract. Consent to government is simply one among the many freedoms which liberalism attributes to the individual. The conservative objection is not simply that freely given consent could never be the source of the legitimacy of political power because the very point of exercising it, not in every instance but certainly in some, is to restrain and to compel. It is also that the exercise of freedom is only possible in the first place if a sufficient concrete order exists within civil society.

The use to which modern conservatives put the authority of the state is to support a civil society composed of individuals seeking negative freedom. As Scruton put it: 'it is the individual's responsibility to win whatever freedom of speech, conscience and assembly he may; it is the politician's responsibility to define and maintain the arrangement in which that freedom is to be pursued' (Scruton 1980: 19). If there is a difference between conservatives and liberals in respect of individual freedom that has to do with an argument about the nature of negative liberty. John Gray, for instance, insists that conservatism proper is 'anti-reductionist' in the sense that it upholds 'the primacy of cultural forms'. What this entails is that rights, notably, are not, despite doctrinaire liberalism, universal entitlements. They are the legal abridgements of culturally specific practices and institutions. Conservatism is not opposed to negative liberty, according to Gray who, speaking as a conservative, advocates the 'subtlest liberal uses of the idea of autonomy'. Where such subtlety is used 'it is recognized that the exercise of autonomous choice depends for its value on a cultural environment that is rich in choiceworthy options and inherently public goods' (Gray 1997: 43–5). In other words, the practice of negative liberty is not possible in just any culture and even where there have arisen the institutions which are the conditions for its possibility it does not follow that autonomous actions should be performed by everyone and on every available occasion.

Negative liberty, then, is limited by 'cultural forms' but only because they make it possible in the first place. Two significant political implications follow from this. One is that conservatism proper is anti-universalist. Gray notes that 'even this subtler liberal conception of autonomy unreasonably privileges a particular Western ideal' (Gray 1997: 45). As we shall see in the case of Michael Oakeshott, the state itself, as traditionally understood, is a particular 'cultural form' peculiar to modern western Europe. Secondly, culture may only limit autonomy to the extent that it possesses authority or, as Gray puts it, 'norms' (1997: 44). Gray's sober conclusion is that in contemporary Britain, as elsewhere in the West, 'the effect of market liberalism has been to run down our common stock of cultural traditions by propagating the absurd legalist view that we do not need a common culture only common rules' (1997: 48). For Gray, its affiliation with 'neo-liberalism' has hollowed out conservatism proper and 'the notion that established conservative parties can be reclaimed' is 'a mere illusion' (1997: 3–8). The extent to which liberalism and conservatism remain conjoined is evident when even Gray entertains the hope that 'renewing genuine conservative values and passing on the traditions of a *liberal* civilization' may still be possible for the undeceived conservative (1997: 8, Emphasis added).

## Theorists

### Michael Oakeshott

In an essay first published in 1929, Michael Oakeshott expressed his view of authority in the most candid terms as 'absolute,

## Conservatism: Authority in the Modern State

irresponsible, inescapable power', and showed how, for a conservative, the state is an idea of authority. He dismissed the 'rationalist' notion that one should accept the authority of the state on the grounds that it is the sole legislative power with the observation that 'laws can be changed or governments overthrown'. Nor can political authority be derived, as liberals imagine, from contract or consent, Oakeshott claimed, because 'mere consent may be given or withheld, but whatever is really authoritative is absolute and independent of our acceptance or recognition: consent itself requires an authority upon which to rest'. Oakeshott's conclusion was that 'the authority of the state can reside nowhere save in the state itself as such' and that it 'resides solely in the completeness of the satisfactions which the state itself affords to the needs of concrete persons' (Oakeshott 1993: 86–7; 84). As we have seen in Chapter 7, this conservative vision of the state as a 'conception' and an order without which the concrete personality of the individual is impossible proceeded from Idealist premises shared with some varieties of fascism (Franco 2004). However, whereas fascist political theory was destructive of the idea of the modern state described in Chapter 1, by emphasising the provision of mundane 'satisfactions' as both its *raison d'être* and the source of its legitimacy, even when ascribing absolute power to the state, Oakeshott's early work foreshadowed his later characterisation of the state as 'civil association' in *On Human Conduct*, a work which should be seen as an attempt to recover the idea of the modern state.

*On Human Conduct* distinguishes between two types of human association: 'enterprise association'; and 'civil association'. Enterprise association, the most common type, is directed towards the satisfaction of particular substantive objectives which may be moral, religious, merely recreational, or, most suited to this form of relationship, economic. In contrast, civil association has no purpose extraneous to itself. Not directed towards the fulfilment of substantive needs or wants, it is association in the terms of generally acknowledged rules. These rules, which Oakeshott called *lex* ('law' in general rather than this or that particular piece of legislation) are sustained by a political order of which they are the reflection, a *civitas* or state. Because enterprise association is the more familiar, there is a temptation, according to Oakeshott, to conceive of political order in its terms. However, the ideal political relationship, the distinctively *political* form of human association, is civil association. Being essentially voluntary, enterprise association cannot manifest the compulsory character that belongs to specifically political arrangements. Authority, 'absolute, irresponsible, inescapable power', can belong only to civil association, that is, to the state which alone bears the power to compel obedience because it commands allegiance and not because it possesses the capacity to coerce the citizen. The state may coerce its citizens only on the condition that it first possesses authority and that derives from the fact that it is a civil association, a body of generally acknowledged rules to which citizens assent as a whole. The bond of community is nothing more substantial than the citizens' common recognition of the authority of those laws, the fact that they conceive of them as providing for them a shared political identity.

The state, then, is a 'conception'. No common purpose is required, no national 'project' and no ethnic identity or shared religious faith. The authentically political society, on Oakeshott's account, is one bound together by the sentiment of 'civility', that is, the recognition of others as fellow members of the same legal community regardless of ethnic, religious or other differences in style of life. Such a civil association or state is an historic achievement that will emerge only among particular peoples whose collective experience has been such as to endow them with a practical sense of civility. It is as if, for Oakeshott, the state proper, rather than the mere apparatus of government, will appear only within a community that has developed certain 'manners'. Indeed, the concept of 'the state' is nothing other than an abstraction from the historical experience of such a 'civilised' community. As a contingent historical development, the existence of the state is precarious. The force of its laws depends finally upon the approval of its citizens, their recognition that those laws do indeed provide for them such 'satisfactions' as will leave them contented. Once that approval vanishes, the state appears to be fundamentally illegitimate, and laws lose their force, the compulsory character that made them *lex*. Hence, the 'rationalist' project of subjecting law to 'ceaseless criticism never did anyone or anything any good' (Oakeshott 1989: 115). General approval of state authority is the result of 'political education' which, for Oakeshott, is neither a training in political 'science' nor ideological indoctrination but the transmission across the generations of that practical knowledge which permits the individual a tacit recognition of what counts as reasonable within the public sphere thereby transforming the individual into a citizen (Oakeshott 1991: 43–69). As the

## Conservatism: Authority in the Modern State

understanding of a particular tradition, the effect of 'political education' is to form the popular will.

'The rule of law' has always been appealed to by liberals, Oakeshott's 'rationalists', who make use of the machinery of government, observing procedure scrupulously, to invade the social sphere, modifying habits and traditions in the name of 'enlightenment' or 'progress' (Oakeshott 1991: 5–42). Such aggressive liberal constitutionalism is incompatible with Oakeshott's civil association since some or other enterprise, such as creating 'gender equality' or a 'multicultural society', is advanced using the law as an instrument. The non-instrumental *lex* to which Oakeshott ascribed political authority, however, was not something really separate from society but society itself politically organized. It could not be available for use as a tool to adjust the habits of the community because it is no more than the political arrangements that simultaneously reflect and condition those habits. The real model for *lex* is common law. If the state is sustained by established moral sentiment in the way described by Oakeshott, then a question naturally arises: how can civil association survive the abandonment of traditions of civility? In effect, this is the question asked of Oakeshott by the American neo-conservative historian Gertrude Himmelfarb. She finds in Oakeshott no response and that in itself, she believes, throws doubt on the political value of Oakeshott's conservatism in modern circumstances (one presumes she is thinking primarily of the United States) where the habit of civility described by Oakeshott either never existed or has been eroded (Himmelfarb 1986: 210–28). The solution to Himmelfarb's problem adopted by American neo-conservatives has been to use the machinery of state to create or restore 'civility'. Although the objective is widely regarded as 'conservative', the way in which it is pursued and, indeed, the fact that it is pursued at all as a 'problem' in need of a technical 'solution', shows neo-conservatism to be a species of what Oakeshott called 'rationalism'. Himmelfarb's presumption that the decline of civility is a malaise for which a remedy is urgently required is not one that Oakeshott would have shared. For him, if habits of civility die within a community it is no longer fit for civil association. The machinery of government will persist. Indeed, it will grow in power relative to the social sphere. According to the modern European concept of the state as an autonomous structure of government, separate from both those who rule and those who are ruled, such a community is no longer a *political* society and, in that sense, no matter how powerful its government, it is stateless. The neo-conservative criticism of genuine conservatism such as Oakeshott's is beside the point. For Oakeshott, civil association, the modern European state, was a product of a certain type of civilisation. If the lived experience which sustained it declines, so too will the state.

## Carl Schmitt

The centre-piece of Schmitt's state theory is a definition of 'the political': 'The specific political distinction to which political actions and motives can be reduced is that between friend and enemy' (Schmitt 1996: 26). The friend/enemy criterion permits us to to contrast specifically political relations with other forms of association, whether moral, religious or economic. A person's orientation is political in the proper sense to the extent that they recognise themselves as belonging to a community composed of like-minded 'friends', that is, those who also recognise themselves as belonging to the same community. Schmitt's terms 'friend' and 'enemy' are eminently social in that they do not refer to individual sympathies or enmities but to relations within and between communities. However, the distinction is more than merely social in that it is intended to identify distinctively political action from among other types of social relation. The essence of the political lies in the fact that, when someone acquires a political identity, they may be required to risk their life in defence of the community. The type of community which calls for such sacrifice is a political society. The recognition that you belong to a community of friends, all of whom may equally be called upon to risk their lives in defence of the community, is simultaneously a recognition that other communities exist, composed of persons with different values and allegiances. The perception that you belong to a political society, that you are among friends, arises and is intensified to the degree that you perceive others as comprising a community of enemies. At one level Schmitt's friend/enemy criterion seems a perfectly commonplace description of conflict between political societies, whether tribes, nations, empires or modern mass movements such as fascism, communism and fundamentalism.

Clearly, this understanding of the political stands in opposition to the typically liberal view that the purpose of political action is peace. As against the liberal emphasis on negotiation and compromise in terms of generally acknowledged rules and procedures, Schmitt took

## Conservatism: Authority in the Modern State

the view that concrete communities exist in the shadow of crisis. If crises are to be resolved, this will require decisions which override normal procedures and express an intense experience of solidarity. Schmitt's 'decisionism' is manifest in his definition of sovereignty: 'Sovereign is he who decides on the exception' (Schmitt 1988: 5). It follows from this that there can be no rule of law in the sense of a nomocracy. Law cannot *rule*. Concrete persons, rulers, are required who must decide, especially under the exceptional circumstances which always threaten to irrupt, what law is, how it should be applied and, most importantly of all, who may apply it. If, for Schmitt, the liberal vision of politics as the quest for the *juste millieu* leaves out of account the fact of ever impending crisis, critics such as Giovanni Sartori have argued that Schmitt's political theory represents an opposite extreme in which politics are identified with conflict (Sartori 1989). In contrast, Paul Hirst has observed that 'the exception is different from anarchy and chaos' and that Schmitt's principal motive was to preserve the state and to defend constitutional politics . Because of this, Schmitt 'is certainly a conservative concerned with defending a political framework in which the "concrete order" of society can be preserved' (Hirst 1987: 20). The state must possess the type of authority which Oakeshott also ascribed to it.

Chris Thornhill has shown how, even when Schmitt appeared most to act as a mouthpiece for the Hitler state, his ideas matched neither genuine Nazi ideology nor the reality of Nazi power which ensured that 'contrary to Schmitt's fond projections, by 1935 the state, in the traditional sense of the word, had ceased to exist' (Thornhill 2000: 85). As we have seen in Chapter 7, Nazism substituted the party for the state. The distinctively political action which, for Schmitt, only the state may perform, is representation. In liberal-democratic orthodoxy, representation involves the articulation and, ultimately, the satisfaction of particular interests. Like Rousseau, Schmitt understood the concept of political representation in another way, as the articulation, indeed, the formation, of the general will, the political identity by means of which members experience their participation in the community, not as an accident or mere convenience, but as essential to them. The state can only represent society in this sense if it is distinct from its particular parts, standing over and above them as an autonomous legal structure which both reflects and determines the concrete order of the social totality. A people possesses political identity only to the extent that it is given representation in this sense by a state. That is, the state's primary function is to form the will of the people. All of its authority depends upon its success in accomplishing this. For Schmitt, the liberal vision of the representation of particular interests, even if all particular interests were included, fails to be representative in the full political sense because, on such a view, the object of political representation, the will of the people as a whole, its pure political identity, vanishes from sight. There can be no democratic representation because the concept of democracy implies an absolute identity between rulers and ruled, representatives and represented (Schmitt 1985: 26). The notion of a fully democratic state, then, is an illusion. In this respect Schmitt's political theory converges with elitism as we saw in Chapter 3.

## Leo Strauss

Although Strauss once wrote that 'liberal or constitutional democracy comes closer to what the classics demanded than any alternative that is viable in our age' (Strauss 1959: 113), even this statement shows that his estimation of the merits of liberal democracy was heavily qualified. Strauss knew that, in modern circumstances, the consent of the ruled was a practical requirement of government but the principle of consent can only be reconciled with what Strauss called 'natural right', the putative objective order known only by the truly wise (Strauss 1953), if such consent is not directed towards any particular political decision but given, rather, in response to a constitution which allegedly wise rulers have designed and to which the people pledge allegiance. That is, the constitution should be the corner-stone of a civil religion. Moreover, the terms of the constitution must be such as to allow those who control the state to act on behalf of the people. It is the system of representation to which citizens consent in a liberal democracy, not each and every action performed by representatives. Agreement to those particular concrete decisions need not be given because consent to the system of representation amounts to according to representatives the intellectual or moral superiority which authorises them to use the discretion required to take decisions for those incapable of grasping their own genuine interests. The historical importance of Strauss lies in his rehabilitation of the elitist vision of the state in the uncongenial circumstances of twentieth-century America.

Democracy proper, for Strauss, was as he took the ancients to have conceived of it, a 'universal aristocracy' (Strauss 1989: 314). This reflection led Strauss to consider the question which, as we have seen, preoccupied both Oakeshott and Schmitt, the question of the formation of the popular will in a modern society. If 'the people' are to rule, they must exhibit the virtues traditionally associated with 'the best', such as wisdom, courage and, above all, public-spiritedness. Such virtues will be present within the population at large only if what Strauss called 'liberal education', knowledge of the 'greatest minds', especially the classics, is provided as 'the necessary endeavor to found an aristocracy within democratic mass society' (1989: 314–15). Such an aristocracy will be composed of 'free men' who possess the type of wealth that affords them the leisure to acquire a 'liberal education'. These 'gentlemen' may rule on the basis of popular election (1989: 323–4, 326). However, Strauss noted that early modern theorists of government by consent, such as Locke, simply assumed that those with 'good breeding' would act as representatives of the people in a well-ordered political society. He also pointed out that the same assumption was made by the founding fathers of the American republic who took the view that, 'if the electorate is not depraved', it would select its representatives from among 'the best' (1989: 332–3). Because 'just government is government which rules in the interest of the whole society, and not merely of a part', those who are able to recognize and act for the sake of the social totality should be accorded power (1989: 325).

The predicament of modern republicanism, for Strauss, is twofold. On the one hand, there is 'the decay of religious education of the people'. It was not accidental, Strauss observed, that one of Locke's crucial assumptions was that the people's right of consent was conditional on the popular will having been formed by Christian teaching which induced 'everyone to regard himself as responsible for his actions and for his thoughts to a God who would judge him' (Strauss 1989: 331). In the absence of such traditional religious indoctrination, the people would be unfit for representative government. On the other hand, there is 'the decay of liberal education of the representative' (1989: 336). For Strauss, modern education has almost uniformly capitulated to some form or other of relativism. It is no longer capable of providing a liberal education in Strauss's sense, that is, the type of education appropriate to a free person whose liberty derives from his acquaintance with the

## The Modern State

objective moral order. Far from equipping some with the knowledge required if they are to represent others, the prevalence of relativism means that even 'the best' receive a merely technical education that has the politically disastrous effect of eliminating knowledge of natural right. Strauss's hope lay in the recovery of the ancient tradition of natural right. As the source for liberal education, it would instill, he believed, 'unhesitating loyalty to a decent constitution and even to the cause of constitutionalism', encouraging a spirit of 'moderation' which alone, he urged, would 'protect us against the twin dangers of visionary expectations from politics and unmanly contempt for politics' (1989: 345). Like Oakeshott's 'political education', 'natural right' would provide a support for political authority without which it would not stand.

## Practical politics

### Post-war conservatism in Europe

Nineteenth-century conservatism was the political expression of traditional elites which strove not to eliminate but to contain industrial society within the bounds of a civilisation in which their predominance was assured. However, industrialisation was to bring with it consequences fatal to that conservatism. Compelled by culture and allegiance to resist the rise of liberal democracy, from the end of the nineteenth century until 1945 conservative elites refused to accept representative institutions as the legitimate means of distributing and exercising power (Girvan 1994: 95). As we saw in Chapter 7, in choosing to ally themselves during the inter-war era with mass political movements recruited from the middle and lower-middle classes, fascism, national socialism and authoritarian nationalism, traditional elites throughout continental Europe hoped to harness 'the people' to an order in which those elites would remain dominant.

After 1945, as a result of the victory of the liberal democracies, the old conservatism was effectively extinguished in what became 'Western Europe'. New political elites emerged which were not nearly so readily identifiable as either 'left' or 'right' as those terms had been used in the nineteenth century. It has been said that after 1945 European conservatism was dead (Weiss 1977: 261). It would be more accurate to say that a new form of conservatism came into existence. Although the new conservatism was very different, it deserves the name 'conservatism' all the same. With two exceptions, the application of the term requires heavy qualification when used in reference to the post-war political parties, governments or regimes to which it has often been applied. This is because the new European conservatism was democratic as a matter of principle. The exceptions were Franco's Spain and Salazar's Portugal where traditional elites controlling the military were able to maintain power in the most economically backwards nations of western Europe until the 1970s when those nations too turned towards democracy. The short-lived post-war dictatorships of the Iberian peninsula might well be seen as manifestations of the type of conservatism endorsed by Schmitt. Charles de Gaulle, often regarded as the greatest of all post-war statesmen of the right, no matter how personally distasteful he found political parties, embraced electoral democracy. If the constitution of the Fifth Republic increased the powers of the President in a way consistent with Schmittian conservatism, de Gaulle 'like all republicans . . . accepted the programme of the law-based state, the sovereignty of the people, and all political and civil liberties' (Agulhon 1995: 388). Gaullism should be seen as a nationalist French equivalent to Christian democracy.

Of all those to whom the label continues to be applied, the Christian Democratic parties which have dominated the politics of post-war continental Europe seem least 'conservative'. As mass parties with a broad electoral appeal which are secular in practice, if not by profession, closely linked with trades unions and welfarist in social policy, it is difficult to describe European Christian democracy as 'conservative' in any ideological sense (Kalyvas 1996: 1). If social democracy can be said to 'socialise' capitalism from 'the left', the historical function of Christian democracy, the most politically significant force in post-war European politics, has been to reform it from 'the right' (Girvan 1994: 122). The fact that Christian Democratic parties tend to be reformist and gradualist must be seen in the light of the fact that they have held power more often than social democrats or socialists, as should their inclination to emphasise economic growth and pursue anti-inflationary policies rather than redistribution. It is not evidence of ideological conservatism. Apart from nationalism, especially in the case of France, and a tendency to implement social policies which may be seen to endorse traditional Christian beliefs in respect of the family, what their socialist opponents think of as the 'conservative' aspects of Christian democracy in the hands of a man like Adenauer might be more accurately described, like Gaullism, as managerialist (Watson 2003: 251; Williams 2003).

However, this attitude towards the state endorsed by post-war parliamentary conservatives in Europe is conservative in Oakeshott's sense. The authority of the Christian Democratic or Gaullist state rests on its capacity to protect and to provide 'satisfactions' for the civil society over which it presides, conceived of as a concrete social order. To consider arguably the most politically significant case, that of German Christian democracy, from the Adenauer era to the present day, the CDU and Bavarian CSU have been instrumental in creating institutions which direct the market economy towards social purposes, most notably generous welfare provision, worker participation, apprenticeship training, regional autonomy and a banking system that protected industry from predatory finance capital (Crouch 1995). Those contemporary European states which have been most shaped by the politics of Christian democracy, Germany, Austria, Belgium and the Netherlands are 'conservative' in a distinctively twentieth-century sense. They are states that, by sheltering them from unrestrained capitalism, have relatively successfully conserved their societies. The British Conservatives performed a comparable function up until 1979. However, Thatcherism represented a radical departure from conservatism (Green 2004: 280–90; and see Chapter 10 of this book). Under Margaret Thatcher the Conservative Party became effectively a British version of American neo-conservatism.

## American neo-conservatism

First-generation Americans from New York and Chicago, children of the Depression who at one time or another had been Marxists, by the mid-1960s the original 'neo-cons', Irving Kristol, Daniel Bell, Seymour Martin Lipset and Norman Podhoretz, had converted to meritocratic liberalism ostensibly because they came to view Johnson's Great Society as a betrayal of genuine liberalism. Trained in the social sciences, the neo-conservatives used the language of economics, sociology and political science to show that the progressive welfare state created dependency rather than freedom and, far from embodying an ideal of distributive justice, confiscated the tax dollars of the virtuous to reward the indolent and the criminal. Progressive education, whether through its denunciation of canonical texts or the introduction of quotas, threatened to destroy high culture. Insisting that the cause of growing anti-patriotic sentiment was not the war in Vietnam but a pervasive moral relativism, which the state did nothing to combat if, indeed, it did not inculcate it through the education system, neo-conservatives set great store by 'virtue'.

In this there is an unmistakeable affinity between neo-conservatism and the thought of Leo Strauss. Oakeshott, in contrast, repudiated the politics of virtue (Oakeshott 1996). The moralising emphasis characteristic of neo-conservatism marks it out as liberal but anti-libertarian. In a distinctively American fashion neo-conservatives are statist. As Irving Kristol has commented, whereas Hayekian libertarians conceive of the welfare state as 'the road to serfdom', neo-conservatives regard it as 'natural, indeed inevitable' (Stelzer 2004: 35). They object to a particular type of welfare state, one that produces what they regard as perverse moral consequences. In his most frequently referenced essay, Kristol declared himself in favour of the welfare state provided that its policies distinguished beween deserving recipients and the undeserving: the old, children and widows on the one hand; and the underclass composed of 'welfare mothers' and able-bodied but feckless males on the other hand (Stelzer 2004: 147–8). In practice, such an understanding of welfare by no means diminishes the extent of state action.

At the same time, neo-conservatives support tax cutting. Their 'basic assumption', as Kristol has explained, is that reducing the tax rate promotes economic growth that, in turn, will create general affuence. Large budget deficits as a consequence of reducing levels of taxation while maintaining government spending may have to be tolerated as a temporary measure. However, increasingly affluent taxpayers will naturally become 'more sensible about the fundamentals of economic reckoning' (Stelzer 2004: 35). It is the implementation of such neo-conservative thinking that accounts for an otherwise mysterious fact. Despite presenting itself as the anti-government party, Republicans have become 'the party of big government' (Micklethwait and Wooldridge 2005: 259). It has been estimated that the federal government's budget deficit will run at 3 per cent of GDP for the next decade, a figure which does not take into account a projected massive rise in the cost of funding social security and health care. Government spending under the current Bush administration at 8 per cent of GDP is higher than it was during Clinton's presidency. Federal spending on defence, education and social services increased as in 2000 George W. Bush implemented the largest tax-cutting programme since Ronald Regan (Micklethwait and Wooldridge 2005: 255–6). Such policies are explicable only if the 'basic assumptions' of the Bush administration are those of neo-conservatism.

The purpose of Bush's tax cuts was to stimulate economic growth. Those who derive disproportionate benefit from them are the wealthiest members of American society, that is, those who according to neo-conservative ethics are already virtuous and who will be the agents for economic growth and, therefore, affluence for American society at large. Similarly, government spending has been targeted towards the virtuous Republican-voting 'heartland', the South and the Mid-West. Hence, in 2001 US$25 billion was granted in direct subsidies to farmers and more federal spending funded infrastructure in rural areas. In 2002 tariffs on steel and lumber were introduced and the farm bill of the same year 'separated tax payers from some $180 billion over the next ten years, most of which will end up with big agribusiness of one sort or another' (Micklethwait and Wooldridge 2005: 257). The Republican Party has become the party of big business, not the free market. In return for funding its electoral campaigns, the Republican Party rewards corporate America with tax cuts and de-regulation.

Welfare spending under Republican administrations should be seen as a means of mitigating the social distortions that are a consequence of the corporate capitalism they support. Under the Clinton administration education spending rose from US$30 billion in 1993 to US$36 billion in the 2001 financial year. Under George W. Bush it rose to US$56 billion in 2003 and is estimated to increase to US$70 billion in 2008 (Micklethwait and Wooldridge 2005: 259). An example of the type of project which accounts for this enormous increase is the National Fatherhood Initiative through which hundreds of millions of dollars are spent in inner cities teaching 'relationship skills' to unmarried couples in order to 'strengthen marriage' (Micklethwait and Wooldridge 2005: 260). As John Gray has noted, the political fallacy of neo-conservativism derives from its astonishing assumption that there is something called 'virtue' which it is the responsibility of politicians to cultivate while simultaneously denying that the state has a duty to attend to the economic structures which shape behaviour (Gray 1997). The claim that unregulated and lightly taxed business will create affluence 'among all classes', as Kristol insisted (Stelzer 2004: 35), reveals an equally striking tolerance of economic inequality intelligible only given a uniquely American disposition to believe that wealth is the material expression of virtue. The commonly held but mistaken view that American neo-conservativism shares a suspicion of capitalism with European conservatism (Ball and Dagger 2006: 107–8) comes from accepting at face value the moralistic language which neo-conservatives use without attending either to the divergence between that language and the actual effects of neo-conservative policy or to its ideological function as a means of obscuring those effects.

A certain militarism is also considered to be the sign of a virtuous state by neo-conservatives and, as a consequence, Republican administrations under both Ronald Regan and George W. Bush increased defence spending. During the Cold war neo-conservatives outside and within government advocated military build-up, accusing those who preferred to use diplomacy with the communist enemy of appeasement. After 1989, neo-conservatives identified terrorism as the new enemy. In this the influence over American conservatism exercised by the followers of Leo Strauss was no less evident, an influence which became most apparent with the announcement of the policy of pre-emptive war known as the Bush doctrine. Referring with approval to Strauss by name and Schmitt by implication, in 2003 Kristol defined the neo-conservative attitude towards foreign policy as patriotic, opposed to 'international institutions that point to an ultimate world government', that is, the United Nations, and supportive of 'statesmen' who 'have the ability to distinguish friends from enemies'. Kristol did not hesitate to name George W. Bush as one such statesman (Stelzer 2004: 36–7).

The interpretation of American politics given by the followers of Leo Strauss, when it has not directly or indirectly influenced it, further reveals the political logic that governs the policies of the Bush administration. Harvey Mansfield has interpreted the *Federalist Papers* as containing, in addition to an appeal to the vulgar appetites of a commercial society, a call to political fame, nobility and greatness on the part of a natural aristocracy who should exercise leadership precisely because their principal motivation is the desire for political immortality. According to Mansfield the constitutional separation of powers was designed with two ends in view: one was to prevent tyranny; and the other was to allow the president to achieve glory. Hence the doctrine of the separation of powers advanced by the founding fathers established executive prerogative in foreign policy and in times of domestic crisis.

In Mansfield's opinion, it was the intention of the founders of the republic to permit the president to transcend both law and customary moral norms in order to achieve fame by leading the nation towards greatness. Such authority on the part of a natural aristocracy was viewed by the founders as the necessary counterpart to a republic otherwise dedicated to commerce and the satisfaction of lowly desires (Mansfield 1989, 1991). As Strauss himself had written, 'morality is possible only after its condition has been created, and this condition cannot be created morally; morality rests on what to moral men must appear to be immorality' (Strauss 1978: 255). The Straussian argument was that modern democracies required leadership no less than any other type of polity and that democratic leadership was legitimated by reference to an authority created by the achievement of greatness by statesmen acting outside the rule of law on behalf of the nation.

During the 1950s and early 1960s Straussians contested the pluralism most often associated with Robert Dahl according to which democracy is analysed as a means by which the people are represented. Against this the Straussians argued for the necessity of political leadership in a democracy. What pluralism left out of account, for the Straussians, was the fact that the properly political task to which statesman are called is not merely to register and satisfy the popular will but to create it (Devigne 1994: 55). The supposition here is that, in America, 'the people' will not exist as a coherent entity and social atomisation will result unless the state, through the office of the presidency, endows it with an identity and forms its general will. In order to do so, neo-conservative constitutional theorists have claimed, 'the chief executive must be a unitary power fettered neither by law nor Congress' (Devigne 1994: 70). It has surely been in alignment with this political logic that George W. Bush 'engineered the biggest shift of power from the congressional to the presidential branch in a generation' becoming thereby 'the most powerful president since Watergate had humbled the president in 1974' (Micklethwait and Wooldridge 2005: 132).

The most impressive achievement of the neo-conservative president has been the National Security Strategy or Bush Doctrine of 2002. This has three elements. First, it assumes unassailable American military power, committing the state to maintaining forces so strong that potential adversaries will be 'dissuaded' from attempting to rival the United States. Secondly, it commits American foreign policy to the promotion of 'freedom, democracy and free enterprise' as the 'single sustainable model for national success'. Thirdly, it prescribes unilateral pre-emptive warfare against terrorism (Mann 2004: 329). It is clear that the moralistic characteristic of neo-conservative domestic policy has been transferred to foreign policy in this vision of US military power serving as an instrument of democratic nation-building throughout the world. As Alan Dershowitz has pointed out, there is nothing new in the notion of pre-emptive action as an option in extreme circumstances. What is unprecedented is that according to the Bush Doctrine pre-emption is a central feature of national security policy. Moreover, whereas previous US presidents had anticipated the possibility of and occasionally sanctioned pre-emptive attacks, the Bush Doctrine justifies pre-emptive *war* (Dershowitz 2006: 157).

Neo-conservative politics is directed towards the establishment of a certain style of authority – the authority of negative freedom. In every other respect American conservatism is a species of liberalism. Domestically, this means that neo-conservatives use the power of the state to support big business. In foreign policy intense nationalism is a consequence of the fact that neo-conservatives believe themslves to be under a duty to preserve at all costs economic freedom in the homeland and an obligation to spread it abroad. The neo-conservative Robert Kagan has insisted on the necessity of what he calls the 'projection' of American military power as the means towards the creation of a 'liberal international order'. The metaphor resembles Emmanuel Todd's description of contemporary American foreign policy as 'theatrical micromilitarism' (Todd 2004: 15). The difference is that Kagan does not view what is projected as an illusion but as a messianic vision of America as the 'indispensable nation' 'Americans are idealists', he insists, believers in the destiny of their nation as a power which 'may be the best means of advancing human progress – and perhaps the only means' (Kagan 2003: 95, 100). This human progress toward a liberal international order will require the exercise of American military power. Whereas Europeans have grown used to the notion of a rule of law which constrains even the state and imagine that relations between states might be conducted under the auspices of international law, Kagan adopts the Hobbesian view endorsed by Schmitt that a sovereign power acting initially outside the rule of law must first establish the conditions under which legality applies. Within the international order, it is the duty of America, Kagan claims, to act as that extra-legal sovereign power. For Kagan this duty is a destiny, a call towards national greatness, which it would be un-American to resist.

From the European point of view such an attitude towards international relations is incompatible with conservatism. Schmitt explicitly opposed the notion of a global international order of any type. For him the proper field of application for sovereign power traditionally lay within the limits of the nation-state and to attempt to distinguish friends from enemies on a global scale could only lead to unlimited warfare (Schmitt 2003). The primary function of the state for Schmitt, as for Oakeshott, is to protect a concrete social order or, as Gray put it, a particular 'cultural form' within a world composed of a plurality of such forms. The universalism of American neo-conservative foreign policy represents not conservatism in the original European sense but a species of liberal imperialism. In terms of Oakeshott's political thought, neo-conservatism appears as a form of 'rationalism', the antithesis of genuine conservatism. The fact that the term 'conservative' is used by Americans in ways that are increasingly unrecognisable to Europeans indicates a difference in political culture so profound that mutual misunderstanding has become common. For instance, Todd's claim that American foreign policy 'is about as directed as the current of a river' simply reveals how disinclined a European social scientist will be to take seriously the purely political vocation which men like Kagan experience as a matter of the greatest urgency. American neo-conservative foreign policy has a direction. It is to recreate the world in the image of the indispensable nation or, as Irving Kristol once referred to that nation of immigrants, 'an ideological nation' (Stelzer 2004: 35). Just as Bolshevism could not survive without seeking to export revolution, the political power of neo-conservatism derives from its recognition that the very identity of America requires that it Americanise the world. Without that vocation political authority within America itself would collapse. Similarly, in respect of domestic policy, whereas European conservatives use the state to protect civil society, the fact that neo-conservatism has been able to expose American society to unrestrained capitalism shows how very different from European societies the American social order is. There are no American equivalents to the cultural forms which European conservatism seeks to preserve. America has become what Karl Polanyi termed a 'market society', one in which the principles of capitalism have penetrated every sphere of society (Polanyi 1944).

## Bibliography

Agulhon, M. (1995), *The French Republic 1879–1992*, trans. A. Nevill (Oxford: Blackwell).
Ball, T. and Dagger, R. (2006), *Political Ideologies and the Democratic Ideal*. (New York: Pearson).
Crouch, C. (1995), 'Co-operation and competition in an institutionalized economy: the case of Germany', in C. Crouch and D. Marquand (eds), *Ethics and Markets* (Oxford: Blackwell).
Davis, N. (1997), *Europe: A History* (London: Pimlico).
Dershowitz, A. M. (2006), *Preemption: A Knife That Cuts Both Ways* (New York: Norton).
Devigne, R. (1994), *Resisting Conservatism: Oakeshott, Strauss and the Response to Postmodernism* (New Haven CT: Yale University Press).
Franco, P. (2004), *Michael Oakeshott* (New Haven CT: Yale University Press).
Freeden, M. (1986), *The New Liberalism* (Oxford: Clarendon Press).
Gilmour, I. (1978), *Inside Right: A Study of Conservatism* (London: Quartet Books).
Girvan, B. (1994), *The Right in the Twentieth Century: Conservatism and Democracy* (London: Pinter).
Gray, J. (1997), 'The undoing of conservatism', in J. Gray and D. Willetts (eds), *Is Conservatism Dead?* (London: Profile Books).
Green, E. H. H. (2004), *Ideologies of Conservatism* (Oxford: Oxford University Press).
Greenleaf, W. H. (1983), *The British Political Tradition Volume Two: The Ideological Inheritance* (London and New York: Methuen).
Himmelfarb, G. (1986), *Marriage and Morals Among the Victorians* (London: Faber).
Hirst, P. (1987), 'Carl Schmitt's decisionism', *Telos*, 72: 15–26.
Honderich, T. (1991), *Conservatism* (Harmondsworth: Penguin).
Huntington, S. (1957), 'Conservatism as an ideology', *American Political Science Review*, 51: 454–73.
Kagan, R. (2003), *Paradise and Power: America and Europe in the New World Order* (London: Atlantic Books).
Kalyvas, S. N. (1996), *The Rise of Christian Democracy in Europe* (Ithaca NY: Cornell University Press).
Mann, J. (2004), *Rise of the Vulcans: The History of Bush's War Cabinet* (Harmondsworth: Penguin).
Mansfield, H., Jr. (1989), *Taming the Prince: The Ambivalence of Modern Executive Power* (New York: Free Press).
Mansfield, H., Jr. (1991), *America's Constitutional Soul* (Baltimore MD: Johns Hopkins Press).

McClelland, J. (1996), *A History of Western Political Thought* (London: Routledge).
Micklethwait, J. and Wooldridge, A. (2005), *The Right Nation* (Harmondsworth: Penguin).
Muller, J. Z. (ed.) (1997), *Conservatism: An Anthology of Social and Political Thought from David Hume to the Present* (Princeton NJ: Princeton University Press).
Oakeshott, M. (1975), *On Human Conduct* (Oxford: Clarendon Press).
Oakeshott, M. (1989), *The Voice of Liberal Learning* (New Haven CT: Yale University Press).
Oakeshott, M. (1991), *Rationalism in Politics and Other Essays* (Indianapolis IN: Liberty Fund).
Oakeshott, M. (1993), *Religion, Politics and the Moral Life* (New Haven CT: Yale University Press).
Oakeshott, M. (1996), *The Politics of Faith and the Politics of Scepticism* (New Haven CT: Yale University Press).
Polanyi, K. (1944), *The Great Transformation*, (London: Gollancz).
Quinton, A. (1978), *The Politics of Imperfection* (London: Faber).
Sartori, G. (1989), 'The essence of the political in Carl Schmitt', *Journal of Theoretical Politics*, 1 (January): 63–75.
Schmitt, C. (1985), *The Crisis of Parliamentary Democracy*, trans. E. Kennedy (Cambridge MA: MIT Press).
Schmitt, C. (1988), *Political Theology*, trans. G. Schwab (Cambridge MA: MIT Press).
Schmitt, C. (1996), *The Concept of the Political*, trans. G. Schwab (Chicago IL: University of Chicago Press).
Schmitt, C. (2003), *The Nomos of the Earth in the International Law of the Jus Publicum Europaeum*, trans. G. Ulmen (New York: Telos Press).
Scruton, R. (1980), *The Meaning of Conservatism* (Harmondsworth: Penguin).
Selden, A. and Snowdon, P. (2001), *A New Conservative Century?* (London: Centre for Policy Studies).
Stelzer, I. (ed.) (2004), *Neoconservatism* (London: Atlantic Books).
Strauss, L. (1953), *Natural Right and History*, (Chicago IL: University of Chicago Press).
Strauss, L. (1959), *What is Political Philosophy?* (Chicago IL: University of Chicago Press).
Strauss, L. (1978), *Thoughts on Machiavelli* (Chicago IL: University of Chicago Press).
Strauss, L. (1989), *An Introduction to Political Philosophy*, H. Gildin (ed.) (Detroit MI: Wayne State University Press).
Thornhill, C. (2000), *Political Theory in Modern Germany* (Cambridge: Polity).

Todd, E. (2004), *After the Empire: The Breakdown of the American Order*, trans. C. J. Delogu (London: Constable).

Watson, J. (2003), 'The internal dynamics of Gaullism 1958–69', in N. Atkins and F. Tallett (eds), *The Right in France* (London: I. B. Tauris).

Weiss, J. (1977), *Conservatism in Europe 1700–1945* (London: Thames and Hudson).

Williams, C. (2003), *Adenauer: The Father of New Germany* (London: Abacus).

CHAPTER NINE

# Feminisms: the Gendering of the State

*Erika Cudworth*

The emergence of feminist theories of the gendered quality of state institutions and practices is of relatively recent origin. This chapter contextualises feminist approaches in terms of the exclusion of women as citizens in Western 'liberal democracies' and debates in the nineteenth and early twentieth centuries. The regional character of this phenomenon will also be noted with respect to post-colonial state formation. In many non-Western states, feminism and nationalism were closely entwined and the post-colonial state was seen as gender inclusive.

Varieties of feminism have problematised mainstream definitions of the state, but given the significant differences in feminist theory a variety of feminist definitions can be found. Theories discussed include Catherine Mackinnon's radical feminist model of the state as an agent of patriarchal interests, Carole Pateman's understanding of the liberal state as gender dichotomous, Sylvia Walby's assessment of the state as an arena of competing interests and demands biased along gendered, racialised and class lines and Iris Marion Young's 'radical pluralist' understanding of the state. The phenomenon of 'state feminism' will be the basis of much of the discussion of the practical implications of such theorising including: the way Iranian women have negotiated with a 'patriarchal state'; the 'anti-pornography' ordinances in parts of the United States which have divided feminists; and the impact of feminism on the British Labour Party administrations since 1997.

## Feminisms: the Gendering of the State

Feminism is currently perceived as being in some form of crisis or decline, and some of the 'rights' for which Western feminists of the 'second wave' of activism in the early 1970s campaigned are now taken for granted practices. The challenge of post-modern thinking has meant that some of the intellectual energies of feminism have been preoccupied with obtuse debate rather than critical engagement with political institutions and practices. Yet, a dismissal of the feminist project is premature. The majority of the women do not live in liberal democracies and vast numbers lack any basic rights. The increased influence of religious fundamentalism, both in the West and without, may have meant at deterioration in the life chances of many women. Apart from the Netherlands and Scandinavian countries, women are, relatively, starkly absent from political elites (Lovenduski 1999). All kinds of feminism have argued that gender relations are problematic, that inequalities are political, and that these are evidenced in a range of the institutions of the state.

## Context

There is a rich diversity of approaches within feminism, and Maggie Humm (1992) rightly notes that the plural form, 'feminisms', is a more accurate descriptor for the corpus of feminist theorisations. While typologies of feminism almost inevitably underestimate the nuances and complexity of the work of individual theorists (Evans 1995: 8), some kinds of feminist thought have been more explicitly engaged with the political than others, which explains the emphasis here on particular strands – liberal, radical and socialist feminism.

Feminist approaches to the political have problematised the public–private divide. In liberal pluralist understandings of the democratic state, the freedom of individuals is linked to the limits on state power, specifically, keeping 'politics' out of the private lives of citizens as far as possible. Feminists have questioned the extent to which this distinction is universal, arguing that it is a culturally specific phenomenon (Sassoon 1987) and a distinction that is at best, unclear, (Landes 1998). The normativity of this distinction has obscured both the work that takes place within the household and the exploitation and violence that may be embedded in 'private lives'. Nancy Fraser (1989: 168) has referred to a process of depoliticisation of the private sphere, where domestic 'institutions depoliticize certain matters by personalizing and/or familiarizing them'. This process is understood as itself, political. The boundary of the public and private shifts over time and the distinction has been used to bolster established relations of gendered power (Fraser 1998). Some writers of the early second wave argued for a dissolution of the public/private divide (Greer 1970), while others have been more cautious in their appraisal of the liberal tradition and argued for a recasting of the public-private division in ways which open up the public sphere to competing interests and pressures of a revived pluralism (Elshtain 1981: 352). This position has been more pertinent latterly in feminist thinking about the state.

In the politics of liberal democracies, women's collective political behaviour has been seen as exceptional and attempts by individual women to influence or enter the political elite, anomalous (Currell 1974). Women have not had the same relationship as men to the institutions of liberal democratic governance as, in much of Europe and the United States, they did not have the political rights of the citizen (to vote and stand for elected office) until the 1920s, nor did they have features of civil citizenship (such as the right to own property and sign contracts) until the late nineteenth century. In many emerging liberal democracies, citizenship was not constituted in one period. Rather, different kinds of citizenship rights and obligations were secured for different social groups excluded on grounds of class, ethnicity and gender in variant combinations (Walby 1997: 171–8). The demand for political citizenship was part of a range of issues which formed the basis of a struggle for women's 'equality'. The diverse rights for which women campaigned included those of professional employment, jury service, property ownership, initiation of divorce proceedings and protection from domestic violence (Banks 1981). Walby (1988) argues that the rights of voting proved in the British case to be a crucial step from which further rights of civil and social citizenship could be attained. It is not only the case that the women of most Western states came later to citizenship, but feminists have raised questions as to what sort of citizens women were. Women's private work of caring for the young and the elderly has proved particularly problematic in welfare states in which paid employment is the main route to accessing health care and support in old age (Lister 1997, 1999). The casting of the citizens in the form of a male full-time paid worker has meant that women are a 'problem' as citizens of liberal states with welfare systems.

Recent disputes in feminism, particularly in the United States have focused on what has become known as the 'ethics of care debate'. Liberal states pay insufficient attention to the demands of 'biological time' (Mellor 1997), and thereby perpetuate gender inequalities. Sarah Ruddick (1990) argues that political priorities need to change. We need a politics based on 'maternal thinking', an empathetic understanding which considers the care of the most vulnerable in policy debate and decision making, and would result in a check on militarism and environmental damage. Susan Okin suggests that if more men were to take a greater level of caring responsibility in the family, this 'would increase that capacity to identify with, and fully comprehend the viewpoints of others' (Okin 1990: 18) and would improve their actions in public life. Such ideas have been both influential and contested. Mary Dietz (1985), for example, considers that the way in which mothers 'think' is often selfish (based on particular family needs and circumstances), individualistic and patronising (often itself a product of subordination (Segal 1987)), and its inherent limits cannot provide a satisfactory basis for considering citizenship and political morality.

The history of women's relationship with the formal politics of liberal democratic states may explain persistent patterns of marginalisation and under representation throughout the twentieth century (Randall 1987: 95–115). In developing countries, however, the situation was rather different. In most cases, women gained the franchise at the same historical period as men – there was a 'moment' within which the nation-state was 'created' – at the point of national independence from the colonial power. Floya Anthias and Nira Yuval-Davis (1989: 7) suggest that women are implicated in the processes of nation-state building in several important ways. Women are biological reproducers of ethnic collectivities and social reproducers of culture and ethnic–national boundaries, and they often actively participate in national economic, political and also military struggles. Kumari Jayawardena (1986) shows that feminists actively pushed for the inclusion of women and women's rights in nationalist politics in the late nineteenth and early twentieth centuries. She argues that feminism has endogenous roots in such countries and cannot be dismissed as a Western imposition (1986: 2–3), while also examining the impact of Westernisation on feminist debates, which in some countries was very strong.

There are variations in the extent of change in gender relations in post-colonial societies, and the freedoms of a new post-colonial gender regime may have been irrelevant to the lives of the majority of poor women. This said, attaining formal equality at the point of nation building has meant a different focus for feminists in the poorer regions of the post-colonial world. In particular, they have considered the extent to which women share the same national project as men. Anthias and Yuval-Davis (1989) suggest that women may be just as committed to the same national project, whereas Jayawardena (1986) suggests there may be different priorities according to gender. Cynthia Enloe (1989) goes further in suggesting that the project of nation building *per se* is gendered. In the post-colonial context, some countries have lost the semblance of democracy they might have had following decolonisation, and this is not a gendered phenomenon – all voting rights are usually lost in the institution of a military government. There have been exceptions to this, however, where the establishment of certain kinds of 'Islamic states', for example, in Iran after the 1979 revolution and Afghanistan after the Soviet occupation, has meant the loss of civil and political rights for women alone.

In order to contextualise feminist state theory, feminist understandings of social and political power need consideration. Radical feminism has argued for a notion of gender relations as structured in terms of male domination in all spheres of social and economic life. The concept of 'patriarchy' has often been deployed to describe gender relations in terms of a system of male domination (Millett 1977). Radical feminists have been particularly concerned with women's sexual exploitation (within families, through prostitution and pornography) and with issues of violence against women (including rape, domestic battery and sexual harassment). The focus on the state has been relatively absent from radical feminist analyses as writers of the early second wave did not consider electoral and party politics of much relevance in securing social change or analysing power relations. Radical feminists have argued for a redefinition of the political, and for Kate Millet (1977: 23), the term 'politics' encompasses all power-structured relationships. Many of the arenas deemed private and excluded from political analysis are arenas fraught with power relations of gender, including sexual preference (Rich 1980) and practice (Dworkin 1988; Jeffreys 1990), and women's relationship with their bodies (Bartky 1990; Weitz 2003). Problematically, the implication that politics is 'everywhere' and everything is political effectively makes the term 'politics' meaningless, as one cannot discriminate between that which has political characteristics and that which has not.

While this remains a dilemma, some radical feminists have attended to the role of the state with regard to issues of fertility control and reproductive technologies, and violence against women. For Jalna Hanmer (1978) the lack of state intervention (in terms of the police and courts system or welfare services) in cases of domestic violence means that the state is collusive with male power, with its non-intervention functional for the maintenance of a system of 'heteropatriarchy'. Little is said of any pressures other than the interests of heterosexual men in terms of whose social power the state is viewed as an instrument. While radical feminists have been sceptical of engagement with mainstream politics, they have identified a range of patriarchal interests served in different ways by state institutions, and identified possibilities for political struggle and engagement with formal institutions.

Marxist feminist accounts from the early second wave tended to treat women's oppression or as they preferred, exploitation, as a by-product of the systemic relations of capitalism (Breugal 1979), focusing particularly on the function of women's unpaid domestic labour for the capitalist system. Mary McIntosh (1978) grafts an analysis of the social reproduction of gender onto an analysis of the capitalist state, which acts in the interests of the dominant class relations and assists capital accumulation. Gender inequality is derived from an understanding of the logic of capitalism for the state upholds the subordination of women by its promotion (through taxation and welfare systems) of a specific family form in which women overwhelmingly undertake unpaid and unvalued domestic service. This arrangement ensures the cheap reproduction of labour power; women literally reproduce the future labour force, and their domestic work both reproduces the conditions of labour and compromises their position in paid employment. Such an analysis does not take account of the specific benefits to men from the contemporary structure of the heterosexual family (Delphy 1984; Jeffreys 1990), or explain why the state should seek to secure male dominance and privilege (Pringle and Watson 1992: 58). More recently, socialist feminism has debated the ways in which both capitalism and racism intersect with gender relations. Most socialist feminists have eschewed the notion of patriarchy (Bottero 1998), although some sophisticated accounts have attempted to combine a systemic analyses of patriarchy with systemic relations of capitalism, racism and post-colonialism (Mies 1984, 1998). The predominant view is that gender relations cannot be reduced to relations of capital (Brenner 2000) and, thus, the state is seen as a site where multiple relations of power are in evidence.

For liberal feminism, the differential treatment and social, economic and political marginalisation of women in Western liberal states has been ameliorated by legal reform, and liberals seek to secure the same treatment under the law as men receive (Friedan 1983). Although the liberal state has been a vehicle of gender discrimination, the pressures from various marginalised social groups are making the state more properly pluralist. While post-modern feminism appears at odds with the liberal tradition, questioning its foundation as an Enlightenment project, in some ways post-modern influenced analyses of the political have much in common with liberal approaches. Post-modern feminists are concerned with gender as a form of difference, but also make much of the extent to which gender should be seen as a contested category. They have questioned the concept of women as a coherent entity whose 'needs' or 'rights' are denied in some way, arguing that the category 'woman' is highly fractured (Fraser and Nicholson 1990) and uncertain as a basis for making political claims (Coole 1993: 222). Ironically perhaps, notions of women's political interests and of the state as a set of coherent institutions are 'under challenge just at the point when feminist political scientists are getting a hearing in their discipline' (Pringle and Watson 1992: 54).

## Definition

Feminist engagement with the discipline of politics has tested the accuracy of many concepts: citizenship; justice; representation; and equality, for example, have all been the subject of critique and the development of new conceptualisations (Hirschman and Di Stephano 1996; Squires 1999). In non-feminist political science, the state has often been defined in terms of a set of specific institutions associated with governance, rule making and regulation or as a body with particular functions, such as the maintenance of social order (Dunleavy and O'Leary 1987: 1–3). There are difficulties with both kinds of definition. The organisational or institutional definition contains a number of presumptions problematic for gender relations. The state is seen as differentiated from the rest of society – such things as public and private spheres of life are recognisably separate, whereas feminist understandings of politics have questioned this dichotomous assumption of a public sphere of state activity, the market and paid employment, in contrast to a privatised realm of domestic and household activity (Elshtain 1981). Secondly, this definition sees the state as a set of insitutions, which is sovereign and authoritative within a given territory and has a monopoly of legitimate coercion. As research on domestic and other intra-personal violence indicates, some men are able to deploy considerable amounts of physical violence against women, and they do so with relative impunity given the inadequacies of state policies to prevent and address this (Kelly 1999).

Functional definitions presume that the state undertakes certain activities and objectives and can be empirically identified with such activities, and/or that state institutions undertake certain practice that result in desired effects (stability, coercion, legitimacy). These understandings are a feature of Marxist attempts to expand liberal parameters (see Chapter 4), so that the media, education system and the 'family' become incorporated as elements of the state. The state is seen as a body mediating between class groups and/or understood primarily in terms of its functions for a system of capitalism.

The key element of feminist definitions has been to question the assumptions of a range of non-feminist theorisations in stressing that the state has other interests in addition to those of class, and is engaged with and shaped by a complex array of social forces including those of ethnicity, nation, race and, particularly, gender. Some of the best known accounts are those that add a gendered dimension to liberal pluralist conceptions. Liberal analyses of the early second wave argued that the state is gendered due to the sex of its personnel – women were underrepresented in politics due to cultural bias (Epstein 1970), gender role constraints (Kirkpatrick 1974) and political socialisation (Currell 1974). Radical feminists have implicitly defined the state as a series of patriarchal institutions. They consider the state to be a product of gendered relations of unequal power and the oppression of women. The structures and institutions of the state and law have been developed by men and protect their collective interests. Thus, the liberal feminist concern with the gender of policy makers is misplaced. The patriarchal nature of the state will not be remedied by getting more women into politics, as individual representatives in state legislatures are almost irrelevant to policy outcomes. The liberal state rarely concedes to feminist demands, and where it does, this is very limited (Greer 1999). Some argue political reform may actually provide some kind of legitimation for the liberal state itself and for women's oppression, equal opportunities sometimes appear to have been achieved, while there has been little alteration of relations of political power (Mackinnon 1989). Marxism has seen the state as a capitalist formation, an agent of the interests of capitalists or functioning to perpetuate the conditions for the reproduction and maintenance of the capitalist system. More recent socialist feminism, however, sees the state as an arena in which gender inequalities play themselves out alongside other kinds of social stratifications. Post-modern influenced accounts, which sometimes draw on the Foucauldian notion of 'governmentality', and see the state as a distinct sphere of activity in which power relations are made and remade, and in which various political actors engage in strategic alliances, compromises and struggles in order to secure policy goals (Pringle and Watson 1992).

Shirin Rai argues that much feminist state theory has been Western in inception, and reflects the experiences of those living in secular liberal democracies. States in the 'third world' have particular definitional characteristics such as weak infrastructural powers, corrupt practices and inabilities to enforce policy (Rai 1996: 33–4). Compared with Western states, states in poor countries have limited welfare systems and provide women in particular with little support. Weak states often place political expediency above any claims made regarding social justice, and often women encounter the state when they transgress it, an encounter that may well involve violence. While I acknowledge the specific characteristics Rai raises, I am not convinced we might set 'first' world against 'third world' states in this way – there is a complex array of state forms in poorer countries. Many of these characteristics apply to some first world states also. The four theorists selected for detailed discussion are first world feminists who draw most strongly on liberal democratic examples, but many of the points they make are pertinent to a variety of state forms.

## Theorists

Catharine Mackinnon (1989) has theorised the state from a radical feminist perspective, illustrating with examples of policy and law with respect to equal opportunities, abortion, domestic violence,

## Feminisms: the Gendering of the State

pornography and rape. Mackinnon does not argue for a theory of 'patriarchy', but understands gender relations as a social system of oppressive relations, which cannot be reduced to the operation of class. For Mackinnon there is little, if anything, which is non sexualised, non-power dichotomous and thus non-political (1989: 1, 60–1, 128–34). Gender is a 'sexualised hierarchy' which is socially constructed and based on social relations of male power that pervade popular and high culture, sexual and intimate relationships, forms of public and private life in politics and work. This system of gendered oppression reproduces its relations – it is relatively static over time (1989: 127–30). When such analytics are applied to the state, there are strong similarities with 'instrumentalist' Marxist accounts wherein the state is run by capitalists and reflects their interests, for example, 'The liberal state . . . constitutes the social order in the interest of men as a gender – through its legitimating norms, forms, relation to society and substantive policies' (1989: 162). However, in liberal democracies, the state must appear gender neutral, objective. The state both reflects and reproduces social relations; it incorporates a 'male' standpoint and institutionalises the collective interests of men. The liberal state has been institutionally designed with the presumption of male citizenry and on the basis of legitimate male social power (1989: 238). The privatisation of women and prohibition within the liberal democratic model on states intervening in civil society, means that 'the domain in which women are distinctively subordinated and deprived of power, has been placed beyond the reach of legal guarantees' (1989: 165). Liberal legalism cannot account for structural social inequalities because it assumes that society is already fundamentally equal. Equal opportunities policies are actually a means through which gendered social power is maintained, because such policies maintain sexual inequalities by appearing to address them, and thereby, provide legitimation for male social power (1989: 237). Again, there is similarity here with some Marxist accounts, which see the state as legitimating itself through the manufacture of 'false consciousness' (see Chapter 5). For Mackinnon, women cannot be 'equal' to men, for equality means getting the same things for women as can be secured for men, while at the same time prohibiting little or nothing that socially disadvantages women exclusively (1989: 222). Critics have alleged that she has 'backed herself into a corner' (Watson and Pringle 1992: 62) here, for it is difficult to see on what grounds the patriarchal state can be challenged. I think

Mackinnon would respond that her position is tenable while also agreeing that it is contradictory. Feminists must fight for change despite the odds being stacked overwhelmingly against feminist policy solutions that might secure any significant change.

Mackinnon's critics are concerned that she does not allow for other types of social inequality that the state may reflect, and thereby reduces the state to the effect of one kind of relationship – gender (Walby 1990). While Mackinnon is sometimes less careful than she might be, she makes clear that the state is classed as well as gendered. Her point is to address the lack of explicitly feminist theorising about the state rather than to dismiss class as an analytic tool. She is well aware of the paradoxes of her position and it is in her endorsement of and engagement with political struggles for women's 'equality' in the face of the impossibility of such projects that distinguishes her from the more pessimistic cast of elite theory (see Chapter 3). Mackinnon is accused of apparent essentialism in seeing interests as gendered, yet as Phillips notes (1995: 68, 76) the argument that women or men are diverse constituencies, in complex relationships with each other across multiple differences does not counteract the notion that interests can be gendered. Rosemary Pringle and Sophie Watson (1992: 64) also accuse Mackinnon of assuming that the state reflects gender inequalities rather than also constituting them, but my reading is that Mackinnon explicitly makes this very point. Critics might still point to a lack of dynamism, but it is more of the case that for Mackinnon small changes are not enough to constitute a remaking of relations of social power.

The arguments made by Carole Pateman have strong resonance. In *The Sexual Contract* (1988) Pateman critiques contract theory in the history of modern political thought for ignoring the unwritten, uncodified and mystified, contract between the sexes. Contract theorists spoke often of the contract between the citizens and the liberal state, while ignoring the gender divisions in society associated with a rigid dichotomy between public and private spheres (Pateman 1988: 20–4). Pateman argues that the political world appears to be about the contractual relations between the state and the citizenry, while the 'sexual contract' (the key social form of which is marriage and/or heterosexual cohabitation) is seen as private and non-political. The original social contract (between 'citizens' and government) was also a sexual contract in which men overthrew the rule of the fathers (for example, the heredity monarchy) and instituted a fraternal agreement (unwritten, but normative) which guaranteed men access to women's bodies. Pateman argues that the liberal democratic state is underpinned by the notion of 'fraternity', and this part of the French revolutionary mantra 'means exactly what it says – brotherhood' (1988: 74). The fraternal state presumes that men are political actors, have established the state and civil society, and act in the interests of the population as a whole (1989: 32–4).

Liberal feminist demands for political equality have led to what Pateman (1988) refers to as 'Wollstonecraft's dilemma'. In the eighteenth century, Mary Wollstonecraft (1792), in seeking to extend liberal ideas to the situation of women, was caught on the question of how domestic responsibility might bear on women's participation in the public sphere. Wollstonecraft's solution was that women were equal with men in terms of educational and occupational opportunities up to the point of marriage, when they would 'choose' to be equal but different, and undertake the work of the household and child care. Pateman (1989: 17) argues citizenship rights and responsibilities have been based on a paradigm in which women can be considered as equals only to the extent they are able to behave like male citizens. While choice is essential in the notion of citizenship, for many women choices may be so constrained that they are not 'free'.

Questions Pateman raised in the late 1980s are salient in the current 'ethics of care' debate within feminism, particularly in relation to the question of how the state should respond to the inequities attendant on privatised and feminised 'care' of children, elders and the infirm (Lister 1999). However, Wendy Brown (1993) considers that Pateman's historical account of the incorporation of patriarchy into liberal politics is not helpful in understanding the continuation of patriarchal relations in contemporary times. Because Pateman locates women's subordination in contract, she looks to contemporary forms of contract with some basis in law – such as marriage, surrogacy and prostitution. Many of these examples are not entirely convincing, and Pateman is on firmer ground when drawing on those from the eighteenth and nineteenth centuries. It is difficult, therefore, for her to sustain her argument that patriarchal relations were little changed over the twentieth century. We do not need contracts in order to sustain patterns of social relations which disadvantage women, for women's historical material and ideological association with the private-domestic has resulted in powerful discourses of domesticity which have adapted to suit contemporary social practices (Squires 1999). In some ways more pessimistic than Mackinnon, there is no space in Pateman's patriarchal state for feminist engagement and change. Other theorists have suggested that state feminism has shifted gender relations in important ways in some regions of the globe, and that feminism is engaged with the re-shaping of gender through pressure on local, national and supranational states. The accounts of Sylvia Walby and Iris Marion Young are similar in this respect, but Walby retains the notion of the states as implicated in systemic relations of class, ethnicities and gender, whereas Young provides an account influenced by post-modern theory.

Walby's earlier work is situated within what she and others (Bryson 2003) refer to as 'dual systems' theory, which draws on Marxist and radical feminism in considering that the state is both capitalist and patriarchal. Zillah Eisenstein, for example, saw the state as a site where the interests of capitalism and patriarchy cohere – patriarchal interests are represented by male capitalists who dominate decision making (Eisenstein 1984: 92). Walby also conceptualises the state as both capitalist and patriarchal, but also sees it as an arena for the conflict of interests between the imperatives of gender domination and capital, and argues that 'the actions of the state should not simply be read off from the interests of logic of the system; rather, there is a degree of autonomy . . . political struggle is important in determining the state's actions' (Walby 1990: 159). The state is systematically structured as patriarchal, however, and its actions at national level are more often in line with the interests of men than those of women in a variety of policy locales such as employment, family law, welfare imperatives and criminal justice issues.

Walby stresses that the way the state represents and responds to patriarchal interests alters over time, differs cross-culturally and is the outcome of competing pressures. The role of the state in maintaining gendered relations of power was stronger at the end of the twentieth century, she argues, than at the end of the nineteenth because there has been a shift in the form of patriarchy from a predominantly private system of control of women (within the household) to a predominantly public mode. Women are less privatised in liberal democracies than they were. Women's access to political power has meant key changes, many of which are positive (although not unambiguously so), have been secured in the areas of employment and divorce law, equal opportunities, educational achievement, the welfare state and interpersonal violence. However, she also considers that '(w)omen's exclusion from the state was replaced by their subordination within it' (Walby 1990: 179), for in the public world of politics and employment women are still occupying less important niches.

This said, she argues that women's collective political action has played a major role in shifting patriarchal relations, and changes in the gendering of the economy have been structured by the actions of national and supranational states (Walby 1997: 13). While globalisation has widened inequities associated with class through the prioritisation of credentialised education, and increased nationally based, ethnically associated forms of inequality in the economic North, it has 'often speeded the modernization of the gender regime' (Walby 2003: 5). Supranational states have delivered equality in some areas through legislative mechanisms, notably in the case of paid employment over which the European Union has considerable powers (Walby 2004a: 16–18). Thus, democratic states have been open to the articulation of women's political interests, and the 'regulatory state' (Walby 1999) of the EU facilitates and enables the articulation of 'women's views' through mechanisms such as the European Women's Lobby (2004a: 15). Although nation-states remain formations of intense power, they are increasingly compromised in important ways by international political organisations. The state at various levels is implicated in reproducing and remaking gender relations and is a site of contestation where feminists have won arguments and influenced decisions.

The way Walby's understanding of politics has developed is not a common trajectory in socialist feminism. The analytic and strategic shift of the 1980s and 1990s was predominantly a move from 'big' theories of causative explanation, to those emphasising a politics of difference and identities fragmented by the complex intersections of social diversity. Iris Marion Young is concerned with 'identity' in respect to a range of marginalised 'groups' (1990: 7). She uses the term 'group oppression' in referring to sexism, racism, homophobia, ageism and ableism (1990: 132). Politics is about groups, and those groups are political actors motivated by collective identity. Groups shift in composition, non-politicised groups become politicised and enter the political process and others depart from the political scene. This appears to be little different from early pluralism, yet for Young groups are not aggregates of individuals

## The Modern State

but are patterns of relationships arising from inequities in social power (1990: 44).

Young is also concerned with democratic mechanisms for participation and accountability. Her view of contemporary liberal democratic states is that the representation of certain groups is impeded, often severely. Groups are not able to articulate their interests and are thus oppressed, and the democratic system requires modification so that groups can be strengthened and have channels of access (Young 1990: 40). For Young, structural inequalities are a series of oppressions and privileges for particular groups, and must be eliminated by institutional change at state level. Despite formal legal equality, social goods are distributed most unequally. Procedural fairness is required, which compensates (only those) groups with a history of exclusion, with a view to equalising political influence in the policy process. Whether this renders a state representative is not particularly clear. Anne Phillips (1993: 93–101) has questioned the extent to which members of Young's 'groups' would be representative, because Young does not specify that these groups must mirror or be a representative sample of the groups from which they came. A further difficulty, acknowledged by Young, is that groups are extensively and complexly 'cross-cutting' and 'people' are members of a range of potential groups.

There is overlap here with liberal approaches, which have been increasingly concerned with the ability of the liberal democratic state to cater for culturally plural societies. Will Kymlicka (1989), for example, has made a sustained argument for the 'group rights' of a 'stable and geographically distinct historical community' such as aboriginal and Inuit communities, arguing for special protection for threatened cultural communities (see Chapter 2). Both Kymlicka and Young struggle with the questions of what might be done when differences within groups emerge, how decisions might be made on which groups might be represented and which might not, and what mechanisms there are for establishing what a particular group wants at a given time and in a given context. Whatever the difficulties, this notion of group representation has been influential in the practical politics of many liberal democracies. Such group representation is not seen as a means of replacing the more general representation of ideas, provided by political parties in liberal democracies. Rather, this 'politics of presence' (Phillips 1995) is supplementary, complementing representation by attending to the needs of relatively disadvantaged groups, and enhancing the input of collective ideas in the policy process.

Critics on the left are right to point out that Young now shows no concern with the politics of class (Bradley 1996). Others feel she deploys 'the same language of difference and multiple cleavage which dominate postmodern accounts' (Bottero 1998: 485). While some post-structuralist feminists have argued that the concept of the state is an homogenising abstraction of little relevance to feminist concerns (Allen 1990), Young wants to reconsider the state in the light of post-modern theory, integrate gender and other differences in an analysis of structured social power, and call political processes to critical account. Young's radical pluralism suggests the influence of post-modernism, but is nowhere near a post-modern account of the political, wherein the subject, political or otherwise, is too fragmented to be 'represented'. In the work of Judith Butler, for example, the politics of groups and identities do not necessarily enhance the democratic process, for groups are internally differentiated to the point that we cannot generalise about what women are or what their interests might be for example (Butler 1993: ix–xi). For Butler, the only possibility for feminist politics seems to be cultural disruption by 'performing' other kinds of gendered behaviour (Butler 1990: 137–8, Butler and Scott 1992). I agree with Evans (1995: 137) that Butler and those like her have nothing (certainly nothing more) to contribute than the work of Young on women, difference and the complexities of representing these.

## Practical politics

Feminist concern with the absence of women in political elites has made its presence felt in liberal democratic politics from the mid-1980s. The 'equal rights' feminism espoused by many liberals has sometimes been referred to as 'power feminism' (Wolf 1993: 152). It is articulated, for example, by the world's largest feminist organization, the National Organization of Women (NOW) which has effectively mounted pressure on the American political establishment to end any forms of gender discrimination and achieve full equality of opportunity in all areas of life. Since the late 1960s, NOW has become a formidable political player, and has had success particularly within the American Democratic Party, for example, in 1988 campaigning vigorously to ensure the selection of

Geraldine Ferraro as the Democrats' vice-presidential candidate (Bryson 2003: 143). In Britain, liberal feminism has been less influential, although campaigning in the late 1960s led to the passage of equal pay and sex discrimination legislation in the 1970s, and the setting up of the Equal Opportunities Commission.

The language of equal rights has raised difficulties for campaigns around maternity rights and benefits in liberal democracies, for these are not gender neutral. The difficult relationship between arguing for political and social equality and considering the history and practice of different gender roles and practices, has led some to reconceptualise equality in a way that recognises social interdependence and avoids the polarising debates about sameness and difference (Lister 1997). This kind of thinking has informed the campaigning of Scandinavian feminism, which has been successful in shifting state policy towards more 'family friendly' employment policies which recognise the familial responsibilities of both male and female workers (Bryson 1999).

Organisations like NOW support affirmative action programmes to increase women's political representation. These are justified on the grounds that the existing procedures and practices in political institutions reflect subjective and gender biased assumptions about merit and, in practice, favour white men. Phillips (1995: 5–7) argues that this politics of presence presents a profound challenge to liberal democratic theory that has seen political representation in terms of the 'politics of ideas' (albeit often mapped onto class interests). In this politics of ideas, the social characteristics of the elected representatives are irrelevant. However, from the campaigns of first wave feminism in Europe and the United States, some feminists argued that women have particular political views and distinct interests that are not represented by male politicians (Gleadle 1995). Women were seen as being able to represent women's interests and reflect these in the policy-making process. Such notions have been politically influential, for example, within French feminism in the 1990s where demands for quotas of political representatives were made by the 'parity movement' which campaigned for legislation which would make it obligatory for political parties to field equal numbers of male and female candidates (Gaspard 2001).

The arguments on which such campaigns are based are not drawn on 'essentialist' notions of women's particular attributes, but on the basis of historically specific and contingent reasons (Mansbridge 2001). Phillips argues that an historically excluded community with limited political leverage in contemporary institutions are unlikely to be properly represented unless its members are present, thus 'Changing the gender composition of elected assemblies is a major, and necessary, challenge to the social arrangements which have systematically placed women in a subordinate position' (Phillips 1995: 82). Young's notion of group representation assumes disagreements within groups and a high level of mobilisation, which is difficult to see in the current context of public apathy and estrangement from the representative institutions of the liberal democratic state. However, the notion of quotas, an element of group representation within the 'politics of ideas', seems a small and plausible step. We would not be drawn down a path to 'state feminism', for most women are not feminists, and as Phillips notes, as we are talking about representing over half the population more adequately, Balkanisation is hardly an issue (1995: 56).

In the early 1970s, there was considerable optimism in left feminist circles that radical revolutionary change was possible in Western societies. By the mid-to late 1970s, this was replaced by a more pragmatic focus on radical reform from within the existing state system via a coalition of progressive forces in social movements. In Britain, eighteen years of New Right government (1979–97) saw that the achievement of a feminist influenced Labour administration became an important feminist goal. The shift in ideas and policy within the Labour Party from the late 1980s has been in part attributed to increased feminist influence (Perrigo 1996), and certainly the (New) Labour Party courted women voters (Lovenduski 1999). It acceded to some liberal feminist arguments with the brief adoption of all women shortlists in the run-up to the 1997 General Election (Squires 1996). However, feminists have been concerned with the increased pressures on lone parents to work without concomitant investment in childcare infrastructure (Lister 1997: 193), with policies aimed at reducing state welfare and promoting self-help (McRobbie 2000: 110), and with a failure to properly recognise domestic responsibilities or tackle structural inequalities which have proved persistent (Segal 1999; Ward 2002). British socialist feminism, having invested in the New Labour project, seems now to be drawing back (Franklin 2000). More radical activism can be seen in anti-capitalist, anti-corporate and environmental campaigning where feminist issues are advanced (Brenner 2000, Ward 2002), but feminist pragmatism cannot be completely dismissed. There are more positive encounters and, arguably, areas of feminist policy success.

In Britain, feminist concepts and theories of domestic violence have become increasingly mainstream. The police have responded to feminist critiques from the mid-1980s, and by the end of the 1990s, female staffed specialist units in local constabularies were unremarkable and 'good' practice. The British state now adopts a broad definition of domestic violence, including psychological and emotional abuse, and between current and ex-partners or family members whatever their sex or sexuality. It has recently, in collaboration with the radical feminist NGO, Women's Aid, set up a twenty-four-hour help line for female victims of domestic assault and abuse (Women and Equality Unit). Domestic violence legislation in 2004 was based on feminist research on the pattern of such violence in the United Kingdom (Walby and Myhill 2004), and the cost to the state, with the intention of 'mainstreaming' state policy on domestic violence issues (Walby 2004b).

At times, the relationship between feminism and the state has been fraught with various tensions and contradictions. Mackinnon's most controversial written work, ironically titled *Only Words* (1994), relates to her practical political engagement in the United States. With Andrea Dworkin, Mackinnon was influential in pressuring state and city legislatures in Indianapolis and Minneapolis to pass anti-pornography ordinances, using civil rights arguments and precedent in anti-discrimination law. In the mid-1980s, they were partly successful in having civil rights law define pornography in what they saw as feminist terms, as involving the representation of human beings in situations of sexualised subordination. The ordinances, however, fell foul of the Supreme Court which judged them to be unconstitutional on the grounds that they contradicted the right to free speech (Tong 1989: 111–23). The campaign against the Dworkin/Mackinnon Ordinances was promoted by well known liberal feminists, and divisions over a feminist response to pornography were so marked that the clash of feminist activists became referred to as the 'porn wars' (Dines et al. 1998). Given Mackinnon's own theory of the state as patriarchal, she was perhaps not surprised, although certainly disappointed by the reversal in fortune – that defence of pornography as free speech was a means of 'silencing' an analysis of gender inequality (Mackinnon 1994: 65–9).

Feminism has encountered opposition from politicians, political parties and interest groups, and this has often been understood in

## Feminisms: the Gendering of the State

terms of a 'backlash'. Susan Faludi (1992) argued that New Right administrations of the 1980s, and much of the media, claimed that women had achieved equality, that feminism was responsible for a range of social ills, including the 'breakdown' of the nuclear family, increased juvenile delinquency and had even been damaging to women themselves. Although many radical and some socialist feminists share this pessimistic appraisal of state anti-feminism (Greer 1999; Oakley 2002), some younger feminists are asserting the success of feminism, while also, ironically, reiterating many of the unsatisfied demands of feminists from the early 1970s (Walter 1998; Wolf 1993).

Elsewhere around the world, feminist notions can be seen to have suffered more dramatic setbacks. The Islamist state established under the government of Ayatollah Khomeni in 1979 proved, initially, incredibly difficult for Iranian women as it embarked on a series of legislative moves which excluded women from the public sphere. Women were unable to give uncorroborated evidence in court, their murder resulted in lesser penalties, fathers gained custody rights of children on divorce and were recognised 'guardians' of the household, with the power of life and death over children and the right to kill their wives if they were charged with adultery. As Afshar comments 'with the arrival of the Islamic Republic, with the notable exception of the vote, Iranian women lost all they had struggled for over a century' (1996: 126).

Ziba Mir-Hosseini (1996) argues, however, that it is a mistake to see the Iranian revolution as entirely negative for women. Rather, the state remains an arena of contestation. Women, including feminist women, have drawn on Islamist discourse to demand policy solutions for problems incurred by women, and a bargain with the Islamic state was struck in order to gain reforms. Elite Iranian women have accepted the veil while also demanding that the state fulfils certain obligations to enable them to be 'good mothers'. It does this by providing access to education and effective childcare, shorter and flexible hours for mothers who work part-time in the gender segregated labour market. Iranian women's movements contain a strong current of critique of 'Western feminism' as colonialist and as offering a spurious version of gender equality (Afshar 1996: 121–2) and Haleh Afshar considers that this Islamist feminism has been far more effective than Western secularism in securing practical political goals. Mackinnon's and Pateman's model of the patriarchal state is exemplified in many ways here, and the social situation and powerlessness of many Iranian women is desperate. Yet as Walby and Young suggest, however strongly it articulates male interests, the state is an arena in which some degree of negotiation can take place. Iranian women have negotiated better terms by 'bargaining' with 'patriarchy' (Kandiyoti 1988: 277). They have forced a patriarchal state run by a religious elite to engage with secular discourses around gender and the public sphere with some success.

Critics accuse feminism of a narrow focus on political equality and rights which ignores the context of economic, cultural and sexual exploitation. Such concerns are said to reflect the interests of middle-class relatively young, well-educated white women – who are socially privileged in every way except for their sex. In the 'developing world', this equal rights discourse has been criticised by both feminists and male political elites. Although regional differences and local patterning need accounting for, as Georgina Waylen (1996) points out, in almost all nation-states women are politically marginalised and the organisation of politics is male presumptive.

However, hierarchical, competitive, capitalist society is not questioned by such notions of 'equal rights'. Without more fundamental change of social structures, most men and most women are little liberated within the competitive market-place, be it of the political elite or otherwise (Brown 1993; Oakley 2002). In addition, critics on the right argue that feminist demands of all kinds, which often compel the state to move in a welfarist direction, are naive in failing to understand the problematic qualities of state power. There is a clear tension between New Right demands to 'roll back' the frontiers of the (welfare) state and feminist demands for intervention to secure equity. Feminists of various kinds and in various kinds of states have increasingly come to see the state as a facilitator of individual freedom, rather than a threat to it (Siim 1991). In liberal democratic states, this means that much feminism has moved in a social democratic direction. Pateman and Mackinnon see the state as structured around gendered interests. For Walby, the interests of the state reflect the social complexities of domination and the state is shaped by a range of interests in addition to gender. The state is, therefore, not some neutral tool that feminist can simply deploy, but is often inherently opposed to feminist ends. While state provision might free women from their dependence on individual men, it creates another form of dependence.

## Bibliography

Afshar, H. (1996), 'Women and the politics of fundamentalism in Iran', in H. Afshar (ed.), *Women and Politics in the Third World*, (London: Routledge).
Allen, J. (1990), 'Does feminism need a theory of the state?', in S. Watson (ed.), *Playing the State* (London: Verso).
Anthias, F. and Yuval-Davis, N. (eds) (1989), 'Introduction', in *Woman-Nation-State* (Basingstoke: Macmillan).
Banks, O. (1981), *Faces of Feminism: a Study of Feminism as a Social Movement* (Oxford: Martin Robertson).
Bartky, S. (1990), *Femininity and Domination: Studies in the Phenomenology of Oppression* (London: Routledge).
Bell, D. and Klein, R. (eds) (1996), *Radically Speaking: Feminism Reclaimed* (London: Zed).
Bottero, W. (1998), 'Clinging to the wreckage? Gender and the legacy of class', *Sociology*, 32, 3: 469–90.
Bradley, H. (1996), *Fractured Identities: Changing Patterns of Inequality* (Cambridge: Polity).
Brenner, J. (2000), *Women and the Politics of Class* (New York: Monthly Review Press).
Breugal, I. (1979), 'Women as a resource army of labour', *Feminist Review*, 3: 12–23.
Brown, L. (1993), *The Politics of Individualism: Liberalism, Liberal Feminism and Anarchism* (London: Black Rose Books).
Bryson, V. (1999), *Feminist Debates: Issues of Theory and Political Practice* (Basingstoke: Macmillan).
Bryson, V. (2003), *Feminist Political Theory*, (2nd edn) (Basingstoke: Palgrave).
Butler, J. (1990), *Gender Trouble: Feminism and the Subversion of Identity* (London: Routledge).
Butler, J. (1993), *Bodies that Matter: On the Discursiue Limits of 'Sex'* (London: Routledge).
Butler, J. and Scott, J. (1992) *Feminists Theorize the Political* (London: Routledge).
Coole, D. (1993), *Women in Political Theory* (Hemel Hempstead: Harvester Wheatsheaf).
Currell, M. E. (1974), *Political Woman* (London: Croom Helm).
Delphy, C. (1984), *Close to Home: A Materialist Analysis of Women's oppression* (London: Hutchinson).

Dietz, M. (1985), 'Citizenship with a feminist face: the problem with maternal thinking', *Political Theory*, Vol. 13.

Dines, G., Jensen, R. and Russo, A. (1998), *Pornography: the Production and Consumption of Inequality* (London: Routledge).

Dunleavy, P. and O'Leary, B. (1987), *Theories of the State: The Politics of Liberal Democracy* (Basingstoke: Macmillan).

Dworkin, A. (1988), *Intercourse* (London: Arrow Books).

Eisenstein, Z. (1984), *Feminism and Sexual Equality: Crisis in Liberal America* (New York: Monthly Review Press).

Elshtain, J. (1981), *Public Man, Private Woman: Women in Social and Political Thought* (Oxford: Martin Robertson).

Enloe, C. (1989), *Bananas, Bases and Beaches: Making Feminist Sense of International Relations* (London: Pandora).

Epstein, C. (1970), *Woman's Place: Options and Limits in Professional Careers* (Berkeley CA: University of California Press).

Evans, J. (1995), *Feminist Theory Today: an Introduction to Second-wave Feminism* (London: Sage).

Faludi, S. (1992), *Backlash: The Undeclared War Against Women* (London: Chatto and Windus).

Franklin, J. (2000), 'What's wrong with New Labour politics?', *Feminist Review*, No. 64.

Fraser, N. (1989), *Unruly Practices: Power, Discourse and Gender in Contemporary Social Theory* (Cambridge: Polity).

Fraser, N. (1998), 'Sex, lies and the public sphere: reflections on the confirmation of Clarence Thomas', in J. Landes (ed.), *Feminism, the Public and the Private* (Oxford: Oxford University Press).

Fraser, N. and Nicholson, L. (eds) (1990), *Feminism/Postmodernism* (London: Routledge).

Friedan, B. (1983), *The Second Stage* (London: Abacus).

Gaspard, F. (2001), 'The French parity movement', in J. Klausen and C. Maier (eds), *Has Liberalism Failed Women? Assuring Equal Representation in Europe and the United States* (Basingstoke: Palgrave).

Gleadle, K. (1995), *The Early Feminists* (Basingstoke: Macmillan).

Greer, G. (1970), *The Female Eunuch* (London: Paladin).

Greer, G. (1999), *The Whole Woman* (London: Doubleday).

Hanmer, J. (1978), 'Violence and the social control of women', in G. Littlejohn, B. Smart, J. Wakeford and N. Yuval-Davis (eds), *Power and the State* (London: Croom Helm).

Hirschmann, N. and Di Stephano, C. (eds) (1996), *Revisioning the Political: Feminist Reconstructions of Traditional Concepts in Political Theory* (London: Westview Press).

Humm, M. (ed.) (1992), *Feminisms: a Reader* (Hemel Hempstead: Harvester Wheatsheaf).

Jayawardena, K. (1986), *Feminism and Nationalism in the Third World* (London: Zed).
Jeffreys, S. (1990), *Anti-climax: a Feminist Perspective on the Sexual Revolution* (London: Women's Press).
Kandiyoti, D. (1988), 'Bargaining with patriarchy', *Gender and Society*, 2, 3: 271–90.
Kelly, L. (1999), 'Domestic violence: a neglect of policy or a policy of neglect?', in S. Walby (ed.), *New Agendas for Women* (Basingstoke: Macmillan).
Kirkpatrick, J. (1974), *Political Women* (New York: Basic Books).
Kymlicka, W. (1989), *Liberalism, Community and Culture* (Oxford: Clarendon Press).
Landes, J. (ed.) (1998), *Feminism, the Public and the Private* (Oxford: Oxford University Press).
Lister, R. (1997), *Citizenship: Feminist Perspectives* (Basingstoke: Macmillan).
Lister, R. (1999), 'What welfare provisions do women need to become full citizens?', in S. Walby (ed.), *New Agendas for Women* (Basingstoke: Macmillan).
Lovenduski, J. (1999), 'Sexing political behaviour in Britain', in S. Walby (ed.), *New Agendas for Women* (Basingstoke: Macmillan).
Lovenduski, J. and Randall, V. (1993), *Contemporary Feminist Politics: Women and Power in Britain* (Oxford: Oxford University Press).
Mackinnon, C. A. (1989), *Toward a Feminist Theory of the State* (Cambridge MA: Harvard University Press).
Mackinnon, C. A. (1994), *Only Words* (London: HarperCollins).
Mansbridge, J. (2001), 'The descriptive political representation of gender: an anti-essentialist argument', in J. Klausen and C. Maier (eds), *Has Liberalism Failed Women? Assuring Equal Representation in Europe and the United States* (Basingstoke: Palgrave).
McIntosh, M. (1978), 'The state and the oppression of women', in A. Kuhn and A. M. Wolpe (eds), *Feminism and Materialism: Women and Modes of Production* (London: Routledge).
McRobbie, A. (2000), 'Feminism and the third way', *Feminist Review*, 64.
Mellor, M. (1997), *Feminism and Ecology* (London: Routledge).
Mies, M. (1984), *Patriarchy and Accumulation on a World Scale* (London: Zed).
Mies, M. (1998), *Patriarchy and Accumulation on a World Scale* (2nd edn) (London: Zed).
Millett, K. (1977), *Sexual Politics* (London: Virago).
Mir-Hosseini, Z. (1996), 'Women and politics in post-Khomeini Iran: divorce, veiling and emerging feminist voices', in H. Afshar (ed.), *Women and Politics in the Third World* (London: Routledge).
Oakley, A. (2002), *Gender on Plant Earth* (Cambridge: Polity).

Okin, S. M. (1990), *Gender, Justice and the Family* (New York: Basic Books).
Pateman, C. (1988), *The Sexual Contract* (Cambridge: Polity).
Pateman, C. (1989), *The Disorder of Women* (Cambridge: Polity).
Perrigo, S. (1996), 'Women and change in the Labour Party 1975–1995', in J. Lovenduski and P. Norris (eds), *Women in Politics* (Oxford: Oxford University Press).
Phillips, A. (1993), *Democracy and Difference* (Cambridge: Polity).
Phillips, A. (1995), *The Politics of Presence* (Oxford: Oxford University Press).
Pringle, R. and Watson, S. (1992), 'Women's interests and the post-structuralist State', in M. Barrett and A. Phillips (eds), *Destabilising Theory: Contemporary Feminist Debates* (Cambridge: Polity).
Rai, S. (1996), 'Women and the state in the Third World', in H. Afshar (ed.), *Women and Politics in the Third World* (London: Routledge).
Roudall, V. (1987), *Women and Politics: An International Perspective* (Basingstoke: Macmillan).
Rich, A. (1980), 'Compulsory heterosexuality and lesbian existence', *Signs*, 5, 4: 631–60.
Ruddick, S. (1990), *Maternal Thinking: Towards a Politics of Peace* (London: Women's Press).
Sassoon, A. S. (1987), *Women and the State: The Shifting Boundaries between Public and Private* (London: Hutchinson).
Segal, L. (1987), *Is the Future Female? Troubled Thoughts on Contemporary Feminism* (London: Virago).
Segal, L. (1999), *Why Feminism? Gender, Psychology, Politics* (Cambridge: Polity).
Siim, B. (1991), 'Welfare state, gender politics and equity principles – women's citizenship in the Scandinavian welfare state', in E. Meehan and S. Sevenhuijsen (eds), *Equality Principles and Politics*, (London: Sage).
Squires, J. (1996), 'Quotas for women: fair representation?', in J. Lovenduski and P. Norris (eds), *Women in Politics* (Oxford: Oxford University Press).
Squires, J. (1999), *Gender in Political Theory* (Cambridge: Polity).
Tong, R. (1989), *Feminist Thought: A Comprehensive Introduction* (London: Routledge).
Walby, S. (1988), 'Gender politics and social theory', *Sociology*, 22, 2: 215–32.
Walby, S. (1990), *Theorizing Patriarchy* (Oxford: Blackwell).
Walby, S. (1997), 'Is citizenship gendered?' and 'Women and nation', from *Gender Transformations* (London: Routledge).
Walby, S. (1999), 'The new regulatory state: the social powers of the European Union', *British Journal of Sociology*, 50, 1: 118–40.

Walby, S. (2003), 'Modernities/globalisation/complexities', paper presented to the British Sociological Association Conference, University of York.

Walby, S. (2004a), 'The European Union and gender equality: emergent varieties of gender regime', *Social Politics*, 11, 1: 4–29.

Walby, S. (2004b), *The Cost of Domestic Violence* (London: Department of Trade and Industry), p. 7558.

Walby, S. and Myhill, A. (2004), *Domestic Violence, Sexual Assault and Stalking: Findings From the 2001 British Crime Survey* (Home Office Research Study 276, London: Home Office).

Walter, N. (1998), *The New Feminism* (London: Little, Brown).

Ward, L. (2002), ' "Globalization" and the "third way": a feminist Response', *Feminist Review*, No. 70.

Waylen, G. (1996), *Gender in Third World Politics* (Buckingham: Open University Press).

Weitz, R. (ed.) (2003), *The Politics of Women's Bodies* (2nd edn) (Oxford: Oxford University Press).

Whelehan, I. (1995), *Modern Feminist Thought: From the Second Wave to Post-'Feminism'* (Edinburgh: Edinburgh University Press).

Wolf, N. (1993), *Fire with Fire: The New Female Power and How it Will Change the 21st Century* (London: Chatto and Windus).

Wollstonecraft, M. (1978 [1792]), *A Vindication of the Rights of Women* (Harmondsworth: Penguin).

Women and Equality Unit, www.womenandequalityunit.gov.uk/domestic.violence.

Vogel, L. (1983), *Marxism and the Oppression of Women* (London: Pluto).

Young, I. M. (1990), *Justice and the Politics of Difference* (Princeton NJ: Princeton University Press).

CHAPTER TEN

# The 'New' Right: the Minimal State

Erika Cudworth

The term 'New Right' was associated with the politics of the 'Thatcher era' in the United Kingdom and the Conservative governments from 1979 to 1990. In continental Europe, the term 'neo-liberalism' is often used to describe the politics of limited government and fiscal restraint, and talk of the politics of neo-liberalism abounds in the literature on globalisation. In the United States, however, the association of right-wing politics with certain kinds of Christianity and Cold War rhetoric led to the appellation 'neo-conservative' for the kind of Republican Party politics associated with Senator Barry Goldwater in the 1960s and with Ronald Reagan in the 1970s, initially as governor of California, and then as President from 1981 to 1989 (and subsequent governments, see Chapter 8). Some may consider 'neo-liberalism' or 'neo-conservatism' more contemporary, but I find 'New Right' to be a more accurate descriptor of a distinctive politics that brings together two seemingly incongruous positions: a paternalistic support for state intervention; and a commitment to the free market strongly influenced by classical liberal economics. Both critics and proponents consider that there is a cogent body of theory behind the politics of fiscal restraint, limited government and the restoration of authority. Yet the name given to this politics varies both regionally and when the national or international context is considered.

This chapter begins by discussing the emergence of the New Right as a critique of the politics of liberal democratic states in the

## The 'New' Right: the Minimal State

1960s and 1970s. The development of New Right theory is linked to right-wing anarchism, but it is most usually seen as either a form of conservatism or a form of liberalism. What distinguishes the New Right from either of these established positions is its contribution to theorising the modern state and, in particular, its application of economic methods to the understanding of political institutions. Key theorists are selected with a view to illustrating different strands and themes. James Buchanan and others have used public or rational choice theory to understand paradoxes of voting and their effects on party politics in liberal democratic states. Gordon Tullock has suggested liberal states have distorted democratic inputs through the influence of pressure groups and William Niskanen considers that the role of the bureaucracy in particular leads to an 'over supply' of government. The well known New Right solution of the 'minimal state' will be elaborated with reference to Fredrick von Hayek's critique of social democracy, and the arguments for limited governance made by Robert Nozick.

Since the early 1980s, New Right ideas have borne directly on practical politics in Western liberal democracies. Particularly significant were the governments of Ronald Reagan in the United States and Margaret Thatcher in Britain and their legacies. The final section will focus on these cases, considering the extent to which these political phenomena represent New Right state theory in practice. Partly due to the extent of its influence on practical politics, the New Right has weathered sustained critique. Some consider that the New Right has become the dominant paradigm of politics in our age of 'neo-liberal democracy', which has been reflected in the policy decisions of important international organisations such as the International Monetary Fund and the World Trade Organization. This theme will be elaborated when considering the possible futures of the state in the context of debates on globalisation – the subject matter of Chapter 12. In its practical attempts to dismantle the social democratic project, however, it has not only been theorists of social democracy who have responded to the challenge of the New Right, but Marxists and feminists also. In its political distaste for long established institutions and practices, the New Right has also raised the ire of many conservatives.

## Context

The intellectual origins of the New Right lie in mainstream liberal and conservative political philosophy, and the purpose of this section is to consider what elements of such thinking the New Right draws upon. What arguably is 'new', is the particular combination of ideas, and the fact that this is given analytic rigour through a social science-based critique of the assumptions of pluralism (Dunleavy and O'Leary 1987: 72), and this section will end with an elaboration of the distinctiveness of New Right theory with a discussion of public choice methodology and its theoretical implications.

The New Right is committed to the notion that political life is primarily concerned with individual freedom, adopting the broadly liberal position that societies arise from the actions of individuals pursuing their own interests. Any groups or associations individuals might enter into are understood in contractual terms, and an emphasis is placed on such contracts being entered into freely. Both the New Right and traditional conservatism share a belief in a natural social hierarchy and see social equality as both undesirable and unachievable either on grounds of meritocratic liberalism or elitist paternalism. However, some traditional conservatives have seen the New Right as a break from conservatism. For example, British politician and intellectual, Ian Gilmour, was bitterly critical of the shift in British conservatism from the late 1970s. He argues that conservatism is not a zealous, radically reformist politics (Gilmour 1978: 132), but is concerned with the preservation of national unity and national institutions. He endorses Michael Oakeshott's understanding of a free society as one that is guided by principles of continuity and consensus (1978: 92–100, see Chapter 8), and sees state intervention as convenient and practical (1978: 236). Gilmour (1992: 271) is also scathing of what he considers to be a universalistic, simplistic and mistaken presumption of a self-interested human nature, which is foundational for New Right theory. In addition, for Oakeshott or Gilmour, the rationalist presumptions of New Right theories would be erosive of a conservative politics that understands political change as necessarily incremental.

For other British conservative thinkers, however, the New Right is not 'new'. Rather, it is a continuation of a well-established tradition of British conservatism that brings together a defence of market freedom with the notion of duty and moral obligation to 'fellow citizens' (Willets 1992: 52). While Gilmour protested the 'dogmatism' of Thatcherism, there is also an argument that this is not without precedent in the conservative tradition (Adonis 1994: 149). Some consider that the British Conservative Party had for some time been disquiet about the creeping 'statism' of Conservative governments of the 1950s and 1960s and the power of organised labour (Evans and Taylor 1996: 2–3). For traditional conservatives and New Right thinkers alike, there are social advantages associated with property ownership. Private property, particularly in the form of housing, provides security in an uncertain world and promotes a number of important social values such as respect for law, authority and social order (Heywood 2003: 82). For Robert Nozick (1974), property reflects individual tastes and each individual has an absolute right to use their property as they choose. Other elements of similarity include a 'moral' agenda, which seeks, for example, to resist and reverse egalitarian policy in education, welfare and gender relations (Scruton 1981). New Right thought was also influenced by conservative desire to restore the authority of the state. Conservative critics from the United States, such as Irving Kristol, argue that a 'rights-based' culture led to a declining sense of duty and responsibility within the citizen body.

In terms of the historical political context, the New Right's emergence has been associated with a critique of the politics of social democracy in liberal states. In the British case, it emerged as a reaction to Conservative governments which accepted, from the 1950s on, a version of social democracy and 'planned capitalism', similar to that of European Christian democracy. One of the reasons why the emergence of the New Right is so strongly associated with Britain and the United States is that both countries have seen the historical impact of classical liberal ideas, and for some, the 'New Right' is essentially reactionary, drawing upon these pre-social democratic traditions in British conservatism and American republicanism (Jacques 1983: 53). Yet the rise of the New Right as a distinct politics is really something to be associated with the 1970s and the development of a set of radical ideas, which directly challenged the Keynesian orthodoxy of a post-war European social democratic consensus, particularly in the context of its apparent failure, and the 'New Deal' and 'Great Society' programmes in the United States.

The New Right is, therefore, a political hybrid and one in which there are often seen to be two 'schools' of thought. Quite what those strands are, however, is debateable. For Andrew Gamble (1994: 34–8), there is a liberal tendency that argues for a 'freer' and more competitive market economy (as represented by Hayek and Nozick), and a conservative tendency that is more interested in restoring the authority of the state. This is a more conventional understanding of the New Right as a composite on the political spectrum. Another way of differentiating the strands in New Right thinking is to consider methodological approaches. Here, we might differentiate the normative political theory of those such as Nozick, from theorists who seek to substantiate their understandings of the state empirically, often through the use of statistical data. This latter 'public choice school', is also referred to as collective choice, rational choice or mathematical political theory (Dunleavy and O'Leary 1987: 75).

While the adoption of public choice as a methodology is not an exclusive preserve of the New Right (Dunleavy 1985) it is most commonly associated with the articulation of these political values and policy recommendations. Public choice theory derives from elements of economic theory in which private individuals are seen as making choices in the market-place based on their own preferences. Similarly to mainstream economics, public choice theorists assume that people are self-interested and act in a utility maximising manner. They further assume that such interest and action is rational. For Gordon Tullock (1976: 5), 95 per cent of human behaviour is self-interested. Not all public choice theorists would attempt to put a figure on the extent of our self-interest, but all make the similar presumption that the preferences people have and the choices that they make, strongly reflect their own interests. While in economics, theorists are concerned with private choices, that is, the choices made by private individuals in the context of the market; public choice theory involves the study of social or non-market choices (Dunleavy and O'Leary 1987: 76). For Hayek (1979), however, social life is too subjective and social systems too complex and unpredictable to be studied in the same way that we study non-human nature. Although Hayek considers the experience of the private individuals as the foundation of knowledge, he is also keen to emphasise that individual political actors cannot be reduced to a collection of quantifiable political preferences in the manner public choice theorists assume.

The public choice school has been concerned with collective decision making in the social and political sphere and has concentrated its attention on state institutions and related political practices such as voting and party activity. The assumptions on which it is based involve these phenomena being studied in a particular way, and have resulted in a particular set of arguments about the state. It is this assumption of self-interest which underpins the hostility to the state, particularly in its social democratic form. Mancur Olson (1971) argued that self-interest utility maximising citizens 'free ride' upon the provision of public goods, such as welfare services, provoking a fiscal crisis. Olson does not presume that all individuals are always self-interested and will exploit state services, nor does he think that the state itself is incapable of steering its self-interested citizens in the direction of the common good. It is not only significant numbers of citizens who 'free-ride' on state benefits, so do many politicians and bureaucrats. Public sector workers seek to maximise their budgets and competitive elections involve politicians seeking to maximise their electoral base, for example, by promising further public services, or making promises in line with short-term gains for certain population groups rather than the longer-term 'public interest' (Buchanan and Wagner 1977: 23).

James Buchanan, one of the doyens of public choice theory in the United States is associated with the use of mathematical modelling and what become known as 'game theory'. This has examined the permutations and combinations of political preference and outcomes in terms of political decision making and the irrational and democratically questionable results of electoral processes. The features of 'games', such as winning and losing, calculation, co-operation, collaboration, bargaining and betrayal can be applied to most forms of political activity (Dunleavy and O'Leary 1987: 78). As public choice theorists assume that human beings are rational utility maximisers, they argue that despite the many situations where mutual welfare is best served by co-operation, a lack of trust in other members of the citizen body means that it is individually rational to opt for policies which serve individual needs most immediately, albeit that such decisions have potentially undesirable effects (Buchanan and Tullock 1962: 323). The logic and applicability of games analysis has been a pre-occupation for public choice theory, yet while there is novelty and rigour, the institutional, historical, cultural and power relational context in which decisions are (actually) made is absent.

The findings of public choice theorists, such as James Buchanan, Gordon Tullock and William Niskanen are elaborated in the

Theorists section below. It is worth noting here, however, that public choice stands or falls on the notion of self-interested behaviour. Despite their adherence to a positivistic (quasi-)scientific methodology, public choice theorists make no rigorous theoretical or empirical attempt to substantiate this normative claim. They do not demonstrate, for example, that a public service ethos does not exist, or that it is not commonly held among politicians and bureaucrats. This is an assumption which appeals to a cynical 'commonsense' but not one which is anyway verified. Thus, the cynicism of public choice theorists is as much a romantic fiction as the elements of social democratic politics they so accuse and seek to 'de-bunk'. Further, the apparent schism in New Right thinking between the normative theories of Nozick and Hayek and the positivist empiricism of the public choice theorists is perhaps more a difference of presentation than substance.

## Definition

The way in which New Right theorists understand the state is premised on the particular conception of human nature outlined above. Most would concur that the state is an arena of unnecessary coercion in which the initiative and rights of sovereign individuals are undermined. Given that all strands of New Right thinking explain politics in terms of individual preferences and actions, social collectivities can be understood only in terms of aggregates of individuals. To argue that social collectivities have goals, needs, functions or purposes is a 'holistic fallacy' (Dunleavy and O'Leary 1987: 90). As we have seen in previous chapters, some elite theorists, Marxists and feminists attribute functions and intentions to the 'state' as an agency of an elite group, gender or class. New Right theorists apparently reject all such functional explanations, arguing that explanations in politics must be based on the intentional actions of the individual. Further, there is the view that what we think of as large-scale political phenomena, such as the state, is premised on small-scale political phenomena – the behaviour of individuals. Thus, what composes 'the state' is a net result of the actions of individuals as voters, party members, politicians and different kinds of bureaucrats. All these individuals make non-market choices and the state is an arena in which 'public' choice occurs.

## The 'New' Right: the Minimal State

The analogy most often used in pursuing this notion is that of the market. Following Adam Smith's *The Wealth of Nations* (1776), there is the assumption that the net result of the multiplicity of individual decisions in a competitive market will result in the general interest of all. Problematically for New Right theorists, however, the state is a different kind of entity to the market because it behaves as if it were a collectivity separable from the individual actants that compose it with purposes of its own. Smith's argument was that human beings have an inherent tendency to exchange goods in order to promote their own interests. The 'invisible hand' of the competitive market will ensure that producers maximise sales and thus profits by improving quality and lowering price, developments which are likely to benefit the consumer. While Smith saw the state undertaking some minimal social provision and regulation, he considered that intervention could upset the market mechanism and undermine a nation's prosperity. Much contemporary New Right theory consists of a reassertion of elements of Smith's ideas in (a crude) *laissez-faire* economics. What they take from Smith is the notion that the 'free' economy gives rise to a spontaneous harmony of interests generated through the free exchange of goods and services between free and autonomous individuals (Barry 2004: 12–13). New Right theorists concentrate on liberal democratic states, which from the 1930s adopted some form of social democratic model of governance. It is this model which New Right theorists see as 'failing' as a direct result of attempts at social engineering with the goal of reducing inequalities.

The role of the state is to provide stability and order to the 'spontaneous order' generated by the market, and this is a contradiction at the heart of the New Right model of the liberal democratic state. States require 'vigilance and firm action to enforce laws impartially so that competition might be fair, exchange voluntary and the fruits of enterprise secure' (Gamble 1994: 37). Yet as Gamble points out, the strong state justified, in practical political terms, incredibly high expenditure on areas such as defence and measures required to reduce the overburdening of government would engender political struggle in which strong law enforcement was likely to be necessary. The strong state, therefore, forces the disengagement of the people from the state – forcing them to be free from dependence on welfare provision and to be entrepreneurial. This is highly contradictory, for it means that the New Right does see the state as a collectivity with a purpose, with a function. That function is the policing of markets.

There is a further difficulty with New Right definitions in that different kinds of theorists envisage a different entity when they speak of 'the state'. For Robert Nozick, a state can be defined in Weberian terms as having the 'requisite sort of monopoly over the use of force in the territory' (Nozick 1974: 113). In some ways this definition is value neutral – the state is not by definition seen as serving any particular interest. David Held (1996: 235) refers to the New Right model of the state as a 'legal democracy' where, following Hayek, we have a minimally liberal legalism that impinges little on the actions of free individuals. Public choice theorists tend to conflate government, policy making and 'the public sector' as an amorphous and undesirable public sphere. They define the state as a sum of theses various processes such as voting, party politics, pressure group activity and policy making, all of which are seen to serve office holder and (certain kinds) of elite groups, and thus be self-interested.

## Theorists

Even critics have seen Friedrich Hayek as the most commanding figure in New Right theory (Gamble 1996). Hayek challenged the very idea of a planned economy and pointed to the inefficiencies of those of eastern European state 'communism' as well as those of social democratic liberal states. Whatever the institutional structure and political order, the state, for Hayek, is a bureaucracy incapable of allocating resources fairly and efficiently in a modern industrialised economy. The market can provide a more sensitive mechanism; involved as it is in the daily minutiae of allocating goods and services in line with the demand for them. Perhaps Hayek's most famous work, *The Road to Serfdom* (1944) provided a critique of all state regulation as implicitly totalitarian in character. The more social provision to which the citizen body is subject, the more dependent on such provision it becomes and the basis of a 'free' society is eroded by a culture of dependence on government.

Hayek (1960) sees fundamental dangers in the political processes of modern democratic states. There is constant pressure on the state to purposefully interfere with the distribution of wealth, an activity that suppresses the conception of individual liberty in deference to the social good. This is a critique of the social democratic project, which sees the state as an important tool in maximising 'liberty' through economic redistribution. He argues that a properly liberal state should be defined in terms of its capacity to prevent the coercion of its citizens, and the purpose of law is to regulate but not to direct their behaviour (Hayek 1960: 1–5). Hayek (1982) appeals for a restoration of 'legal democracy' in which the coercion of social redistribution and regulation is severely curtailed. As David Miller (1991: 14–15) points out, this ignores the very real limits placed on liberty by economic misfortune. Hayek would consider the conflation of poverty with unfreedom to be a falsity for 'we must recognise that we may be free and yet miserable . . . to be free may be freedom to starve' (Hayek 1991: 87). However, Hayek also claims that private property is crucial to individual liberty (Hayek 1991: 96), oblivious to those whose economic situation does not enable them to acquire such protection. It is clear that Hayek's liberty is liberty for the few – those residing in the wealthy regions of the globe, with sufficient personal wealth to be independent of social provision (of education, transport, health care, welfare benefits and so on). These ideas influenced the economist Milton Friedman (1962), whose critique of Keynesian economics strongly influenced New Right governments in the 1980s. The Keynesian position is that the state is responsible for reducing unemployment and should do so by injecting money into the economy through public spending. Friedman argued that the consequent budgetary deficit was unacceptable, particularly as there was little a state could do to influence the 'natural rate' of unemployment. For Friedman, following Hayek, the most serious economic difficulty is high levels of inflation and states must seek to eradicate this in their search for sound money (that is, with a stable value). For Friedman, monetarism is a solution to the fiscal crisis of democratic states, and limited public spending is in the best interests of citizens.

Hayek's confidence in the efficacy of a minimal state is founded on his view of the market. Markets are tools through which social learning can take place, as new products, methods and processes of production, distribution and marketing are sought and redefined in response to constant changes (Gamble 1994: 58). By contrast, mass democratic procedures result in arbitrary and oppressive majority rule and concentrate power in the hands of politicians and bureaucrats (Hayek 1960: 103) who are not adept at constantly shifting in response to changes in public demand and are insensitive to the preferences of individuals. For Hayek, state driven attempts to secure 'social justice' are bound to fail for they impose a particular conception of what is 'just' on a diverse citizen body (1960: 231) and because they cannot learn to adjust. The dichotomous conception of states and markets here, however, is overdrawn. On Hayek's own admission, markets require policing by (albeit minimal) states and must, one assumes, be at least fit for that purpose. In addition, in order to maintain such incredible distinctiveness between states and markets caricature and stereotype are deployed (Kay 2004: 77). Hayek will not admit that markets are also prone to 'failure'.

While philosopher Robert Nozick is a highly ambiguous thinker, his ideas, as articulated in his best known work *Anarchy, State and Utopia* were profoundly influential on New Right theorists. Nozick argued for a 'rights-based' libertarianism and against the social liberalism of John Rawls (see Chapter 2). Nozick argues that the rights of the individual citizens are so far reaching that there is only political legitimacy for a minimal state in order to protect the citizen body against theft, fraud, coercion and violence (Nozick 1974: ix), anything further is 'intrinsically immoral'. While strongly influenced by what he calls 'individualist anarchist theory' and, I consider, anarcho-capitalism (see Chapter 6), Nozick draws back from the abolition of the state. He is concerned that the market provision of law and order, which anarcho-capitalists favour, may become subject to powerful territorial monopolies that would have no regulatory mechanism to ensure the fair administration of justice (Nozick 1974: 51, 101–10).

Like Hayek, Nozick is opposed to the state having redistributive functions. In no sense will Nozick support the idea that there is a 'social good', rather 'There are only individual people, different individual people, with their own individual lives' (1974: 33). Human beings are so extraordinarily diverse; there is no one community or indeed, politics, which might serve all of our interests (1974: 310). Appealing to individualism and probably to egotism, Nozick asserts that it is only we unique individuals who are able to decide what we would prefer. We discover this by experimentation and, thus, have the right to take significant risks, and to decide what those risks might be (1974: 75). Any attempt to understand redistribution in the interests of 'social welfare' is an assault on the liberties of the individual because for Nozick, income tax is a form of 'forced labour' and a violation of individual rights (1974: 169). Redistributive taxation makes the false assumption that we work to maximise our income rather than our lifestyle. People may choose to earn less in order to have less responsibility or more leisure time, but a 'progressive' taxation system takes no account of this choice and unjustly punishes those who choose to work in order to maximise their income (1974: 169–70, 248–50). A riposte here, of course, would be that within capitalism workers do not freely choose their occupations. Finally, he argues that only a minimal model of the state can ensure that elite jobs in politics or the bureaucracy are relatively undesirable, and given the small scope of state activity, groups will not seek to manipulate the state machine for economic benefits (1974: 272).

Nozick's defence and advocacy of a minimal state operates at a high level of theoretical abstraction, and considering all the attention *Anarchy, State and Utopia* has received, it is surprisingly thin. Perhaps this has been part of its attractiveness – unsubstantiated generalisations that appeal to the libertine in all of us. The natural rights that are so inviolable are asserted but not argued for. The assumption that a minimal state, unlike a social democratic state, will behave in a neutral way and equally protect the 'natural rights' of its citizens rather than behave arbitrarily, is not substantiated. There is also, of course, an inability to account for extreme disparities of wealth in this conception of liberty. In Hayek, Friedman and Nozick there is no understanding of markets as powerful forms of organisation shaped, for example, by the rivalry of trade blocks, the power of corporations and by monopolistic and oligopolistic structures. Finally, these very general theories are apparently unaware of the extent to which they reflect the context of their emergence in western Europe and the United States.

Public choice theorists are less prone to theorising abstractly or generally, and their state theory is composed from a series of understandings of particular political processes based on empirical observations. For James Buchanan, the problem of liberal democracy is that state actors pursue their self-interest (in getting elected and staying in office), opting for policies that increase public expenditure and the provision of public services. Knowing that the public will be antithetical to raised taxation in order to fund such service provision, however, political parties rarely have an incentive to raise taxation, or, once elected, to cut public expenditure in a period of economic boom. Indeed, the 'grafting of Keynesian economics onto the fabric of a political democracy' has resulted in the undesirable combination of budgetary deficit and inflation (Buchanan and Wagner 1978: 23). Self-interested political parties and politicians are concerned only with short-term political fortunes but have rarely reason to care about the fiscal constitution after that and the long-term impact of economic recession to which their low tax/high spend policies lead.

Buchanan and Gordon Tullock (1962) echo Hayek and Friedman in their concern with arrangements for citizen participation and decision making, which they see as limited and insensitive to the range of options and preferences in the political market place. They consider the way politicians may 'make deals' to secure mutual advantage and often also, the advantage of those constituents who vote for them. This analysis of 'vote trading' has been important in explaining one of the persistent and problematic features of American politics – the politics of 'pork barrel'. Buchanan and Tullock (1962) argue that most politicians, in order to secure re-election, need to 'bring home the bacon' for their constituents and the various local interest and pressure groups. Groups of politicians agree to support legislative initiatives in return for the same favour at a future date. This allows politicians to demonstrate their ability to deliver on policies favouring the interests of their constituents, but often boosts public expenditure and is undemocratic because it discriminates against the constituents of politicians not party to such deals. Tullock (1989) also has a particular contribution to make in his notion of 'rent seeking', which is concerned with the relationship between pressure groups and the state. Tullock argues that firms, pressure and interest groups all invest resources with the expectation of securing privileges as a result. The problem with 'rent seeking' is that it encourages state intervention, distorts competition and disrupts the market. For example, it might be electorally unpopular for governments not to come to aid of ailing industries and nationally-based firms, and thus companies, trades unions and public opinion might encourage government to 'bail out' such businesses. Further, such pressures might encourage governments to establish, maintain and preserve monopolies in the production of certain goods and services (such as transport or energy).

For Buchanan and Tullock then, a key problem with the political processes of liberal democracies is that electoral competition and pressure group activity are fundamentally open ended. There are strong pressures on politicians, parties and party leaderships to compete in ways that over time create unrealistic and unrealisable expectations of government intervention. Individual voters, and in particular, powerful interest groups, lobby for purely sectional purposes and seek to extract the maximum advantage from the state budget to secure their goals or preferences. There is then a scaling up of state intervention and spending which eventually precipitates fiscal crisis.

William Niskanen (1971, 1994) develops the notion that the state has its own interests in maximising the public purse. This is because state bureaucrats will seek to maximise the size of their budgets in order to secure desirable goods such as salary raises, patronage, power and reputation (Niskanen 1971: 38). Whatever the area of policy making with which they are engaged, bureaucrats will seek to maximise the spending of their particular department, division or bureau. Niskanen (1994) is interested in how the structure of bureaucracies enables bureaucrats to be so successful at this budgetary inflation. Bureaucracies are compartmentalised – set up as individual departments with particular remits. Each department has significant monopoly power, responsible as they are for their individual policy areas. The lack of intra-departmental competition means that bureaucrats have no interest in efficiency or quality, so the structure of bureaucracies encourages monopoly, and promotes over-spending and over-provision and thus 'state failure'. The burgeoning nature of bureaucracy, as we have seen, has been a subject of concern for elite theorists, but the scientific elite of Vifredo Pareto (see Chapter 3) or the scientific estate of John Galbraith (1996) does not paint such a picture of bureaucratic incompetence. Niskanen (1973) proposes an over-supply thesis – bureaucracies over supply us with government. Bureaucracies are self-sustaining and expansive, and unlike private firms, they have a low rate of organisational deaths and a high rate of organisational 'births' as new departments are founded and new functions undertaken. In sum, the inflated demands of citizens, the vote maximising behaviour of politicians and the budget maximising efforts of state bureaucracies force the liberal democratic state towards crisis.

For all these theorists then, there is an excess of governance and the liberal state itself is 'overloaded' (Held 1996: 241). The way in which state institutions and the political processes of liberal democracy operate serves to alienate the public from the state and is dysfunctional for the capitalist economy. Buchanan's ideas are an over-simplified caricature of a complex political reality – reducing the analysis of politics to that of economics. Many New Right theorists understand behaviour by analogy – by suggesting that behaviour in states can be compared with and likened to economic descriptions. Whether they have verified such assertions is another

## The Modern State

matter. Rather, there is evidence of factors other than self-interest motivating political action. These include beliefs and ideology, social identification and intrinsic motivation (such as 'doing the right thing', see Taylor 1996). In addition, there are questions raised about the empirical validity of the findings of Buchanan and others, for example, the analysis of lobbying in the American political system precludes the 'reality' of a range of groups competing for influence in the same policy arena and the often uncertain outcome of the lobbying process (Green and Shapiro 1994).

What pluralism is to liberalism, so public choice theory has been to the politics of the New Right. It has provided a methodological framework of clarity and apparent rigour, as well as a framework seeped in a normative ontology. In the late 1990s British critics such as Tony Lawson (1997) suggested that public choice methodology might dominate the discipline of politics just as the assumption of self-interested behaviour has dominated economics. In the United States in 2001 there was a petition supporting a critique of the extensive influence of public choice theory on the discipline of politics. In Britain and the United States particularly 'these ideas almost became an orthodoxy powerful enough to displace pluralism as the conventional wisdom of academic and mass media analyses' of politics (Dunleavy and O'Leary 1987: 72). Certainly, the New Right has sought not only to theorise but also to change the world in challenging political orthodoxy in the 1970s and 1980s and drawing our attention to the failures of the liberal democratic model. Andrew Hindmore notes with reference to the governments of Margaret Thatcher and Ronald Reagan that:

> Theirs was not a conversion on the road to Damascus prompted by a reading of James Buchanan or Gordon Tullock. But public choice theory did provide the New Right with a particular language in which the failings of the state could be dissected and a set of policy recommendations to deal with them. (Hindmoor 2006: 97)

That language, however, sometimes had the air of faith about it:

> The Old Testament prophets did not say 'Brothers I want a consensus'. They said: 'This is my faith, this is what I passionately believe'. If you believe it too, then come with me. (Margaret Thatcher, cited Evans 1997: 16).

## Practical politics

In the 1980s, some governments sought to reverse the social democratic model embodied by many liberal democratic states after 1945. While examples could be drawn from Germany or Australia, perhaps the most controversial were those in the United Kingdom and the United States. The policies adopted by the governments of Reagan and Thatcher drew strongly on concepts of overloaded government. The economic policies of both these administrations placed an emphasis on cutting inflation by reducing government spending and, in the case of Britain, a policy of privatisation which effectively dismantled the mixed economy. 'Reaganomics' was characterised by significant cuts in personal and corporate taxation as an incentive to the creation and sustenance of an entrepreneurial culture. The liberty of the individual was also seen as being undermined by collectivism and a key intention was to achieve the 'rolling back' of the state as Margaret Thatcher liked to describe it (Thatcher 1993: 745). Particular concerns were the mechanisms for social welfare, which were seen, following Hayek, to be contributing to a culture of dependency.

In the United Kingdom, intellectuals within the Conservative Party provided an important link between New Right thinking and government policy. Keith Joseph was a close associate of Thatcher, and at that time the 'intellectual leader' of the party (Evans 1997: 6). Like Nozick, Joseph disputed the notion that the state should have a 'duty to supervise the distribution of wealth' and that it should do so in favour of social and economic equality (Joseph and Sumption 1979: 1). Joseph similarly considered the redistribution of wealth via income tax to be unjust and ineffective, because inequality is 'natural' (1979: 38, 103) and redistribution destroys the competitive ethos needed for wealth creation. Joseph was opposed to measures adopted to eradicate poverty on the grounds that in 1970s Britain such a thing did not exist:

> A family is poor if it cannot afford to eat. It is not poor if it cannot afford endless smokes and it does not become poor by the mere fact that other people can afford them. A person who enjoys a standard of living equal to that of a medieval baron cannot be described as poor for the sole reason that he has

chanced to be born into a society where the great majority can live like medieval kings. (1979: 27)

Joseph echoes Hayek in his presumption that moves for political equality require a 'concentration of political power' in the state, and expansion of its institutional size and social and economic reach (1979: 52–4). He was also of the opinion that the market is a more sensitive mechanism for allocating wealth and assessing value (1979: 73). Finally, like Buchanan and others, there is a deeply pessimistic view of human nature in which political behaviour is seen to be self-interested and utility maximising (1979: 119). How then, did such ideas make themselves apparent in policy terms?

In both the United Kingdom and the United States, Niskanen's theory of bureaucratic budget maximisation encouraged the development of bureaucratic reorganisation in the interests of 'efficiency' (Evans 1997: 53–64), competitive tendering and privatisation (Evans and Taylor 1996: 298). Niskanen himself was a member of Reagan's council of economic advisers during his first term of office (Riddell 1994: 31). In the late 1970s the British Conservative Party committed itself to the firm management of government expenditure, control of the growth of the money supply, reduced levels of taxation on savings and earnings and removals of various kinds of restrictions on business. In addition, they wanted to reverse a welfarist culture of 'dependency', and to limit the propensity of both organised labour and professional interest groups to 'distort' the operation of the market (Evans 1997: 3). Thatcher and her allies saw this as 'monetarist', and in the United States, 'Reaganites' had similar policies and commitments (Riddell 1994: 20). However, while there was much party support in Britain for cutting the money supply (after Friedman) this was carried out incrementally rather than drastically, as was the case in the United States (as recommended by Hayek (see Evans and Taylor 1996: 207)). Nevertheless, as Gamble points out, this, and significant control and reduction of public expenditure, was achieved between 1979 and 1984 (Gamble 1994: 111). Yet the introduction of internal markets, for example, in British health care, proved costly and actually expanded health service bureaucracy (Evans 1997: 67–9), and the audit explosion which has checked the autonomy of the professions has likewise proved expensive and bureaucratically expansive (Marquand 2004: 59).

In addition to such economically liberal measures there was a concern with social fragmentation and a breakdown of law and order. The conservative aspects of the New Right agenda include attacks on the 'permissive society' particularly in the form of liberal education, tough policy stances on 'law and order' issues and rhetoric in support of nuclear families and nationalism. The late 1980s saw the reintroduction of the death penalty in a number of American states, and in Britain, 'short, sharp shock' regimes were promoted in tackling offenders in youth custody centres. In the British case, the matter of 'disciplining' organised labour could be seen to encompass both these concerns. A policy of weakening trades union powers through legislative change also involved the characterisation of organised labour as economically, socially and politically disruptive and the striking miners in Britain in 1984–5 became characterised as 'the enemy within'. The problematic powers of organised labour are strongly articulated in some of Hayek's later work, where unions are seen to promote the fiscal crisis of the state by collective bargaining in the public sector, disrupting the sensitive market mechanism and undermining the freedom of individuals through coercion of employers and individual workers (Currie 1983: 75–9). Hayek was to personally congratulate Thatcher on her 'defeat' of the National Union of Mineworkers on the collapse of their strike.

Superficially, there was a commitment in the United Kingdom to what Thatcher considered 'Victorian values', which involved deference to authority figures such as teachers and a hierarchical and gender dichotomous model of the family. Thatcher's dictum that there is 'no such thing as society' but 'individuals and families' in local communities is entirely consistent with Nozick. Gillian Peele (1994: 70–1) argues, however, that while Margaret Thatcher personally supported what she saw as traditional 'morality', socially liberal opinion in the party meant that Thatcherite morality drew most heavily on entrepreneurship and a lack of 'dependency culture'. The Church of England found itself increasingly at odds with the government in regard to a social policy that ignored deprivation in inner city areas. In the United States, however, the Christian right contributed to the political values of neo-conservatism and there were crossovers in supporters and ideas between the Moral Majority led by Jerry Falwell and elements of the Republican Party (see Chapter 7). These shared a concern that an elite had captured key cultural institutions and were making policy decisions reflecting liberal values that would undermine the fabric of American national and family life (Peele 1994: 77). This has been a constant feature of American politics, and the Christian right aided the re-election of George W. Bush in 2005. Thus, the 'traditional morality' agenda has been consistently important to the practical politics of the New Right in the United States but has featured only periodically in Britain.

A raft of policies were adopted to buttress national identity from internal and external threats, real or imagined. Here the New Right is on traditional conservative territory, seeing the nation as an organic unity with a common cultural and civic identity. Threats from within include the fragmentary impact of mass migration for which governments sought harsh controls. In the 1980s, the external threat came from the east in the forms of the former Soviet Union, seen by Reagan as an 'evil empire'; while 'rogue states' in the Middle East became the pre-eminent threat of the later 1990s. Currently the preoccupation is the 'war on terror'. This commitment to the 'strong state' means ironically, that 'New Right' governments in the 1980s and 1990s simultaneously increased aspects of the state's power while also restricting scope for action in others (Held 1996: 254). For Colin Crouch (2004: 104) the 'neo-liberal' state in Britain and the United States should also be seen as a 'security state' where the reduction in the welfare state has resulted in a concomitant rise of the 'warfare state'. Ironically then, the New Right has been associated with the most expensive, centralised, uncompromising and invasive form of state action – war. The current 'war on terror' has resulted in an enormous budgetary deficit in the United States, and both there and in Britain, there has been increased surveillance and compromise of civil liberties.

Many of the ideas and policies of the Reagan and Thatcher governments have been sustained. Neo-liberal managerialism has replaced high blown rhetoric and, in the British case, intense conflict with organised labour. Liberal critics, such as Dennis Kavanagh (1990: 302), who provide a cautious assessment of the impact of Thatcherism in Britain, nevertheless argue that it 'created a new agenda' which successors have not been willing or able, to reverse. While the Bush (Senior) and Major governments distanced themselves from the rhetoric of the Thatcher/Reagan period, the legacy remained largely intact (Adonis and Hames 1994: 1). The governments of the Clinton era and of 'New' Labour under Tony Blair accepted much of the New Right paradigm. This said, these governments, while ideologically motivated, were tempered by the political realities induced by the requirements of government and external restraints.

There are various interpretations of 'Thatcherism'. For example, Peter Riddell (1985) suggests that the Thatcher governments did not pursue consistent ideological objectives, and policies were determined by national and international contexts rather than some 'grand design'. Jim Bullpit (1986) also considers Thatcherism to be a practical politics, arguing that it constitutes a form of 'statecraft', the key value of which was stable government. Marxist and left critics in the 1980s shared with conservative dissenters the view that Thatcherism was a dogmatic political 'project'. Stuart Hall and Martin Jacques argue that Thatcherism created a new constituency for suppressed sentiments and discontents hitherto not catered for by the establishment, such as dislike of immigrants and welfare dependents (Hall and Jacques 1983: 11). Such views strengthened authoritarianism and justified a growth in state power. Although some of this may be so, Hall and Jacques considerably undermine their credibility by making careless comparisons between Thatcherism and 'fascism', which as discussed in Chapter 7, is far more than an experiment in 'authoritarian populism' (see also Jessop et al. 1984). Key to many left and left-feminist critiques, is the notion of Thatcherism as a retrenchment, primarily of class struggle in terms of its ability to 'disorganise the labour movement' (Hall and Jacques 1983: 13–14), but also of gender relations (Gardiner 1983; Segal 1983) in its attacks on 'permissiveness', approach to working women and emphasis on family values. Andrew Gamble sees Thatcherism as both ideological and practical. It intended to revive market liberalism as the dominant public philosophy and limit the scope of the state regarding economic policy in order to reverse economic decline (Gamble 1994: 4–6). Drawing heavily on Gramsci, Gamble argues that Thatcherism was an attempt to establish a new hegemony in a context of a crisis in both social democracy and global capital accumulation (1994: 13–18, 22–5; also Currie 1983: 85–9, Ross 1983). This notion that Thatcherism was adept at propagating New Right ideas as a form of common sense is well made, and the evidence of economic and social restructuring and change in political values bears out the argument that Thatcherism was a project of the New Right. The extent to which this was a response to difficulties in capital accumulation, however, is more difficult to sustain.

For some, the political interventions of Thatcherism were so profound, that 'New' Labour has been forced to adapt to a new kind of politics and a new set of expectations about the state (Finlayson 2003: 21). For others, the adoption of the rhetoric of the market is just that, a device stressing continuity of the New Right agenda while 'New' Labour have, in fact, been faithful to the statism implied in social democracy (Marquand 2004: 52). Others see external constraints as more significant. New Labour can be seen to have shifted the values and ideas of a social democratic party 'in accordance' with a 'new political economy' (Kenny and Smith 1997: 229). The Western state of the twenty-first century is not in retreat, but is more reflective of market driven politics. The ideas of the New Right have become part of 'common sense' thinking and have found resonance in the understandings of good governance promoted by international organisations. Some on the left see 'neo-liberalism' as the most successful ideology in modern history, and consider that limited government, free markets and a residual welfare state will be the dominant state form of the twenty-first century (Anderson, cited Plant 2004: 24). Colin Leys (2001: 3) argues that the changes wrought by Thatcherism have meant that the pressures of market forces on national politics are 'unusually open and efficacious'. It is not simply that New Right governments have restructured the state along market lines, rather, they have opened up the state to a range of interactive relationships with aspects of the market, which is gradually shifting the state–market balance in complex and unpredictable ways.

James Buchanan's (1984) own assessment of the political success of the New Right is that it has made people think differently about states, public policy and the democratic process. Buchanan has presented us with a politics of self-interested citizens, politicians, parties and governments, and bureaucrats and public sector workers who manipulate governments and maximise their personal privileges. Those in political authority behave opportunistically, and the vast majority of citizens in liberal democracies are excluded from, and disadvantaged by, the political process. These ideas struck a chord with those citizens disillusioned with the 'red tape', bureaucratisation, surveillance and curtailment of individual liberty in 'liberal democratic' states, and for many, this has become a 'commonsense' view of the modern state.

In examining popular disenchantment with democratic politics, Gerry Stoker (2006: 121) gives public choice theory the appellation 'an academic framing for cynicism' and argues that this, along with the impact of New Right policies and politics, has manufactured a level of cynicism that is unfounded and excessive. Scepticism about politicians and the political process can be seen as a healthy sign in liberal democratic states. However, the New Right analysis of selfish and self-serving individuals and institutions is overdrawn. It universalises self-interest as a sole motivational factor in politics (and in life) and extrapolates this in analysing elements of (some) liberal democratic states. In practical terms, restructuring the welfare state and increasing the scope of market forces has lessened the protection of vulnerable people. In a world where divisions of wealth are increasing and significant minorities exist in conditions of extreme poverty, where inequalities around various social divisions pertain, it is difficult to see how the liberty beloved of Hayek and Nozick might flourish. We are not 'free' if we starve, and we need the access to cultural and material resources in order to pursue the very individual tastes, desires and talents of which the New Right is so fond.

## Bibliography

Adonis, A. (1994), 'The transformation of the Conservative Party in the 1980s', in A. Adonis, and T. Hames (eds), *A Conservative Revolution? The Thatcher–Reagan Decade in Perspective* (Manchester: Manchester University Press).

Adonis, A. and Hames, T. (eds) (1994), *A Conservative Revolution? The Thatcher–Reagan Decade in Perspective* (Manchester: Manchester University Press).

Barry, N. (2004), 'The rationale of the minimal state', in A. Gamble and T. Wright (eds), *Restating the State* (Oxford: The Political Quarterly in association with Blackwell).

Buchanan, J. (1984), 'Politics without romance', in J. Buchanan and R. Tollinson (eds), *The Theory of Public Choice II* (Ann Arbor MI: University of Michigan Press).

Buchanan, J. and Tulloch, G. (1962), *The Calculus of Consent* (Ann Arbor MI: University of Michigan Press).

Buchanan, J. and Wagner, R. (1977), *Democracy in Deficit* (New York: Basic Books).

Buchanan, J. and Wagner, R. (1978), *The Consequences of Mr Keynes* (London: IEA).

Bullpit, J. (1986), 'The discipline of the new democracy: Mrs Thatcher's domestic statecraft', *Political Studies*, 34.

Crouch, C. (2004), 'The state and innovations in economic governance', in A. Gamble and T. Wright (eds), *Restating the State* (Oxford: The Political Quarterly in association with Blackwell).

Currie, D. (1983), 'World capitalism in recession', in S. Hall and M. Jacques (eds), *The Politics of Thatcherism* (London: Lawrence and Wishart).

Dunleavy, P. (1985), 'Bureaucrats, budgets and the growth of the state', *British Journal of Political Science*, 15: 299–328.

Dunleavy, P. and O'Leary, B. (1987), *Theories of the State: the Politics of Liberal Democracy* (Basingstoke: Macmillan).

Evans, B. and Taylor, A. (1996), *From Salisbury to Major: Continuity and Change in Conservative Politics* (Manchester: Manchester University Press).

Evans, E. J. (1997), *Thatcher and Thatcherism* (London: Routledge).

Finlayson, A. (2003), *Making Sense of New Labour* (London: Lawrence and Wishart).

Friedman, M. (1962), *Capitalism and Freedom* (Chicago IL: University of Chicago Press)

Galbraith, J. K. (1996), *The Good Society: The Human Agenda* (New York: Houghton Mifflin).

Gamble, A. (1994), *The Free Economy and the Strong State: The Politics of Thatcherism* (Basingstoke: Palgrave).

Gamble, A. (1996), *Hayek* (Cambridge: Polity).

Gardiner, J. (1983), 'Women, recession and the tories', in S. Hall and M. Jacques (eds), *The Politics of Thatcherism* (London: Lawrence and Wishart).

Gilmour, I. (1978), *Inside Right* (London: Quartet).

Gilmour, I. (1992), *Dancing with Dogma: Britain under Thatcherism* (London: Simon and Schuster).

Green, D. and Shapiro, I. (1994), *Pathologies of Rational Choice Theory* (New Haven CT: Yale University Press).

Hall, S. (1983), 'The great moving right show', in S. Hall and M. Jacques (eds), *The Politics of Thatcherism* (London: Lawrence and Wishart).

Hall, S. and Jacques, M. (1983), 'Introduction', in S. Hall and M. Jacques (eds), *The Politics of Thatcherism* (London: Lawrence and Wishart).

Hay, C. (2004a), 'Theory, stylized heuristic or self-fulfilling prophecy? The status of rational choice theory in public administration', *Public Administration*, 82, 1.

Hay, C. (2004b), 'Re-stating politics, re-politicising the state: neo-liberalism, economic imperatives and the rise of the competition state', in A. Gamble and T. Wright (eds), *Restating the State* (Oxford: The Political Quarterly in association with Blackwell).

Hayek, F. A. (1960), *The Constitution of Liberty* (London: Routledge and Kegan Paul).

Hayek, F. A. (1979 [1953]), *The Counter Revolution of Science* (Indianapolis IN: Liberty Press).
Hayek, F. A. (1982), *Law, Legislation and Liberty: Volumes I–III* (London: Routledge and Kegan Paul).
Hayek, F. A. (1991), 'Freedom and coercion', reprinted in D. Miller, *Liberty* (Oxford: Oxford University Press).
Held, D. (1996), *Models of Democracy* (2nd edn) (Cambridge: Polity).
Heywood, A. (2003), *Political Ideologies* (3rd edn) (Basingstoke: Palgrave).
Hindmoor, A. (2006), 'Public choice', in Hay, C. et al. (eds), *The State: Theories and Issues* (Basingstoke: Palgrave).
Jacques, M. (1983), 'Thatcherism – breaking out of the impasse', in S. Hall and M. Jacques (eds), *The Politics of Thatcherism* (London: Lawrence and Wishart).
Jessop, B., Bonnett, J., Bromley, S. and Ling, T. (1984), 'Authoritarian populism, two nations and Thatcherism', *New Left Review*, 147: 32–60.
Joseph, K. and Sumption, J. (1979), *Equality* (London: John Murray).
Kavanagh, D. (1997), *The Reordering of British Politics: Politics After Thatcher* (Milton Keynes: Open University Press).
Kavanagh, D. (1990), *Thatcherism and British Politics: The End of Consensus?* (2nd edn) (Oxford: Oxford University Press).
Kay, J. (2004), 'The state and the market', in A. Gamble and T. Wright (eds), *Restating the State* (Oxford: The Political Quarterly in association with Blackwell).
Kenny, M. and Smith, M. (1997), '(Mis)understanding Blair', *Political Quarterly*, 68, 3.
Lawson, T. (1997), *Economics and Reality* (London: Routledge).
Lees, C. (2001), *Market-driven Politics: Neoliberal Democracy and the Public Interest* (London: Verso).
Marquand, D. (2004), 'False friend: the state and the public domain', in A. Gamble and T. Wright (eds), *Restating the State* (Oxford: The Political Quarterly in association with Blackwell).
Miller, D. (1991), 'Introduction', in D. Miller, *Liberty* (Oxford: Oxford University Press).
Niskanen, W. (1971), *Bureaucracy and Representative Government* (Chicago IL: Aldine).
Niskanen, W. (1973), *Bureaucracy: Servant or Master?* (London: IEA).
Niskanen, W. (1994), *Bureaucracy and Public Economics* (Aldershot: Edward Elgar).
Nozick, R. (1974 [reprinted 1984]), *Anarchy, State and Utopia* (Oxford: Basil Blackwell).
Olson, M. (1971), *The Logic of Collective Action* (Cambridge MA: Harvard University Press).

Peele, G. (1994), 'Culture, religion and public morality', in A. Adonis and T. Hames (eds), *A Conservative Revolution? The Thatcher–Reagan Decade in Perspective* (Manchester: Manchester University Press).

Plant, R. (2004), 'Neo-liberalism and the theory of the state: from *Wohlfahrtsstaat* to *Rechtsstaat*', in A. Gamble and T. Wright (eds), *Restating the State* (Oxford: The Political Quarterly in association with Blackwell).

Riddell, P. (1985), *The Thatcher Government* (2nd edn) (Oxford: Blackwell).

Riddell, P. (1994), 'Ideology in practice', in A. Adonis and T. Hames (eds), *A Conservative Revolution? The Thatcher–Reagan Decade in Perspective* (Manchester: Manchester University Press).

Ross, J. (1983), *Thatcher and Friends* (London: Pluto).

Scruton, R. (1981), *The Meaning of Conservatism* (London: Macmillan).

Segal, L. (1983), 'The heat in the kitchen', in S. Hall and M. Jacques (eds), *The Politics of Thatcherism* (London: Lawrence and Wishart).

Stoker, J. (2006), *Why Politics Matters: Making Democracy Work* (Basingstoke: Palgrave).

Taylor, M. (1996), 'When rationality fails', in J. Friedman (ed.), *The Rational Choice Controversy* (New Haven CT: Yale University Press).

Thatcher, M. (1993), *Downing Street Years* (London: HarperCollins).

Tullock, G. (1989), *The Economics of Special Privilege and Rent Seeking* (Boston MA: Kulwer Academic).

Willets, D. (1992), *Modern Conservatism* (Harmondsworth: Penguin).

CHAPTER ELEVEN

# Fundamentalism: the Godly State

*John McGovern*

If so-called fundamentalism has been discovered among Jews, Hindus and Buddhists, the two most politically significant forms taken by what is often considered to be a global resurgence of religion (Kepel 1994) are American Protestant and Islamic fundamentalism. Although fraught with political implications, I shall argue that neither are authentically political movements. However, provoked by political circumstances which have made it possible to conceive of the impoverishment, insecurity and humiliation endured by many Muslims as caused by states that have strayed from the true faith, Islamic fundamentalism has given birth to an intrinsically unstable offspring, an anti-political political movement, 'Islamism', which has attempted, often violently, to make politics from religion. As a 'political religion', Islamism shows striking affinities with totalitarianism.

## Context

The Qur'an has 'very little to say on matters of government and the State' (Ayubi 1993: 1–2). Classical Islamic thought had a different focus. It was concerned with the personal moral and religious qualities of leaders, an emphasis which has constrained the capacity of traditional Islamic thought to develop a theory of the state (1993: 7, 14–16). According to 'the Pious Sultan theory' endorsed by the traditional clergy or *ulama*, what is essential is that the ruler should be an observant Muslim or, failing this, that he should do nothing to hinder the devout in the practice of their faith. That is, Islam was to be the 'civil theology' of Muslim states. Traditionally, the *ulama*, claiming the right not to exercise but to censure power, have urged the implementation of the *Shari'a*, Islamic law, 'without regard to the nature of the political system', thereby instilling within Islamic societies a quietist reserve towards politics which permitted the emergence of 'a secular space: the place of power' (Roy 1994: 29).

With the exception of the Iranian revolution, the Islamic clergy have never served as heads of state, leaving the task of 'Islamising' society to secular leaders. The common belief that Islam is a 'political religion', therefore, is misleading. Western intellectuals who have derived this notion from Tocqueville should have noticed that it was French revolutionary ideology which he regarded as a political religion. Whereas religion proper aims

> to regulate both the relations of the individual man with his Maker and his rights and duties towards his fellow men on a universal plane, independently, that is to say, of the views and habits of the social group of which he is a member (Tocqueville 1966: 42)

a political religion identifies the spiritual relationship between the believer and God with the political relationship between a 'citizen' and the state and confuses the 'universal' rules of ethics with the rights and duties which belong, not to the human being as such, but to the member of a particular political society or state. As we saw in Chapter 7, fascism, inheritor of the modern Western revolutionary tradition, is a political religion in this sense.

The notion that Islam is a political religion, said to be both a religion and a state (*din wa dawla*), may be current but this is testimony to the influence of fundamentalism on contemporary Muslims (Ayubi 1993: 4). Far from infusing politics with the intensity proper to religious experience, traditional Islam effectively withdrew from the political sphere. This does not imply, absurdly, that the politics of Muslim societies have no relation to Islam. Islam is the only source from which politics may derive authority for an observant Muslim. Rather, the effect of removing itself from the mundane exercise of political power has been to render Islam the civil theology of Muslim societies, that is, the body of religious meanings already existing within a society that defines a membership transcending social differences, and which, in consequence, may be appealed to by rulers to lend authority to the power they are able to exercise in virtue of their good standing in relation to that pre-political religious authority. A civil theology may also become a civil *religion* when the state actively imposes belief. Occasionally, it has been possible for Muslim states to prescribe an Islamic orthodoxy. Wahabbism has been the civil religion of the kingdom of Saudi Arabia from its formation in 1930 and, during the 1970s, the government of Pakistan attempted to impose an Islamic orthodoxy by declaring the Ahmadis 'non-Muslims' (Piscatori 1986: 5; Watt 1986: 46). However, traditionally Islam, especially the majority Sunni tradition, has always resisted the attempt of Muslim states to impose orthodoxy. Modern Islamic fundamentalism, in breaking with that tradition, has been responsible for creating a civil religion in Saudi Arabia, Pakistan and the Sudan.

By declining to stipulate an Islamic orthodoxy and emphasising instead the religious necessity of consensus within the *umma* or community of the faithful, the *ulama*, especially among the majority Sunni community, ensured that, traditionally, Islam was the civil theology of Muslim states rather than a civil religion. By endorsing 'the Pious Sultan theory' the *ulama* offered resistance to the emergence within the Islamic world of a political religion, that is, the millennialist attempt to translate the idiom of faith into the language of politics. The 'secular space' left behind by the retreat to ethical universalism would be filled by a pragmatic politics towards which the pious could be indifferent. Islamists, 'obsessed with the state', begin with an urgent political objective which distinguishes them from fundamentalists, to seize the power of the state as the indispensable instrument without which the truly Islamic society cannot be recreated (Roy 1994: xi, 61). However, Islamists are inevitably, according to Olivier Roy, drawn back towards the religious vision which they share with fundamentalists. The political society which they aim to institute is one in which the legal and ethical precepts of a purified Islam, the *Shari'a*, guide the behaviour of each and every Muslim. This means that Islamist politics contain an inherent and insuperable contradiction. They are politics dedicated to the abolition of the political sphere in favour of the religious and the ethical. That is, they are anti-political politics. Within Islamism there is a version of the

Marxist and anarchist notion of the 'withering away' of the state. As Roy has observed, 'if everyone is virtuous, why should institutions be necessary?' In fact, 'a successful re-Islamisation would bring an end to political society' (Roy 1994: 63). In effect, the *Shari'a* itself acts as an ideological brake on the emergence of the genuinely Islamic state, which would be, for Islamists, its embodiment.

Similarly, ever since the 1920s modern American fundamentalists have preferred to substitute the imperatives of religious ethics for the choices, calculations and compromises that make up secular politics. When Jerry Falwell declared in 1980 that 84 per cent of his fellow Americans 'believe that the Ten Commandments are still valid for today' it is not clear that he exaggerated entirely (Falwell 1980: xi). The US Census Bureau published figures in 2001 which suggest that about 80 per cent of Americans would describe themselves as Christians, the majority Protestant. Although not all of those Americans are as concerned as Falwell to prove the 'validity' of the Mosaic law for contemporary politics, a recent study by one American political scientist suggests that the 'religious right' can count on the support of between 10 and 15 per cent of the American public (Wilcox and Larson 2006: 5). Fundamentalism has historical roots in America, originating in the ascetic Protestantism brought to America in the seventeenth century by Presbyterian and Baptist settlers from the British Isles. Escaping what they regarded as persecution by the religious establishment, seventeenth-century non-Conformists committed themselves to a certain understanding of religious freedom. The political implications of early colonial American Protestantism were that religion was not to be, as it was in Europe, an instrument by means of which the state dominated society but 'a medium of *social* self-organization and *social* control' (Riesebrodt 1998: 33, emphasis added). As Tocqueville remarked, 'an American sees in religion the surest guarantee of the stability of the State and the safety of individuals' (Tocqueville 1966: 174). The First Amendment to the Consitution of 1789, adopted in 1791, provided a legal basis for the religious pluralism that already characterised American society.

Despite the evident theological differences, in its relation to mundane government ascetic Protestantism resembles traditional Islam in so far as the same tendency to leave political power in the hands of what, during the Reformation, were called 'civil magistrates' characterises both. By the first half of the nineteenth century

Protestantism had become the settled civil theology of the American nation, 'an ideology of integration for the new nation' (Riesebrodt 1998: 36), just as Islam serves to integrate diverse social, ethnic and tribal groups in Muslim nations. There, however, the resemblance ends, for what Protestantism provided was religious legitimacy for the American system of representative government and capitalism. Legally separated, the spheres of religion and politics were symbolically united by Protestantism as America's civil theology, a set of meanings through which all 'good' Americans discovered a shared purpose and a common national destiny (Coleman 1996: 25–7). Throughout American history Protestant Christianity has performed the mythic function, which, after Sorel, fascists insisted is essential for the life of any nation, people or race. It could not have provided its distinctive mythical vision of a 'nation dedicated to freedom' had it not excluded others. American religious pluralism did not, at least not until the twentieth century and only then for 'liberal' Americans, imply a vision of unlimited tolerance. It certainly did not signify to Protestants the emergence of a secularist state as that came to be envisaged in France after 1789, and especially after 1905 when the separation of the Church and state passed into French law. The French revolutionaries were avowedly and aggressively anti-Catholic, confiscating Church property and compelling the priesthood to swear allegiance to the state. If in America the private sphere of society and religion is seen as in need of protection by the state from the state, the French state has always sought to neutralise the religious power of the Catholic Church and, latterly, Islam.

During the late nineteenth century the social predominance of Protestantism, its capacity to define membership of American society, began to decline as a result of the effects of industrialisation, mass immigration and modern science, evolutionism in particular. Protestant denominations reacted to these upheavals in different ways. An inherent feature of Christianity is 'the potential for criticism of society' (Riesebrodt 1998: 36). Some Protestants used this potential to preach a 'social gospel', which emphasised that social conditions could be responsible for sinful behaviour and that reforming those conditions was a Christian duty. Others, the forerunners of contemporary fundamentalists, took the view that sin was the result of a lack of faith on the part of the individual and that, in consequence, the role of Protestant America was not to improve social conditions but to convert sinners. For the fundamentalists, criticism of society amounted to the rejection of secular values in the name of a return to the religious basis of the reformed faith (Riesebrodt 1998: 38, 49).

The division within American Protestantism between 'modernists' or 'liberals' and 'traditionalists' or 'fundamentalists', revealed by the publication between 1910 and 1915 of what is often taken to be the founding charter of twentieth-century American fundamentalism, a series of pamphlets authored by Protestant theologians and pastors entitled *The Fundamentals*, was political from the beginning. The 'modernists' who interpreted the Bible in the light of the 'Higher Criticism' were social reformers who supported the expansion of the state required to remedy the market failures of early twentieth-century American capitalism. In seeking to return Protestantism to its 'fundamentals' (scriptural inerrancy, creationism, the Virgin Birth, the bodily resurrection of Christ and His imminent Second Coming) the fundamentalists were also opposing the growth of an interventionist state which, they argued, was a secularist state. The emergence of fundamentalism in the 1920s was a protest against the decline of Protestantism as America's civil theology and the rise of a new 'ideology of integration' more suited to the requirements of an increasingly socially divided, multicultural and multiethnic society that invited vastly increased state supervision, regulation and intervention. Fundamentalists call this ideology 'Humanism'.

## Definition

Fundamentalism has been defined as 'a strategy, or set of strategies, by which beleaguered believers attempt to preserve their distinctive identity as a people or group' (Marty and Appleby 1993: 3). A visceral attachment to the community of which one is a member is also a feature of conservatism, as we saw in Chapter 8, and this affinity explains why it is that American fundamentalists have allied themselves with conservatives and why, as we shall see, radical Islamism tends to return to a more conservative 'neo-fundamentalism'. Moreover, 'like nationalism, fundamentalisms possess hegemonic political ambitions and demand colossal sacrifices from their devotees' (Marty and Appleby 1993: 623). What distinguishes fundamentalism from conservatism or nationalism, however, is its

## Fundamentalism: the Godly State

dependence upon a 'sacred past', invariably a sacred text, from which it derives beliefs and practices for use in the future (Marty and Appleby 1993: 3). There is a revisionary, 'modernising', element within fundamentalism. Fundamentalists discover within sacred tradition the material from which they hope to recreate a social order directed towards the future. This should not be confused with modern progressivism. The future towards which fundamentalists look is conceived of in millennialist terms as an 'end-time'.

The term originated in America where it has always been used to refer to Protestants who are committed to a literalist interpretation of the Bible. In this sense it would be 'meaningless' to apply it to Islam, according to Malise Ruthven, 'since all observant Muslims believe the Koran . . . to be the unmediated Word of God, all are committed to a doctrine of scriptural inerrancy' (Ruthven 2004: 5). Similarly, Bernard Lewis has claimed that what is distinctive about 'so-called Muslim fundamentalists' is their ambition 'to restore the full panoply of the Islamic state and the Islamic holy law'. Because of this using 'fundamentalism' in the context of Islam is 'inaccurate and misleading' (Lewis 2005: 384–5), and 'Radical Islamism' (Lewis 2004: 20) is a more appropriate description. There are good reasons for referring to such movements as the Muslim Brotherhood, the Indo-Pakistani *Jamaat-i Islami* party, *Hezbollah*, *Hizb al-Tahrir* and Islamic *Jihad* as 'Islamist' rather than 'fundamentalist'. 'Islamism' refers to radical Muslim groups that construe Islam as a political ideology. Indeed, Islamists were responsible for introducing the term 'ideology' to the Islamic world (Roy 1994: 40). For the *ulama* the term is anathema, since it implies that Islam is comparable to secular modes of thought such as Marxism. For their part, Islamists view the *ulama* as traitors to the faith (Olesen 1996: 400). It is now well established that Islamist activists are rarely clerics, tend to come from urban milieux and to have been trained in the sciences at modern universities. They are not socially representative of the broader Muslim populations whom they claim to represent politically (Riesebrodt 1993: 177–8). The organisational structure of Islamist groups resembles the Leninist-style vanguardist party. Their political aim is to seize the power of the state as an instrument for 'Islamising' societies they believe to have been corrupted by alien Western values and morally lax Muslim leadership.

None the less, it does not follow that 'fundamentalism' should not be used at all in an Islamic context. Islamism should be distinguished from the broader religious movement of which it is a part (Ayubi 1993: 68–9). 'Islamic fundamentalism' remains an appropriate description for this movement (Choueiri 1997: xvii). Fundamentalists, whether Muslim or Protestant, even when the traditional order is threatened, tend 'not to seek political office but to appeal to the government to remedy the situation', aiming to exercise moral influence over society 'from below' (Riesebrodt 1993: 195). In contrast, radical Islamist movements aim to take over the state in order to 'Islamise' society 'from above'. This 'Islamisation from above', the millennialist hope of radical movements struggling against existing Muslim states, must be distinguished from the authoritarian state-sponsored 'Islamisation from above' practised in Saudi Arabia, Pakistan and the Sudan where 'projects . . . to "Islamize" law are calculated and instrumental initiatives by regimes to consolidate their own power' (Halliday 1996: 150). Whereas authoritarian regimes use Islam as a 'civil religion', an instrument of state power, just as European monarchies once established national churches, Islamism is a political religion seeking to create an 'Islamic state' as a means to 'Islamise' society.

## Theorists

### *Individualist fundamentalism in America: Jerry Falwell and Tim LaHaye*

Jerry Falwell, the founder of the 'Moral Majority Movement' and America's most prominent fundamentalist leader during the 1980s, insisted that the 'founding fathers' of the American republic did not intend to create a democracy in which 'mob rule' or 'a social minority prevails' (Falwell 1980: 52). The form of millennialism most popular among contemporary American fundamentalists, 'premillennialism', according to which the end of the world will come, with only the righteous saved from destruction, before the advent of the millennium or thousand-year reign of Christ, has always been associated with anti-democratic sentiments (Riesebrodt 1993: 66–7). For Protestants like Falwell, without divine intervention human beings are incapable of creating a just state. Associated with this view of the state is a belief about the nature of political sovereignty which American fundamentalists share with Islamists. As Falwell insisted, 'the only sovereign over men and nations was Almighty God' (Falwell 1980: 52). In other words, the law in accordance with which the American republic is governed is God's law.

Divine 'nomocracy' is also the political objective of Islamic fundamentalists. However, nomocracy in America has an individualist accent where Islamic fundamentalism is intensely collectivist (Bruce 2000: 9–10). Falwell claimed that the superiority of a republic over a democracy derives from its greater propensity to safeguard the rights of the individual. The doctrine of the separation between Church and State is provided for in two clauses contained in the First Amendment of the American Constitution. These are that 'Congress shall make no law . . . prohibiting the free exercise (of religion)' and that 'Congress shall make no law . . . respecting an establishment of religion' (Garvey 1993: 38). Falwell's interpretation of the second of these clauses is that it was the intention of the 'founding fathers' to rule out the 'favoritism' embodied in an established church, such as the Church of England. The 'founding fathers'' opposition to civil religion, however, 'does not mean they intended a government devoid of God' (Falwell 1980: 54). On the contrary, they appreciated what Falwell sees as the true purpose of government: 'to protect the God-given rights of the people'. Among such 'natural rights', 'the lives, the liberties, and the property of the citizens' come first to mind for Falwell as, indeed, they did for John Locke (Falwell 1980: 70). 'God's law' requires a republican constitution, in which popular sovereignty takes the form of representative government rather than direct democracy, 'to ensure individual freedom' (Falwell 1980: 70).

'Individuals should be free to build their own lives without interference from government', Falwell declared (Falwell 1980: 70). He had in mind policies favoured by the Democratic Party such as redistributive taxation, increased welfare spending and anti-discrimination legislation, which fundamentalists view as invasions of individual freedoms that no state may either concede or abolish because they are God-given. In that it would interfere with individual freedom in matters of faith, any civil religion is also ruled out. What Falwell argued for, in effect, was the restoration of Protestantism as America's civil theology.

The expansion of the welfare state during the twentieth century is viewed by fundamentalists as an illegitimate extension of governmental power bordering on tyranny. The politics of fundamentalism at this point merges with the nostrums of the 'New Right' and contemporary 'neo-conservatism' (see Chapters 8 and 10).

Whereas the founding fathers sought to disperse political power, according to Falwell, welfarism depends upon unprecedented centralisation. In Falwell's view Roosevelt's 'New Deal' Democratic administration was a watershed. Belief in individual initiative was traded for 'social responsibility' with the result that a highly centralised managerial state emerged which not only eroded the basis of individual freedom but also showed itself to be incompetent, fraudulent and corrupt. The source of these evils, for fundamentalists like Falwell, lies in the fact that the welfare state deprives citizens of the free and full exercise of property rights: 'property rights are human rights' (Falwell 1980: 74).

Tim LaHaye, another prominent fundamentalist thinker, has also claimed that the constitutional provision for the separation of Church and State in America was never intended 'to separate government from God' (LaHaye 1980: 207). A central term in LaHaye's political thinking is 'Humanism', 'the world's greatest evil' (LaHaye 1980: 57). Fundamentalists believe that 'Humanism' is the ideology of powerful bureaucratic, managerial, media and literary elites. Moreover, they claim that it is propagated by the state through the public education system which is said to be controlled by 'social change agents', officials and teaching professionals who, subscribing to an 'amoral, humanistic philosophy', wield the power of the state in order to modify behaviour, preaching beliefs about 'sexual activity, contraceptives, birth elimination, and permissiveness to children, whether parents want it or not' (LaHaye 1980: 67). 'Political Correctness', the phrase invented by neo-conservatives, coincides to some extent with this 'Humanism'. The difference is that neo-conservatives do not rail against 'political correctness' because they think it impious. Fundamentalists fear 'Humanism', then, not only because it has displaced Protestantism as America's civil theology but because they recognise that, supported by the vastly increased administrative and legislative power of the twenty-first-century state, it has become a civil religion. For LaHaye, Humanism is a *'state-controlled religion'* (original emphasis) (LaHaye 1980: 67). It is vital to recognise that fundamentalists conceive of themselves as defending the traditional separation of Church and State, that is, nothing less than the American Constitution itself, against the penetration of public life by a new and aggressively secularist civil theology. State sponsored initiatives to protect 'childrens' rights', for instance, are interpreted as tactics designed to remove responsibility for family life from parents and transfer control to the state (LaHaye 1980: 67).

## Sayyid Qutb, Jihad and the Jahiliyya state

Generally regarded as the single most influential Islamist ideologue of the twentieth century, Sayyid Qutb interpreted traditional Islamic sources in such a way as to create a revolutionary Islamist political theory. Qutb described contemporary Islam with the term used by Muhammad to refer to the polytheistic religion against which the Prophet himself warred, *jahiliyya* or 'paganism', a form of spiritual ignorance. Qutb, however, applied the term to his Muslim contemporaries and used it not in a spiritual but in a political sense very close to the Marxian notion of 'false consciousness'. The whole of contemporary Islam, its laws, customs and ideas is *jahiliyya*, according to Qutb. Only a vanguard of true believers can lead the Muslim world back to the values of true Islam (Qutb 1981: 11–16).

Qutb read the Qur'an as a set of literally true, divinely authored commands addressed to the believer whom he likened to a soldier on the battlefield (Qutb 1981: 27). The purpose of such commands is to guide the true Muslim in the conduct of a holy war or *jihad*. Qutb insisted that *jihad* could not be interpreted as 'defensive war'. It is, he wrote, 'a movement to wipe out tyranny, and to introduce true freedom to mankind, using resources according to the actual human situation'. The 'true freedom', which Qutb had in mind, was 'the establishment of the sovereignty of God and his Lordship throughout the world, the end of man's arrogance and selfishness, and the implementation of the divine Shari'a in human affairs' (Qutb 1981: 111). In this way he contrived to redefine the concept of 'defence' so that it meant not protecting the faith of Muslims but 'the defence of man'. It would follow that the Muslim who wages holy war 'defends' those who imagine themselves to be his victims. In transferring the ethical universalism of religion to the political sphere, Qutb construed Islam as a political religion that could license suicidal 'martyrdom' and political terrorism (Ruthven 2002: 97). Though such actions themselves would not overcome *jahili* activity, indirectly, by provoking the retaliation of the godless state, they would reveal its oppressive nature, mobilise the faithful and so create the conditions for an apocalyptic confrontation between true Islam and 'the enemies of God'.

It has been observed that the concept of a revolutionary vanguard is a Western import without precedent in Islamic political thought (Roy 1994: 41; Ruthven 2002: 91). Qutb's Islamism shows remarkable structural similarities with totalitarianism. Whether Rousseau's 'general will', Marx's revolutionary proletariat, the fascist total state, the racially pure nation of national socialism or, in Qutb's case, a purified and militant Islam (Ruthven 2002: 91–3), as we saw in Chapter 7, the totalitarian imagination posits a type of community in which the individual achieves 'freedom' through complete submission, a community in which 'peace' is identified with a condition where conflict is removed by violent repression. A revolutionary vanguard is the initial representation of the total community and, thereafter, the agent by means of which it irrupts into history.

If there are no traditional Islamic precedents for his notion of the Islamist vanguard party, Muslim tradition did provide material for Qutb. Michael Cook has noted 'the ready availability' within that heritage 'of a particular tradition of religiously sanctioned violence' which 'may be seized upon by small, fanatical groups' (Cook 2005: 347). Although Bernard Lewis has insisted that 'Christians and Muslims share a common triumphalism' (Lewis 2004: 4), Malise Ruthven has drawn attention to the historical fact that, whereas Muhammad established what was to become an expansionist empire, Christianity was persecuted for the first three centuries of its existence and 'learned to survive, even to flourish, under non-Christian governments' (Ruthven 2000: 284). When in the fourth century it was adopted as the official creed of the Roman Empire, under the influence of Saint Augustine the distinction between spiritual power and temporal power became established, a duality which persisted up until the Protestant Reformation. With the 'City of God' defined as a spiritual destination, the authority of Augustine within the Western Church inhibited the emergence of 'the dangerous belief that the Kingdom of God would be fulfilled on earth' (Ruthven 2002: 247). The millennialism that appeared with the Reformation and reappeared within American Protestantism, has always been neutralised by the Catholic Church. Islam, not a 'Church', possesses little organisational means with which to resist millennialism and it must also be said that, unlike Christianity, 'Islam is a religion "programmed for victory"' (Ruthven 2000: 284) in which a millennialist impulse was bequeathed to his successors by Muhammad himself.

## Practical politics

*Fundamentalism and contemporary American politics*

During the late 1970s and early 1980s fundamentalist Christians turned towards political activism, believing that they had a duty to exercise moral influence within society. It should be noted that fundamentalist activists do not intend to enforce Christian morality by extra-constitutional means but, working through the legislative, judicial and electoral systems, to inhibit the increasingly powerful state from imposing secularist values upon their families, communities and the wider American society. That is, their intention is to defend the constitutional separation of Church and State. Fundamentalists are conservatives in this respect. Thus, LaHaye gave explicit support to the fact that, under United States law, churches cannot endorse political candidates or raise funds for campaigns without jeopardising their non-profit status (LaHaye 1980: 209). Since they turned towards activism, fundamentalist Christian churches have been careful not to infringe upon the law in these ways. For instance, when the 'televangelist' Pat Robertson stood for nomination as the Republican Party's presidential candidate in 1988, he did so as a private individual and not as the official representative of any church. In accordance with American law, LaHaye made clear, ministers of religion are not prohibited, as private citizens, from endorsing 'pro-moral' candidates in elections, churches are permitted to mount legislative campaigns, and there is nothing in the least unconstitutional in Christians voting as a bloc for candidates whom they believe will be likely to represent them.

By endorsing, indeed defending, the separation of the public sphere of politics from the private sphere of religion, fundamentalists limit themselves in the pursuit of their political objectives. The judicial and legislative record of activists in relation to issues such as prayers in state schools, the teaching of creationism, prohibiting abortion and outlawing homosexuality has been unimpressive. This is practically inevitable, given the combination of the highly diverse nature of American society with the fact that fundamentalists themselves invariably present their case in terms of the rights of the individual and 'the fairness principle', employing a concept of justice as 'fairness' from which a contemporary American liberal follower of John Rawls would not, in principle, demur. Thus, they argue in favour of school prayers or against abortion, for instance, by claiming to be 'pro-choice' (Bruce 2000: 76–8). Nor is recourse to political violence, within America at least, attractive to fundamentalists. At home their millennialism remains in the 'spiritualised' condition prescribed by Augustine. While in some religious traditions, Judaism for instance, 'Forcers of the End' have believed that by their own actions they can hasten the return of the Messiah, historical Christianity has prevented the irruption of immanentist eschatology by construing millennalist prophecy as symbolically rather than literally true (Barkun 2004: 63). Even though they interpret the millennialist prophesies in the Book of Revelation literalistically, none the less fundamentalist Protestants tend towards 'absolute cultural and political pessimism' (Kepel 1994: 121), understanding Christianity as an alternative to political engagement and the antithesis of terrorism (Bruce 2000: 100–1). As Michael Cook has observed, in Christian societies where there is terrorism, 'terrorists have no religion and the fundamentalists have no politics', whereas 'what is distinctive about the Muslim world is the extent to which the two have come together, and the explosiveness of the mixture' (Cook 2005: 348).

Moreover, there is evidence to suggest that a candidate too closely associated with fundamentalism may suffer electorally (Kepel 1994: 129). Fundamentalists have clearly been successful in infiltrating the Republican Party but, as Steve Bruce notes, it does not follow from this that Republican politicians, once in power, will actually implement a Christian moral agenda. In respect of the most important items on that agenda fundamentalists have signally failed to recreate America in the light of Biblical Christianity (Bruce 2000: 79–81). It would seem that the conclusion to be drawn from this is that fundamentalism proper, the movement to Christianise American public life, is not a political movement at all. Fundamentalists are genuinely committed to constitutional government. By no constitutional means, however, whether judicial, legislative or electoral, could the fundamentalist moral agenda be implemented unless the politically significant sections of American society already subscribed to it. They do not. As Olivier Roy commented in relation to Islamic fundamentalism, in order for the state to be virtuous society must already be composed of virtuous individuals but in that case the state and politics are rendered entirely unnecessary.

Nevertheless, there is an area of American foreign policy – its unstinting military, diplomatic and financial support for Israel – where fundamentalism has had a real effect. The global significance of this cannot be underestimated. Fundamentalists lobby for, proselytise on behalf of and raise funds for Israel. Jerry Falwell has enjoyed close personal relations with leaders of the Likud Party and successive Israeli prime ministers. As Dan Cohn-Sherbok has shown, this support for the Israeli state stems from fundamentalist theology (Cohn-Sherbok 2006: 161–84). Interpreting the end of the world literally as a global nuclear holocaust, men like Falwell, LaHaye, Robertson and millions of like-minded Protestants believe that the establishment of the state of Israel and its settlement of the Occupied Territories signifies the Second Coming. For them supporting Israel and fighting Israel's enemies is a Christian duty. More than that, it involves personal salvation since, according to the form of millennialism subscribed to by contemporary American fundamentalists, true believers will receive their eternal reward, being 'raptured' to Heaven, before the outbreak of the battle of Armageddon which will be fought on the soil of Israel. To support Israel is to 'force the end', the end of the irremediably corrupt, godless world of which contemporary 'humanist' America is a part. It would appear that Ronald Regan's presidency was openly influenced by such beliefs (Cohn-Sherbok 2006: 165–6). The same pessimism, which inhibits fundamentalism from genuinely engaging with domestic politics, permits it to exercise a certain influence in respect of American foreign policy.

It might be argued, then, that fundamentalism is a political movement in foreign policy. Cohn-Sherbok has suggested that it was not a desire to reform American domestic policy that lay behind Falwell's decision to found the Moral Majority movement but Israel's victory in the Six Day War (Cohn-Sherbok 2006: 161–2). The political meaning of fundamentalist support for Israel lies in its providing a religious justification, attractive to millions of Americans who might otherwise have cause to question it, for a policy which also corresponds to the rather more mundane political and economic interests of powerful sections of American society. It so happens that fundamentalist millennialist fantasies have converged with the interests of the right wing of the Republican Party, neo-conservative ideologues, multinational construction firms, the petroleum and arms industries and the Jewish American pro-Israeli lobby (Cohn-Sherbok 2006: 166). In the context of American foreign policy, its apparently limitless support for Israel and determination to defeat Israel's enemies in a 'war on terrorism', Christian fundamentalism resembles a political religion. If its constitutionalism has, so far, prevented it from appearing as one within America itself, that does not prohibit it from serving as an ideological focus for military action undertaken against nations and peoples whose chief characteristic, according to those who make American foreign policy, is the absence of constitutional politics in the American style, an absence which may be rectified by the use of American military power. It might be the case that terrorists have no religion and fundamentalists no politics within America itself but its foreign policy, unleashing terror in the name of 'freedom', suggests that this can be reversed in America's dealings with other nations and peoples.

Domestically, however, fundamentalism proper is best seen as a conservative protest movement the aim of which is, not to seize state power in order to Christianise America but to evangelise American society in such a way as to defend a particular way of life the status of which has been progressively eroded for a century and a half. For fundamentalists 'politics is only an epiphenomenon, an effect, not a cause' and what they seek is not to overthrow or even to control the state but 'a cultural victory . . . over the "Liberal" intelligentsia, which must be defeated on its own ground' (Kepel 1994: 132). In this, like all conservatives, fundamentalists are swimming against the tide. They are not likely to win a cultural war fought on ground of the enemy's choosing. In so far as it has a genuinely political objective, that is to diminish the power of the welfare state that many American Protestants view, not without justification, as acting against their economic interests and instilling values to which they cannot consent. Leaders like Jerry Falwell or Pat Robertson represent not only the relatively affluent fundamentalists of the North, urban Midwest and southern California whose opposition to welfarism is motivated by moral considerations, loss of social status and fears for personal security in a society both atomised and racially divided but, as Gilles Kepel has observed, also the 'poor whites' of the South and rural Midwest. These were the people who, having provided the United States Army with recruits in disproportionate numbers during the Second World War, after 1945 'received nothing from the social welfare programmes but had to pay for them through taxes, and who were excluded from the networks of political, cultural and social power' (Kepel 1994: 134). In their hostility towards 'big government' it has been possible for fundamentalists to make common cause with other powerful sections of American society who nowadays parade under the banner of 'neo-conservatism'. In this way, pious American Protestants continue to provide foot soldiers, activists, campaigners and voters for a political movement that attacks the welfare state in order to promote an economic and political system that must defeat the most cherished moral and religious ideals of Evangelical America.

In short, American fundamentalist politics are internally contradictory. The moral evils that fundamentalists inveigh against are conditioned by the same market freedom they think of as God's law. Protestant fundamentalism is an ideology in Marx's sense, a set of beliefs that permit late capitalism and the system of government that is its political expression to go unchallenged by misrecognising their real significance. The effective political agenda to which the 'Christian Right' contributes its considerable electoral support is provided by a genuinely political movement which, unburdened by a Christian conscience, can control the power of the American state – neo-conservativism. The neo-conservative agenda, it is true, contains much talk of morality. As we have seen in Chapter 8, however, neo-conservative morality is restricted to rules that those who derive benefits from market freedom prescribe for those to whom such freedom is a source of suffering, such as 'poor whites'. It is not a Christian morality.

## The myth of the 'Islamic state'

Turkey, Egypt and most other Muslim states, when they became independent after colonialism, proclaimed constitutions that formally resemble those of Western nations. Such constitutions contradict the *Shari'a*. For instance, Article 3 of the Egyptian Constitution abolishes the traditional *Shari'a* distinction between Muslims, *dhimmis* (tolerated subject peoples of a different faith) and unbelievers by granting full legal equality to all Egyptian citizens, while Article 12 declares that 'freedom of conscience is absolute', contradicting the *Shari'a* prescription that apostates must be executed (Ruthven 2000: 306). Islamists have always distinguished between 'Muslim states' and the 'Islamic state', as their explicit political aim is to destroy the former in order to institute the latter. It is precisely because they are secular that modern Muslim states are violently attacked by Islamist groups. But those states could not exist without being secular.

The 'Islamic state' imagined by Islamists is a myth (Roy 1994: 27). If a predominantly Muslim nation succeeds in creating for itself a state, that could never be 'Islamic', while the result of implementing the ideology of radical Islam would be the creation of a stateless Islamic society. As Roy has argued, the vision of an Islamic state in which the *Shari'a* occupies in full the legal sphere 'is condemned to serving as a mere cover for a political logic that eludes it' (1994: ix). As well as being an ideology in the political sense, an ostensibly more or less coherent political programme, it is 'ideological' in the Marxist sense of 'false consciousness', a set of ideals the real function of which is not to disclose but to disguise social realities, the more so the greater the conviction of those who subscribe to the ideals. Islamic fundamentalism resembles Christian fundamentalism in this respect. In the case of Islamism, the social reality hidden from view by a vision of the *Shari'a* as a timeless set of truths to be implemented as a matter of sacred duty is the condition of statelessness, caused by the presence of traditional ethnic, tribal or communal divisions which continue to characterise much of the Islamic world, 'the horizontal bonds of solidarity groups' which inhibit the emergence of a modern state (Roy 1994: 11). In so far as it aims to overthrow the *jahilyya* state and Islamicise society 'from above', Islamism may be said to be a political movement. But its politics are inherently contradictory, for the achievement of those political aims would signify the end of politics. The 'Islamic state' would not be a state.

Initially supported by secular radicals and a wide range of religious groups, revolution in Iran led to the proclamation of the Islamic Republic in 1979 under the leadership of the Ayatollah Ruhollah Khomeini. During the early 1940s the young Khomeini criticised the then Shah, Reza Khan, on religious fundamentalist, not political Islamist, grounds, blaming him for undermining religion by introducing into Iran a disease, 'occidentosis' or 'Westoxification' (Bruce 2000: 51). At this stage, Khomeini appeared to adopt the traditional Muslim view that the duty of the clergy was to exercise religious supervision, not to rule. He came to political prominence in the early 1960s when, implicated in protest movements against a government perceived by most Iranians as corrupt and repressive, he was deported. It was in exile that Khomeini delivered lectures in which Islam was presented as a political religion, the faith of 'militant individuals who are committed to truth and justice' for whom there is no more a separation now between religion and politics than there was for Muhammad. In the

'Islamic state', governed by *Shari'a* law, the clergy were to be the rulers (Abrahamian 1992: 118).

However, in the period just before the revolution he shied away from any mention of theocracy in the knowledge that this would have alienated not only the secular middle classes but the traditional clergy, using instead his 'extraordinary ability to unify the various components, religious and secular, of a movement whose single point of departure was hatred of the shah and his government' (Kepel 2002: 112). While refraining from revealing his theocratic ambitions, Khomeini made abundant reference to the *mostazafin*, the 'disinherited', using the millennialist language of Third World anti-colonialism and Marxism to appeal especially to the young and the lower classes with vague populist promises to end oppression and establish God's rule on earth because, he declared, 'Islam belongs to the mostazafin' (Abrahamian 1992: 119–22).

On his return to Tehran in February 1979, Khomeini 'set about eliminating all of his secular allies and establishing a theocracy' with himself as 'God's Representative on Earth' at its head (Kepel 2002: 113). This did not take longer than a few months. All dissent was prohibited in accordance with the doctrine of *vahdet-e kalimeh*, 'the oneness of discourse' (Kepel 2002: 116). When war with Iraq broke out in 1980, Khomeini seized the opportunity to sacrifice Iran's youth and working classes in the name of Islam, thereby breaking the political will of the 'disinherited'. Having offered up the lives of a generation, Khomeini was able to make use of them as 'martyrs' to the Islamic Republic. In speeches and murals the sacrifice of the 'martyrs' was celebrated. The families of 'martyrs' were granted special privileges. For instance, siblings of the dead were permitted to take up a place at university without needing to pass an entrance exam.

Once God's rule was established on earth, the wearing of the veil and full Islamic dress became compulsory, with miscreants, generally women from the secularised middle classes, hounded and beaten or arrested by a newly instituted 'morality police' recruited from the working classes who were encouraged to regard themselves as defenders of the faith. The 'disinherited' were given the opportunity to be persecutors as compensation for being excluded from political power and remaining economically disadvantaged. As Malise Ruthven has argued, in Iran, as in the Sudan since 1989, it has not been 'civil society' but 'the post-colonial state and the interest groups controlling it' that have benefited from radical Islamic revolution. Promising freedom ('under God'), economic development and prosperity Islamist regimes, such as Iran, turn quickly 'from economics to morality' without this at all diminishing the power of the state, 'rather the reverse' (Ruthven 2004: 148). State power in Khomeini's Islamic Republic remains at least as authoritarian as the regime of the Shah. The Islamist revolution became an authoritarian neo-fundamentalist state in which Islam was used as a civil religion.

Borrowing from modern Western political thought, especially Marxism, Islamists bend traditional Quranic terms to give them an alien political meaning. Though often called 'conservative', there is none of the reverence for tradition characteristic of the authentic conservative in Islamism. For Khomeini and others *mostazafin* ('meek') becomes 'disinherited' or 'exploited'. Qutb treated *jahiliyya* as the equivalent of another Marxist notion, 'false consciousness'. One of the most important of all Islamic theological concepts, *tawhid*, the 'divine oneness' attributed to God alone, has been interpreted by Islamists as applying to human society, the *tawhidi* society being a 'total order' from which social, ethnic, national and, of course, religious differences are to be eliminated (Roy 1994: 40–1; see also Stenberg 1996: 150). In applying *tawhid* to society, Islamists have effectively imported into Islamic discourse the concept of the total state common to both fascism and communism.

There are further parallels with modern Western revolutionary ideology. Islamists also subscribe to a cult of the leader or *amir*, a 'charismatic chief', 'his own indicator', who 'by merely appearing . . . would be instantly recognizable' because 'the idea of voting and of election seems to weaken the unity of the *umma*' (Roy 1994: 43). In Iran, among the Shia, the leader is the *imam*. It was widely believed that Khomeini was the twelfth or 'hidden' *imam*, an eschatological figure whose reappearance on earth would herald the consummation of history. The Ayatollah did not go out of his way to deny it (Abrahamian 1992: 111). The *amir* is the equivalent of the totalitarian leader, the *umma* whose unity he is said to represent resembles far more the Fascist notion of 'the people' as the nation, the Nazi identification of the *volk* as a racial entity or the 'progressive' elements declared to be 'the people' by Marxists than the traditional *umma*, the community of the faithful. Neither the *amir* nor what Islamists propose as the Islamic equivalent of democracy, the *shura*, a council which has no legislative powers but serves merely to advise or counsel the *amir*, are conceived of as autonomous institutions, providing for government as an 'office' independent of the individuals who happen to hold power. Though Islamist parties, such as the Algerian *Front Islamique du Salut*, interpret the *shura* as 'Islamic democracy', this means no more than that laymen, providing they are Muslims, and not only the clerical elite, might be elected to the assembly. 'Democracy' in this context signifies a power struggle between two elites, educated lay Islamists and the traditional *ulama*. It does not imply the doctrine of popular sovereignty. On the contrary, irrespective of who are the representatives composing the *shura*, this assembly should not make law because only God is sovereign and His law, the *Shari'a*, is already present and complete, requiring nothing more than interpretation and application. The *shura*, then, presupposes an already God-given consensus that it is its purpose to maintain. The opposite of consensus is said to be 'arbitrariness' or 'despotism' and this is related to 'oppression' (Stenberg 1996: 151–2). An 'oppressor' or 'despot' is, therefore, anyone who departs from Islamic law and 'freedom' is identified with accepting it without question.

Islamism represents just the condition from which the modern state, striving for autonomy from both rulers and ruled, has delivered those societies in which it has flourished, the same condition of statelessness to which Islamism's ideological predecessors, Fascism and Communism, regressed. Again, like those movements, because the presence of a plurality of political parties is incompatible with Islamism, the Islamist party is an 'anti-party', the purpose of which is to represent, not one among a variety of interests, but 'the people of God' as an indissoluble whole (Stenberg 1996: 151). Just as Mussolini's PNF identified itself with the Italian nation, the Nazis with the Aryan race and Communist parties everywhere with 'humanity', the Islamist parties are always understood by their members, each one 'born again' as a 'true Muslim', to be prefigurations of the future Islamic state which it is their purpose to bring into being. If Islamists, inevitably, turn back from politics towards religious fundamentalism this may be more true of their relations with fellow Muslims than with non-believers. Here there is a similarity with the American religious Right. Ideologues such as Qutb and Khomeini, for whom America was 'the Great Satan', have interpreted *jihad* as war waged against 'the enemies of God', giving a political and military meaning to traditional Islamic millennialist belief in the 'cosmic struggle of good and evil' (Lewis 2005: 394–6). Osama bin Ladin is reported as having charged the faithful with a duty of holy war against 'the armies of the American devils and against those who are allied with them from among the helpers of Satan' (quoted in Lewis 2004: xxv). The terrorist tactics recommended by Qutb and employed by the disparate groups commonly referred to as 'Al Qa'ida', designed to provoke confrontation in order to militarise Islam, show them to be 'Forcers of the End'.

Olivier Roy has argued that within the Islamic world, however, Islamism is no less a political failure than Christian fundamentalism has been in America. The *mostafazin* have not inherited the earth. In the majority of Islamic nations traditional clerical and political elites remain in power. It may, however, be too early to pronounce Islamism a political failure. In July 2006 Israel declared war on the Iranian-backed *Hezbollah* in Lebanon. The consequences of this struggle cannot be foreseen. On the other hand, Roy's claim that its failure has been religious seems more secure. In 1988, Khomeini issued the diktat that the authority of the Islamic Republic over which he presided was the same as the Prophet's. Thus, if a policy deemed essential to the interests of the state contradicted the *Shari'a*, the latter could be abrogated (Ruthven 2004: 148). For instance, in the case of the *fatwa* that he promulgated against Salman Rushdie, Khomeini claimed, contrary to Islamic tradition that the fatwa would persist after his death. He broke with the tradition of collegiality among grand ayatollahs and promoted clerics because they were activists owing allegiance to him and not on the basis of their religious rank. Because the Shi'ite clergy have also been persecuted in Iraq, Khomeini's politicisation of the clergy has emptied its ranks, with clever young clerics preferring political activism to religious devotion. Khomeini not only physically but also spiritually diminished the Shi'ite clergy by eliminating 'the transcendent, autonomous space from which the clergy spoke: the clergy was brought down to the level of the state' (Roy 1994: 180). Nor does the clergy even control the state, as a hierarchy of Islamist political activists has supplanted the religious hierarchy. By making the *Shari'a* subordinate to the revolution, the only successful Islamist revolution succeeded in going some way towards abolishing Islam itself.

## Bibliography

Abrahamian, E. (1992), 'Khomeini: A fundamentalist?', in L. Kaplan (ed.), *Fundamentalism in Comparative Perspective* (Amherst MA: University of Massachusetts Press).

Ayubi, N. (1993), *Political Islam: Religion and Politics in the Arab World* (London: Routledge).
Barkun, M. (2004), 'Religious violence and the myth of fundamentalism', in L. Weinberg and A. Pedahzur (eds), *Religious Fundamentalism and Political Extremism* (London: Frank Cass), pp. 55–70.
Bruce, S. (2000), *Fundamentalism* (Cambridge: Polity).
Choueiri, Y. (1997), *Islamic Fundamentalism* (London: Continuum).
Cohn-Sherbok, D. (2006), *The Politics of Apocalypse: The History and Influence of Christian Zionism* (Oxford: Oneworld).
Coleman, S. (1996), 'Conservative Protestantism, politics and civil religion in the United States', in D. Westerlund (ed.), *Questioning the Secular State: The World-Wide Resurgence of Religion in Politics* (London: C. Hurst), pp. 24–47.
Cook, M. (2005), *A Brief History of the Human Race* (London: Granta).
Falwell, J. (1980), *Listen, America!* (New York: Doubleday).
Garvey, J. H. (1993), 'Fundamentalism and American law', in M. Marty and R. Scott Appleby (eds), *Fundamentalism and the State* (Chicago IL: University of Chicago Press), pp. 28–49.
Kepel, G. (1994), *The Revenge of God: The Resurgence of Islam, Christianity and Judaism in the Modern World* (Cambridge: Polity).
Kepel, G. (2002), *Jihad: The Trail of Political Islam* (London: I. B. Tauris).
LaHaye, T. (1980), *Battle for the Mind* (Old Tappan NJ: Fleming H. Revell).
Lewis, B. (2004), *The Crisis of Islam: Holy War and Unholy Terror* (London: Phoenix).
Lewis, B. (2005), *From Babel to Dragomans: Interpreting the Middle East* (London: Phoenix).
Marty, M. and Appleby, R. Scott (eds) (1993), *Fundamentalism and the State* (Chicago IL: University of Chicago Press).
Olesen, A. (1996), 'The Islamic movement in Afghanistan: National liberation and the challenge of power', in D. Westerlund (ed.), *Questioning the Secular State: The Worldwide Resergence of Religion in Politics* (London: C. Hurst), pp. 392–410.
Piscatori, J. F. (1986), *Islam in a World of Nation-States* (Cambridge: Cambridge University Press).
Qutb, S. (1981), *Milestones* (New Delhi: Ishaat-e-Islam Trust Publications).
Riesebrodt, M. (1998), *Pious Passion: The Emergence of Modern Fundamentalism in the United States and Iran* (Berkeley CA: University of California Press).
Roy, O. (1994), *The Failure of Political Islam*, trans. C. Volk (London: I. B. Tauris).
Ruthven, M. (2000), *Islam in the World* (Harmondsworth: Penguin).
Ruthven, M. (2002), *A Fury for God: The Islamist Attack on America* (London: Granta).
Ruthven, M. (2004), *Fundamentalism* (Oxford: Oxford University Press).

Stenberg, L. (1996), 'The revealed word and the struggle for authority: interpretation and use of Islamic terminology among Algerian Islamists', in D. Westerlund (ed.), *Questioning the Secular State: The World-Wide Resurgence of Religion in Politics* (London C. Hurst), pp. 140–66.

Tocqueville, A. de (1966), *The Ancien Regime and the French Revolution*, trans. S. Gilbert (London: Fontana).

Watt, W. M. (1986), *Islam: A Short History* (Oxford: Oneworld).

Westerlund, D. (ed.) (1996), *Questioning the Secular State: The World-Wide Resurgence of Religion in Politics* (London: C. Hurst).

Wilcox, C. and Larson, C. (2006), *Onward Christian Soldiers: The Religious Right in American Politics* (3rd edn) (Boulder CO: Westview Press).

CHAPTER TWELVE

# Futures: Theorising the State in a 'Global Age'
*Erika Cudworth*

The phenomenon of globalisation has been contested and proved to be contentious, and various theories of the state have demonstrated their plurality and internal contradictions as they grapple with the key questions posed by globalisation theory. Is there such a thing as globalisation, or is this a different term for some well-known phenomena? If globalisation is something relatively new and distinctive, how has the organisation of political life changed as a result? Have any changes in state form and powers been generally positive, negative or mixed in their impact?

The organisation of modern politics has for at least the last three hundred years been associated with the 'nation-state'. As we saw in Chapter 1, the notion of territoriality is key to the concept of the nation-state – states have jurisdiction over legitimate violence and political power (often based on a claim of representation) within a particular geographical space (Anderson 1974). Developments and conflicts in the nineteenth and twentieth centuries seemed to suggest that the rise of the nation-state as the key formation of modern politics was inexorable. For sceptical voices within globalisation theory, regional and national politics is very much alive in the twenty-first century. In what pass for 'international' political organisations, it is bargains between nation-states that are being struck and the interests of nation-states that structure debate and decision making. The world order is not a pluralist forum where the interests of multiple states are represented, but an arena that is defined and shaped by the interests of the most powerful states. For others, however, globalisation either has transformed or is transforming the organisation of politics as we have known it. In this view, we have seen since 1945 a growth in the number of international and transnational economic and political organisations, and pressure groups. NGOs and social movements are seen to campaign on a 'global level', and nation-states are arenas of compromised sovereignty extensively penetrated by the demands and regulations of international networks and institutions. Diverse issues (such as trade, security and environmental protection) are increasingly managed at regional and global level.

This chapter sets the context for contemporary debates on 'globalisation' in relation to those in 'world systems' and 'dependency' theory from the 1960s. An emergent question here is whether there is anything distinctive about more contemporary theories of 'globalisation'. The following section clarifies the concept of globalisation and considers the definitions linked to various perspectives in the globalisation debate. Theorists are drawn from different positions in this debate and from different schools of state theory. For example, neo-liberal Kenechi Ohmae has argued that the nation-state has no future in a 'borderless world', whereas Marxist Alex Callinicos sees the politics of 'globalism' as a new form of imperialism. Some Marxist and socialist theorists have been concerned about the inability of the state to secure social justice within the parameters of a global capitalism, whereas liberal internationalists like Ronald Robertson have been encouraged by the cultural effects of globalism as a mechanism of restraining 'national' and parochial interests in international decision making. In addition, sceptical left theorists such as Leslie Sklair and Paul Hirst have argued that a 'global system' is not a recent development, whereas David Held considers that the nation-state is undergoing a process of radical institutional transformation in a changed context. Practical political consequences are considered in terms of the global nature of certain aspects of policy making, the role of 'global' political institutions and political activism. In considering the possible globalisation of politics, this chapter will conclude by drawing together and evaluating what different theories have to say about the health of the nation-state in the twenty-first century. The debate on globalisation is key to understanding possible futures for the state, and as David Held and Anthony McGrew (2002: 58) remark: '. . . the globalisation debate projects, into a new context, the cardinal

## Futures: Theorising the State in a 'Global Age'

questions of political life concerning power and rule, namely: who rules, in whose interests, by what means and for what ends?'

### Context

The concept of globalisation has historical antecedents in the theories of modernisation and dependency developed in the 1960s within politics, sociology and development studies. Modernisation theorists generally adhered to a 'convergence hypothesis' – capitalism was to spread around globe, accompanied by the development of liberal democracy. Critics contended that modernisation was an apparently neutral term for a highly political process: the global expansion of capitalist market relations through economic and cultural imperialism.

The theories of modernisation that emerged in the 1950s drew upon the approaches to social change in Europe developed by the 'classical' sociologists. Talcott Parsons drew on Durkheim in proposing an 'evolutionary' approach to social change where 'societies' adapt to become more functional in changed circumstances. Those influenced by Weberian sociology, such as Walt Rostow (1962), emphasised the cultural prerequisites for 'development'. Economic growth follows the pattern of the industrialised countries towards a 'mass consumption' society, and the historical experience of the West can be used to explain how the 'Third World' would develop. The neo-Marxist tradition argued, however, that the 'Third World' was not impoverished because it had 'failed' to develop. Rather, poorer countries have been 'underdeveloped' to the economic benefit of Western nations.

An early critic of mainstream modernisation approaches was André Gunder Frank (1969) who claimed that developing countries have long been incorporated into world capitalist relations. He developed a model of a world 'metropolis' consisting of a global governing class with 'satellites' consisting of governing elites in the 'peripheries' (poorer countries) and at sub-national level. He suggested a chain of dependent relations from the centre of the world capitalist system to the peripheries, the key feature of which is that the world metropolis and Western national metropolises accumulate resources from the Third World – 'underdeveloping' it. Critics argued that Third World societies are too different and complex to be considered with such a single model of social change

(Randall and Theobald 1985: 123) but, despite a recess in interest in global theorising in the 1980s, the 1990s saw their resurgence in theories of the 'global system'.

Immanuel Wallerstein (1974) similarly divided the globe, but into three categories: the core; periphery; and semi-periphery. The core was formed in the seventeenth century from the modernising states of northern Europe, which exploit the countries of the periphery, and hold back the development of the semi-periphery. Wallerstein (1979) stressed that from the early phase of its development, capitalism has been an international system. The division of the world into state socialist and free market/liberal democratic camps in the Cold War period was historically something of an aberration. Rather, we have had a global economy with high levels of mobility of capital and labour, and high levels of international trade benefiting global and regional capitalist classes (Braudel 1984; Frank and Gills 1996; Wallerstein 1974). For Frank (1998: xvi), however, Wallerstein and Braudel remain trapped in 'Eurocentric ideology'. Frank argues that European hegemony was not established until the nineteenth century, and he presents an incredible mass of detail in order to suggest the dominance of Asia in an international network of economic relations from 1400 to 1800. In this kind of theorising, the state is relatively unimportant – merely a connective node in a worldwide system of relationships. It is the points of connection between regional power formations that are important (Frank 1998: 338). Wallerstein and Frank are agreed, however, that what is analytically important is the global level – they have no concept of 'free standing' relatively autonomous societies or states, for all social, political and economic relations are interconnected through the capitalist world system.

In all these accounts the state seems unimportant, it is analytically marginal, reduced to an instrument of corporate capital. Yet Wallerstein argues that the changes in the political system around 1500 led to a centring of the world system on European capitalism. Frank also wants us to believe that the mercantilism of European states had a fortuitous role in the apparent dominance of the 'West' in the emerging modern state system. World systems theory is not entirely distinct from some of the approaches to 'globalisation', and certainly both preceded the latter and continue to be an important approach in understanding the global political context.

Anthony Giddens (1990) argues less strongly, that the processes of modernisation in Europe, the impact of colonialism and neo-colonial relations and the emergent new social economic and political forms in globalised society are not distinct phases but are closely interconnected. Others suggest that globalisation is 'relatively autonomous' from modernisation, and that there are a series of distinct processes associated with it (Robertson 1992: 60). Jan Aart Scholte (2005: 85–120) considers that Wallerstein, Frank, Sklair and even Giddens, overstate the case for continuity. What is different about the theorising of globalisation is that from the late nineteenth century and through the twentieth century we have seen a progressive and rapid intensification of 'supraterritorial' links across the globe, that is, connections which transcend territorial geography, which are not clearly linked to a 'place'. Such different readings of history bring us to the vexed question of how globalisation might be defined in the first place.

## Definition

In the last fifteen years, talk of globalisation and the politics of 'anti-globalisation' has reached a fevered pitch and burgeoning literature of sometimes dubious quality fills library shelves. There are few brave souls who claim that theorising 'globalisation' is 'folly' and that the concept, as deployed by many in the field, has no theoretical worth or empirical utility (Rosenberg 2001, 2005). Certainly, within the literature, different theorists mean different things when they speak of globalisation. Ulrich Beck (1999) distinguishes between what he calls the 'planetary perspective' adopted by the critics of globalisation ('globality' or 'globalism'), the neo-liberal ideology and practice of 'globalisation', and the subjective cultural understanding of what globalisation might be. There are, therefore, a range of ways in which globalisation is both understood and defined, and the definitions themselves reflect different theories of both politics and the state.

Some have a subjectivist definition, and consider that the peoples of the globe are increasingly seeing themselves as part of a globalised world (Waters 1995: 3). Ronald Robertson (1992) argues the world is increasingly 'compressed' by our ability to travel around it quickly and to 'know' it through new forms of information and communication technology such as the Internet. Most people now have a sense of global oneness that he refers to as 'the consciousness of the world as a single place' (1992: 183). For others, globalisation is essentially 'about' space, more specifically, the changing nature/qualities of space, or 'respatialisation'. For David Held and Anthony McGrew (2002: 1) the changing nature of geography is crucial for globalisation:

> ... denotes the expanding scale, growing magnitude, speeding up and deepening impact of transcontinental flows and patterns of social interaction. It refers to a shift or transformation in the scale of human organization that links distant communities and expands the reach of power relations across the world's regions and continents.

Political and cultural geographers in particular have argued that social and political relationships show a tendency towards 'deterritorialisation' (Massey and Joss 1995; ÓTuathail 2000; Short 2001). For Held et al. (1999: 16) globalisation is a complex concept implying a 'set of processes' involving this changing spatialisation. These have differing levels of 'extensity, intensity, velocity and impact' – so the effects of globalisation are not presumed to be evenly spread. I find this the most convincing of definitions in that it attempts to capture something distinctive. We can then evaluate whether this apparently 'new' phenomena is actually taking place.

Various other definitions conceptualise globalisation as a new term for established processes. Globalisation is sometimes seen as a process of univeralisation, associated with the spread of cultural objects, consumer capitalism and political practices associated with Westernisation or Americanisation (Spybey 1996). The social structures of Western modernity, including bureaucratisation, industrialism and rationalism, are spreading across the globe and this usually involves the destruction and/or displacement of indigenous cultures. George Ritzer, famous for his thesis that the social world is becoming increasingly 'McDonaldized' (Ritzer 1993) has more recently suggested that we are witness to a process involving the 'globalisation of nothing' as we move from indigenous, local and distinctive social forms to standardised 'McDonaldization' (Ritzer 2004). Globalisation has also been understood either as a process of economic liberalisation (Sander 1996: 27) or as an alternative term for internationalisation, that is, for cross-border relations and international exchanges and dependencies (Hirst and Thompson 1999: 48). Finally, there are those on the left who define globalisation as a new 'stage' in the historical processes of imperialism

(Callinicos et al. 1994) and others for whom globalisation is 'not a particularly useful term . . . it can be counterposed with a term that has considerably greater descriptive value and explanatory power: *imperialism*.' (Petras and Veltmeyer 2001: 12, original emphasis). Even those with a less strong analytic claim have deployed the term 'empire' in order to describe what Michael Hardt and Antonio Negri (2000: xii) see as a 'deterritorializing apparatus of rule'.

Many of the different definitions offered reflect the analytic positions and ideological commitments of the theorists concerned. What I like about the spatial definition is that it gives the concept of globalisation distinctive content as a process of 'deterritorialisation', rather than putting a new gloss on established notions. We are then perhaps, in a better position to assess if this distinctive phenomenon is indeed distinctive. We do not necessarily have to concur with a particular theory of, or position on, globalisation in order to define it in this way.

## Theories

While many liberal pluralists accept the definition of globalisation as a form of internatialionalisation, other groups of state theorists, Marxists for example, are divided as to whether globalisation is historically distinctive and whether it requires new approaches to understand the rapaciousness of international capital. Feminism has also produced mixed responses. Some have been supportive of regional trans-territorial developments, such as the employment policies of the European Union; while others have been concerned that globalisation has sharpened the differences between rich and poor countries and further contributed to the feminisation of poverty. On the right, there are those who see the free market vindicated and the state rendered powerless by the powerful economic processes of globalisation, while others argue against regional and global political projects and are concerned about the Americanisation of local cultures. For extreme nationalists, it is national culture that is eroded by globalisation. For example, the current leader of the National Front in France, Jean-Marie le Pen, has considered 'French culture' to be a victim of the 'abattoirs of Euro-globalisation' (cited in Scholte 2005: 18). Meanwhile, the politics of anarchism has enjoyed media coverage unprecedented for decades, due to the involvement of anarchist groupings in the 'anti-globalisation movement'. Because of the complexity and contradiction involved in theorising the state in a 'global' context, I have chosen a number of theorists here who exemplify different approaches and reflect a range of the theories of the modern state found in the rest of this book.

'Hyperglobalisers' (Held et al. 1999) or 'globalists' (Held and McGrew 2002) see globalisation as a new development in the history of human social organisation. Deep structural changes are taking place, so that contemporary social relations have become thoroughly 'globalised'. An important development is the increase of activities that operate at interregional, trans- and intercontinental scales. These relationships are not seen as inevitably hierarchical. Global political organisations such as the United Nations are not necessarily the most 'important', because power relationships depend on the specific arena in question (Dicken 1998). Globalists identify three areas of change – socio-economic organisation, the reach and impact of decision making and a challenge to the territorial basis of the nation-state system. While globalists agree on the extent to which the social and political world is 'globalised', their views on the nature of the process differ strongly.

The neo-liberal Kenechi Ohmae (1995: 5) argues that we are living in a new 'era' in which globalisation is de-nationalising our economies through international networks of finance, production and trade. We now have a 'borderless economy' where the political authority of nation-states is negligible. The operations of multinational corporations integrate into regional and global production networks, the notion of a national economy is no longer sustainable, and the distinction between national and international economic activity is blurred at best (Ohmae 1990). To extrapolate from the notion that sovereignty is compromised by international economic activity, to argue that it is neglible and the state is redundant is over-drawn. Ohmae actually says little of the political institutions whose obituary he is so keen to write. We might argue that the nature of political sovereignty has shifted remarkably in some areas (Sørenson 1999) without concluding this indicates the demise of nation-statehood.

Martin Albrow (1996: 85) argues that political globalisation is ushering in a new world order in which the dominant political form is liberal democracy, and we have a common global culture in which democracy and consumer capitalism are key values. Ohmae also recognises this shift, and suggests the role of the politician as a national representative is now outmoded (1995: 149). For Ohmae, global institutions of governance such as the International Monetary Fund (IMF) and the World Trade Organization (WTO) are capable of providing the necessary regulation of the global market as we move towards the grand destination of a 'world civilisation'. With developments in global communications, others argue that NGOs and groups in civic society are engaging in new forms of effective political engagements. International institutions of governance like the United Nations and the WTO have created new political spaces in which the voices of 'citizens' and interest groups can be heard, and these engagements shape the practices of global governance (Rosenau 1990). A characteristic of both liberal pluralist and neo-liberal explanations seems to be their apparent lack of specificity, justification and verification. Why this might be is uncertain, but I would concur with Scholte's hunch (2005: 125) that this is because such accounts have been less subject to critique, forming, as they do, part of the established status quo in powerful states, financial institutions and the UN.

Hyperglobalisers on the left such as William Grieder (1997) agree that the magnitude and scale of global economic interaction is historically unprecedented. National economies are no longer effectively national, for they are increasingly enmeshed in global systems of production and exchange. We are in an era of 'supraterritorial capitalism'. Capital has become 'footloose' – liberated from the restraints of national states and their territorial boundaries (Dicken 1998). This process has increased exponentially with the collapse of state socialism as a viable alternative to the market system. Although there remain harsh inequalities between the global north and south, we are also seeing divisions within nations and regions – a new global division of labour in which we see the increasing poverty of certain groups within what have been thought of as the rich and poor regions (Amin 1997). States are increasingly forced to adopt a political agenda that supports economic neo-liberalism, and what concerns Grieder is that this will prevent any attempt to redistribute wealth through progressive taxation, or to provide social service provision for the less well off. Governments in liberal democratic states are increasingly unable to maintain existing levels of social welfare and protection. In this sense, globalisation can be seen to represent the 'triumph' of global capitalism over social justice, where the needs and priorities of global capital and the interests of the transnational corporations impose a neo-liberal ideological commitment and policy framework on all national governments.

For some Marxists, the development of international institutions is about the promotion of global capitalism. The UN and the other organisations of economic and social co-operation advance the project of a liberal democratic and capitalist world order (Sklair 2001). Liberal global governance takes as given the universal applicability, suitability and value of the institutions and practices of liberal democracy and the market economy. What we are currently witness to is the coming together of a range of elite groups – political, bureaucratic, corporate and technical – in networks of global policy making to form a 'transnational capitalist class' wedded to the enhancement and sustenance of global capitalism. However, not all on the left are so pessimistic. James Mittleman provides a neo-Gramscian account that emphasises the significance of struggles by the global underclass in resisting globalisation. Mittleman (2000) argues that the conditions for radical change are endemic in the contradictions of the world capitalist system, and anti-globalisation social movement organisations (SMOs) are 'engines of change' that will eventually transform or even 'destroy' the current global capitalist system (2000: 242). In this view, global institutions cannot regulate globalisation; it must be transformed through collapse. Mittleman uses the traditional Marxist argument here that the (supraterritorial) 'superstructure' cannot keep pace with the changes in the economic base. Thus, the spread of the market outstrips the pace of 'democratisation' and it is in 'the space opened up by this disjuncture' (2000: 165) that the politics of anti-globalisation is taking off.

Some feminists, such as Maria Mies (1986, 1998), also consider capitalism to be an inherently globalising system. However, to argue that what we are seeing is the increased impoverishment of working-class and 'underclass' groups in 'developing countries' is to ignore the phenomenon of the feminisation of poverty (see also Dalla Costa and Dalla Costa 1993; Rai 2004). The actions of multinational corporations, particularly those concerned with industrial agriculture are disrupting traditional production with gendered effects (Shiva 1998). In addition, the process of globalisation involves the imposition of Western norms of rationalism that supplants indigenous knowledges (Chowdhry and Nair 2002) and feminists have read this as a gendered phenomenon (Shiva 1988). Globalisation is also seen to have contributed to the expansion of a commodified form of 'care' services for the elderly, disabled, ill and young in the absence of state provision. Mies (1998) argues that women's caring labour has long been crucial to the maintenance of the labour relations of capital, but this is increasingly commodified (private nursing homes and nurseries, commercial health services and house cleaning in the West) and sometimes operates globally (medical services, sex tourism, the migration of female 'domestics' from developing counties) (Ehrenreich and Hoschchild 2002; Hoschchild 2000; Yeates 2004).

Whatever their perspective, 'hyperglobalisers' see globalisation as either a decisive break in economic, political and social arrangements and processes, or a significant change in such processes, with international economic and political institutions supplanting the roles and powers of nation-states. We are moving inexorably towards a global liberal 'democratic' capitalist consumption-orientated culture. This might be a triumph or an apocalypse depending on one's politics.

The sceptical thesis contends that there is nothing conceptually distinctive or historically unprecedented about globalisation (Hirst 1997). Theories of globalisation are a myth, global governance is weak, and nation-states still have significant power despite economic internationalisation. For those on the left, globalisation may merely be a less controversial term for the justification of neo-liberal economic policy through the influence of the transnational corporations (TNCs). Sceptics have been particularly concerned to 'prove' the invalidity of globalist claims through empirical investigation (Held and McGrew 2002: 3), and this has often been focused on the question of whether or not there is such a thing as a global economy and whether or not this is a development of recent origin.

The work of Paul Hirst with Graham Thompson (1999) argues that, in historical context, the claims for economic globalisation cannot be substantiated. The acid test hinges on whether or not there is a pattern of increasing global integration able to substantiate a claim that there is a single world market (1999: xiii). They examine finance, technologies, labour and production and conclude that there is no evidence that a global economy exists or is emerging. Many of the economies which were open to trade and migrants in the early twentieth century are no longer so open, and this also applies to many developing states and regions, making them in effect less and not more dependent on foreign investment capital. Most economic transaction is either local (national) or regional

(1999: 66–97). Elements of the capitalist system (finance, for example) are increasingly mobile, but this does not mean we have entered into a new phase of global capitalism that is 'hyper' or 'manic' (Greider 1997; Luttwak 1999). Rather there are still varieties of capitalism (see Hall and Soskice 2001), which are nationally rooted and interlinked with political regulation by states.

National governments remain central to the governance of the world economy, because it is they who have both the power and authority to regulate increased flows of trade and finance. Even where the sovereignty of nation-states appears to be under threat, for example for states of the European Union, the way in which the EU works is that political elites of member states engage in 'multilateralism', they amalgamate their political sovereignty on a specific issue and at a specific point in time in order to enhance their positions both collectively and individually (Hirst and Thompson 1999: 230). The EU may exhibit 'state like features', but it is a complex and highly organised confederation of states not actually a unified confederal state (1999: 232–3). Governance beyond the state is not 'above' the state, but is an intergovernmental affair, and any form of 'global governance' exists because it is in the interests of the most powerful states that it should continue. There are formal and informal kinds of veto that strong states can exert over the poor and weak in decision making, and international institutions effectively constitute global domination of the strongest states (Callinicos et al. 1994). The structural power of the United States in the international state system is, therefore, underpinned by the existence of 'global political institutions'. For Hirst and Thompson (1999) there is also considerable overstatement of the powers and significance of transnational corporations (1999: 12). Hyperglobalisers are seen as naive in their presumption that globalisation is a result of inevitable economic tendencies. Levels of interconnections between states are intensifying, but this process is politically constructed by the policies of nation-states.

Marxist and socialist sceptics are concerned that current political agreements and economic practices have intensified the North/South international divide with trade flows benefiting the rich states of the Northern Hemisphere. Some see the most pressing issue as the new division of international labour. TNCs are exporting jobs to the states of the Southern Hemisphere because lack of health and safety regulations and statutory employment rights means that workers can be more heavily exploited (Krugman 1996). Rather than the

## Futures: Theorising the State in a 'Global Age'

nineteenth-century imperial systems of empires and colonial rule, current 'global' mechanisms for economic regulation (such as the G8, World Bank and IMF) are institutions for imperial management in the twenty-first century (Petras and Veltmeyer 2001). In this view, globalisation theory is itself functional for the political legitimacy of capitalism, for it is a discourse that justifies and legitimates the neo-liberal project of a global free market. On the right, Samuel Huntington (1996) also argues that globalism is 'mythic', particularly in its presumption of a common 'global culture', for increased economic inequality has contributed to religious fundamentalism and aggressive nationalism. Interestingly then, whether right, liberal or left wing, sceptics of the globalisation hypothesis collectively argue that global governance is a project of affluent Western states which is deliberately constructed, is not historically unprecedented and is designed to maintain Western economic and political supremacy.

'Transformationalists' see globalisation as a powerful force transforming contemporary society over the long term. Unlike the hyperglobalisers, they do not specify the end point towards which the process of globalisation is travelling. Rather, they argue economic and political formations are shifting. Some accounts have stressed the uneven incidence of globalisation on particular regions of the globe, within countries and/or its impact on particular communities within them.

Giddens (1990) sees the emergence of a 'New World Order' where modern nation-states are becoming reflexive in relation to their sovereignty, that is, where states now recognise their sovereignty is not a 'fixed' phenomenon and changes over time. He argues that global bodies are assuming the function of maintaining law and order. Warfare has become globalised to the extent that it is impossible for states to wage war in bloc or alliances has they have done in the past. Weapons of mass destruction make multi-state warfare unlikely, as does membership of the UN. Warfare of the twenty-first century in Giddens's view, will not become a thing of the past, but will be transformed into local and peripheral conflicts, usually of single nation-states against global alliances such as NATO.

For David Held, globalisation has led to a series of new opportunities, first and foremost of which is a transformation in democracy, particularly through the reform of 'transworld' institutions such as the UN and its many agencies. The impact of regional and global decision-making bodies on the policy making of individual nation-states has led to a series of 'disjunctures' in the sovereignty of nation-states and the development of new 'sovereignty regimes' (Held 1996: 337–50). For example, the ability of nation-states to control national economic programmes is compromised and while some markets and countries can isolate themselves from transnational networks, others find that their decision-making scope is very much compromised by these. A range of developments taken collectively signals a shift from a purely state-centred system of governance to 'novel forms of geo-governance' (Held 1996: 347). By this he means that key areas of high politics for nation-states (such as defence and national security) may be voluntarily 'surrendered' to collective and co-operative ventures. For Held (2002) there have also been significant changes in the scope of international law. In the latter part of the twentieth century, we saw the emergence of what he calls a framework of 'cosmopolitan law' that limits the powers of individual states to treat their citizens as they wish. International law in areas such as the conduct of warfare, human rights, environmental protection and 'crimes against humanity' collectively limit the sovereignty of states over their subjects/citizens.

However, states are suffering various kinds of crises of legitimacy because it is often difficult to deliver on key goods and services (often the subject of electoral pledges by governing parties) either because of conflicting international obligations, or because delivery is premised on international co-operation. We now have a system of global governance which is multi-layered, multi-dimensional and involves multiple actors (Held 2005: 23). At the global level, making and implementation of policy is a highly complex matter, involving the co-ordination and co-operation of global regional, national and local agencies. Rather than the institutions of global governance being home to a constellation of elite groups operating in the interests of transnational capital, levels of power differ throughout the system, and policies are a result of bargaining, negotiation and compromise involving 'representatives of transnational civil society' (international pressure groups such as Greenpeace or Jubilee 2000). Held and McGrew call this understanding 'essentially pluralist' and in this they are right, but they are critical enough to note that this does not mean an equality of group influence.

Georg Sørenson (2006) suggests that we are 'all' transformationalists now, at least when it comes to globalisation. However, it is often the case that those with such a perspective present their work as some 'reasonable' and 'balanced' assessment through a caricature of 'globalism' and 'scepticism'. They chart a considered middle way between these two apparently intransigent positions. Yet the picture painted of state 'transformation' (see in particular Sørenson 2004, box 9.2) is itself a caricature. The modern state never was as 'transformationalists' portray it – a coherent, utterly 'sovereign' body with a self-sustained national economy and a clear unity of sentiment underpinning the 'nation'. In addition, like globalists, 'transformationalists' such as Sørenson do have teleology – we are moving to a 'postmodern' state where the certainties of the 'modern state' are compromised. Transformationalists are closer to the globalists than they might think, and the model of change they posit is rather like those outlined by classical sociologists wherein we move from one 'ideal type', in this case 'the modern state' to another, 'the postmodern state'. States have never possessed uncompromised sovereignty, being always enmeshed in global patterns of trade and political influence. The sceptics are right to argue that the case for globalisation is over-drawn (exaggerated) and badly drawn (empirically insubstantial, theoretically weak). However, whatever the problems of some of the highly diverse perspectives on and understandings of 'globalisation', some of these have proved influential in terms of how policy makers and political institutions evaluate the contemporary political context. They have also informed non-state actors – financial institutions, companies, NGOs and social movements.

## Practical politics

Theories of globalisation asserting the inevitability and desirability of a 'global market' have been incredibly influential and politically consequential. Ohmae is part of a movement expressing what is becoming orthodoxy in some elite Western circles. According to this, the vitality of the global market will be enhanced by the removal of state intervention, especially through privatisation, deregulation and an absence of fiscal constraint. The economist John Williamson referred to the adoption of such a policy package by the governments of the wealthiest states as the 'Washington Consensus' (Held 2004). Neo-liberals have successfully contested the statist strategies of economic management that prevailed across the world from the 1930s to the late 1970s, whether those involve welfarist social democracy, fascism or socialism. Since the 1980s, most governments in the developed world have adopted some version of the neo-liberal agenda, although this is arguably a weak version. Global institutions such as the IMF, WTO, World Bank and OECD have linked globalisation with liberalisation, and in the 1990s, the agencies of the UN also adopted a similar stance. International business forums, such the World Economic Forum have also strongly promoted a neo-liberal agenda.

Hirst and Thompson (1999) have argued that those who propose further deregulation of domestic economies and liberalisation of international trade have influenced policy makers to a disastrous end. Such policies led to economic crises and consequently mass unemployment and poverty in south-east Asia in the late 1990s. These policy initiatives are shrouded in the globalisation myth that 'exaggerates our degree of helplessness in the face of contemporary economic forces' (1999: 6). Certainly the application of liberalisation has been shaped by a politically conservative agenda. Deregulation and liberalisation would logically also involve the removal of restrictions on cross-border movements of workers as well as capital, goods and services but this has been 'rarely pressed' (Scholte 2005: 38). It is work not workers which moves across borders. Workers, with their citizenship demands and welfarist needs are kept relatively immobile, while their labour can be exchanged fairly freely.

For other sceptics, social equality and social justice can only take place within the boundaries of the nation-state, and Hirst and Thompson (1999) have argued for a reinvigorated social democracy on such grounds (see Chapter 5). They argue, for example, that Scandinavian states have retained progressive taxation, elaborate welfare state provision and significant intervention in economic life. In these cases, states are seen to exercise considerable discretion in their economic and social welfare choices. For others, the inequalities of global power relations cannot be restrained only by a reinvigoration of national political life (Hutton 1996). Rather, expanded and radically reformed institutions of global governance are seen as necessary in order to make a revived social democratic project a reality (Held 2004). The World Social Forum, although a linchpin of the anti-globalisation movement, should also be seen as promoting increased global governance with the ends of social and environmental justice in mind.

Global politics has significantly increased its institutional presence since the end of the Second World War. A range of multilateral agreements, treaties and forms of international law has come into being, and networks of policy makers meet in a variety of global institutional contexts. The UN is at the core of this network with its institutions of justice, the Security Council and representative and deliberative General Assembly. The last fifty years have seen the proliferation of UN programmes in the areas of development, the environment, refugees, drug control, children, education and trade. Perhaps most controversial in the current context are the specialist agencies of the UN most of which are concerned with economic development. While the actions of welfare agencies (UNESCO, WHO) have been less subject to sustained critique, those involved in economic regulation have become a focus of activity for both globalisers and opponents of globalisation. Such organisations include the World Bank Group and the IMF. While the UN is able to set global parameters and priorities for policy making, it does not operate like a centralised and co-ordinated set of institutions that comprise national state governments. For this reason, many sceptics doubt that we are seeing the transformation of politics, while also allowing that international organisations are increasingly attempting to regulate the actions of nation-states.

An organisation which is seen by many as accruing both power and influence, is the World Trade Organization that emerged in January 1995 from the Uruguay round of the General Agreement on Tariffs and Trade (GATT). The WTO has a considerable membership (140 countries) and concerns itself with cross-border exchanges of goods, traded services, competitive arrangements, intellectual property law and e-commerce. Member states commit themselves to alter national statutes in order to comply with suprastate trade law. The WTO carries out periodic surveillance of member states to ensure they comply with the latter and investigates allegations of breaches, often brought by transnational corporations. The G7/G8 process is a forum for transnational co-operation on financial and economic matters, which began in 1975 with the 'Group of Five' (Scholte 2005: 201). Held would point to such developments and networks of influential policy makers as forming a different site or level of governance in the global sphere, but he would admit that the extent of control compared with a 'traditional' nation-state is very limited.

For those involved in the protests against 'globalisation' it is seen as a project managed by the world's political and economic elite in the interests of the few. Some see a 'cosmocracy' centred on and in the United States, which promotes and manages globalisation through networks of global institutions, primarily the IMF, the World Bank, the WTO, the G7/G8 and Bank for International Settlements (BIS) (Hardt and Negri 2000). It is certainly the case that the trade regime is focused on liberalisation, without considering the possibility those free trade regimes might work to the benefit of northern-based companies and interest.

Effective critiques have come from 'insiders', such as the economist Joseph Stiglitz, once adviser to President Clinton, then chief economist and vice president at the World Bank. Stiglitz considers globalisation as an active creation not of governments but of international organisations, and argues that it is chronically 'mismanaged'. The result has been increased levels of poverty and both economic and political instability in developing countries, for which international economic institutions such as the WTO, IMF and World Bank must take much of the credit (Stiglitz 2002: 214). He portrays the IMF as an institution far removed from its Keynesian origins and dominated by 'market fundamentalists' (2002: 196). He makes much of the 'democratic deficit' in these global institutions that are both public yet entirely unaccountable (2002: 12). IMF policies demonstrate an ignorance of local conditions, a contempt for local political contexts, a preference for 'one size fits all' programmes and financial conditions – in effect, a colonial form of international governance in both style and content (2002: 30–47). Most damning perhaps is the extent of hypocrisy in the policies of trade liberalisation, which ensure protection for the markets of the richest countries (2002: 176, 269). Stiglitz considers that the inequities endemic in the process of globalisation can be ameliorated by radical reform of international organisations, including a move away from a neo-liberal understanding of governance as a minimalist activity. In this he is not alone.

The radical politics associated with the protests against globalisation has drawn together a range of single-issue concerns. Particularly interesting are the recent moves to a quasi-institutional setting for the generation of both protest and alternative policy and programme. The World Social Forum (WSF) is often portrayed as a 'site of resistance' to global capitalism, a 'democratic alternative' to colonialist policy. Yet, while global social movement organisations are unanimous in denouncing neo-liberalism, debt, poverty, the power of transnational corporations and promoting regional and local autonomy, human rights, democracy and citizen participation, there is also an emergent reformist consensus (de Sousa Santos 2004; Hardt 2002; Mestrum 2004; Rupert 2000). The WSF tends to 'approve' policies for restructuring globalisation rather than directly combating corporate power. It supports the reform of and working with/in the UN system and suggests increased management of a deregulated market. The opposition to globalism may itself be coming close to a transformationalist position; such an understanding of globalisation is increasingly reflected in the collective agendas of the organisations that constitute this international movement.

Of perhaps more substance in supporting the arguments of globalists, are institutions of macro-regional governance, the most remarkable example of which is the European Union. The EU is the result of fifty years of widening and deepening of regional regulation in an expanding territorial collective body. The EU has gone beyond mere economic co-operation with its own Commission, Parliament, Court of Justice, Central Bank and currency (Hix 1999). However, while the enlarged EU has extended its powers over a range of policy domains, it is only over economic regulation that the EU has 'considerable powers', its ability to regulate welfare and engage in social justice initiatives is limited (Walby 2004). As Brigitte Young (2000) argues, the project of the EU is one of neoliberalism, and fiscal conservatism limits its ability to extend its influence over other areas of policy making. The recent rejections of the EU constitution and the delay in the process of its ratification has perhaps lent some support to those who would argue that the EU is the product of elite negotiation and does not command any significant level of popular support among the citizens of its member countries. The limits of its policy reach may also confirm the view that supra-territorial powers in one arena do not a 'super state' make.

Some political issues do seem to be increasingly global in policy-making terms. Such issues include human rights, which although contested, have become enshrined in a UN declaration (Beetham 1998), and environmental protection. It might be assumed that environmental issues are inevitably global given that the atmosphere and the climate are common eco-systems for the planet, but a minority of affluent states and rapidly industrialising ones such as China, may be responsible for much of the pollution that degrades them. Environmental problems do not have uniformly global consequences and there is fierce debate about who is to 'blame' for damage. Much of the development of international environmental policy has taken place under the auspices of the UN. Over three decades, UN reports of 1972, 1987 and 1992 assumed we are a global community, wherein our interests are similar, and universal policy application is possible (Yearley 1996). However, when the first 'Earth Summit' (an intergovernmental conference representing nearly every UN member state) was held in Rio de Janeiro in 1992 to establish agreements on environmental protection, there was clear dissatisfaction expressed by governments of poorer countries with the Western domination of decision making (Miller 1995), and the way in which IMF tied environmental protection agreements to Western models of development (Sachs 1993). Many environmental campaigners see transnational corporations as the most significant players in causing environmental hazards. Even when national governments oppose the intentions of multinational corporations, such companies are able to appeal to the WTO, which has the power to ensure national compliance. One is left to ponder, however, were the policies and institutional arrangements of the WTO and IMF reformed, whether a more fairly and fully managed capitalism might emerge, and to what extent (if at all) social and environmental justice might be enhanced as a result.

## The nation-state in the twenty-first century

For sceptics, the terminology of globalisation is a rebadging of some very old concepts and practices. On a global level, it is as it has been for centuries, the richest and most powerful states in the global system govern, and in some accounts this is linked to the power of nationally based class elites. The interests of such groups form the basis for dispute and bargaining in international organisations, and decisions generally maintain Western interests. For those who adhere to some sort of 'globalisation' hypothesis, the wealthy and powerful exert influence in line with their interests, but these are increasingly unlikely to be based within the parameters of the nation-state. The power of different agencies, and pressure varies across time and space, in different kinds of institutions and at various level of the policy-making process in some accounts. In others, it is the 'transnational capitalist class' that effectively governs and whose interests are best articulated and represented.

On the political right, neo-liberalism sees politics as it sees economics. Politics should reflect individual freedom and initiative.

## Futures: Theorising the State in a 'Global Age'

A free market, guided by a 'minimal state' is a key political objective, and in terms of an international political agenda, the extension of the market into new regions and encompassing more areas of our lives, is possible and desirable. For Ohmae (1995: 5) 'traditional nation states have become unnatural, even impossible'. We are witness to the creation of a global market system in which the state is redundant. A new world order is emerging in which the individual, unimpeded by bureaucratic mechanisms and power politics can best survive and prosper (Ohmae 1995: 149). For liberal pluralists, increasing global interconnectedness paves the way for a more co-operative world order based on the increasing interdependence of regions and the common adherence to liberal democracy. This is likely to be achieved by an enhancement of the role of international organisations, particularly the UN. International institutional reform and empowerment, and increased mechanisms for participation, transparency and accountability might help achieve a more just world order. The nation-state is not facing its demise in this order, but a reconfiguration of relationships of sovereignty, power and authority. For Held (1996) new forms of democratic engagement are necessary and emergent. We will have to learn to become 'cosmopolitan citizens', as well as citizens of a national polity. 'Global transformers' such as Held have much in common with liberal pluralist analyses – they want cosmopolitan democracy, a transformed UN system open to and able to articulate the interests of those across the globe, and they want more effective and transparent governance, in particular, regulation of corporate capital.

There have been re-articulations of state power. This has not, as Held and McGrew (2002: 124) argue, been a 'zero-sum game'. However, it has been a game in which wealthy states have been able to skew international decision making in the direction of their own interests. Most would agree that institutions of global governance have demonstrated a persistent failure to ameliorate, let alone turn the tide on ever-increasing levels of inequality. The UN claims, as a vital part of its mission, its intention to reduce levels of poverty and secure social justice. These aims are so far from being achieved that it makes little sense to talk of global political institutions as supplanting the power and authority of nation-states. Until the UN can convince dominant interests in the international order that social justice is key to prosperity and security and environmental justice is required for the maintenance of our planet as a global system, the idea of global governance seems mythic. As Castells (1996) has powerfully argued, any moves we may have seen in the direction of ameliorating the power of nation-states and establishing workable international organisations of governance will fail on the questions of poverty and injustice.

International institutions have expanded their influence and the bureaucratic machinery by which to generate and implement policy, but this is still of limited effect in the face of a nation-state with immense power and wealth. What is certain is that 'globalisation', 'internationalisation' or the new form of 'imperialism' does not involve the demise of the state – at most, a reconfiguration of its power relations. In this context, the state will remain crucial to the politics of the twenty-first century, and the kind of politics we hold will depend very much on how we understand the state itself, for this still answers many key questions in political life: who governs? in who's interests? by what means? and to what end?

## Bibliography

Albrow, M. (1996), *The Global Age* (Cambridge: Polity).
Amin, S. (1997), *Capitalism in the Age of Globalisation* (London: Zed).
Anderson, P. (1974), *Lineages of the Absolutist State* (London: New Left Books).
Beck, U. (1999), *What is Globalisation?* (Cambridge: Polity).
Beetham, D. (1998), 'Human rights as a model for cosmopolitan democracy', in D. Archibugi, D. Held and M. Kohler (eds), *Re-imagining Political Community: Studies in Cosmopolitan Democracy* (Cambridge: Polity).
Braudel, F. (1984), *Civilization and Capitalism 15th–18th Century. Volume III: The Perspective of the World* (New York: Harper and Row).
Callinicos, A. (2002) ,'Marxism and global governance', in D. Held and A. McGrew (eds), *Governing Globalisation: Power, Authority and Global Governance* (Cambridge: Polity).
Callinicos, A., Rees, J., Harman, C. and Haynes, M. (ed.) (1994), *Marxism and the New Imperialism* (London: Bookmarks).
Castells, M. (1996), *The Rise of the Network Society* (Oxford: Blackwell).
Chowdhry, G. and Nair, S. (eds) (2002), *Power Postcolonialism and International Relations: Reading Race, Gender and Class* (London: Routledge).
Dalla Costa, M. and Dalla Costa, G. F. (eds) (1993) *Paying the Price: Women and the Politics of International Economic Strategy* (London: Zed).

de Sousa Santos, B. (2004), 'The world social forum: towards a counter-hegemonic globalisation', in F. Polet and CETRI (eds), *Globalizing Resistance* (London: Pluto).
Dicken, P. (1998), *Global Shift* (London: Paul Chapman).
Ehrenreich, B. and Hochschild, A. R. (eds) (2002), *Global Woman: Nannies, Maids and Sex Workers in the New Economy* (New York: Metropolitan Books).
Evans, P. (1997), 'The eclipse of the state? Reflections on stateness in an era of globalisation', *World Politics*, 50, 1: 62–87.
Frank, A. G. (1969), *Capitalism and Underdevelopment in Latin America: Historical Studies of Chile and Brazil.* (New York: Monthly Review Press).
Frank, A. G. (1998), *ReOrient: Global Economy in the Asian Age* (Berkeley CA: University of California Press).
Frank, A. G. and Gills, B. K. (eds) (1996), *The World System* (London: Routledge).
Giddens, A. (1990), *The Consequences of Modernity* (Cambridge: Polity).
Greider, W. (1997), *One World, Ready or Not: The Manic Logic of Global Capitalism* (New York: Simon and Schuster).
Hall, P. A. and Soskice, D. (eds) (2001), *Varieties of Capitalism: The Institutional Foundations of Comparative Advantage* (Oxford: Oxford University Press).
Hardt, M. (2002) 'Porto Alegre: today's Bandung?', *New Left Review*, 14: 112–18.
Hardt, M. and Negri, A. (2000), *Empire* (Cambridge MA: Harvard University Press).
Held, D. (1995), *Democracy and the Global Order: From Modern State to Cosmopolitan Governance* (Cambridge: Polity).
Held, D. (2002), 'Law of states, Law of peoples: three Models of sovereignty', *Legal Theory*, 8, 1.
Held, D. (2004), *Global Covenant: The Social Democratic Alternative to the Washington Consensus* (Cambridge: Polity).
Held, D. (2005), 'Principles of the consmopolitan order', in G. Brock and H. Brighouse (eds), *The Political Philosophy of Cosmopolitanism* (Cambridge: Cambridge University Press).
Held, D., McGrew, A., Goldblatt, D. and Peraton, J. (1999), *Global Transformations: Politics, Economics, Culture* (Cambridge: Polity).
Held, D. and McGrew, A. (eds) (2000), *Governing Globalisation: Power, Authority and Global Governance* (Cambridge: Polity).
Held, D. and McGrew, A. (2002), *Globalisation/Anti-Globalisation* (Cambridge: Polity).
Hirst, P. (1997), 'The global economy: myths and realities', *International Affairs*, 73(3).

Hirst, P. and Thompson, G. (1999), *Globalisation in Question: the International Economy and the Possibilities of Governance* (Cambridge: Polity).
Hix, S. (1999), *The Political System of the European Union* (Basingstoke: Palgrave Macmillan).
Hochschild, A. R. (2000), 'Global care chains and emotional surplus value', in W. Hutton and A. Giddens (eds), *On the Edge: Living with Global Capitalism* (London: Cape).
Hulton, W. (1996), *The State We're In* (revised edn) (London: Vintage).
Huntington, S. P. (1991), *The Third Wave: Democratisation in the Late Twentieth Century* (Norman OK: University of Oklahoma Press).
Huntington, S. P. (1996), *The Clash of Civilizations and the Remaking of the World Order* (New York: Simon and Schuster).
Krugmou, P. (1996), *Pop Internationalism* (Cambridge MA: MIT Press).
Luttwak, E. (1999), *Turbo-Capitalism* (New York: Basic Books).
Massey, D. and Jess, P. (eds) (1995), *A Place in the World? Culture, Places and Globalisation* (Oxford: Oxford University Press).
Mestrum, F. (2004), 'The World Social Forum: a democratic alternative', in F. Polet and CETRI (eds), *Globalizing Resistance* (London: Pluto).
Mies, M. (1986), *Patriarchy and Accumulation on a World Scale* (London: Zed).
Mies, M. (1998), *Patriarchy and Accumulation on a World Scale* (2nd edn) (London: Zed).
Miller, M. A. L. (1995), *The Third World in Global Environmental Politics* (Buckingtom: Open University Press).
Mittleman, J. H. (2000), *The Globalisation Syndrome: Transformation and Resistance* (Princeton NJ: Princeton University Press).
O'Tuathail, G. (2000), 'Borderless worlds? Problematising discourses of deterritorialisation', *Geopolitics*, 4, 2: 81–93.
Ohmae, K. (1990), *The Borderless World* (London: Collins).
Ohmae, K. (1995), *The End of the Nation State* (New York: Free Press).
Petras, J. and Veltmeyer, H. (2001), *Globalisation Unmasked: Imperialism in the 21st Century* (London: Zed).
Pijl, K. van der (1998), *Transnational Classes and International Relations* (London: Routledge).
Rai, S. (2004), 'Gendering global governance', *International Feminist Journal of Politics*, 6, 4: 579–601.
Ritzer, G. (1993), *The McDonaldization of Society* (Thousand Oaks CA: Pine Forge/Sage).
Ritzer, G. (2004), *The Globalisation of Nothing* (Thousand Oaks CA: Pine Forge/Sage).
Robertson, R. (1992), *Globalisation: Social Theory and Global Culture* (London: Sage).

Rosenau, J. N. (1990), *Turbulence in World Politics* (Hemel Hempstead: Harvester Wheatsheaf).
Rosenau, J. N. (1998), 'Government and democracy in a globalizing world', in D. Archibugi, D. Held and M. Kohler (eds), *Re-imagining Political Community*, (Cambridge: Polity).
Rosenberg, J. (2001), *The Follies of Globalisation Theory: Polemical Essays* (London: Verso).
Rosenberg, J. (2005), 'Globalisation theory – a post mortem', *International Politics*, 42, 1: 2–74
Rostow, W. (1962), *The Stages of Economic Growth: A Non-Communist Manifesto* (Cambridge: Cambridge University Press).
Rupert, M. (2000), *Ideologies of Globalisation: Contending Visions of a New World Order* (London: Routledge).
Sachs, W. (1993), *Global Ecology* (London: Zed).
Sander, H. (1996), 'Multilateralism, regionalism and globalisation: the challenges of the world trading system', in H. Sander and A. Inotai (eds), *World Trade after the Uruguay Round: Prospects and Policy Options for the Twenty-first Century* (London: Routledge).
Scholte, J. A. (1997) 'Global capitalism and the state', *International Affairs*, 73(3).
Scholte, J. A. (2005), *Globalisation: a Critical Introduction* (2nd edn) (Basingstoke: Palgrave).
Shiva, V. (1988), *Staying Alive: Women, Ecology and Development* (London: Zed).
Shiva, V. (1998), *Biopiracy: the Plunder of Nature and Knowledge* (Dortington: Green Books).
Short, J. R. (2001), *Global Dimensions: Space, Place and the Contempory World* (London: Reaktion Books).
Sklair, L. (2001), *The Transnational Capitalist Class* (Oxford: Blackwell).
Sørenson, G. (2004), *The Transformation of the State: Beyond the Myth of Retreat* (Basingstoke: Palgrave).
Sørenson, G. (2006), 'The transformation of the state', in C. Hay, M. Lister and D. Marsh (eds), *The State: Theories and Issues* (Basingstoke: Palgrave).
Spybey, T. (1996), *Globalization and World Society* (Cambridge: Polity).
Stiglitz, J. (2002), *Globalisation and Its Discontents* (London: Penguin).
Walby, S. (2004), 'The European Union and gender equality: emergent varieties of gender regime', *Social Politics*, 11, 1: 4–29.
Wallerstein, I. (1974), *The Modern World System: Capitalist Agriculture and the Origins of the European World Economy in the Sixteenth Century* (London: Academic Press).
Wallerstein, I. (1979), *The Capitalist World Economy* (Cambridge: Cambridge University Press).

Wallerstein, I. (1990), 'Societal development, or development of the world system', in M. Albrow and E. King (eds), *Globalisation, Knowledge and Society* (London: Sage).
Waters, M. (1995), *Globalisation* (London: Routledge).
Yearley, S. (1996), *Sociology, Environmentalism, Globalisation* (London: Sage).
Yeates, N. (2004), 'Global care chains: critical reflections and lines of enquiry', *Internaltional Feminist Journal of Politics*, 6, 3: 369–91.
Young, B. (2000), 'Disciplinary neoliberalism in the European Union and gender politics', *New Political Economy*, 5, 1: 77–98.

# Index

absolutism, 26–7, 28
Adenauer, Konrad, 204
Afghanistan, 218
Afshar, Haleh, 233
agency/structure dualism, 98–9, 101–2, 105–7, 110
Al Qa'ida, 286
Albrow, Martin, 296–7
Algeria, 285
Allerdyce, Gilbert, 166
Althusser, Louis, 101
American Revolution, 31, 41
Americanisation, 77, 282, 294, 295
AN (*Alleanza Nazionale*), 183, 184
anarchism, 3, 6, 8, 29–30, 34, 43, 137–8, 159, 162–3
    context, 139–42
    definition, 142–3
    fascism, 162–3, 173–4
    globalisation and, 295–6
    practical politics, 150–1
    right-wing, 241
anarcho-capitalism, 139–40, 149–50, 250
anarcho-communism, 139, 141, 143
anarcho-syndicalism, 152, 162–3, 167–72
Ancient Greece, 64–6
Angry Brigade, 151
Anthias, Floya and Yuval-Davis, Nira, 217, 218
anti-conservatism, 163–4, 182
anti-globalisation movement, 109, 138, 154, 293, 298, 304
anti-pornographic legislation, 232
anti-semitism, 180
Apel, Karl Otto, 121
Arendt, Hannah, 180
Argentina, 119
aristocracy, 67–8, 69, 177, 189, 201, 207–8
Aron, Raymond, 70
Arrow Cross, 165
associationalism, 43, 53, 124–5, 128–30, 134–5, 195–7
Augustine, Saint, 276, 278

Austria, 166, 183, 184, 204
authority, 191–2, 195–6, 199, 209
autonomous states, 20–34, 138, 145, 147–8, 159, 163, 178, 181, 185, 192–4, 197–8, 199–200, 284–5; *see also* anarchy; conservatism; fascism
autonomy, 43, 49, 54–5, 60, 107–8, 110, 125, 178, 180, 194, 204
Ayubi, Nazih, 21

Baader-Meinhof Gang, 151
Bachrach, Paul and Baratz, Morton, 51, 81
Bad Godesberg programme, 117, 126
Bakunin, Michael, 139, 140, 145
Barclay, Harold, 137–8
Beck, Ulrich, 126, 293
Belgium, 183, 204
Bell, Daniel, 204
Berlin, Isaiah, 74
Berth, Edouard, 163, 171
bin Laden, Osama, 285–6
Birch, Anthony, 63
BIS (Bank for International Settlements), 306
Blair, Tony, 59, 83, 258
Blanqui, Louis Auguste, 162
BNP (British National Party), 182–3, 184
Bodin, Jean, 23
Bookchin, Murray, 140, 143, 145–7
Bossuet, Jacques Benigne, 29
Bottomore, Tom, 77, 86
bourgeoisie, 94–5, 96, 147, 163, 168, 171, 172
boycotts, 152
Bracher, Karl Dietrich, 30
Brandenburg-Prussia, 27
Brazil, military elite, 85–6
Bretton Woods system, 119, 122; *see also under* individual institutions
broker states, 45
Broszat, Martin, 181
Brown, Wendy, 225
Bruce, Steve, 278
Buchanan, James, 241, 245, 251–2, 256, 260

**315**

Bullpit, Jim, 259
bureaucracy, 46–7, 71–3, 83, 84, 144, 146, 241, 253, 256
Burke, Edmund, 38, 67, 69–70
Bush, George W., 205–6, 207
Butler, Judith, 229

Cahill, Tom, 154
Callinicos, Alex, 290
capitalism, 3, 100, 147–8
  development of, 144
  elite theory and, 80, 86
  gender inequality, 219
  neo-conservatism, 210
  patriarchy and, 226–7
  political inequalities and, 52–3
  social democracy and, 119–21
  spectacle and, 153–4
  stakeholder, 43
  supraterritorial, 297
care debate *see* 'ethics of care' debate
care services, 299
Carter, Alan, 138, 147–8
Castells, Manuel, 309
Castoriadis, Cornelius, 96
China, 148, 180, 307
Chirac, Jacques, 183
Christian Democratic parties, 203–4, 243
Christian Right, 257–8, 281
Christianity, 24, 169, 179, 181, 201, 203–4, 276, 278; *see also* Protestant fundamentalism
citizenship, 40, 55, 116, 155, 306
  Ancient Greece, 65
  conservatism, 196
  exclusion from political process, 260
  fascist state, 176
  gender equality, 216, 224–5
  social contract, 160–1
  tests for, 56
civil religion, 200, 267, 269, 270, 272, 273, 274, 284
civil rights, 31, 51, 232
civil society, 3, 32, 42
  associationalism, 43, 53, 124–5, 128–30, 134–5, 195–7
  conservatism, 192–4, 210
  increased state power over, 33–4
  Iranian, 283
  Marxist critique of, 91, 92–3, 110
  nineteenth-century, 38
  positive welfare and, 127
  social democracy and, 121
  totalitarianism and, 176
civilisational decline, 167–8
civility, decline of, 196–7
class warfare, 169, 170
classical anarchism, 140
Clinton presidency, 206, 258
co-operativism, 154–5
Cohen, Gerry, 96
Cohn-Sherbok, Dan, 279
Cold War, 39, 44, 113, 207
Cole, George Douglas Howard, 43, 128
Coleridge, Samuel Taylor, 68
colonialism, 292
common good, 74–5, 161, 169, 170, 199, 208, 245, 276
communism, 160, 163, 164, 184, 248, 284, 285
communitarianism, 139
competitive tendering, 256

consensus, 51, 53–4, 59, 78, 80–1, 114, 121, 124, 131, 242
conservatism, 4, 6, 7, 8, 67–8, 182, 242–3
  context, 188–9
  definition, 190–4
  fascism, 163, 182
  fundamentalism, 270–1, 280–1, 284
  liberalism, 188–9, 192–4
  New Right, 241, 242–3
  practical politics, 202–10
  theorists, 194–202; *see also* neo-conservatism; New Right
Conservative Party (UK), 204, 240, 243, 256
constitutionalism, 26–7, 31, 41, 189
consumerism, 153, 294
contract theory, 224–5
Cook, Michael, 276, 278
corporate governance, 53, 80, 128, 134
corporatism, 114, 118, 123, 166, 172, 176
counter-culture movement, 153
Creveld, Martin van, 33
Crosland, Anthony, 116–17
Crouch, Colin, 258

Dahl, Robert A., 39–40, 42, 43, 45, 46, 50–3, 77, 81, 99, 208
Dahrendorf, Ralf, 113
Davies, Norman, 189
De Felice, Renzo, 159, 179
Debord, Guy, 153–4
decentralisation, 123, 128, 139, 153
decision making, 78–9, 81, 142, 217, 290, 296, 300, 302
democracy, 5, 25–6, 30, 163, 177
  accountability, 132
  Ancient Greece, 64–6
  associative, 43, 53, 124–5, 128–30, 134–5, 195–7
  corruption of, 168–9, 170
  Dahl's theory of, 50–3
  elitism, 71–4
  modern state and, 29–33
  neo-conservative foreign policy, 209
  nineteenth-century thinkers on, 68–70
  protective/developmental models of, 42
democratic deficit, 46, 132, 306
Democratic Party (US), 229–30, 273
deregulation, 303, 304
Dershowitz, Alan, 209
deterritorialisation, 294, 295
developing countries, 217, 222, 291–2, 298, 306
Dewey, John, 44
dictatorship, 39, 177–8, 203
Dietz, Mary, 217
Diniz, Eli, 86
direct action, 153, 154
Disraeli, Benjamin, 189
diversity, 40, 176–7
division of labour, 21, 96, 104, 297, 300
divorce law, 226
Djilas, Milovan, 84
Domhoff, G. William, 64, 78, 81, 82
Dunleavy, Patrick and O'Leary, Brendan, 2–3, 75, 81
Dunn, John, 65
Durkheim, Emile, 121, 128, 291
Duyn, Roel van, 154
Dworkin, Andrea, 232
Dworkin, Ronald, 40, 42

316

# Index

eastern Europe, 84–5
Eatwell, Roger, 166
ecologism, 154
economic interdependence, 114, 118, 122–3, 125, 130–1; *see also* globalisation
economic liberalism, 149, 189, 192, 247, 295
education, 124, 146, 196–7, 226
   Humanism, 274
   neo-conservative budget, 206
   political, 202
   progressive, 205
   religious, 201
egalitarianism, 139, 148, 150, 243
Egypt, constitution of, 281
Eisenhower, President, 82
Eisenstein, Zillah, 226
electoral system, 31–2, 45, 68, 72–3, 182–4, 216, 252–3
elite theory, 2, 3, 4, 5, 7, 30, 145, 147, 200, 202, 224, 246, 253
   competitive, 45, 50
   context, 64–70
   definition, 70–5
   multiple, 46
   practical politics, 82–6
   theorists, 75–81
employment, women, 226
Engels, Friedrich, 91, 94, 140, 142
English Civil War, 28
Enlightenment, 47
Enloe, Cynthia, 218
enterprise association, 195–6
entrepreneurship, 127, 247, 257
environmental politics, 6, 108, 126, 131, 145, 147, 154, 217, 302, 307–8
equal opportunities, 223, 226, 229–30
Ertman, Thomas, 27
Estates, polity of the, 21–2, 26, 28
'ethics of care' debate, 216–17, 219, 225
ethnocentrism, 184
ethnocultural minorities, 55–6
Etzioni, Amitai, 59, 60
European Union, 114, 119, 123, 125, 130–5, 227, 295, 300, 307
Evans, Judith, 229
exchange of goods, 91, 102, 141, 247

Falangism, 165
Faludi, Susan, 233
Falwell, Jerry, 8, 257, 268, 272–4, 279, 280
fascism, 5, 7, 8, 30, 74, 152, 159, 284, 285
   after 1945, 182–5
   anarchy, 171–2, 173
   communism, 164
   conservatism, 163, 182
   context, 160–3
   definition, 163–7
   fundamentalism, 185, 269, 284–5
   liberalism, 163–4
   Marxism, 163–4, 172–3
   myth, 269
   practical politics, 179–85
   socialism, 164–70, 172
   Thatcherism and, 259
   theorists, 167–79
feminism, 2, 3, 7, 108, 139, 154, 214–15, 259
   anarchism, 141
   context, 215–20
   definition, 220–2
   elite theory, 82

globalisation, 295, 298–9
   liberalism, 220, 221–2, 223, 229–30
   Marxism, 219, 221, 222, 226
   New Right, 231, 233, 241
   post-structuralist, 229
   practical politics, 229–35
   social democracy, 234
   socialist, 219–20
   statehood, 4
   theorists, 222–9
fertility control, 219
fetishism, 107–8, 110–11
feudalism, 21, 144
Figgis, John Neville, 43
Finer, Samuel, 30, 31, 32
Fini, Gianfranco, 183
FN (*Front National*), 183, 184, 295
Foucault, Michel, 109
Fraenkel, Ernst, 181
France, 25
   anarcho-syndicalism, 162–3, 167–72
   Bonapartist, 94–5, 102
   Constitution (1793), 32
   feminism, 230
   French Revolution, 31, 41, 162
   Gaullism, 203, 204
   populist-nationalist parties, 183, 184, 295
   royal absolutism in, 28–9
   secularism, 269
Franco, Francisco, 152, 203
Frank, André Gunder, 291, 292
Fraser, Nancy, 215–16
free-riders, 245
freedom, 74–5, 92, 116, 150, 151, 173, 192, 242, 244, 248–9, 255, 257, 273
Freedom Party, 183, 184
French Revolution, 31, 41, 162
Friedman, Milton, 249, 256
friend/enemy distinction, 198–200, 207
functionalism, 78, 96, 101, 102–3, 107, 126, 128, 221
fundamentalism, 4, 5, 8, 34, 215, 301
   conservatism, 270–1, 280–1, 284
   context, 265–70
   decadent modernity, 168
   definition, 270–2
   fascism, 185, 269, 284–5
   Marxism, 267–8, 284
   practical politics, 277–86
   theorists, 272–6
   totalitarianism, 276

G7/G8, 305, 306
Galbraith, John, 253
Galston, William A., 56, 60
Gamble, Andrew, 244, 256, 259
game theory, 245
Gandhi, Mohandas, 152–3
Gaulle, Charles de, 203, 204
gender relations, 216, 217–20, 259; *see also* feminism
general will, 74–5, 161, 169, 170, 199, 208, 245, 276
Gentile, Giovanni, 159, 171, 172–9, 180, 181
Germany, 28, 30, 151
   Christian democracy, 204
   neo-fascism, 182–3
   nineteenth-century political liberalism, 189
   social democracy, 115–16, 117; *see also* fascism; National Socialism

**317**

Giddens, Anthony, 122, 125–7, 128, 129, 133, 134, 292–3, 301
Gilmour, Ian, 242, 243
globalisation, 1, 4, 119, 122, 129, 184, 289–91
  context, 291–3
  definition, 293–5
  economic inequality, 109
  practical politics, 303–8
  theories, 295–303
globalists, 296–9, 300, 307
Godwin, William, 140
Goldwater, Senator Barry, 240
governance, 2, 4, 142
  corporate, 53
  EU, 132
  global, 300, 301–2, 304, 309–10
  sub-national, 120, 123
  supranational, 114–15, 119, 120, 123, 125, 135
Gray, John, 113–14, 122, 193–4, 206, 210
Greenpeace, 126, 302
Gregor, A. James, 165, 178
Grieder, William, 297
Griffin, Roger, 164–5, 166
Grotius, Hugo, 23
group oppression, 227–8
group rights, 49
Guérin, Daniel, 140

Habermas, Jürgen, 121, 124
Haider, Jörge, 183
Hall, John, 24
Hall, Stuart and Jacques, Martin, 259
Hanmer, Jalna, 219
Hansen, Mogens, 65
Hardt, Michael, 295
Harrison, Frank, 149
Hay, Colin et al., 105
Hayek, Frederick von, 241, 244, 248–50
Hegel, Georg Wilhelm Friedrich, 47, 92–3, 109–10, 121, 172
Held, David, 52, 248, 290, 294, 301–2, 309
Hellawell, Keith, 59
*Hezbollah,* 271, 286
Higher Criticism, 270
Himmelfarb, Gertrude, 190, 197
Hindmore, Andrew, 254
Hintze, Otto, 26–7, 28
Hirst, Paul, 43, 53, 123, 128–30, 133, 134, 199, 290, 299, 300, 304
historical utilitarianism, 190
history, philosophy of, 96–7
Hitler, Adolf, 181
*Hizb al-Tahrir,* 271
Hobbes, Thomas, 23, 24, 29–30
Honderich, Ted, 190
House of Commons, 83
human association, 195–7
human nature, 140–1, 191, 244–6, 256
human rights, 39, 302, 306, 307
Humanism, 270, 274
Humm, Maggie, 215
Hungarian revolts, 28
Hungary, 27, 28, 165
Hunter, Floyd, 75
Huntington, Samuel, 190, 301
Husserl, Edmund, 40
Huxley, Thomas Henry, 144
hyperglobalisers, 296–9, 300

IMF (International Monetary Fund), 119, 241, 297, 304, 305, 306, 307
immigration, 258, 259
imperialism, 68, 294–5, 310
inclusiveness, 126–7
incrementalism, 57–60, 145
India, 138, 152–3
individual freedom, 116, 242, 244, 248–9, 255, 257, 273
individualism, 125–6, 127, 139–40, 159, 173–4, 176–7, 250
industrialisation, 202
inflation, 118, 181, 249, 255
instrumentalism, 97, 98, 99–101, 104–5, 140, 147, 223
interest groups, 47, 252, 283, 290, 297, 298, 302
international law, 305
internationalism, 294, 310
Investiture Conflict, 24
Iran, 266, 282–4
  feminism in, 218, 233–4
Islam, 265–8, 268–9, 271–2, 275–6; *see also* fundamentalism
Islamic states, myth of, 281–6
Israel, 279–80
Italy, 151, 152, 159
  city-states in, 21–3
  extreme right parties, 183
  Fascism, 164, 166, 167, 172, 178, 179–80, 181
  neo-fascism, 182

*Jamaat-i Islami* party, 271
James, William, 44
Japan, 151
Jayawardena, Kumari, 217, 218
Jefferson, Thomas, 67
Jessop, Bob, 104–5
*jihad* (holy war), 168, 275, 285
*Jihad* (Islamist group), 271
Johnson, Lyndon B., 204, 243
Joseph, Keith, 255–6
Jubilee 2000 (pressure group), 302
justice, 53–4
  anarcho-syndicalism, 169–70
  early modern states and, 24–6, 34
  ethnocultural, 49
  fairness principle, 277
  liberal equality and, 48–9; *see also* social justice

Kagan, Robert, 209–10
Kant, Immanuel, 42–3, 47, 60, 92
Kavanagh, Dennis, 258
Kepel, Gilles, 280
Keynes, John Maynard, 116
Keynesian economics, 243, 249, 251, 306
Khomeini, Ayatollah Ruhollah, 233, 282–4, 285, 286
Kristol, Irving, 204, 205, 206, 207, 210, 243
Kropotkin, Peter, 138, 140, 142, 143–5, 153
Kymlicka, Will, 40, 49, 55–6, 228

labour market, 123–4, 147, 219
Labour Party (UK), 152, 231, 258, 260
LaHaye, Tim, 274–5, 277, 279
*laissez-faire* economics, 149, 189, 192, 247, 295
Lane, David, 84–5
Larmore, Charles, 60
Laski, Harold J., 43, 128

# Index

law, 30, 33
 international, 302, 305
 and order, 257, 301
 public sphere, 32
 rule of, 67, 94, 189, 196–7, 199, 209
law-states, 24–6, 160
Lawson, Tony, 254
Le Pen, Jean-Marie, 183, 295
leadership, 74, 162, 164, 177–8, 184, 207–9, 284
Lebanon, 286
Legion of the Archangel Michael, 165
legitimacy, input-orientated/output-orientated, 132, 134–5
Lenin, Vladimir, 97, 145
Lewis, Bernard, 271, 276
Leys, Colin, 260
'liberal culturalist' position, 49, 55
liberal equality, 39–40, 41, 42, 44, 47–9
liberalism, 6, 37–41
 conservatism and, 188–9, 192–4
 context, 41–4
 definition, 44–9
 fascism, 163–4, 173
 feminism, 220, 221–2, 223, 229–30
 group rights, 228–9
 New Right, 241
 practical politics, 57–61
 theorists, 50–6
Libertarian Party, 151
liberty of conscience, 54
lifestyle politics, 146–7
Lindblom, Charles, 39, 43, 44, 46, 52, 57–60
Lipset, Seymour Martin, 204
Locke, John, 41, 201, 273
Lowi, Theodore, 46
Lukács, Georg, 107, 110, 111

McCann, Frank, 85
McGrew, Anthony, 290, 294, 302, 309
Machiavelli, Niccolò, 66–7, 74
Mackinnon, Catherine, 214, 222–4, 232, 233–4
McLennan, Gregor, 52
Madison, James, 31, 41–2, 67
Maistre, Joseph de, 160
Makhno, Nestor, 152
Malatesta, Errico, 142
Manicheanism, 170
Manin, Bernard, 65–6
Mann, Michael, 165, 166
Mansfield, Harvey C., 207–8
Mao Tse-Tung, 180
Margulis, Lyn, 144
market economy, 20–2, 108, 116–18, 124, 176, 244–6, 249–50, 257, 260
Marquand, David, 114
marriage, 224, 225
martyrdom, 275, 283
Marx, Karl, 55, 71, 91–2, 102, 106–7, 108, 121, 123, 145
Marxism, 3, 6, 7, 75, 76, 77, 81, 86, 91–2, 147, 173, 182, 223, 268, 276
 anarchist theory and, 140, 141, 142
 context, 92–5
 definition, 95–9
 fascism, 163–4, 172–3
 feminism and, 219, 221, 222, 226
 fundamentalism, 267–8
 fundamentalism and, 284
 globalisation, 290, 295, 298, 300
 New Right, 241

practical politics, 108–9
social democracy and, 115
Sorel's rejection of, 168
Thatcherism, 259
theorists, 99–108
means of production, 91, 101, 102
media, 83, 152
Mexico, 151
Michels, Robert, 63, 71
middle class, 170, 189, 234
Mies, Maria, 298–9
Miliband, Ralph, 76, 96, 99–101, 103, 109
militarism, 207, 208, 217
Mill, John Stuart, 38, 42, 60, 68, 190
millennialism, 271, 272, 276, 278, 279, 283
Miller, David, 249
Millet, Kate, 218
Mills, C. Wright, 38, 64, 75–8, 82, 85, 148
Mir-Hosseini, Ziba, 233
Mittleman, James, 298
modernisation, 291, 293
Mommsen, Hans, 181
monarchy, 33, 41, 188–9
monetarism, 256
Montesquieu, baron de, 41
moral duty, 42–3, 243
Moral Majority movement, 257, 272, 279
moral pluralism, 40, 47–9, 53–5, 56
morality, 257, 281
Mosca, Gaetano, 63, 71
multiculturalism, 40, 41, 44, 55–6
multinational corporations, 80, 83, 109, 296, 298
Muslim Brotherhood, 271
Mussolini, Benito, 152, 159, 167, 171, 172, 173, 179–80, 181
myth
 fascism, 167, 169, 171
 fundamentalism, 269
 of globalisation, 299, 301, 304

'Narodaya Volya,' 151
nation-states, 289–90, 296, 308–10
National Fatherhood Initiative, 206
National Socialism (Nazism), 30, 152, 163, 164, 165, 166, 167, 180–2, 184, 199, 284, 285
National Syndicalism, 165
nationalism, 33, 166, 171, 172, 174–5, 177, 203, 209, 258, 295, 301
NATO, 125, 301
natural rights, 201–2, 251, 273
negative integration, 114–15, 130–2
negative liberty, 173, 192–4, 209
Negri, Antonio, 295
neo-conservatism, 148, 149, 197, 198, 204–10, 240, 257–8, 274, 281; *see also* conservatism
neo-fascism, 182–5
neo-liberalism, 2, 86, 130–1, 134, 184, 194, 240, 258, 260, 293, 297–8, 306, 307
 EU constitution, 133
 globalisation, 301, 303–4
 globalists, 296
 politics, 307–8
neo-Marxism, 4, 147, 291
neo-pluralism, 4, 6, 45, 46–7, 53
Netherlands, 204, 215
Neuman, Franz, 181
New Deal, 101
New Labour, 258, 260
New Left, 153

**319**

New Right, 3, 6, 34, 37, 86, 114, 138, 151, 231, 240–1
  bureaucracy, 46–7, 241, 253
  conservatism, 241, 242–3
  context, 242–6
  definition, 246–8
  feminism, 231, 233, 241
  overload theory of, 124
  practical politics, 255–61
  public-choice theory, 244–6, 251, 254, 261–2
  social democracy, 241, 243, 245, 246, 247
  Thatcherism, 204, 243, 259–60
  theorists, 248–54
  welfare state, 234; *see also* conservatism
NGOs (non-governmental organisations), 290, 297, 303
Nietzsche, Friedrich, 68–9, 70
Niskanen, William, 241, 245, 253, 256
Nolte, Ernst, 163, 164, 182
nomocracy, 273
NOW (National Organization of Women), 229–30
Nozick, Robert, 150, 241, 243, 244, 248, 250, 255
NPD (*Nationaldemokratische Partei Deutschlands*), 182–3, 184

Oakeshott, Michael, 190, 194–8, 199, 202, 204, 205, 210, 242
'objective Will,' 174–5
OECD, 304
Offe, Claus, 120, 121, 122, 123–5, 133
Ohmae, Kenechi, 290, 296, 297, 303, 309
oil crisis (1973-4), 118, 122
Okin, Susan, 217
oligarchy, 77, 139, 145
Olson, Mancur, 245
Ostergaard, Geoffrey, 153
O'Sullivan, Noel, 160, 178
overlapping consensus, 53–4

Pakistan, 267, 272
palingenesis, 164
Pareto, Vilfredo, 63, 70–1, 73, 74, 85, 253
parliaments, 21, 28, 83
Parson, Talcott, 95–6, 291
partisan mutual adjustment, 58
Pateman, Carole, 214, 224–6, 233–4
patriarchy, 218, 219–20, 221, 223, 225, 226–7, 234
Payne, Stanley, 163, 176, 179
Peel, Sir Robert, 189
Peele, Gillian, 257
permissive society, 257, 274
Phillips, Anne, 224, 228, 230–1
Pious Sultan theory, 265–6
pluralism, 6, 8, 99, 124
  context, 41–4
  definitions, 44–9
  elite theory, 75–80, 86
  moral, 40, 47–9, 53–5, 56
  multiculturalism, 49
  political leadership, 208
  practical politics, 57–60
  theorists, 50–7
  Yale, 39, 40. 41, 42, 43, 44–7, 50–3, 56
Podhoretz, Norman, 204
Poland, 27, 28
Polanyi, Karl, 210
policy analysis, incrementalist model of, 57–60
policy consensus, 78, 80–1
'policy tsars,' 59

political competition, 38, 39, 43, 45–6, 50–1, 53, 72–4, 78–9
political correctness, 274
political education, 196–7, 202
political office-holders, 63
political pluralism, 39, 40, 41, 42, 43, 44–7, 50–3, 56
political religion, 170, 174, 265, 266, 269, 272, 275–6, 280, 283
political violence, 167, 169–70, 178–9, 181
poltical religion, 173–5
Polyani, Karl, 123
polyarchical states, 40, 41, 50–1
popular sovereignty, 22–4, 30–3, 94, 177, 273, 285
populist-nationalist parties, 183
pornography, 218, 232
Portugal, 27, 165, 203
positive integration, 114–15, 130–2
positive welfare, 126, 127, 134
post-colonialism, 108, 217–18
post-modernism, 220, 222, 226, 228–9, 303
post-structuralist feminism, 229
Poulantzas, Nicos, 94, 95, 96, 101–4, 105, 109, 145, 147
poverty, 249, 255, 304, 306, 309
power dualism, 21–2, 26
premillennialism, 272
pressure groups, 47, 252, 283, 290, 297, 298, 302
Pringle, Rosemary and Watson, Sophie, 224
private property rights, 91, 102, 128, 150, 192, 243, 249, 274
privatisation, 149–50, 184, 255, 256, 303
production of goods, 21, 91, 106, 124, 155
propaganda, 180
property rights, 91, 102, 128, 150, 192, 243, 249, 274
prostitution, 218, 225
Protestant fundamentalism, 268–75, 272–3, 277–81
Proudhon, Pierre-Joseph, 141, 142, 162–3, 170
public choice theory, 244–6, 248, 251, 254, 261–2
public–private spheres, 32, 47, 55, 196, 215–16, 221, 224, 277

Quinton, Anthony, 191
Qur'an, 265, 271, 275
Qutb, Sayyid, 168, 275–6, 284, 285, 286

racism, 167, 180–1, 184–5, 219
radical feminism, 218–19, 221, 222–4
radical Islam, 271–2, 275–6, 282
Rai, Shirin, 222
railway networks, 129
Rawls, John, 39–40, 42, 47–9, 53–4, 250, 277
Reagan, Ronald, 206, 207, 240, 241, 254, 255, 256, 279
Red Army (anarchist group), 151
Red Brigades (anarchist group), 151
regulation, 123, 124, 129–34, 248–9
reification, 107–8, 110–11
relativism, 201–2
religion, 169, 173–5, 179, 181, 203–4, 265, 266; *see also* civil religion; political religion
religious education, 201
religious tolerance, 47, 54, 189
Renaissance, poltical elite, 66–7
representation, 28–9, 45, 67, 144, 199–200, 230–1
Republican party (US), 205–6, 240, 257, 277, 278
republicanism, 3, 23–4, 31–2, 67, 201–2, 273
responsive states, 44–6

# Index

revolution, 28–9, 31, 41, 162
revolutionary fundamentalism, 168
Riddell, Peter, 259
risk-taking culture, 127
Ritzer, George, 294
Robertson, Pat, 277, 279, 280
Robertson, Ronald, 290, 293
Roman Empire, 68, 69, 276
Romania, 165
Roosevelt, Franklin Delano, 59, 274
Rosenberg, Alfred, 181
Rostow, Walt, 291
Rothbard, Murray, 138, 139–40, 149–50, 151
Rousseau, Jean-Jacques, 32, 42, 47, 160–2, 170, 176, 199, 276
Roy, Olivier, 267–8, 278, 282, 286
Ruddick, Sarah, 217
rule of law, 67, 94, 189, 196–7, 199, 209
rulers, 21–2, 24–5, 31, 33, 41, 71, 188–9, 265–6
Rushdie, Salman, 286
Russia, 68, 84, 151, 152, 184
Ruthven, Malise, 271, 276, 283

sabotage, 152, 154
Salazar, Antonio, 203
Sampson, Anthony, 83
Sarvodaya movement, 153
Saudi Arabia, 267, 272
Scandinavia, 28, 117, 123, 215, 230, 304
scepticism, 299, 300, 303, 304, 307
Scharpf, Fritz W., 114, 121, 122–3, 125, 132, 133
Schmitt, Carl, 198–200, 203, 207, 210
Scholte, Jan Aart, 293, 297
Schumpeter, Joseph, 64, 73–4, 75
Scott, John, 64, 79–81
Scruton, Roger, 188, 193
self-management, 139, 152, 155
semi-autonomous states, 138, 145
separation of powers, 31, 41–2, 45, 94, 207–8, 274
sexual exploitation, 218, 225
*Shari'a* (Islamic law), 266, 281–2, 283
Shell, 126
Sieyès, Abbé, 32
situationism, 153–4
Skinner, Quentin, 3, 23
Sklair, Leslie, 290
Skocpol, Theda, 82
Smith, Adam, 247
SMOs (social movement organisations), 298, 303
social anarchism, 139, 141, 143
social class, 78–9, 94–5, 117
social contract, 140, 141, 161, 224–5
social Darwinism, 143–4
social democracy, 4, 6, 8, 34, 37, 53, 113–15, 203, 304
  context, 115–19
  definition, 119–21
  feminism, 234
  New Right and, 241, 243, 245, 246, 247
  practical politics, 130–5
  theorists, 121–30
social domination, 97, 103–5, 107, 140, 143–7
social justice, 39, 53, 131, 145, 304, 309
  global, 109, 290, 297
  New Right theory and, 249
  positive welfare, 126–7
  voluntary sector and, 128
social science, 70
socialism, 69–70, 116, 160, 163–4, 167–72
socialist feminism, 219, 222, 227, 231

societal culture, 55–6
Sorel, Georges, 167–72, 173, 175
Sørenson, Georg, 302–3
sovereignty, 43
  friend–enemy distinction, 198–200
  globalisation, 296
  individual, 140
  loss of, 125
  political, 296, 300
  popular, 22–4, 30–3, 94, 177, 273, 285
  religious, 272–3, 275
Soviet Union, 148, 180
Spain, 27, 138, 152, 165, 203
SPD (Social Democratic Party), 115–16, 117
Spencer, Herbert, 144
stagflation, 118
stakeholder capitalism, 43, 53, 128–9, 134
Stalin, Joseph, 180
state institutions, 97–8, 99–100, 103–4, 107
statehood, concept of, 2–5
statism, 38, 117, 120, 122, 124, 145, 149, 172, 173, 205, 242, 243, 260, 270
Sternhell, Zeev, 165, 171–2
Stiglitz, Joseph, 306
Stoker, Gerry, 260–1
strategic-functionalism, 106
strategic-relationalism, 97, 98–9, 103–5
strategic-relationism, 108
Strauss, Leo, 200–2, 205, 207, 208
strikes, 152, 169, 171, 257
structuralism, 97, 98, 101–4, 108
Suarez, Francisco, 23
subsidiarity principle, 132–3
Sudan, 267, 272, 283
suicidal martyrdom, 275
supply and demand, 106
surrogacy, 225
Sweden, 117, 118
symbiogenesis, 144
syndicalism, 152, 162–3, 165, 167–72, 179

Talmon, Jacob, 33, 170–1
taxation, 27, 125, 147, 255
  cuts, 205–6, 255
  France, 29
  New Right theory, 250–1
  redistributive, 273
technocracy, 86, 114, 117–18
territoriality, 20–4, 289, 293, 296
terrorism, 109, 207, 209, 258, 275, 278, 286
Thatcher, Margaret, 59, 83, 113, 241, 254, 255, 257
Thatcherism, 204, 243, 259–60
theocracy, 283
Thompson, Graham, 299, 300, 304
Thornhill, Chris, 199
Tilly, Charles, 21, 27
Tocqueville, Alexis de, 29, 31, 38, 42, 68, 266, 268
Todd, Emmanuel, 209, 210
totalitarianism, 30, 33, 159, 164, 172, 175–6, 177, 179–80, 181, 248, 276, 284
towns, growth of, 21–3
trade, 21, 25, 77, 149, 189, 192, 247, 295
trade unions, 152, 243, 257
traditionalism, 190–2
transformationalists, 301–3, 307
transnational corporations, 300, 306, 307
Truman, David, 39
Tullock, Gordon, 241, 244, 245, 252

**321**

Turkey, 281
tyranny, 31, 39, 42, 68, 207, 273, 275

Ukraine, 184
ultra-nationalism, 164, 184–5
underclass, 126, 205, 298
unemployment, 118, 122, 182, 249, 304
United Kingdom, 26, 27, 28
   anarchist group, 151
   anarcho-syndicalism, 152
   anti-terrorism legislation, 109
   domestic violence poliicies, 232
   elite theory, 79–80
   equal opportunities policy, 230
   incremental model of policy analysis, 57, 58, 59
   neo-fascism, 182–3, 184
   New Right, 243, 254, 255–7
   political power in, 83–4
   religious freedom, 54
   social democracy, 115, 117
   socialist feminism, 231
   Thatcherism, 118, 123, 204, 240, 259
   Whig aristocracy, 189
United Nations, 39, 151, 207, 297, 298, 301, 304, 305, 309
United States
   anarchist issues, 152
   anti-pornographic legislation, 232
   anti-terrorism legislation, 109
   civil rights, 51
   Constitution of the, 41–2, 67–8, 207, 268, 273
   death penalty reintroduction, 257
   elite theory, 75–9, 82
   foriegn policy towards Israel, 279–80
   founding fathers, 201, 207–8, 272, 273, 274
   fundamentalism, 268–70, 277–81
   global political institutions, 300, 306
   'Great Society' programme in, 204, 243
   liberal feminism, 229–30
   Libertarian Party, 151
   neo-conservatism, 149, 204–10, 240, 257–8, 281
   New Deal, 59
   New Right, 243, 256
   'pork barrel' politics, 252
   Protestant fundamentalism, 272–3
   public choice theory, 254
   religion and the private sphere, 47
   'the Great Satan,' 285–6
Universal Declaration of Human Rights (1948), 39
universalisation, 294

Valois, Georges, 167, 171
Vaneigem, Raoul, 153–4
Veblen, Thorstein, 75
Victor Immanuel III, 180
violence, 4, 184
   domestic, 218, 219, 221, 227, 232
   terrorist, 109, 207, 209, 258, 275, 276, 278, 286
virtue, political, 66–7, 205, 206–7
voluntary co-operation, 139

Wahabbism, 267
Walby, Sylvia, 214, 226–8, 234
Wallerstein, Immanuel, 292
war on terror, 258, 280
Ward, Colin, 154
warfare, 26–7, 34, 209, 301, 302
Washington Consensus, 303
Waylen, Georgina, 234
wealth redistribution, 248–9, 255, 297
Weber, Max, 3–4, 8, 20, 29, 64, 74–5
   bureaucratic elites, 71–3, 84
   definition of the state, 95
   status, 75
   warfare, 26
Weberian sociology, 291
welfare state, 101, 122–3, 123–4, 125, 146, 176, 216, 227, 234, 245, 260
   fundamentalism and, 273–4
   neo-conservatism and, 205
   New Right, 255, 256
Wells, David, 93, 107–8, 110
Westernisation, 282, 294, 295
Wetherly, Paul, 96
Williamson, John, 303
Wollstonecraft, Mary, 225
Women's Aid, 232
working class, 101, 117, 168, 170, 298
World Bank, 119, 304, 305, 306
World Economic Forum, 304
world systems theory, 292
WSF (World Social Forum), 306–7
WTO (World Trade Organization), 241, 297, 304, 305, 307

Yale pluralism, 39, 40, 41, 42, 43, 44–7, 50–3
Young, Iris Marion, 214, 226, 227–9, 231, 234
Yugoslavia, 41, 84

Zapata, Emiliano, 151
zero-sum game, 309